STRANGER IN TOWN
The Musical Life of Del Shannon

Howard A. DeWitt
Ohlone College

D1616842

KENDALL/HUNT PUBLISHING COMPANY
4050 Westmark Drive   Dubuque, Iowa 52002

CONTENTS

Preface

When Del Shannon hit the **Billboard** number one slot in April 1961 with "Runaway," he seemed to be a rock and roll act that came out of nowhere. In reality, the young Michigan singer had worked in a highly popular Battle Creek group, the Charlie Johnson Band. His residence at the Hi Lo Club was the stuff of legend. Before he attained national stardom, Shannon was already a local music legend.

There is a side to Shannon's life from the days in his hometown of Coopersville and later in Battle Creek, Michigan that explains a great deal about his life and music. In many respects he was a storyteller. One who took the experiences of his youth and early adult life and crafted them into meaningful songs. The tragedy to his career is that he came of age in the early 1960s when the myth persisted that it was a period of vacuum rock.

In 1960, Shannon, then known as Chuck Westover, using the stage name Charlie Johnson, and wrote a song with his keyboard player Max Crook. Not only did the tune, "Runaway," make him a star but it began a life in rock and roll music.

No one expected a great rock and roll song. Drummer Dick Parker who told Westover, "we aren't going anywhere, so let's try a new musical direction," had brought Max into the band. Chuck agreed and hired Crook. Max brought to the group a genius for sound. His musitron, a forerunner of the synthesizer, created the eerie sound that made "Runaway" so unique.

THE ORIGINS OF DEL SHANNON

The combination of Shannon's lyrics and music, and Crook's musitron, paved the way for one of the classic rock tunes of all time. "Runaway" remains on the play list in oldies stations and on general AOR radio. The movie and television industry recognizes the power of "Runaway" and it has earned a fortune licensed to the entertainment industry.

The Del Shannon story is a complicated one. He had to change his name from Charles Westover and shave five years off his age in 1961 to fit into the teen market. But the key to his life is in his songs. When Shannon wrote "Stranger In Town," it reflected his life long feeling that he didn't fit in or belong. He always felt alienated from the mainstream. His life was one of frenetic ups and downs.

His close friends in Battle Creek described him as "sometimes suicidal." One of the members of the Charlie Johnson Band remarked, "I saw Chuck's manic side; depression was a lifelong problem. So Westover was something of an enigma. His life doesn't fit into neat patterns."

In the mid-1950s Westover married a young girl whom he had met when she was 15. Her brother, Dick Nash, lived in Coopersville and his sister Shirley came from Custer to visit for a few weeks. Eventually after courting Shirley for two years, Chuck convinced her to get married. The marriage was a solid one and produced three lovely children, Craig, Kym and Jody. Then, after 31 years of marriage, Shirley divorced her husband. Rock star Del Shannon found himself on his own. According to Del's closest friends, his career was a contributing source to his marital breakup. But his life is about the music. What has hindered Shannon's artistic recognition is the publicity surrounding his personal life. Some of it was true while other tales were false. What can't be overlooked are the hit records.

From 1961 to 1965 Shannon placed seven songs in the **Billboard** Top 40, including "Runaway," "Hey! Little Girl," "Hats Off To Larry," "Little Town Flirt," "Handy Man," "Keep Searchin' (We'll Follow The Sun)" and "Stranger In Town." In England Del was an even stronger chart presence with thirteen songs on the various U. K. charts. "Del Shannon was a presence who influenced the English rock sound," Ray Coleman, a British journalist, remarked.

Contrary to popular myth, Shannon's hits didn't end in 1965. Although he was seldom at the top of the pops, his records continued to chart. From 1966 until his death in 1990, Del continued to make some of the best music of his career. He also produced "Baby It's You" for Smith and "Gypsy Woman" for Brian Hyland. Shannon was a multi talented performer who had the ability and write and produce hit records.

There were many sides to Del Shannon. To many of his close friends, he was a stranger in town. They weren't sure whether or not he was Chuck Westover, the good old boy from Michigan, or Del Shannon, the international rock and roll star.

STRANGER IN TOWN: CHARLES AND DEL

His friends often remarked that there were two Del Shannons. One grew up as Charles Westover in Coopersville, Michigan and came of age playing in the bars in Battle Creek. The other was an international rock and roll star. One who spent three decades as the consummate rock and roll artist. In between Shannon married twice. His first wife, Shirley, was his high school sweetheart. His second wife, LeAnne, he had known since she was 11.

One of the problems with Del Shannon was his mercurial personality. At one point he was a loving and doting husband. At another juncture he could be withdrawn, cruel and at odds with the world.

Like some entertainment figures he had problems with drugs and alcohol. He wasn't always the perfect husband. But in the larger scheme of life he wasn't a wife beater. For a time he was a philanderer, but his overall loyalty to his family remained unquestioned.

In matters of money, Shannon was a contradiction. He was generous to a fault with family and friends. But he was also parsimonious. His daughter Jody quit her job to attend junior college and he pulled the plug on the $500 a month he was giving her for school. To some observers this appeared cruel. The reality is that it was the old Charles

Westover. As Del Shannon, he feared a return to the poverty in Coopersville and the meaningless jobs that he endured during the years he lived in Battle Creek.

As a songwriter, Shannon was first rate, as a producer he didn't get the respect he deserved and as a performer he stood audiences on their heads for three decades. But Shannon remained a personal contradiction. He was alternately moody. His championing of Alcoholics Anonymous and his sessions with psychologists and psychiatrists helped him to eliminate his drug and alcohol problems. But just five days after playing at a Buddy Holly Memorial Concert in Fargo, North Dakota, he killed himself with a .22 caliber rifle. The shock was overwhelming. His family and friends were stunned.

At the time of his death there were rumors that Shannon would join Bob Dylan, Tom Petty and Jeff Lynne in the Traveling Wilburys. He was also back on the road and bringing in $300,000 a year. What killed Del Shannon? The answer is obvious, it was the record business. During his early years in Coopersville, Michigan, he talked about not getting the respect that he deserved. If there is a signature line to Shannon's career it is his continual search for respect in another hit record. He had more hits than most performers could imagine, but the burden of stardom never ceased.

Del Shannon was a stranger in town. He never fit in Coopersville or Battle Creek, Michigan. He moved to a Detroit suburb and felt out of place there. In the mid-1960s he moved his family to California where he remained until his untimely death.

One of the elements of the rock and roll lifestyle is unwarranted media attention. Del Shannon had more than his share of media intrusion in his life. None more so than when he died. There were unwarranted tales of drug abuse. The majority of which were inaccurate and his supposed love affair with Prozac was splashed all over the newspapers. Shannon was neither addicted to drugs or using Prozac in any appreciable manner.

DEL SHANNON'S FAMILY AND FRIENDS: THE GENESIS OF THE STORY

Many of Del Shannon's family and friends have remarked that he had a continual creative impulsive. One that ran like a rapid river and flowed continually with new songs. The creative drive was incessant and Del always had new tunes. Until his premature death, Del never gave up on having another hit record. From the time that he started performing as Charlie Johnson in Battle Creek, he pointed toward stardom. Consumed by the music business, he was sensitive to criticism, the vagaries of the music business and the personal affronts that rock and roll stars faced.

When he committed suicide, Del Shannon was in a precarious mental state. Del was emotionally ill. Whether or not he was on prescription drugs or over medicated,   is a subject for the Internet. In our research we found little evidence of drug abuse. There was, however, strong indications that his mental state was a precarious one. To ignore that condition would be to overlook the reason for Shannon's death.

After his death his first wife, Shirley, and his children rallied together as a family. The children Craig, Jody and Kym have all turned out well with families and jobs.

Whatever the pressures of rock and roll stardom, Del and Shirley raised a normal and well-adjusted family. This is mentioned because many of the articles on Shannon suggest an abnormal family life. Nothing is further from the truth. His family was crushed by his death. The story of Del Shannon's career begins and ends with his music. But it would be irresponsible to ignore the controversy over the drug Prozac. Did it ultimately lead to Shannon's death? No one will know for sure.

THE MEDIA CIRCUS AND PROZAC

One of the problems of rock and roll biography is the tendency toward hagiography. Rock stars are heroes and their behavior is generally forgiven in the media. They eventually reach mythical proportions. What has been reported in the rock press generally ignores Shannon's personal life. Much of what was printed about his family and relationships in the general media is incorrect. When Shannon committed suicide there was a media feeding frenzy.

It was widely reported that Shannon committed suicide while taking Prozac. The coroner found no sign of Prozac or any other drug in Del's body. His wife LeAnne brought suit against Eli Lilly, the manufacturer of Prozac, and the media circus continued to swirl around Shannon.

LeAnne Westover, Del's second wife, testified in September 1991 in Washington D. C. at the Federal Drug Administration hearing on Prozac. Peter R. Breggin, M. D., described LeAnne's testimony as displaying "a rather sophisticated knowledge about the drug and its effects." Then Breggin and his book, **Talking Back To Prozac**, appeared on the Opray Winfrey Show and became a best seller. The tragedy was that Del Shannon and his music were all but forgotten in the media circus. Most reporters remarked that he had the number one hit "Runaway" and then they brought out the drug connection. The truth was that Shannon was alcohol and drug free when he ended his life. The answer to his death is a simple one. He was killed by the music and entertainment business. This book will tell that story.

Del's wife of more than three decades, Shirley, remained the love of his life until he died. The story of her marriage has never been told and this book weaves her influence through his career.

THE REAL DEL SHANNON

The real Del Shannon was an elusive figure. He was a husband, a father, a musician, a creative person and an internationally known rock star. But, he was born Charles Westover in the small town of Coopersville, Michigan and never forgot his rural roots. When he apprenticed in the music world at the Hi Lo Club in Battle Creek, Michigan, Chuck's music took its initial direction.

He was a songwriter who could evoke teen angst in his songs and he was something of a poet. As Del Shannon he lived in the musical fast lane. The temptations of the rock and roll lifestyle were everywhere and he was much like his contemporaries, a hell raising rock and roller.

There was also a compassionate and sensitive side to Shannon. He loved his family, kept in touch with close friends and was always ready to help. Whether it was advise, money or simply listening to a problem Del was there for his friends. When he died everyone was shocked. No one saw his suicide as a possibility. The Del Shannon story tells us a great deal about rock and roll and even more about a remarkable talent.

Del and Buffalo Bob Smith

Del Shannon at Coopersville H.S. Reunion, 1983

PROLOGUE: THE MYSTERIOUS DEATH OF DEL SHANNON

"I don't believe that he committed suicide; it wasn't like Charles,"
Leone Westover, Del Shannon's mother

The spring weather which comes early in Los Angeles hadn't arrived in the evening hours of February 8, 1990. The unseasonably chilly evening caused Del Shannon to walk out into his backyard and look at the moon. This particular night the California evening was as cold as the Michigan nights where he had spent his happiest years. The wind that blew up Saddleback in Canyon Country, California was a cold wave that made Los Angeles drivers irritable as they hurried home.

Del Shannon was a rock and roll star who had hit the number one slot on the **Billboard** Hot 100 with his first release, "Runaway." By the 1980s his career had revived and he was rumored to join Bob Dylan, George Harrison and Jeff Lynne in the super group, the Traveling Wilburys. Everything looked bright for Shannon.

There were pressures, however, which were causing mood shifts in Shannon's personality. He had moved into three different houses in the last few years, and the pressures of real estate speculation caused him unrest. Yet, there were positive aspects of Shannon's life. Gold records hung on the wall and there was money in the bank. He had a new band, and legendary rocker, Tom Petty, produced Shannon's music.

For years Shannon had fought depression. What impact did depression have upon Shannon? It often drained the vital force from his songwriting. The resulting melancholia led to a decline of self-worth and a drop off in work habits. To alleviate his personal hell, Del returned to visit Coopersville, Michigan, the small town where he grew up and Battle Creek, Michigan the factory town where he had lived with his first wife, Shirley. There he had formed the Charlie Johnson Band and became a legend at the Hi Lo Club. But the early Michigan days seemed like a distant memory.

During the last few years, Del had thought a great deal about the good old days hanging out with his friends in small Battle Creek nightclubs, running around the rural Michigan countryside playing in small country and western bars and then having it all taken away with rock and roll stardom. Shannon was never comfortable as a rock star. He was a Michigan kid who had gone on to have a number one **Billboard** hit and a spate of chart records in a career that had spanned thirty years. But, for whatever reason, Shannon was a physically sick man. Shannon's suicidal depression prompted him to write songs, which reflected that his life was turning into a gradual nightmare. Thoughts of suicide are not uncommon in cases of severe depression.

Early in the evening of February 8, 1990, Del was agitated, and within an hour or two of committing suicide. He went in to his small study, which was still full of unpacked boxes, and began singing into a tape recorder: "Songwriter, songwriter, give me back my life," Shannon wailed. This unpublished and unpolished song perfectly described his state of mind. It summed up the turmoil that rock and roll music had caused him in his thirty years in the entertainment spotlight. For the time being his mind drifted from his music and he began to think about the area around Valencia.

Buried just a few miles away, blues legend Roy Brown offered an ominous reminder of the burden of fame. One day Del went out and looked at Brown's grave and then walked down to the grave of Gene Vincent's. The rockabilly artist was one of Del's favorites and he thought a lot about Vincent's early death.

The weather was often a catalyst to Shannon's mood changes. During the winter of 1989-1990, the frigid temperatures hit the area around his newly purchased home. Shannon was an outdoors person. He always reacted to the warm California climate and spent a lot of time riding his bicycle or scooting around the hills and nearby mountains on his motorcycle.

The mountains are on one side of Newhall and the desert on the other, and this often makes the weather extreme. But Newhall, Valencia and Canyon Country were still favored suburbs. They are the type of suburb where even Denny's has a menu acceptable to the locals and includes a low-fat fruit or vegetable plate. "I remember whenever we went out to eat, Charles was careful about his diet," Leone Westover, his mother, remarked. "In fact, he was almost fanatical about it. One day we had to go to five restaurants before he found a menu he liked." His mother suggested that looking back on her son's life, she did notice changes in his behavior. But she didn't believe that they indicated any tendency toward suicide. "

Del's close friends were puzzled by his death. It didn't make sense. Shannon dieted, exercised, watched his weight and appeared ready to reenter the mainstream of the rock and roll world. By the late 1980s, he was back on the charts and touring regularly. But something was wrong.

DID THE REAL ESTATE BOOM KILL DEL SHANNON?

The real estate developers had moved into the Valencia area with a zeal and built new housing tracts. Although the area boomed, some speculators had trouble selling their houses. The recent drop in prices caused many to lose money. Shannon was one of those speculators who could not sell one of his homes because of the wildly fluctuating Southern California real estate market. This depressed Del, because throughout his lengthy musical career he had made many wise real estate investments, and he had never had any trouble selling his homes. For someone who liked to be in charge and who was used to wheeling and dealing, this was a frustrating period. But since the mini-real estate boom of 1989, the market had not only declined but also, in fact, crashed in the Valencia-Newhall area.

Shannon was holding onto a home that he couldn't sell while living at 15519 Saddleback in Canyon Country. The new home was large and comfortable, but this did little to ease Shannon's depression. Although Del had been in his home for just a few weeks, he continually dwelled on the mortgage payment that he made on a house on another hill overlooking Valencia. Shannon worried about finances and being overextended in the turbulent California real estate market. The $670,000 that Del Shannon paid for the Saddleback Road home was more than $100,000 under the asking price.

Del Shannon in England, early 1960s

What happened? No one knows for sure. The secrets behind Del's death remain locked in the room where he shot himself. The 55 years that Charles Westover lived including almost 30 as his alter ego Del Shannon were a mystery. He was often two people. The bald, athletic and business conscious Charles Westover or the rock star who put on a wig, a fur coat and rock star clothes to become Del Shannon. The story is an interesting, if perplexing, one.

DEL SHANNON: THE EARLY YEARS MOLD A ROCK STAR

Chuck Westover never gave up trying to become a rock and roll or country music star. Long before he became Del Shannon, Westover grew up in Coopersville, Michigan pursuing his musical dreams. In the small town of Coopersville, he was constantly reminding people that he was going to make something of himself. Then, after he left the army, Chuck moved his family to Battle Creek and began leading a popular local band. "I'm gonna be a rock and roll star," he told Peter Vice, the owner of the carpet shop where he worked. Charlie Marsh, a popular local disc jockey, remembered the drive to stardom. "There was no doubt that Chuck would make it big," Marsh reflected. Chuck wanted out of the Battle Creek area. He would sit in the carpet shop and play his songs for Vice.

Vice loved Charlie's music and often went to see him perform at the Hi Lo Club. "I told Chuck that he had to get out of Battle Creek; the damned town was killing him. But hell, we had too many good times to leave." The honky tonk atmosphere of the Hi Lo Club appealed to young Chuck Westover and it was also an important training ground.

The Hi Lo Club developed Shannon's early performing skills. He played long hours there and learned to cover every popular rock and roll song. The Charlie Johnson Band, as his group was known, was able to work in original tunes and experiment musically. It was also at the Hi Lo Club where he wrote and performed "Runaway" to a throng of local admirers.

Every night after the Hi Lo Club gig, he went home to his young wife, Shirley, and his rapidly growing family, which soon included two girls and a boy. There were two people in Battle Creek, one was Chuck Westover, the family man and provider, and the other was Charlie Johnson, the rock musician.

He played his music in small clubs, honky tonk western bars and in the few after-hour's clubs that ringed Battle Creek. Then in 1961, Westover changed his name to Del Shannon and his first record "Runaway" went to the top of the **Billboard** pop chart. He was forced to shave five years off his age, leave his wife in a trailer park in Battle Creek and go on the road to become a single, rock and roll idol. Guilt was the inevitable by-product of this life. Periodically, Shannon had trouble coping with stardom and he always felt like he had abandoned his wife. Shirley stuck with him for three decades and then she divorced him. Del quickly remarried and was in a state of turmoil from forces that no one understood. There were personal demons known only to Del and these forces killed him. There were some hints of a problem.

From the time his first hit record in 1961, "Runaway," started climbing the charts, Shannon was a heavy drinker. He kept late hours, worked and caroused, but he was generally a responsible family man who took care of business. As a musician, he wrote, recorded and produced a huge backlog of material. Del Shannon was a one-man band who could do anything. Then, sometime in the last 1970s, Del confronted his life and began to make changes. It took some time, but sobriety became a goal that he worked toward and achieved. He understood his addictions and appeared to have conquered them.

The craziness of the rock and roll lifestyle led to numerous relapses, but, generally speaking, for years Del Shannon had been sober. During his career, heavy drinking almost derailed him personally and professionally, but he had discovered Rafters, an AA group in Newhall. He became an exemplary member of AA. Shannon, known simply as Charlie, was now healthy and a help to other alcoholics.

There were other changes in Shannon's life. He became a dedicated jogger, an avid health food advocate and the old days of cigars, red meat and sweet foods were long gone. But Shannon still suffered periodic depression. He was moody. There were also signs of physical deterioration.

Del Shannon: An Early Publicity Shot

THE SAND CANYON HOUSE AND
DEL SHANNON'S TRAGIC SUICIDE

The first few days that he lived in the house, Del seemed to love it. Each morning the BMW's, the Mercedes, Pontiac Grand Prix's and the Saturns headed down the freeway to Los Angeles. Young professionals, upwardly mobile lawyers, small business people and entrepreneurs populated Sand Canyon. It was the picture perfect suburb. Bright children, well-maintained homes and a sense of prosperity filled the air.

After a few days in his new house, Del smiled at a plaque he had just hung on the wall. There was a special place in his study for awards. Not only did Del have gold records, other awards and personal recognition from the industry, but he had a sense of humor about being screwed out of the credit for producing a million-selling record, Smith's "Baby It's You."

After he developed Smith, the act was taken away from him and someone else was given credit for producing their million-selling record. In a moment of rage, Shannon presented himself with a self-made gold record for the Smith's million-selling disc. There was a delicious irony to the trophy everytime he looked at it. Life appeared perfect for Del Shannon. His career was back on track, he had new music in the can, a new CD was about to be released and he was in demand on the concert circuit.

But the signs of prosperity and career success obscured a sickness dwelling inside Shannon. He was mentally and physically ill and no one could help him. He wasn't the same around his wife and friends. No one knew what to do about it.

Del Shannon's death took place amidst the sun and fun that people associate with Southern California. Befitting the tragedy, it was raining and overcast. The house located at 15519 Saddleback in Canyon Country, California was just a few miles from Magic Mountain. The park was closed, but on weekends the roller coaster and other rides made it a fairyland. Nearby, in downtown Newhall, the Rafters, an Alcoholic Anonymous meeting spot, where Del was known as Charles Westover, a meeting had just concluded. One of the ironies of Del Shannon's life is that he committed suicide while his friends at the Rafters were trying to overcome their alcoholism.

THE REACTION TO DEL SHANNON'S SUICIDE

At 55 years of age, he was in perfect health, a jogger who rode his bicycle daily, and he ate with the vengeance of a dedicated health food advocate. His career was once again back on track. There didn't seem to be any reason for suicide.

But there was a dark side to Shannon. The singer who came to fame and fortune in 1961 with the platinum hit "Runaway," seemed to have a perfect life. He had married a young woman, his old hits continued to sell, a new album was ready and there were rumors that he would join Bob Dylan, George Harrison and Jeff Lynne in the Traveling Wilburys. Lynne. Tom Petty and Mike Campbell were involved in Shannon's most recent recordings. Del had invested his money wisely and owned land in Southern California and Hawaii. With investments in condos and raw land, Shannon was financially secure. So his death made no sense. Yet, there were private demons.

The Los Angeles County Sheriff's Department reasoned that Shannon was depressed over changes in his "finances, work and personal life." The LA County Sheriff's Department report concluded that Shannon was "an apparent suicide." But there was no room for speculation in the official verdict.

THE OFFICIAL VERDICT ON DEL SHANNON'S DEATH

The police report on Shannon's death was an interesting one. It stated that Shannon picked up a 22-caliber Glenfield semi-automatic rifle and pumped a bullet into his head. The report indicated that just after 11:00 p.m. his young wife, LeAnne, went into Del's study and found him. She dialed 911. The call was logged at 11:25 p.m. and Fire Department Engine Number 123, commanded by Captain Seder, arrived quickly on the scene. Shortly thereafter the paramedics, Williams and Allen ran through the front door and were taken to the den in the back of the house.

As the fire department and paramedics arrived, Dr. Kurt Olson, a close friend of the family, was standing in the studio. Dr. Olson lived at the end of Sand Canyon and he and his wife, Bonnie, were crying over Shannon's death.

Del was sitting in a chair with his body slumped to the right and a rifle was resting against his leg. A spent cartridge was on the floor. It was an eerie scene that upset everyone. The police report observed that the "the victim's left hand was across his chest and resting on the rifle barrel. The victim's right arm was extended down over the rifle and his hand was between his legs." Thus leading the police to conclude that it was a suicide.

Del's son, Craig Westover, came over immediately, and the police took Shannon's body out. The death scene was a traumatic one. The gunshot wound had taken place between 7:00 p.m. and 10:30 p.m. When the fire department and paramedics arrived, there was no doubt that Shannon had died instantly from the gunshot.

When Deputy Disbro arrived from the local police department, he found no evidence of forced entry and he checked the house security system. No one had broken in and there was no evidence of foul play.

Del Shannon's life is a microcosm of all that is positive and negative American popular culture. He became a star in 1961, during the second generation of rock and rollers and somehow survived the fickle public taste, which forced many rock acts into retirement. At the time of his death, Shannon was in the middle of another comeback and his sound was once again fresh and contemporary. Unfortunately, Shannon was unable to reap the rewards of the next step in his musical career. He died just as he had prepared an album of new songs. The scandalous tales of Shannon using Prozac were untrue allegations. His suicide obscured the power of his last musical journey. What Shannon meant to his family and friends never reached the press.

Throughout his life he embodied all that was positive and fresh about the rock and roll music revolution. From its earliest days, rock and roll was a music which came from a different person with a skewed direction and innovative sense of musical destiny. A look at Del Shannon's life reveals a great deal about the importance of rock and roll music to American culture. His life also suggests the difficulty of separating fame from his private life and family. The important moments of Shannon's life were celebrated in a fish bowl atmosphere. He was never able to escape fame and fortune. "My husband never felt like he was good enough for the fame he achieved." Shirley Westover continued, "he was a person who could not come to grips with the accolades."

So the question remains: "Who killed Del Shannon?" The answer is a simple one. The rock and roll lifestyle and the music industry. This book will examine the pressures and forces that prompted Shannon to kill himself on an unusually dreary California evening. It will also celebrate his legendary contribution to rock music and his personal legacy. Whatever else can be said about Del Shannon, he was always first and foremost a quality person who seldom let down his family and friends.

To some there is still a mystery surrounding Del's death. His close friends in Coopersville talk of Shannon not liking guns. Sonny Marshall, a boyhood friend, recalled that he didn't like to clean, load or fire guns. "Chuck couldn't have killed himself, he hated guns," Marshall recalled. That Chuck Westover was alone in his study is certain. But whether or not Del Shannon pulled the trigger that killed Charles Westover is open to question. Del was fond of saying: "There is no songwriting without secrecy." This was a reference to his all night, secret songwriting sessions in the mole hole. It was also an insight into his intensely private life.

Shannon is the most elusive and unwilling of subjects. He kept a guarded front during interviews. But Del was a song biographer who wrote his life in lyrical beauty. He knew the dangers of biography. It would destroy your privacy. He also was aware that there were two sides to his character. "Chuck continually lived on the edge," Dick Parker, the drummer who helped him craft "Runaway," remarked. "Del had his feet in two worlds," Chuck Marsh, the Battle Creek disc jockey, remarked. "One was the normal world, the other was the rock and roll lifestyle." In many respects Shannon was a man of secrets. He wrote songs in a small room, he called it the mole hole. He would vanish for an entire day to gather inspiration for his tunes.

Del Shannon: The Teen Idol

PROLOGUE

The mysterious life of Del Shannon is compounded by his equally strange death. It is impossible to explain and suggest the complexity of his life. To some extent, of course, Charles Westover invented Del Shannon, but he could not have written his songs, performed his music and began his journey to the Rock and Roll Hall of Fame without his wife Shirley, his singing and song writing partners, his producer, his performing friends and most of all his fans. Any biography of Del Shannon has to consider all these factors. His life is, in many respects, a case study in the history of rock and roll music.

On February 17, 1990, Del Shannon was scheduled to appear in Merriville, Indiana. This small town, just south of the industrial city of Gary, was the perfect venue for Shannon's music. It was rural, friendly and filled with people like Del who had grown up in a lifestyle much like his hometown Coopersville. His relatives were planning to drive down from Michigan, his close friend Ray Meyer would drive in and a few of his old friends from Battle Creek were looking forward to the concert. But he never made it to the concert.

BIBLIOGRAPHICAL SOURCES

The Los Angeles Sheriff's Department Complaint Report # 090-02006-0630-451 formed the basis for describing Shannon's death. Interviews with Dan Bourgoise, Mike Popenhagen, Peter Vice and a number of sources requesting anonymity helped to place Shannon's tragic death in perspective.

Chuck Marsh provided some interesting observations on Shannon's early life and then recalled some of the difficulties of his last years. In Battle Creek, Sue Gooch, Sue White, Darwin Farr, the Popenhagen family and Ginny Gibbs provided important insights into Del's life. The original drummer on "Runaway," Dick Parker graciously recalled Shannon's life.

Interviews with Shirley Westover, Leone Westover, Craig Westover, Jody Westover, Kym Westover and Max Crook added to this chapter. Also, significant was the help of Battle Creek's Richard Schlatter who provided a wealth of material on the reaction to Shannon's death. Harry Balk, Shannon's early producer, added some important details.

Michael Tennesen, "Did Charles Westover Kill Del Shannon?" **Los Angeles Magazine**, September, 1990, pp. 132-140 was written after an extensive interview with Shannon's second wife LeAnne. It is an interesting piece, which analyzes the turmoil in the last years of Del's life.

An excellent obituary is written by Michael Goldberg, "Del Shannon: 1934-1990," **Rolling Stone**, March 22, 1990, pp. 20, 124. Also see David Hinckley, "Time Ran Out For Runaway Man," **New York Daily News**, February 19, 1990.

Del Shannon in Concert, Lubbock, Texas, 1986

1: DEL SHANNON: THE EARLY YEARS

"He was always playing his guitar, writing songs and singing for anyone who would listen, but he had no idea that he would become a rock and roll star," Leone Westover, Del's mother

On February 8, 1990, rock star Del Shannon was found dead in his home from a self-inflicted gunshot wound. The obituaries referred to his hit, "Runway," which was number one in 1961 and his other top ten chart songs, "Hats Off to Larry, " number five in 1961 and "Keep Searchin (We'll Follow The Sun)," number nine in 1964. These tunes along with the seminal, "Little Town Flirt," a number twelve hit in 1963, defined Shannon's career. To the casual observer, Shannon appeared little more than a multi-hit artist who vanished from the charts after 1965. But this simplistic view is far from the truth.

With eight **Billboard** Top 40 hits from 1961 to 1965, Shannon appeared to fit the stereotype of the rock and roll star that made hits for a short time and then vanished to the oldies circuit. But appearances are deceiving. Unlike his contemporaries from the early 1960s, Shannon wasn't a typical teen idol. He was a singer-songwriter, a consummate businessman and a touring artist who delighted audiences for more than thirty years. He was also much more complex as a person than people realized. His enormous talent was often hidden by a personality that made it difficult to understand him. He was also frustrated by the record business and was angry that his talent wasn't fully utilized. Like many creative people, he had a hidden side. He was often two people. He was born Charles Westover but took the stage name Del Shannon. The name came from combining a Michigan wrestler's name with the Cadillac logo. When he became a star, it was a mixed blessing. Throughout his life, Del made some disastrous decisions and he suffered from clinical depression. Eventually, this may have led to his suicide. What Del Shannon did was to reflect the teen agony of the early 1960s and then continued his career and faced every challenge in the rock and roll music business. His tragic death has obscured his place in the music business. The journey to becoming a rock star was an intriguing and often perplexing one.

CHUCK WESTOVER ON THE ROAD TO BEING DEL SHANNON

No road offers more mystery than the first one that you travel down from your birthplace. There are hidden pressures; unseen values and extraordinary influences that shape one's character. For Del Shannon who was born Charles Westover in Grand Rapids, Michigan on December 30, 1934, there was a happy childhood. His mother, Leone, and his father, Bert had met in the small town of Coopersville, and after they married they lived in a small, nondescript farmhouse.

Chuck Westover, Age 16

DEL SHANNON: THE EARLY YEARS

The two block downtown section of Coopersville is right out of a Norman Rockwell painting. There were three bars, a bowling alley, complete with a small restaurant, and a movie theater that offered family entertainment. Tiny and Tink's Restaurant offered the first all-electric kitchen in that part of Michigan. Chuck Westover loved the town and the people.

As a rock star, interviewers winced when Del told them he was from Coopersville, Michigan. They looked at him like Coopersville was the end of the earth. Yet, this small town remained the ballast, which steadied Shannon's life. He recalled the kindness of the locals, the sense of community spirit and the "Del Shannon Days" held in 1961 and in 1983. Del was always a Coopersville kid and proud of it. It was only if you were a New York music critic that it was difficult to understand this feeling. Shannon viewed this small Michigan community as his savior. Time and time again he would extol its rural virtues.

Chuck and Shirley: Their Wedding Day

It was Chuck's high school friends, Sonny Marshall, Earl Meerman, and Bud Taylor who recalled a playful young man with a drive to succeed in the music business. The Coopersville High School principal, Russell Conran recalled that he spent an inordinate amount of time convincing Chuck to graduate. When he did, Conran remarked; "The next time I see you it had better be on a television show singing a hit record." This remark turned out to be prophetic.

By the time he graduated from high school, Chuck was playing his guitar and dreaming of a musical career. It was in Coopersville that his character was formed. He also met a young girl from nearby Custer, Shirley Nash, and they married in 1954.

During the time Chuck and Shirley lived in Coopersville, they worked at various jobs, but employment was difficult and career jobs were few and far between. Therefore, Chuck decided to enlist into the armed forces. The result was two separate tours in the service before Chuck and Shirley returned to Michigan in the late 1950s. While in the army, Westover was in the Special Forces. Consequently, he joined the U. S. 7th Army band and appeared on a radio show "Get Up and Go." This stimulated his appetite for show business. Westover also discovered that he had a talent for writing songs and performing them.

Chuck Westover in Kentucky

When he returned to live in Battle Creek, Westover continued his life long infatuation with country music. He loved Lefty Frizzell and sang along daily with his Hank Williams records. Jazz was another musical interest. Yet, Westover also listened to Chuck Berry, Elvis Presley, Fats Domino and the Everly Brothers. He had an eclectic interest in music and soon this evolved into a highly personal and unique rock singing direction.

It was 1958 and the first Golden Age of Rock and Roll Music was coming to an end. Elvis Presley was going into the army, Chuck Berry was off to jail, Buddy Holly died in a plane crash in February 1959 and Fats Domino wasn't hitting the charts with the same consistency. Unwittingly, these events led to the rise of white, pop crooners. It was in this atmosphere that Del Shannon emerged as a hit-making artist in 1961. But this was still to come and he remained Charles Westover.

While living in Battle Creek in the 1950s, Westover worked at the Brunswick Corporation in nearby Kalamazoo and at Peter Vice's Carpet Shop. It was here that Chuck wrote the early lyrics to "Runaway."

Chuck also settled with his family at the Brown's trailer park. In the 1950s, Battle Creek was filled with clubs catering to every music taste. At the Hi Lo Club is where Chuck would lead the Charlie Johnson Band, with a blend of country and rock tunes. Green's, which was near the outskirts of town, was strictly for the country music crowd. The Grotto and the Bellman and Waiter's Club were African-American clubs. The Club Bar was for the jazz fan. A dozen other bars created venues for all types of music. It was in this musically nurturing environment that Chuck Westover evolved into Del Shannon.

HI LO CLUB, DOUG DEMOTT AND THE BIG LITTLE BAND

One night, Chuck Westover walked into the Hi Lo Club and saw the Doug DeMott Band on stage. The hulking DeMott was a former football player turned boxer who was a guitar wizard. He performed all the country hits of the day and his band included some of Battle Creek's finest musicians. There was Bob Popenhagen on guitar, an elderly looking mechanic, L. D. Dugger, on slapping bass and whoever was on the drums that night, the DeMott band was a skilled bar band.

It didn't take Westover long to become friendly with DeMott. Before long Chuck was part of the DeMott band. Long nights of playing followed by partying and more music schooled Westover in the craft. Then DeMott left to play strictly country music.

By the late 1950s, Chuck Westover became Charlie Johnson and organized the Big Little Band or the Charlie Johnson Band with L. D. Dugger on bass and Bob Popenhagen on guitar. Then Chuck looked for two other musicians. In Shirley's rusted Saab, Chuck drove out to Dick Parker's house and hired the baby-faced eighteen-year-old drummer. Then Parker introduced Chuck to his first musical partner. He found a keyboardist, Max Crook, who had invented an instrument known as the musitron, and they began to make music. This strange piano-organ device was controlled by a black box and eventually gave "Runaway" its eerie instrumental break. With a new musical outfit in tow, Westover began his ubiquitous march to stardom.

At the Hi Lo Club—between the drinking, the partying and the fighting—Shannon began to write and record songs. By 1960, there were four unissued demos which suggested that Chuck was a future talent. "Little Oscar," "Without You," "The Face of An Angel" and "I'm Blue Without You" were songs that had a hit direction to them.

While Westover played with the Charlie Johnson Band on stage at the Hi Lo Club, Westover loved to cover Chuck Berry classic tunes like "Johnny B. Goode" and "Sweet Little Sixteen," but then he could perform a Hank Williams tune with ease. Westover was versatile and musically innovative. For five hours a night, three nights a week, the Hi Lo Club provided a musical training ground. On Sundays he would drive out to Gun Lake and play country music at Daisy Mae's. They had the best chicken wings and gizzards in Michigan and a host of country artists performed there over the years. This was another training ground for Westover's music.

There was a powerful drive within Westover to make something of himself. He grew up poor in the small Michigan town of Coopersville and felt the slights, real and imagined, of the locals. There were plenty of facilitators for Chuck's original music.

So, when he went on stage at the Hi Lo Club, the Big Little Band burned with intensity. It was as much a roar of defiance against those who doubted his musical genius as it was a march toward stardom.

Del Shannon on Stage with Doug DeMott at the Hi Lo Club

Del Shannon with the Cool Flames, 1956

FACILITATING THE DEL SHANNON SOUND

The Charlie Johnson Band had both followers and fans. A local Battle Creek disc jockey, Charlie Marsh, known on the air as Charlie O., was one of Chuck's constant companions. They hung out in the bars, in the record stores, in the late night coffee joints, and scoured the countryside for new rock and roll music.

There were musicians all over Battle Creek. Doug DeMott continued to lead his own country band. As Westover's first guitar and song writing guru, he was a strong supporter. After playing in the DeMott Band, Chuck met guitarist Bob Popenhagen who was another early musical influence. Then one night a rockabilly looking cat, Darwin Farr, who performed under the name Dar Farr, walked into the Hi Lo Club and began making music after hours with the Charlie Johnson Band. Wes Kilbourne was a local guitar player who was friendly with the Charlie Johnson Band. "Chuck had trouble keeping a guitar player, they were all drinkers," Kilbourne observed, "but Westover was the best guitar player, Popenhagen had nothing on him." Kilbourne listened to early versions of "Runaway" and knew that Westover had a sure hit.

Chuck Westover in Germany

Charlie O. introduced Westover to the stock at Lil's Record Store and it was here that Wade Flemmons' 1958 hit "Here I Stand," became an early influence upon Del Shannon's song writing direction. Then Ollie McLaughlin, a disc jockey and talent scout from Ann Arbor, took an interest in the Charlie Johnson Band. It was McLaughlin who would put Shannon in touch with producer Harry Balk at Embee Productions.

The Battle Creek music scene was alive with a wide variety of sounds. At the Grotto Jackie Beaver, later a well-known soul artist, held forth nightly. The Bellman and Waiters featured Count Basie or Duke Ellington on a Sunday or Monday night in the late 1950s as the bands traveled to Chicago or Detroit. Lloyd Brown, another soul singer, played at the Club Bar and Green's had a country music outfit. There was a great deal of music and it all came together to influence Chuck Westover. Unwittingly, these acts were facilitating the Del Shannon sound.

The patrons at the Hi Lo Club were fans for life. Sue Gooch, Susie White, Ginny Gibbs and John Anglin were fans who remained friendly with Del Shannon. They all recalled the drive and intensity which brought Chuck Westover into the rock and roll limelight. "He had a drive that you admired," Sue Gooch recalled. But the secret ingredient to Shannon's rise to fame was the 18-year-old drummer, Dick Parker. He was a listener, a facilitator, a thinker and ballast for Chuck Westover's dreams.

DICK PARKER: DRUMMER EXTRAORDINAIRE AND THE GESTATION OF THE DEL SHANNON SOUND

The Del Shannon story is one in which Max Crook's musitron and Del's voice came together magically to make "Runaway" a massive hit. The drummer, Dick Parker was one of the unseen, but significant, influences upon the music. When he joined the Charlie Johnson Band at the Hi Lo, Parker didn't look old enough to shave. The truth was that he was already a musical veteran. He became a sounding board and a jam session buddy for Chuck Westover.

When Parker graduated from Richland High School in 1959, he was a veritable musical encyclopedia. He listened to the Four Freshmen, Stan Getz, Kenny Burell and Dave Brubeck. Dick liked the cool jazz drummers and spent an inordinate amount of time on his solo skills. After playing in a number of bands, he became the man who held the beat in the Charlie Johnson Band.

What set Parker apart from the other drummers who passed through the Charlie Johnson Band was the way he meshed with Westover's musical ideas. They could spend a brief time on a song and perfect it. "Little Oscar" was one of Westover's early tunes and Parker helped to put it on tape. He also contributed to other originals including "Living In Misery" and "This Feeling That I'll Call Love."

The early songwriting and recording sessions that Westover initiated were important ones in perfecting his talent. "Chuck always had stories or lyrics, we would play something and he would go off to finish the song. He was always writing a tune," Parker remarked.

Like Westover, Parker was an innovative musician and despite his youth he was a seasoned professional. They would bounce musical ideas off each other and the interplay helped to create the Del Shannon sound. Parker was also a young man who kept a diary and wrote poetry and prose reflecting his experiences.

THE HI LO CLUB AS AN EXPERIMENTAL VENUE

At the Hi Lo club, the Charlie Johnson Band experimented with a jazz, country, or rock and roll music. Part of the magic of the Del Shannon sound was the ability to mix musical styles. In 1959-1960, Chuck and Max Crook put together thirty-eight unreleased recordings. Eventually, these made their way into Del Shannon's first album and one of these songs, "Runaway," rose to number one on the **Billboard** pop chart in 1961.

DICK PARKER RECALLS THE HI LO CLUB DAYS

Of all the people involved with Charlie's band at the Hi Lo Club, I remember Dugger, an old man playing bass. Raising the bar of alcohol behavior to new levels, Dugger would suddenly awake from what appeared to be a deep sleep and play his stand-up bass with a furious energy. There was also Bob Popenhagen, rhythm guitar. I don't remember if Bob was there before or after I was. Dick Pace replaced him on guitar. Then Pace left and went to work at Knott's Berry Farm in California. I first met Max Crook while still in high school. I grew up in the small town of Richland just north of Kalamazoo and most weekends in the summer there would be band jams in the old armory. Exciting times, those early days of rock and roll...young kids honing their growing musical chops with an awareness of the new rock and roll scene, and musicians and their bands were abundant. It was here at the armory in 1958 that I first met Max. It was the late summer of 1959 in Hickory Corners, Michigan. I was holed up in my grandparents house, they were away for the summer and I was there with my drums, some Danish coffee cake and a car with only a couple of bucks for gas. One afternoon a small Saab lurched up over the curb and parked in front of the house. And with a knock on the front door, a cigar in his hand and a smile on his face, Chuck Westover introduced himself and offered me a job. I never knew how he tracked me down. The next thing I knew I was playing in the Charlie Johnson Little Big Band at the Hi Lo Club. I called Max Crook and he joined the band. That was it and then '"Runaway" followed six months to a year later. The Hi Lo Club was a once in a lifetime experience.

The sets at the Hi Lo Club not only inspired Chuck but helped him write his songs. The club regulars were strong Charlie Johnson supporters, but to this day many tell a tall tale of writing songs. Marv Martin, who sang during the break, has repeatedly taken credit for writing a number of Shannon's songs. There is no evidence to back up his claims. What is obvious is that many talented musicians and performers passed through the portals of the Hi Lo Club. The result was a musical cross-pollination, which elevated the Charlie Johnson Band to the ranks of a group ready for a rock and roll record.

For two years, the grueling sets at the Hi Lo Club not only trained Chuck Westover in the skills and requirements necessary for success as a rock and roll musician, but the club also taught him to please an audience. This was a lesson that he never forgot and until the day that he died Del Shannon was the consummate performer. Battle Creek and the Hi Lo Club provided the impetus for this future success.

The groundwork was laid for the writing, recording and merchandising of Shannon's number one hit "Runaway." But in order to facilitate this record there were two important people who had to work into the mix—Max Crook, the musitron inventor and producer, Harry Balk. They would become the two final ingredients in the Del Shannon sound.

Del Shannon: Getting Ready for Stardom

BIBLIOGRAPHICAL SOURCES

Interviews with Sonny Marshall, Earl Meerman and Bud Taylor helped to shape parts of this chapter on Shannon's youth. Peter Vice, Dick Schlatter, Dick Nash, Leone Westover, Craig Westover, Kym Wilkerson, Jody Westover and Shirley Westover all helped to clarify both the Coopersville and Battle Creek years. Brian Young of the Del Shannon Appreciation Society helped to reconstruct the early years through his magazine and archives. Charlie Marsh, a Battle Creek disc jockey, provided local color. Del Shannon's best friend, Dan Bourgoise, helped to reconstruct the early days. Steve Monahan also helped with this period.

Jim and Lillian Budzynski, **Chronicles of Coopersville** (Coopersville, 1996) was an invaluable aid as were the Budzynski's historical comments. Also see, **The First Hundred Years** (Coopersville Area Centennial, 1971) and **History of Muskegon and Ottawa Counties, Michigan Illustrated, 1882** (Chicago, 1992) and the local newspaper, the **Coopersville News** from 1890 to 1983.

In Battle Creek, Ginny Gibbs, Darwin Farr, Susie White, Jim DeMott, Wes Kilbourne, Sue Gooch, Joan Schwner, Lloyd Brown, Pete Anglin, Jim Ray and the late Junior Walker all provided key information.

The drummer on "Runaway," Dick Parker was unusually introspective and perceptive about the Battle Creek days.

See Sue Worden and Brian Young, "Wes Kilbourne Interview," **And The Music Plays On**, no. 14, Summer, 1998, pp. 26-31 for Kilbourne's role in Shannon's musical development.

Max Crook the musitron genius provided hours of material in the Battle Creek days. Thomas Snyder at the Bellman and Waiters Club sat for interviews, as did jazz performer, Bobby Parker.

See also, Graham Gardner, "Del Shannon Interview," **And The Music Plays On.** (Issue 6, Winter, 1995, pp. 8-15).

2: MAX CROOK: THE UNSPOKEN MUSICAL INFLUENCE

"I knew we had something special, musically speaking, the first night I played with Del. He played off my musitron and we had a new sound."
Max Crook

Max Crook walked onto the Western Michigan University campus. He was an eighteen-year-old freshman and he was scared to death. Just three months earlier in June 1954, he had graduated from Ann Arbor High School. Max Crook had a secret. He didn't want to become a doctor. He didn't want to become a businessman. He didn't want to become an engineer. He didn't want to become a teacher. Crook hoped to become a rock and roll musician. He wondered if he could tell his family.

Although rock and roll was in an infant stage, Max was well aware of it. He listened to the early, non-mainstream records, which began part of the rock and roll revolution.

There were other secrets in Max's life. He was an inveterate inventor. Since high school he had fiddled with splicing together an instrument with a secret black box. He would later name his invention the musitron and it was the forerunner to the synthesizer. But there was more to Crook than his technical genius. He was also a keyboard player of extraordinary skill. All of Crook's talents came together behind the emerging rock and roll phenomena.

In 1954, Michigan radio was filled with rhythm and blues sounds and Max loved the blues as well as the rhythm and blues sounds. The early strains of rock and roll burst forth and when Crook heard Bill Haley and the Comets he found part of his musical future.

ROCK AND ROLL AND MAX CROOK

Rock and roll was in its formative stages and Crook loved to invent new sound equipment. Since high school, he had worked on the box which he would call the musitron. It was this then unknown instrument which added the highly identifiable sound to "Runaway."

When Shannon's signature tune "Runaway," hit the charts in 1961, Max Crook's musitron gave it a special sound. The strange synthesizer solo that came out of the musitron was not only an indication of Crook's engineering genius but a picture of his future musical direction. On Del Shannon's first album and early songs, it was the musitron which made Del Shannon's early sound.

For decades Crook stood in Shannon's shadow. He was a good friend who praised Del for his musical innovativeness. Del reacted often by remarking in interviews that Crook was an integral part of the early Shannon sound. With characteristic modesty, Crook found it difficult to talk about his contributions to "Runaway" and other early Shannon songs. He has always been a modest man whose signature synthesizer sound was an identifiable part of early 1960s rock and roll.

What made Del Shannon and Max Crook special friends was that they never parted company. They were friends for life. In the weeks before Shannon's untimely suicide, he drove out to Crook's California desert home to talk and play music. No musician was closer to Shannon than Max Crook and they worked as a team.

However, Max Crook has a musical story in his own right because he was in the forefront of the rock and roll revolution long before he met and played with Del Shannon. Over the years, Max Crook has not only been seriously underrated musically as a composer, but there has been very little attention paid to his body of musical work. Synthesized electronic music owes a great deal to Crook. When he invented an instrument known as the musitron, it was due to Crook's experimental genius. But it was in music theory that Crook influenced Del Shannon. This theory evolved during Crook's early education and his family was instrumental in his musical direction. He helped Del to arrange, produce and record the first dozen tunes, which defined Shannon's musical legacy. But the Max Crook story is a long and complicated one.

THE CROOK FAMILY LEGACY AND THE MUSIC

Max was born in Lincoln, Nebraska, to Dr. Clarence and Helen Crook on November 2, 1936. He was christened Maxfield Dole Crook. Soon the Crooks moved to Michigan. Max's father, Clarence, was a renowned local physician with a fine reputation. His mother was a local society maven and her sense of culture influenced Max's early musical interests. Not only was the family upper class, but sons were expected to become doctors or engineers.

While still in high school, Crook shaped his earliest musical dreams. He was enamored with the rhythm and blues, blues and big band instrumental tunes, which evolved into early rock and roll music. Crook didn't like what he heard on the radio, so he began writing his own rock and roll originals. He thought of forming a band and looked for other like-minded performers. This drive toward instrumental music was a part of Max's personality from his earliest days.

Looking back upon these days, Max recalled the difficulty he had learning scales and reading music charts. But he learned that the popular hits of the day by ear. Max knew early on that he had a talent for interpreting music.

Eventually, he found Chuck Westover, who hired him for the Charlie Johnson Band at Battle Creek's Hi Lo Club. Then Charlie became Del Shannon and Max Crook was lost in the shuffle. But Crook was the interpreter who helped Chuck Westover become Del Shannon.

Crook's musical imprint was stamped all over Del Shannon's sound. As a technician, inventor, arranger, singer and songwriter, Crook had an indelible influence upon those he worked with at the Hi Lo Club. His biggest influence was upon Del Shannon and it was a collaborative effort. For almost two years Max and Del spent an inordinate amount of time working on music.

MAX CROOK: THE FORMATIVE YEARS

The Max Crook music story begins during his formative years. The Crook family had interest in the arts, local history and the Michigan business community. It was a family, which had success and good taste. Max's father, Dr. Clarence E. Crook, a St. Joseph Mercury Hospital surgeon, talked about the value of an education.

The Crook home at 2112 Wallingford Rd. was a warm and bustling place. During these early years, Max practiced intensely and constantly tinkered with his music. The artistic freedom that emerged from his childhood was one of the reasons that Max eventually mastered many musical instruments. In time he learned to play the piano, guitar, drums, accordion, harmonica, bass and ukulele and dabbled with other instruments. When his father accused him of being a dilettante, Max ignored the criticism and continued to pursue his dream.

There was a scholarly tune to Max's early life. Everyone believed that he would achieve professional recognition. But Max had a secret. It was the music world that he wanted to enter.

No one has been more adamant about following his own course in the music world. Max Crook was determined to become a professional musician and an innovative one at that. He succeeded from the first day that he took a music lesson. There was originality to Crook that often frightened his early teachers. He was almost too original and innovative.

Each act of Max's personal drama was played out with class and style. It was also apparent from his earliest musical lessons that Crook would do it his way. He had an independent streak, which earned him a maverick reputation.

While still in junior high school, Max learned to play the accordion. The strict German music teacher introduced Crook to note reading. But Max was more interested in picking up songs by ear. After a great deal of practice, Max played an up-tempo version of the "12th Street Rag" and his teacher almost had heart failure. He was scolded for improvising rather than practicing scales. So Max quit playing the accordion. It was time for high school and Max's parents wanted him to forget the musical craziness and concentrate upon his education.

Max purchased a reel-to-reel tape recorder. It was this instrument which changed Max's life. When Dr. Crook brought home this expensive gadget, it got Max to tinkering with musical sounds. Unwittingly, Max's dad planted the seeds of a musical career. All through high school, young Max developed recording techniques for his musical talent.

But Crook was more than a musical genius. At Ann Arbor's Pioneer High School, Max was a member of the swim team. In 1954, he placed second in the Six-A Conference swimming finals as a springboard diver. But his asthma was acting up and Max realized that he would need to select a college in a warm, dry desert climate.

As an athlete, Max was a skilled one. He practiced diligently and throughout high school excelled in diving and intramural sports. He was also an honor student. Once he completed high school, Max was much like any other Michigan high school student in the early 1950s. He had aspirations to attend a major college. There was a duality to Crook's life as he developed a scientific and a musical direction. Another student at Max's high school, Joann Stollsteimer, would become his wife. Ironically, they didn't date in school.

Joann was a recreational therapist at the University of Michigan Hospital and she put on talent shows in the wards. She not only entertained the patients but also was a diligent education student at Western Michigan University. In time, Joann and Max would meet and marry, but not before Crook migrated to New Mexico to attend college. It was because of his hay fever that Max left for the Southwest.

ON TO THE UNIVERSITY OF NEW MEXICO AND BACK TO MICHIGAN

Max decided to go to college at the University of New Mexico. In 1954, UNM was a small college. However, it was filled with Korean War veterans and had a free and easy atmosphere. In Albuquerque, Crook took an introductory piano class and flunked it. "I would sneak into the practice room and play for hours," Max recalled. But it was popular music that Crook played. Soon a sign went up on the practice room door: "The playing of popular music will not be tolerated on these instruments." Max was always one to follow the rules and he never returned to the piano class.

The nearby restaurants offered Max a chance to hang out with other students. On the local jukeboxes the music of black artists like Billy Ward and the Dominoes, the Clovers, the Drifters and others blended with mainstream sounds. Rock and roll music was forming and Max was there to be influenced by it. Max not only listened to it, but he continued to compose his own songs. Soon, Max quit listening to the radio so that he could write fresh music not contaminated with influences of other musicians.

The University of New Mexico allowed Max to become his own person. He continued to tinker with his music while paying close attention to his studies. At the University of New Mexico, Max was able to control his allergies that plagued him in Michigan. But he missed his home state. His studies had gone well, but he wanted to be near his family and his future bride, Joann. So in 1956, he transferred to Western Michigan University.

Once he entered Western Michigan University in Kalamazoo, Crook was on his way to an extracurricular musical education. During his first week in school, he and his new roommate, Stan Martin, got together at the piano in the lounge of their dormitory. They discovered a common interest in music. Over the years Stan's musical ability was recognized by a wide variety of musicians. In 1961, Martin was one of the backing musicians who played with Del Shannon during his triumphant Coopersville home coming concert. But at this point, Martin was simply a college musician looking for a place to play.

The dormitory at Western Michigan University was a catalyst to Max's musical dreams. For the next year, the Smith-Burnham Hall was a scene of musical experimentation as Max and Stan worked out sophisticated piano arrangements and began to work out instrumental patterns which would eventually influence the course of rock and roll history in the late 1950s and early 1960s.

THE WHITE BUCKS

Soon Max and Stan formed a band, the White Bucks. They began playing local dances, fraternity parties and an occasional roadhouse gig. They also added another musician, Norm Murdock, who played saxophone. A character with an outgoing personality, Norm had a hyena-like laugh that made the crowds laugh. Eventually, this laugh became the idea for their first song. In time they added another member to the White Bucks, Eddie Lynch, who was an excellent guitar player. But the White Bucks were still an incomplete group. However, they did make some recordings. Max was absolutely possessed with the idea of recording.

Max Crook and the White Bucks, 1959

So when the White Bucks made their first recording, it was called "The Laughing Hyena." Norm's infectious laugh was the perfect title for a raucous rock and roll instrumental featuring a burning piano solo. The b-side was "We Gotta Crazy Beat" which owed a great deal to Bill Haley and the Comets' influence. The vocal on the b-side is a great one and one drumstick is used to create a unique sound. Just as the group was jelling at the Smith Burnham-Hall Lounge, a young kid who had joined the crowds watching them practice, Tom Sabada, brought his saxophone into the group. Now the crowds were huge and the White Bucks had to look for venues in which to perform in the quest to continue to perfect their sound. But they still didn't have a drummer. They also needed another guitarist.

Soon they were practicing in the dorm basement and the resident director was threatening them. The dormitory headmaster, Mr. Potter, screamed daily: "You boys won't amount to anything. That damned music sounds like hell."

Like many early rock and roll bands, they fell apart before they started playing. Norm Murdock tired of college quickly and left the band. One night they walked upstairs in the dorm and there was Eddie Lynch playing his guitar. "We started practicing with Eddie," Max remembered, "and I knew that we had the makings of a pretty good band."

The only problem is that they didn't have real drums or a real drummer. On their first record, a small toy-like drum and one drumstick was used. This gave the record an amateur quality. Max was depressed. Then one day a drummer, Brian Woodword, wandered into the dorm and proudly announced that he was unloading his drums from the car.

The White Bucks were getting to a point where they had the instruments and sounded like a professional band. When Tom Sabada told the group that he had a string bass, the White Bucks became an even more complete musical unit. They were finally ready to display their sound. There was no problem with the sound because Max was a person who loved to experiment on tape.

Max Crook loved to make demo tapes. He was a scientific, recording genius who couldn't get enough of the White Bucks musical sound. Then Max drove to Ann Arbor and dropped off some tapes with a local disc jockey, Ollie McLaughlin, and they so impressed him that he brought the group to Detroit for a recording session.

"We began working hard between classes and after classes," Stan Martin continued. "It was Max who had an old reel-to-reel tape recorder that allowed us to make demo tapes." Soon Crook sent some White Buck tapes to a local disc jockey, Ollie McLaughlin. There were two songs "Get That Fly" and "Orny," which Max cowrote with Tom Sabada, that appealed to McLaughlin. With Max on vocals, these songs were perfect ones for the teen market.

In Detroit, McLaughlin booked the same studio where the Lone Ranger had cut his radio show. With a two-track Ampex machine, Max wove his magic by placing the studio microphones to balance the sound perfectly. In many ways Ollie McLaughlin was the man behind the White Bucks' sound. Some years later, he would be the disc jockey who alerted the world to Del Shannon's hit "Runaway."

ENTER OLLIE MCLAUGHLIN

Ollie McLaughlin was an African-American disc jockey who had an enormous impact upon Michigan rock and roll. His radio show on WHRV (now WAAM) was called "Ollie's Caravan" and its theme song, Duke Ellington's "Caravan," was an indication of the show's eclectic musical mix. Eventually, Ollie would bring Del and Max together with their first producer, Harry Balk, and the front man for Embee Productions, Irving Micahnik, this would lead to the recording of and initial success of "Runaway." But at this point McLaughlin was interested in recording the White Bucks and adding their songs to his company, McLaughlin Publishing.

After Ollie had listened to some of Crook's tapes, he suggested that they find a professional recording studio. So Ollie booked a Detroit studio to cut a single. McLaughlin was close to Barney Ales who had worked around Detroit as a representative for Capitol Records and then had briefly worked for Warner Bros. Records before he opened a one-stop Detroit record distributorship. Ales was a good judge of talent and he worked promoting new records with the radio stations, the distributors and the small TV dance shows in and around Detroit. As McLaughlin talked with Ales about the White Bucks, they agreed that the group had a future. But the partnership between McLaughlin and Ales never got off the ground because Berry Gordy, Jr., hired him in 1960 as Motown's first significant white executive. But with Ales' blessing, McLaughlin sent a tape to Hollywood's Dot label and they offered a contract.

That recording "Get That Fly," written by Max Crook and "Orny," written by Crook and Tom Sabada was released on the Dot label in February 1959. While the song didn't hit the charts, it helped the White Bucks to secure bookings. Soon they began to play teen dances and some roadhouses and the press began to notice the White Bucks. The **Kalamazoo Gazette** published an article. The Kalamazoo Armory was a favorite haunt of the White Bucks and it wasn't long before they had a fan club.

The White Bucks began each show with Max Crook remarking: "Good evening and welcome to our show." The band then went into a cover of Duane Eddy's "Rebel Rouser" and segued into Eddie Cochran's "Summertime Blues." But the real purpose of the band was to play original tunes. Max was continuing to write new music.

"I think that we were a little ahead of our time," Max Crook remarked. "A few years later, Danny and the Juniors had a sound much like ours."

But the White Bucks did have their moments. Max used his musitron to cut some songs at Berry Gordy's early Motown studio. With new songs with the not so commercial titles, "G-Jam Blues" and "C-Jam Blues," the White Bucks were primed for 45 record success. Although the White Bucks were one of Michigan's best rock bands, they weren't able to break their Dot 45 nationally. They had a moment of fame in 1959 and soon it vanished.

Shortly after this brief burst of fame the White Bucks broke up. Max married Joann, Stan Martin returned to a summer job to make money for college. But while playing at the Kalamazoo Armory, Max met a young kid, Dick Parker, a drummer, who had the same fanatical zeal for rock and roll music.

At the time Parker was playing in a band, Charlie Johnson and the Big Little Show Band. They had a gig at the Hi Lo Club in nearby Battle Creek. When Parker listened to Max, he was awe-struck at the sound of the musitron. It sounded like an organ but could copy other musical sounds. At the time no one knew that Max had invented a new musical instrument.

ENTER DICK PARKER

It was Dick Parker who brought Max Crook to the Hi Lo Club for a tryout with the Charlie Johnson Band. In less than two years Johnson would become Del Shannon and "Runaway" would rise to number one. At this point in his career, Del, known as Charlie Johnson, was the toast of Battle Creek. After one brief audition, Max was invited to join the group. He accepted.

The initial meeting between Chuck and Max was the perfect start of a friendship and musical partnership. They had many of the same ideas. Max was the consummate soundman and Chuck was the idea person.

What impressed Del Shannon about Max Crook? There were many things. First, Crook told Del that he didn't listen to the radio. He wanted his music to sound fresh. "It's not rock and roll, Charlie." Max continued, "It is a fabricated sound from Philadelphia. If some middle-aged producer is telling us how to play our music, then there is something terribly wrong." Then Crook explained what the musitron could do and demonstrated it. "Shit," Del remarked, "I think we just went to sound heaven."

It was early September 1959 when Max Crook joined the Charles Johnson Band. He lived thirty-eight miles away in Kalamazoo and had to commute each night. Max usually came into the club through a side door carrying his thermos of kool aid and his bag of cookies. He was a handsome, but quiet young man who didn't seem to fit into the Hi Lo Club. That is until the music started. Then Max rocked out with the best of them. His ability to come in behind Chuck's vocals filled out the club sound.

The rough side of the Hi Lo Club often obscured the high musical level. On a given night, Rufus Wines allegedly might beat someone up or his sister might pull a knife and walk somebody into a corner. Max Crook was about to receive the musical education of a lifetime. He was also about to give one to Charles Westover.

MAX CROOK'S ROLE IN DEL SHANNON'S MUSIC

The role that Max Crook played in Del Shannon's career was a seminal one. After he met Shannon and began playing with him, Max not only shaped the sound of "Runaway" and other subsequent Shannon hits, he provided some of the techniques that Shannon used to make his music stand apart from the dull droning tunes of the early 1960s.

Although Crook was a quiet, reserved young man who was the antithesis of Del Shannon, they worked like brothers when it came to music. Max didn't smoke, he didn't drink and he ate cookies and drank punch during the band breaks. Del was just the opposite. What drew these two young men together is a complicated story and it tells us a great deal about the development of rock and roll music.

The studio recording equipment that Crook had in the 1950s was self-manufactured, to the average eye it looked crude and unsophisticated. Nothing was further from the truth. The musitron that Crook built was a prototype of the present-day synthesizer and he was able to create sounds from the funny looking instrument that prompted studio guitarist Al Caiola to remark: "Max Crook is a hidden part of the history of rock and roll. Without his sound on 'Runaway' there would have been no hit." Whether or not this is true is up for debate, but one thing is certain, Del Shannon and Max Crook formed a partnership that lasted until Shannon's death.

The musitron has been credited with originating the eerie sound which made "Runaway" a hit. But there was more to Crook's collaboration. For years Max and Del had spent hundreds of hours making music in the Hi Lo Club and in Max's homemade studio. The first Del Shannon album was the result of this collaboration. For years Del would call Max in to play with him at select California concerts and on television shows. They had a musical partnership, which began in Battle Creek and didn't come to an end until Shannon's tragic suicide.

In a strange irony, Del's second wife, LeAnne, scattered Shannon's ashes in the driveway of Crook's home. It was a strange and eerie sight to watch as Del's remains were scattered in the desert. This is definitely another strange and tragic twist to Shannon's story. As LeAnne rode off on a motorcycle after scattering Del's ashes, Max and Joanne watched from the front door of their house. It made Crook reflect on the early years at the Hi Lo Club. It was here in this Battle Creek, Michigan dive that he learned his trade. Those days not only helped Del but made Crook a consummate professional. He recalled how the patrons provided the material for Del's half a dozen major hits and the other records that hit the charts.

MAX'S MUSICAL EDUCATION AT THE HI LO CLUB

At the Hi Lo Club, Max received not only a musical education in raw, gutbucket sounds; he was able to expand his creativity to new levels. The initial adjustment to working for Del Shannon was not an easy one.

When the Charlie Johnson Band was ready to go on-stage, Del would unplug the jukebox. He was an impulsive person and couldn't wait for the end of a juke box song. "I never saw anybody who wanted to get on stage quicker," Sue Gooch remarked.

If there was a fight, Del told the band to unplug and they walked off stage. A married man with fundamental Christian values, Max still adjusted well to the scene. After all, he loved the music and was there to play it.

There were also people to meet and experiences to gain at the Hi Lo Club. Max met Wayne Carter there. A Detroit native, Carter had some knowledge of the music business. Eventually, he talked Del into managing his band. From this point until the day that Del committed suicide, Carter was a close friend. He was never much of a manager but a drinking buddy par excellence.

```
DEL SHANNON RECORDS: MAX CROOK'S CONTRIBUTION

                    Runaway
                     Jody
                Hats Off to Larry
            Don't Gild The Lily, Lily
               Cry Myself to Sleep
              I Don't Care Anymore
                 Hey Little Girl
                  So Long Baby
                    Misery
                   Day Dreams
                His Latest Flame
                   The Prom
                I Wake Up Crying
                Wide Wide World
                     Lies
                 He Doesn't Care
```

When Del left the Hi Lo Club to tour after "Runaway" became a hit, Max stayed on and led the Maximilian band. Dick Parker remained to play drums, but they never had the same impact as Del Shannon. So a country-oriented artist, Mayf Nutter, was brought in to lead the band. Mayf was a guitar player in the mold of Doug DeMott who had played at the Hi Lo prior to Del Shannon.

By 1961, Max Crook had enough money from his share of the "Runaway" royalties to purchase a 1961 white Ford Thunderbird. Del bought the exact same automobile, only black, a week earlier.

As Max Crook continued to play his music, he had some success on the Michigan nightclub circuit. In 1967-1968, Crook formed a duet with Scott Ludwig called "The Sounds of Tomorrow." Once again Max was ahead of his time. "We were two guys with synthesizers and keyboards," Max recalled, "and we would haul this truckload of electronic equipment in for a gig." They were a popular act and had no trouble with bookings. They played fraternity parties, proms, school dances, country clubs and banquets. The sound was less rock and roll and more often big band or country. Once again this phase of Crook's career suggests his musical diversity.

The Sounds of Tomorrow played regularly at The Pin Room in a bowling alley in Ann Arbor, at the Anchor Inn in Portage Lake and at Len's Restaurant in Arborland. With Scott Ludwig's Moog synthesizer, the first in Michigan, the Sounds of Tomorrow were a hit. At least in the clubs. They also did some recording. They cut some singles for TNT Records. But these weren't rock and roll records; they were square dancing and clogging records.

Although Max and Scott cut some other demos, they never shopped the Sounds of Tomorrow records. "We used them to get jobs," Ludwig remarked. There was no doubt that with songs like "Space Child" and "Our Electronic Bag," Max and Scott were ahead of their times. This often frustrated Crook because he had the feeling for a hit record. The problem was how to incorporate it into the record market. Not only was Max an excellent writer and a fine arranger, but he had the sense of what it took to write and produce. Ironically, he was unable to do so. His friend, Chuck Westover, became a virtual hit factory. Crook never complained; he simply went his own musical way with style and grace.

CROOK'S MUSICAL GENIUS IN THE STUDIO

Max Crook blossomed and flourished after he married Joann. The early years were happy ones for Max and Joann. "Our first Thanksgiving together Max and I were in a small apartment. We put up a card table and carved up a red apple. Then we made legs with toothpicks. It was our turkey and a symbol of our strong marriage."

The stable marriage was a tonic for Max's music. He spent more time on his musitron and intensely wrote songs. Crook remembered "Delilah" as his first composition employing two early reel-to-reel tape recorders and he was hooked from that point. As the years progressed, Max Crook continued his magnificent song writing direction. He has had a career that exudes musical genius.

Over the years, Max Crook has written and performed some amazing music. He also recorded under the name Maximilian and his instrumentals were among the best ever completed in the late 1950s and early 1960s. But some of Crook's better tunes were never released. "Blue Fire," recorded at Bell Sound in New York in the early 1960s, was an example of a hit instrumental that remains unreleased.

Prior to "Runaway's" success Crook had made great music. A good example of this was when Max completed a demo of "Mr. Lonely," an instrumental he wrote for producer Harry Balk. It was given to Johnny and the Hurricanes who had a regional hit with "Jada." "Mr. Lonely" was the b side. Johnny and the Hurricanes also cut Crook's ""Seventh Hour," but it was never released. In 1959, at Berry Gordy, Jr's. Studio, Max cut "Beez Wax" and it impressed the future Motown genius so that he spent hours listening to it.

In the studio Max often achieved a hit sound. A good example was his demo of "Bumble Boogie." It was recorded two years before B. Bumble and the Stingers had a hit with it.

Crook was an experimental genius. He took two well-known standards, "The Breeze and I" and "The Theme To Peter Gunne" and combined them into one song. These tunes were combined in the spring of 1961 and cut at the session which produced "The Twistin' Ghost." This was Max's second Big Top single and suggested his solo brilliance. Although "The Twistin' Ghost" was a b side, it received hit record play throughout Canada. At Toronto's CHUM it rose to number 11; then in May 1962, another Crook song, "Greyhound," charted in Canada. The Canadian music press praised Maximilian,

Max's recording name, and they demonstrated that he had a bright future. But Max always talked about Del and his music and seldom about his own career.

"During my years with Del Shannon, I was proud of my work on 'Runaway.' The musitron really helped the record," Max recalled. Crook also wrote the bridge on "Don't Gild The Lily, Lily." "I wrote that bridge for 'Hats Off To Larry,'" Max remarked, "but we used it on 'Don't Gild the Lily, Lily.'"

After the fame and fortune of the Del Shannon years, Max Crook continued his musical career. By the late 1960s he had played a series of regular gigs in and around Ann Arbor, Michigan and began working at Wedemeyer Electronics and Morrey Richman Industries. For some time in the late 1960s he promoted his new band known as the "Sounds of Tomorrow." They became the regular band at Len's Buffet in Arborland and then they played for months at the Anchor Inn near Dexter, Michigan. Never a person with a big ego, Max performed as well for these small crowds as he did when he faced thousands of people with his musitron percolating behind Del Shannon's massive hit "Runaway." From the beginning Max was intrigued with the music and he never forgot how to excite a crowd.

By the late 1960s, Max and Joann lived at 2570 Seminole Road in Ann Arbor, Michigan and together they had two children, Susan, nine, and David, six and a half. From early in their marriage, the Crook's lived in a household where drugs, alcohol and the craziness associated with rock and roll was not part of the family lifestyle. When Max went into his study he made some of the most revolutionary music of his day.

Max Crook: An Early Publicity Photo

A solid family man, Max realized that he had to earn a better living. So Crook became a sales representative for the Electronic Alarms Company in Ann Arbor and bought and managed four apartment buildings. In his spare time Max continued to work in his home recording studio. His music grew and continued to develop. Finally, in the early 1970s, Max and Joann decided to relocate to the Los Angeles area. Their old friend Del Shannon lived there, and Max worked for Sierra Alarm, a burglar alarm company in the greater Southern California area.

While he lived in the Los Angeles area, Max remained a close friend to Del Shannon. At times Del would hire Max to play the keyboards. But it was Max's sage advice that Shannon appreciated. It was in Los Angeles where Max became even more significant in urging Del to continue recording and touring.

Max Crook: The Sounds of Tomorrow

ON TO LOS ANGELES AND A NEW LIFE

When he moved to the Los Angeles area, Crook installed burglar alarms for awhile and then joined the Ventura County Fire Department. He was stationed at the Potrero Road firehouse but continued to work other jobs. Crook also worked for a Conejo electronics firm and moonlighted part time as a security guard.

Max had a goal in mind and that was to retire and make music full time. It wasn't rock and roll music that was Max's calling. His dream came true in the early 1980s when Max accepted Jesus Christ as his personal lord and savior, retired as a captain and began pursuing his Christian music. While in Southern California, Max occasionally returned to the musical scene.

In January 1974, Max Crook brought out his musitron to play with Del Shannon in a well-received Midnight Special concert in Los Angeles. The 37-year-old Crook's face beamed from the musitron as ABC television's In Concert highlighted a performer on the musitron who looked ten years younger on national television. Del Shannon was so relaxed and jovial in his return concert with Max that there was talk of the duo going back on the road full time. This didn't work out.

A decade later in 1983, Max recorded an "electro stomp" version of "Runaway" with the musitron and a moog studio synthesizer. The process involved Max placing a small speaker about the size of an earphone in his mouth and forming the words without speaking. This electronic wizardry then allowed the instruments to act as the vocal chords. It was a strange, but satisfying version of the classic "Runaway."

When Max joined the Charlie Johnson Band, he and Joann spent many hours dining and talking with Del and Shirley. He was always part of the family.

MAX CROOK: A DISCOGRAPHY

Delilah, a 1949 piano instrumental
We've Got A Crazy Beat/ The Laughing Hyena, 1958 White Bucks
Get That Fly/Orny, 1959 White Bucks
Beez Wax/ Bumble Boogie, summer 1959 recorded at Motown
Home Rock/Mr. Lonely/Seventh Hour, summer 1960, Big Top Records
Runaway/ Jody/The Snake/ The Wandered, Winter 1960 or possibly early 1961; Max was coauthor on these songs
Theme to Peter Gunn and the Breeze and I/The Twistin' Ghost/Greyhound/Autumn Mood/Blue Fire, Spring, 1961
Monsoon/Cookie Jar Blues/Rockin' 88 Monsoon was an instrumental coauthored with drummer Dick Parker
Space Child/Our Electronic Bag; This was from the Sounds of Tomorrow period with Scott Ludwig
Wheels/Razz My Berries/Runaway; These three songs were cut in January 1973 at the Cherokee Ranch Studio in Chatsworth, California
Backdraft (Firefighter's Theme). This song resulted from Crook's Ventura County Fire Department experiences

MAX CROOK AND DEL SHANNON:
THEY COLLABORATED AFTER DEATH

When Del Shannon committed suicide in 1990, Max and Joann Crook were devastated. They had been a part of Del's life prior to "Runaway" and the pain was deep. LeAnne, Del's second wife, had also cut several country gospel tracks at the studio in the Mojave desert home were Crook lived at the time. But Max was not through with Del Shannon. Even after Del's death they collaborated. He found an old reel-to-reel tape where Del had written "Original Tune For Max." This song was from the 1970s and Del had written an instrumental he called "The Last Ride" for Max to hear. Max fittingly reworked it. Much like the Beatles completed John Lennon's "Free As A Bird," Max finished "The Last Ride" which is a rockabilly, Chet Atkins, rock combination original. "I wanted this to be a sort off anthology for my good friend," Max continued. "A liner sheet that I wrote to accompany this song explains the purpose of it. And how I see it representing Del's life and death. This was a tremendous honor for me to find this tape and complete it. It's like a closure for me on the loss of a giant in my life."

Max Crook was a friend, musical collaborator and concert partner to Del Shannon for many years. Their bond was forged by the hard times at the Hi Lo Club and the driving desire to make unique rock and roll music. The songs on Shannon's first album, particularly "Runaway," owe a great debt to Crook's musical creativity.

DEL SHANNON'S, APRIL 4, 1961 POSTCARD TO MAX CROOK

Hi-Thought I'd better get on the ball and write you a line. I'm still at the Paramount and it's a little like being in jail. If you go outside the kids tear you apart, and if you stay in, the walls, all 3 of them, they drive you nuts. I get here at seven in the morning and leave at 11:30 p. m. Well Max I'm looking forward to seeing you at the session. Say hi to everyone. As always, Del S.

This postcard was sent from New York's Brooklyn Paramount Theater where Shannon performed. The session that Shannon referred to on the postcard was the one which led to the recording of "Hats Off To Larry," "Don't Gild The Lily, Lily," "I Wake Up Crying" and "Wide Wide World." These songs had been cut in March, 1961.

The later stages of Crook's life see him continue to write and perform in Christian music. He had published more than fifty church praise and worship songs under his Backdraft music publishing business and has produced six albums of evangelical and worship music under his own label. Max now performs at various special events, and specializes at entertaining in rest homes, retirement centers and other places where senior citizens reside. He is a one-man band utilizing digital midi keyboards and generators (and still the musitron on occasion) in his presentations. Crook, who was rated the number one keyboardists in the world in 1961, according to the Griffin Fund survey, is still in the Top 100 among keyboardists rated on the Internet. Max Crook is still a dynamic force in the music world.

BIBLIOGRAPHICAL SOURCES

Interviews with Max and Joann Crook were instrumental to this chapter. Interviews with Shirley Westover, Harry Balk and Dan Bourgoise filled in much of the information about the personal relationship between Max and Del. Dick Nash and Richard Schlatter also offered perspectives. Brian Young provided some anecdotes. Dick Parker helped to ferret out the relationship between Crook and Shannon. In Battle Creek, Ginny Gibbs, Susie Forest, Sue Gooch and John Anglin offered important anecdotes. Chuck Marsh helped with reconstructing the musical events.

For biographical information on Crook, see, for example, **Thousand Oaks News-Chronicle,** January 18, 1974, p. 3-A and the **Huron Valley Ad-Visor,** July, 1985. The staff of the Poterero Road Fire Station of the Nebury Park, California department was another key source.

Howard A. DeWitt, Dennis M. DeWitt and Brian Young, "Max Crook: The Maximilian Story," **Rock 'N' Blues News,** April-May, 2001 is a biographical sketch of Crook's musical years.

3: THE PRODUCTION GENIUS OF HARRY BALK

"I recognized that Del needed something to make 'Runaway' have a hit sound. So we increased the speed on the master tape and viola. We had a hit." Harry Balk reminiscing about producing "Runaway"

Harry Balk was a Detroit based businessman who loved black music. He hung out at the local clubs and realized that there was a commercial potential in the unknown Motor City performers. Although Balk wasn't sure he wanted the music business.

Balk was happily married, had a family and was the owner of a series of profitable movie theaters. "When I was twenty years old I had theaters in black neighborhoods," Balk remarked. These small movie houses were located in black neighborhoods next to clubs where he heard the music of Detroit's city streets daily.

As a connoisseur of jazz, blues, rhythm and blues and big band music, Balk couldn't escape the lure of the music industry. Then one day Harry met a businessman who had similar musical interest. His name was Irving Micahnik. Micahnik was a tall and slightly overweight man. He was as intense and extroverted, as Balk was calm and analytical. They made a perfect pair. They were like-minded businessmen. Starting out as friends, they eventually combined their interests to form a production company. "We felt that there was more talent in Detroit. After looking around we realized that there was a tremendous amount of undiscovered music that we could record," Balk recalled.

HARRY BALK: DISCOVERING THE MOTOWN SOUND

One of Balk's interests was to find a singer that he could manage. It didn't take long for Harry to discover Little Willie John at Detroit talent contests. As the movie industry fell into decline in the mid 1950s, Balk entered the music business. He became Little Willie John's manager and looked for a record deal.

After hooking up with Sid Nathan's King Record label in Cincinnati, Ohio, Balk convinced legendary producer Henry Glover to handle Little Willie John's sessions. The results were a string of hits including "All Around the World," "Sleep" and "Fever" among others.

At this stage in his career, Balk knew little, if anything, about producing, but he watched Glover with interest. "I didn't know the first thing about cutting a session...I couldn't read music, but I had ideas for the songs," Balk recalled.

Eventually, Balk and Micahnik signed Del Shannon to a contract with Embee Productions. Irv was the manager and Harry the producer. They quickly became responsible for Shannon's earliest successes. It was Balk who had the musical brains behind Embee Productions. His experience in and around Detroit helped Del Shannon reach national stardom.

In sharp contrast, Micahnik had a serious gambling problem. Throughout his life he could never cover his debts. This strained his relationship with Balk and brought an early end to their partnership. For Balk the music was the key thing. His career spanned a long and windy road through all types of music and it began more than a decade before he led Del Shannon and "Runaway" to national stardom.

HARRY BALK'S ROAD TO ROCK AND ROLL FAME AND FORTUNE

The road to fame and fortune for Balk began in the teeming Detroit nightclubs, the after hour spots and the small theaters which graced the Motor City in the late 1940s and early 1950s. It was here that the tall, thin, cigar smoking Balk was seen eyeing the amateur acts, talking to the new musical groups and drinking with the fledgling entertainers who searched for a show business career. The nightlife in Detroit was filled with aspiring singers, comedy performers and would-be actors. Balk decided to take advantage of the talent and organized a series of amateur shows in his movie theaters.

Balk also haunted the local clubs. The Flame Bar was a favorite hangout for Detroit's music aficionados. Balk soon had his own table at The Flame Bar, and it didn't take long for him to realize that he had witnessed acts as good as the professionals.

Soon Balk's small movie theaters were presenting amateur acts like Little Willie John and the Four Tops. It didn't take Harry long to realize that there was potential profit in these performers.

THE LESSONS LEARNED FROM LITTLE WILLIE JOHN

After signing Little Willie John, Balk began promoting and booking the artist whose hits included "Fever," "All Around The World," and "Talk To Me" among others. The well-dressed, handsome Little Willie John had started out as a vocalist with the big bands that played the Detroit Theaters. It was while John was performing with the Paul "Hucklebuck" Williams Orchestra that Balk saw his future act. He knew that he was more than just a concert promoter and nightclub booker.

Not only was Balk a knowledgeable music man but he believed that he could produce some hits. He had an ear and a feel for black music. Henry Glover had produced Little Willie John's hits and Balk envisioned himself in the same role. What he didn't count on was Little Willie John's erratic behavior.

48

HARRY BALK: PRODUCER

"Little Willie John was simply too hard to handle," Balk remembered, "I was always getting him out of jail or out of some jam." Although Little Willie John tested Balk's patience, there was much for Harry to learn in the raucous world of rhythm and blues music from managing John.

Balk watched as small independent labels like King produced a highly profitable product and usually paid the artist next to nothing. When Balk entered the business world, he realized that the small independent labels and managers had a difficult time surviving in the 1950s and Harry Balk was determined not to be a casualty in the rock and roll music marketplace. His contracts were tough, but fair, and the artist could count on good management and careful supervision of their records.

Sid Nathan, the owner of the King label, referred to Balk as, "tough, but honest, by the standards of the 1950s. I never wanted to cross Harry," Nathan remarked. Henry Glover found it easier to have Balk in the studio when the diminutive and tempestuous Little Willie John recorded his hits and this experience undoubtedly influenced Harry. Soon he was cutting his own acetates.

When he watched Henry Glover produce Little Willie John, Balk often made suggestions. It was obvious that Harry had a knack for picking out hit records. It didn't matter whether the artist was black or white; Balk knew a hit sound. He also had some ideas of his own about cutting hit records. So Harry decided to become a producer.

At Joe's Records on Hastings street in the black Detroit ghetto, Balk had already cut demos for Little Willie John. It was here that he met Berry Gordy, who played piano on some of these early demos. When Jackie Wilson gave 6 demos of his songs to Little Willie John, the successful rhythm and blues singer turned them down. Of these, three became top 10 hits for Jackie Wilson and Barry Gordy Jr. who was already formulating the plans which made his Hitsville label, later to become Motown, one of the most successful of the day.

Finally in 1957, Balk released Little Willie John from his contract with two years remaining on it. "I decided that I was never going to fly to another small Southern town to bail Little Willie John out of jail," Balk remembered. "I just cut him loose and looked for a new place in show business."

Among black entertainers, Balk had a fine reputation. Barry Gordy remembered Balk as: "one of the few white guys in Detroit who knew something about black music." Balk also had an eye for the developing teen market. He realized that white acts sold more records, played in better venues and made more money than their black counterparts.

Balk realized that there were many bands and an equally large number of young singers who were ready for commercial success. So he decided to concentrate upon the white, crossover artists. As 1960 dawned, young, white, good looking kids who came out of Philadelphia or New York dominated the charts. Balk was determined to find his own teen idol. He also had the perfect vehicle to promote a teen singer. He co owned his own production company.

It was Embee Productions, which provided the vehicle by which Balk and Micahnik began to promote Del Shannon and bring him ultimate stardom.

THE RISE OF EMBEE PRODUCTIONS

Eventually, along with his partner Irv Micahnik, a local furrier, Balk formed a management company known as Embee Productions. Soon Harry and Irving scoured local nightclubs for talent and were intent upon setting up a management team. Detroit was filled with black rhythm and blues singers and the market was ready for new talent.

"I loved those early days," Balk remembered, "but I couldn't take Little Willie John's behavior. There are only so many times you can bail someone out of jail." As he managed John and broke into the music business, Balk displayed a shrewd sense of the business side of the industry.

"It was song writing and publishing that brought in the money," Balk recalled. "I always took care of business." So Harry formed Vicki Music Publishing, named after his daughter and registered it with BMI. The Vicki Music imprint was all over the place in the 1950s and 1960s and earned Harry a sizable income. It was a common practice for managers to place their names on songs, and Balk and Micahnik were not exceptions to this industry rule. They used the names Ira Mack and Tom King for their own names on songs that they wanted to own a piece of the song writing and publishing royalties.

To find new talent and record it, Harry and Irv employed Embee Productions as the vehicle for their artists. Balk negotiated tough recording contracts and made what he considered fair deals for his artists with major record companies. Eventually, Harry and Irv also set up a small label, Twirl Records, because they found it difficult to secure distribution for their product. "Irv and I founded Embee Productions and then our own record label because no one would distribute Twirl Records, so we became both the record company and the distributor." Soon he was working with Don and Juan and Johnny and the Hurricanes. Unwittingly, these acts helped to reinforce the management skill and musical knowledge, which would allow Balk to move Del Shannon into the mainstream of the rock and roll music industry.

THE ROYALTONES AND HARRY BALK

The initial foray into rock and roll took place when Balk signed a local Detroit band, the Royaltones, to a contract and hit the **Billboard** Top 40 in 1958 with "Poor Boy." Other acts that Balk brought into his management company included Jamie Coe and the Gigolos, Mickey Denton and Johnny Gibson who had minor hits with "Beachcomer" and "Midnight."

The Royaltones were a group that played in and around Dearborn, Michigan. They were a saxophone-based group with five teen musicians who could play their instruments with the feel of seasoned veterans. With two lead saxophones, the Royaltones had a unique sound. As an instrumental band they were legendary and toured before they had record success.

Harry Balk heard them at a teen dance. Soon he worked out a deal with Jubilee Records and during the second week of September 1958 the Royaltones first record was released. It took some time for it to chart and, finally, in November 1958 "Poor Boy" entered the **Billboard** chart rising to number 17 during its 10-week stay. The promotional hands behind the Royaltones were tied to Embee Productions and they pulled out the stops to make it a hit.

In February 1959 Jubilee released: "See-Saw," but the hopes for this Royaltones release to chart were quickly dashed. It vanished from the charts. Jubilee didn't appear to be the label that they needed and Balk pointed this out. For the next two years, the Royaltones cut a number of records. It took two years to find the right sound and this was due to Balk's constant experimentation and technical skill.

Although it wasn't a Top 40 hit, "Flamingo Express" was a chart record in 1961. What made the Royaltones special was their ability in the studio. Often Balk used them to back other singers.

They were one of the best instrumental bands of the day. However, they never achieved lasting national stardom. Yet, from 1958 to 1964 they released a series of singles, which contained some of the best instrumental music of the day. Such Royaltones songs as "Holy Smokes," "Boss Limbo," "Our Faded Love" and "Little Bo" suggest their instrumental genius.

The fact that the Royaltones had a unique sound was in part due to Balk's guidance and inspiration. "I realized early in my career," Balk remembered, "that I had to stay ahead of the crowd and look for an original sound. I went down the dumper if I tried to copy someone else." Harry's words were apocryphal because he discovered an instrumental group with a unique and commercial sound. That group, Johnny and the Hurricanes, was one of the most consistent hit makers of their day. It was with this group that Balk would produce the national hits, which made his reputation as a top-level producer.

JOHNNY AND THE HURRICANES AND HARRY BALK

The road that Johnny and the Hurricanes took to Harry Balk was a long and involved one. Johnny Paris was a young musician in Toledo Ohio. He organized a high school band in 1957, which he christened the Orbits. It was at Rossford's Catholic High School, that John Pocisk, born in 1940 in Wallridge, Ohio, began his musical journey.

While in high school, Johnny listened to jazz incessantly and picked up a great deal from Charlie Parker. It was after he heard Bill Haley that his band, the Orbits, found their sound. He also changed his name to Johnny Paris.

After playing for local high school dances, Paris and the Orbits recorded with a local rockabilly legend, Mack Vickery. The recordings with Vickery were booked in a small Detroit studio and after he returned to Toledo, Johnny Paris decided to move the band to Detroit.

In 1959, Detroit was a hotbed of musical talent and Paris' group had a unique instrumental sound. Like many groups, Johnny Paris and his Orbits sought out Embee Productions. Initially, Harry Balk and Irving Micahnik were not interested in Paris' group. They were intent on signing Fred Kelly and the Parliaments to a recording contract. Once Balk and Micahnik's Talent Artists, Inc., signed the Parliaments, the

Orbits were hired as the back up band. After Balk listened to the Parliaments he fired them and told Johnny Paris and the Orbits that they were Embee Productions' instrumental band.

It was Balk who placed their music in a mainstream commercial context. He crafted the band's sound in a manner which allowed them to play both teen dances and concerts. Once Johnny and the Hurricanes broke away from Balk's production and management arm they never regained their old popularity. He had an ear for a hit record but he wouldn't put up with the artist being temperamental.

It didn't take Balk long to realize that there were enormous sums of money in song writing and publishing royalties. So Balk and Micahnik used the pseudonyms, Ira Mack and Tom King, and the publishing firm Vicki Music was set up to collect their money. It was the perfect vehicle for a publishing company.

Johnny and the Hurricanes first hit in June 1959, "Crossfire," quickly rose to number 23 on the **Billboard** pop chart and remained there for 14 weeks. "I had a plan with Johnny and the Hurricanes," Balk remembered, "I knew their sound was unique and hence commercial." From 1959 to 1961, this commercial path was a successful one as Johnny and the Hurricanes charted nine songs on the **Billboard** Hot 100.

When Balk first recorded Johnny and the Orbits at the Carmen Theater in Detroit, the first thing he did was to change their name to Johnny and the Hurricanes. After recording Johnny and the Hurricanes' "Crossfire," Balk and Micahnik took the demo to New York to shop it to the major labels. Mitch Miller at Columbia Records listened but declined to sign the group. No other major label was interested. "They thought Johnny and the Hurricanes music was kid stuff," Balk recalled. But Harry knew better, because he had watched the reaction to the group at local Detroit sock hops. As Irv and Harry drove their old Chevrolet from New York back to Michigan they were frustrated.

"How much does it cost to put out a record?" Harry asked Irv.

"I don't know, but it can't be that much," Irv replied.

"Let's go for it," Harry remarked.

With that brief statement Twirl Records was born. On a napkin, Harry made notes on what type of music, what type of distribution and the type of artists Twirl would sign. It was all in the planning stage but Balk had confidence. The reason for this optimism was that Harry had discovered a band led by Johnny Paris.

Johnny and the Hurricanes had come a long way since they began in Toledo, Ohio as the Orbits. With Johnny Paris, on sax, whose real name was Johnny Pocisk, Paul Tesluk on organ, Dave Yorko on guitar, Lionel "Butch" Mattice on bass and Tony Kaye on drums, the Orbits had a makings of a hit group. But Balk soon brought in Little Bo Savitch from the Royaltones to replace Kaye on the drums and the sound improved immensely. One of the characteristics of Balk's skill was his ear for a hit record. So he knew when a member of a band needed replacing. Though Balk and Micahnik had some problems getting their product to the general public. They were having trouble finding people interested in their music. No label was interested in signing them. Harry knew that Johnny and the Hurricanes were a sure-hit group. So he took matters into his own hands.

HARRY BALK: PRODUCER

When they returned home form New York, Harry went to a local one stop record distributor, Irv Snider. Over a long lunch Balk talked about Johnny and the Hurricanes and their commercial potential. Snider was interested. He pointed out to Harry that for $250 to $300 a thousand records could be pressed and a local hit was possible. So Harry organized the Twirl Record Company in 1958 and released "Crossfire." The instrumental fire behind "Crossfire" was fueled by a blend of raucous electric guitar and an up tempo saxophone complete with energetic hand clapping. The record hit the charts in and around Detroit and began receiving national airplay. Johnny and the Hurricanes were so hot that every major label wanted to buy the master. Balk was a careful businessman who wanted to deal with someone he could trust.

Harry then contacted his old friend, Morty Craft, at Seven Arts. Craft also owned the newly created Warwick label. A deal was cut and Johnny and the Hurricanes' "Crossfire" was released nationally and reached number 23 on the **Billboard** Top 40. There were three other Warwick releases which charted "Red River Rock" at number 5, "Beatnik Fly," based on the folk song "Blue Tale Fly," at number 15 and "Reveille Rock" at number 25 on the **Billboard** Hot 100. On the **Billboard** Rhythm and Blues chart "Red River Rock" peaked at number 5 in its 14 weeks on the chart in the Summer and early Fall of 1959. In November "Reveille Rock" entered the rhythm and blues chart and remained for 6 weeks rising to number 17.

During this period, Balk learned a great deal about the music business. Embee Productions signed Johnny and the Hurricanes to their Twirl label for a one and one half-percent royalty rate and then leased the material to Warwick Records at an eight-percent figure. Not only did this create a nice profit; it led to an ill will between Balk and Paris that exists to this day. As Harry pointed out, Johnny and the Hurricanes were not forced to sign the contract. They did it of their own free will.

It was Embee Productions who first broke Johnny and the Hurricanes in the Detroit area with their connections to WJBK, which were on both the AM and FM dial, and the disc jockeys at this station, notably Tom Clay, could make or break a record. Micahnik and Clay were frequently seen around town having a drink.

Eventually, Clay was fired for taking payola. There is no evidence that Balk and Micahnik were involved in the payola scandal, but they were helped not only by Clay but other disc jockeys. Perhaps, the Johnny and the Hurricanes' material was strong enough to avoid payola. No one knows and no one is talking.

There was another side to Embee Productions. They realized that the English, European and Australian markets were important ones. What Balk learned about England was as important as Johnny and the Hurricanes American success. In 1959 Harry negotiated a contract with London Records and soon the group was on the United Kingdom charts. As he perused the London music newspapers, Balk realized that there was an unexplored market for American music in the United Kingdom. Due to Balk's sagacious promotion "Red River Valley" rose to number 3 in England in October, 1959, it was also a German hit. This was followed by "Reveille Rock," which peaked at number 14 in December 1959. These experiences in England and Germany were ones that Harry used to promote Shannon's records with enormous success two years later.

Once Johnny and the Hurricanes hit the American charts, Balk began recording their material in New York's Bell Studio. It was the most advanced technological recording studio in America, and it employed some of the best local session musicians. After recording a number of hits with Johnny and the Hurricanes, there were problems finding new material. This is where Harry Balk's expertise came in to rescue Johnny and the Hurricanes.

A take-charge guy, Balk convinced Johnny and the Hurricanes to sign with Big Top Records and give Harry, as producer, total control. Although he signed the deal, this agreement did not sit well with Johnny Paris.

As the leader of the group, Johnny Paris had little sense of the music business. He had a big ego and ideas, which ran contrary to commercial success. So Balk had to take matters into his own hands to keep Johnny and Hurricanes on the charts.

One night while they were in Bell Sound Studio, Johnny and the Hurricanes were having trouble cutting "Red River Rock." Balk remarked: "We took a break. Then the kid on the organ made a crazy sound. That's it." What Balk recalled was the special organ sound that made "Red River Rock" a hit.

Another example of Balk's ear for a hit came when Johnny Paris went to the bathroom one day during a recording session. He wet his sax reed and then blew through it. Harry, who was passing by the bathroom, hollered: "Stop! That's a hit sound." Paris thought Balk had lost his mind. But the strange sound that came from Paris' wet reed turned into the hit "Rockin' Goose."

In 1960, Balk's production brought out the best in an average instrumental group. With the release of "Beatnik Fly" in February 1960, Johnny and the Hurricanes became an in demand concert group. In England, "Beatnik Fly" hit the Top 10 on the British charts and it was even a bigger hit in the United Kingdom than in America. When Johnny and the Hurricanes only album, **Stormsville**, was released in 1960 it continued to sell in England well into the later part of the decade.

Johnny and the Hurricanes were an important part of Balk's baptism in the music business. He preferred black music, but the white acts crossed over into the mainstream and made more money. By 1961 Johnny and the Hurricanes were on a downhill slide. They had a few regional hits with "Down Yonder" and "Ja Da" but there was little demand for their music. With the rise of the Beatles, the Rolling Stones and the Yardbirds, Johnny and the Hurricanes vanished into an oldies act.

After returning from England, Johnny and the Hurricanes signed with Jeff Records. Then, after one single, Paris moved on to Atilla were he released five singles with no chart action. Johnny Paris had remained the only original Hurricane and he took his act to England and Europe for the next three decades. What doomed Paris was his inability to change his musical direction.

One of the problems with Johnny and the Hurricanes was Johnny Paris, who fought tooth and nail with Harry over the production of their records. So there was no love lost when Balk and Paris split company. This was just about the time that Ollie McLaughlin brought Del Shannon to Detroit with his song "Runaway." There was also other talent around Detroit at this time.

It was this talent which validated Balk's production genius. He was much more than a hit record producer and manager. Balk took some unlikely musical groups and made them stars.

JOHNNY AND THE HURRICANES: THE BILLBOARD HIT RECORDS

Crossfire, no. 23, 14 weeks, 1959
Red River Rock, no. 5, 17 weeks, 1959
Reveille Rock, no. 25, 13 weeks, 1959
Beatnik Fly, no. 15, 13 weeks, 1960
Down Yonder, no. 48, 9 weeks, 1960
Rockin' Goose, no, 60, 6 weeks, 1960
Revival, no. 97, 1 week, 1960
You Are My Sunshine, no. 91, 1 week, 1960
Ja-Da, no. 86, 2 weeks, 1961

While Balk was managing and producing Johnny and the Hurricanes, Balk met two house painters. One day a talent agent, Peter Paul, brought Roland Trone and Claude Johnson, who were using the professional name Don and Juan, to see Balk. After listening to their demo of "What's Your Name," Balk quickly signed them to a recording contract. They were New York house painters and Balk met them after learning that they had teamed up at Brooklyn High School with Estelle Williams and Fred Jones to form a group known as the Genies. In 1959, the Genies had a minor hit "Who's Knockin" (Shad 509). After the group disbanded, Roland Trone and Claude Johnson became house painters and then a record agent heard them singing while they were painting a building frequented by music people. This is what led them to cut their demo of "What's Your Name."

Balk wanted to recut "What's Your Name." Balk informed Don and Juan that production changes were needed in the song. So they went to Bell Studios and cut "What's Your Name" backed with "Chicken Necks" (Big Top 3106), it rose to number 7 on the **Billboard** Top 40 in February 1962. Don and Juan's hit came at the time that Balk was working with Del Shannon and it demonstrated his continued hit-making abilities.

ENTER OLLIE MCLAUGHLIN AND RUNAWAY

Ollie McLaughlin then brought Del Shannon to Embee Productions. Since McLaughlin was a friend of Max Crook's, it was easy for Del to find a sympathetic ear with Balk. Ollie had watched the Charlie Johnson Band, Del's group, perform at the Hi Lo Club. Because of the peculiar segregation that existed in Battle Creek, McLaughlin had to come in when the band was practicing. As a result he got to know Chuck and quickly realized that he was a major talent. By sitting in the empty club and watching Chuck perform originals like "Little Oscar" and "Runaway," Ollie realized that there were a lot of hit songs in the Charlie Johnson Band.

So, when McLaughlin contacted Balk and Micahnik, he convinced Embee Productions to listen to Del Shannon's music. It was as a songwriter, as well as a performer, that McLaughlin pitched the songs from this unknown Battle Creek singer. The rest was history as they cut "Runaway" and it soared to number one on the **Billboard** pop chart.

Harry Balk

McLaughlin mentioned to Shannon that the partnership between Balk and Micahnik was a stormy one. While Harry was a tough, but honest businessman, he found out that Micahnik had been collecting past royalties without letting Harry know about it. Irv Micahnik went on to manage Chubby Checker and continued to be a mover in the rock music industry. It was the second phase of Checker's career when Micahnik brought back with commercials, re-recordings of his old hits and concerts on the oldies circuit. Micahnik also put Chubby Checker together with the Fat Boys and this coupling with a contemporary act helped to revive Checker's career.

Soon after, Balk parted company from Micahnik and went his own way. Harry didn't think much about Irv until he found out that his old partner was collecting royalties that he should've been sharing. So Balk began the long process of making Micahnik split what was rightfully owed.

Finally, in 1977, Harry tracked Irv down and Micahnik agreed to pay Balk the past due royalties. They made an appointment to meet the next day. When Harry arrived at Irv's New York apartment, the next-door neighbor lady was crying. Irving Micahnik had died a few hours after agreeing to pay Harry his money. It was a fitting way for Irv to go, as he had avoided paying most people during his lifetime.

Micahnik never married Bobbi Smith, who was the lead singer in Bobbi Smith and the Dream Girls, but she remained his close friend until the end. When Micahnik died, the last chance for Harry to collect his money ended. He could have sued the estate but didn't out of respect for his long time friend. Balk, always the gentleman, let the past-royalties slide and returned to producing new talent.

It was Ollie McLaughlin, the Michigan disc jockey, who realized that Harry Balk was ready to enter the mainstream of the rock music industry. His hits with Little Willie John, Don and Juan and Johnny and the Hurricanes prepared Balk for his eventual success with Del Shannon.

"Del Shannon was the first or second artist we signed after Johnny and the Hurricanes," Balk remembered. "We recorded Del right away-without Max Crook-who was in New York. We cut two sides and it didn't work out. Del was singing too flat." It was after one of these early sessions that Balk realized that Crook's eerie musitron sound was an integral part of Shannon's sound.

When he recalled the background to the "Runaway" sessions, Balk had a sly smile on his face. "I remember that Del was a great songwriter. We took his songs and knew that we would have hits with them."

Balk claims that he knew "Runaway" was an immediate hit. The musicians apparently also knew it was a hit, and Al Caiola offered Balk $15,000 for a piece of it. Harry responded: "I don't need any partners, thank you." As Balk recorded Del Shannon he realized that his newfound star often sounded uneven. It was Del's old friend, Max Crook, who heard the songs before Balk. "He used to sing songs to me he had written while on the road or in his hotel rooms, and these new songs would sound great," Max continued. "Then the same songs would sound flat in the studio. Del was a guy who was up emotionally or was down, never in the middle." The magic of Balk's production was that he could incorporate many ideas and influences. So the Shannon sound was part Del, part Max and part Harry.

After Del cut the final version of "Runaway," Harry not only altered the speed of the master tape but carefully cut the falsetto bridge. "When I played it for Del, he cried and said it didn't sound like him," Harry recalled. "Hell, I said, no one knows what you sound like." Then Balk set up a promotional copy of "Runaway" to one-stop wholesalers and before the song was released there were large orders from New York distributors. "At one point," Balk recalled, 'Runaway' was selling 80,000 a day." Not even Shannon could believe his good fortune.

When "Runaway" first appeared on the **Billboard** Top 40 on March 27, 1961, Del was still working for Pete Vice in his Battle Creek carpet store and he was appearing as Charlie Johnson at the Hi Lo Club.

The myth that the early 1960s was a time of non-talented singers, poor production and a rehashing of old pop tunes is exploded by the Del Shannon story. Not only was Del an original songwriter, and a musical innovator, but he also had a vision for his music. This premonition for success would not have been fulfilled had it not been for Balk.

When Balk looks back upon the early 1960s he has fond memories. "I always thought Del was a better songwriter than singer," Harry remembered. "Another thing about Del is that he always loved country and western music." As Balk recalled his years with Del Shannon, he had primarily positive memories. "The stories about me not being fair with Del or not paying him are bullshit," Balk concluded. What is evident is that Harry Balk was an integral part of Shannon's commercial success. These two businessmen were together from the start with "Runaway" through the mid-1960s; then Balk and Shannon parted company.

The main reason that Del and Harry didn't talk was an album project produced by Balk that was never released. The Shannon album entitled **Move It On Over** was impounded by the recording studio because Micahnik would not pay for the studio time. It seems that Irving lost the money in a card game and wasn't up to telling Balk about his misdeeds. Shannon was furious and left Embee Productions.

In 1965, Balk and Micahnik went their separate ways. They had financial misunderstanding. When Big Top Records folded in the mid-1960s, the cash flow problems prompted them to find other projects. Embee Productions folded and Balk began planning a record label. At this time Del and Harry also parted company. The problem was Shannon's contract and he screamed for years about how unfair Harry was, and then sometime in the late 1970s they made up.

For many years Del Shannon didn't forgive Balk. Then in Dan Bourgoise' Bug Music office one day in the 1970s they reconciled. Del and Harry remained friends until Shannon's untimely suicide. The combination of Balk's production skills and Shannon's song writing and vocal talents produced a series of hit records, which define the early 1960s.

HARRY BALK'S CAREER AFTER DEL SHANNON: THE SOUL YEARS

In 1966, Balk founded the Impact label. Harry also needed an act to get Impact off the ground. As usual he found one in Detroit. There were plans to release a Del Shannon Greatest Hits LP on Twirl, but this never materialized. Just like in the old days, Balk discovered his new act in a Detroit nightclub. They were the Shades of Blue, a one-hit band, who brought Balk right back into the mainstream of the **Billboard** Hot 100.

As Balk searched the clubs for new acts, he found it difficult to pinpoint the right group. Then, in 1966, while hanging out with soul singer Edwin Starr, whose hit

"Agent Double O-Soul" had established him as a major soul act, Harry insisted that they drop into a local club. It was a spur of the moment decision that had professional consequences. As Starr and Balk walked into a local nightclub, they watched a group called Shades of Blue. Balk knew that they had the potential for a hit record. The Detroit based group consisted of three men and a female vocalist. "They had made a demo of a gospel tune "Oh How Happy" and Balk put it out on his own Impact Record label. It was released in May 1966 and rose to number 12 on the **Billboard** Top 40. Once again Balk's nose for a hit proved the critics wrong. He had been told by many industry people in and around Detroit that the Shades of Blue had no future. Harry knew better. The Shades of Blues were turned down by most major record labels, but Impact Records demonstrated that those who knew the industry still had a lot to learn. His reputation as a talent scout, producer and manager was a strong one in the black community. Eventually, Balk's talent brought him a major position as a talent coordinator with Detroit's most prestigious black label.

Del At Home in Southfield, Michigan, October, 1964

In the late 1960s he was approached for a position as an executive with Motown. Barry Gordy, Jr., recognized that Balk was a knowledgeable music person. Therefore, in the late 1960s, Balk went to work for Motown. For two years he advised Gordy and then one day in early 1971 he heard a marvelous demo by Marvin Gaye. "What's Going On" was the tune, which Balk took to Gordy. Then at a board meeting, Balk suggested that they press extra copies of the Gaye song. He was ignored, but Balk wrote his prediction on the blackboard in Motown's office.

When Gaye's "What's Going On" hit the **Billboard** Top 40 in March 1971 the song introduced a new jazz-blues sound to soul music. "It had that jazz feel that I just love," Balk remembered. So did the general public as Gaye took Motown in a new commercial direction. "I worked at Motown for a few years, in the late 60s and early 70s," Balk recalled: "One of my jobs was to develop 'white acts.'

Balk discovered Motown's biggest white act, Rare Earth. In 1969, Harry heard a demo from a white band and knew he had another hit group. When the Detroit based rock group came in for an interview Balk was impressed by the big band and soul quality of these white musicians. Balk knew that they were a professional group. After Rare Earth was signed, they recorded a debut album **Get Ready** (Rare Earth RS 507) which Motown released to platinum sales. Eventually, Rare Earth had six **Billboard** Top 40 hits including three in the top ten in 1970-1971, "Get Ready," "(I Know) I'm Losing You" and "I Just Want to Celebrate."

John Small, the disc jockey at WKNR-FM in Detroit, wrote the liner notes to Rare Earth's debut LP and he predicted stardom. The first single "Get Ready" rose to number 4 on the **Billboard** Top 40 and led to five other hits. Harry Balk's eye for talent continued with other artists.

In the Fall of 1970, R. Dean Taylor, a white singer from Toronto, Canada showed up at Motown with a demo. Taylor was a 31 year-old songwriter who had never recorded anything with commercial success. In 1960 he made a record for Parry Records and continued to release 45s with absolutely no success. When Taylor co-wrote the Supremes "Love Child" in 1968 he came to the attention of Motown's production staff.

Balk listened to Taylor's demo of "Indiana Wants Me" and went to Barry Gordy, Jr., predicting it would be a hit. Gordy wasn't sure but he trusted Balk's instincts. When Taylor's "Indiana Wants Me" was released it went to number 5 in September 1970 on the **Billboard** Top 40. "R. Dean Taylor was a lot like Del Shannon," Harry Balk recalled, "but he didn't have the staying power of Del."

No one had a first hit like Del Shannon. Once Balk got into the studio with Del to make "Runaway," it began one of the most legendary careers in rock music. Harry Balk was a major figure in Shannon's development who helped him navigate the murky waters of the rock music business.

Like many producers in the music business, he has been both praised and criticized. There is little doubt that without his production skills there would have been no Del Shannon. That is reason enough to suggest Balk's importance. He not only understood the subtle nuances of the business, but he knew how to take his people to the top.

BIBLIOGRAPHICAL SOURCES

Harry Balk graciously sat down for a series of interviews which set the record straight about his involvement with the music industry in general and Del Shannon in particular. Interviews with Ike Turner added a great deal to this period of rock music history. Dan Bourgoise filled in many spots in the story from his long association with key figures in the music industry. Dennis DeWitt, "Harry Balk Interview," **And The Music Plays On: Del Shannon Magazine**, Issue 4, Summer, 1995, pp. 4-12 is an important starting point for Balk's career.

Howard A. DeWitt, **Chuck Berry: Rock N Roll Music** (2nd. ed., Ann Arbor, 1985) provided background material. The literature on Motown Records is important in understanding Harry Balk's, see, for example, Berry Gordy, **To Be Loved: The Music, The Magic, The Memories of Motown** (New York, 1994) and an important fact book David Bianco, **Heatwave: The Motown Fact Book** (Ann Arbor, 1998). Also see Dorothy Wade and Justin Picardie, **Music Man: Ahmet Ertegun, Atlantic Records, and the Triumph of Rock 'n' Roll** (New York, 1990) for the contributions of another producer and a rival label to Balk's sound.

On the early 1960s see Howard A. DeWitt, **The Beatles: Untold Tales** (Fremont, 1985) for some essays on the early 1960s that influenced Del Shannon's career. In particular, see the section on John Lennon.

On the role of Johnny and the Hurricanes in Harry Balk's career, see, for example, Bill Millar, "Blowin' Up A Storm," **Melody Maker**, number 54 (March 24, 1979), p. 42: Bill Millar, "Johnny & The Hurricanes," **Goldmine**, number 57 (February, 1981), pp. 10-11. For Little Willie Johnson see, for example, Lou Holscher, "Little Willie John--Fact or Fiction," **Goldmine**, number 72 (May, 1982), p. 189, Bill Millar, "Free At Last," **The History of Rock**, number 17 (1982), 336-337, Steve Propes, "Little Willie John: King of Detroit Soul Music," **Goldmine**, number 171 (February 13, 1987), p. 22.

On the royalty controversy between Del Shannon and Embee Productions see Bob Fisher, "Writs and Royalties," **And The Music Plays On**, number 1, (Fall, l994), p. 16.

Extensive interviews with Jimmy McCracklin, Solomon Burke, Charles Brown, Bob Geddins, Guitar Mac and Lowell Fulson helped to fill in material on the black acts from Balk's Detroit and New York experiences.

For Motown and Harry Balk, see, for example, Nelson George, **Where Did Our Love Go?: The Rise and Fall of the Motown Sound** (New York, 1985); Raynoma Gordy Singleton, **Berry, Me And Motown** (Chicago, 1990) and Gerri Hirshey, **Nowhere To Run** (New York, 1984). See Alan Betrock, ed., **Girl Groups: The Story of the Sound** (New York, 1982) for a section on Motown written by Aaron Fuchs.

A series of interviews with Lavern Baker were helpful in placing Balk in the musical scene in and around Detroit.

On the economics of the music business, see Marc Eliot, **Rockonomics: The Money Behind The Music** (New York, 1989) and R. Serge Denisoff, **Tarnished Gold** (Brunswick, N. J., 1986). Also see, Simon Garfield, **Money For Nothing** (London, 1986) and the sketches in Nick Tosches, **Unsung Heroes of Rock 'n' Roll** (New York, 1984) for tales of how poorly artists were treated when it came to their royalties.

For the Michigan music scene see, David Carson, **Rockin' Down The Dial: The Detroit Sound of Radio, From Jack The Bellboy To The Big 8** (Troy, 2000). Carson's book is a solid contribution with deep research. For allegations of payola, see, for example, "ABC Says Clark Takes No Payola," **Detroit Free Press**, November 19, 1959; "Detroit Radio Star Confesses Payola," **New York Times**, November 23, 1959; "Disc Jockey Tom Clay Fired By WJBK," **Detroit News**, November 23, 1959; "Disc Jockeys Don't Cry-The Wages of Sin," **Time**, December 7, 1959 and "DJs Mum on Charges of Payola," **Detroit Free Press**, November 19, 1959.

Wayne Jancik's book, **One Hit Wonders** (New York, 1998) is a pathbreaking work of excellent historical scholarship that was useful in this chapter. For the early days of rock and roll also, see, for example, Dick Clark, **Rock, Roll And Remember** (New York, 1978); Frederick Dannen, **Hit Men** (New York, 1990); Charlie Gillett, **The Sound of the City** (London, 1983); John A. Jackson, **Alan Freed and the Early Days of Rock 'n' Roll** (New York, 1991); Rick Sklar, **Rocking America** (New York, 1984); Wes Smith, **Pied Pipers of Rock 'n' Roll** (Marietta, 1987) and David P. Szatmary, **Rockin' In Time** (Englewood Cliffs, 1987).

A model work of historical scholarship, Lee Cottten's, **Shake Rattle and Roll: The Golden Age of American Rock 'n' Roll 1952-1955** (Ann Arbor, 1987, volume 1) was important in reconstructing the early years of rock music. Also see Cotton's, **Reelin' And Rockin': The Golden Age of Rock 'n Roll, 1956-1959** (Ann Arbor, 1995, volume II).

Del Shannon At Home With Brian Hyland

4: "RUNAWAY": THE MAKING OF A HIT RECORD, 1960-1961

"Forget everything you have ever heard about 'Runaway.' It was this simple. Max sat down and began tinkling on the piano. I jumped in with the drums and the band worked on the song for the next 15 to 20 minutes on stage." Dick Parker, Del Shannon's drummer at the Hi Lo Club

Del Shannon's "Runaway" was the number one hit record that introduced a soaring new talent into the rock and roll arena. It was January 1961, when Shannon went into the studio with producer Harry Balk and cut the tune that featured Del's high falsetto vocal and Max Crook's unique musitron sound. When "Runaway" entered the **Billboard** and **Cash Box** charts in 1961 it was the result of a three-year musical journey that began when the Charlie Johnson Band took up residence at the notorious Battle Creek, Michigan venue, the Hi Lo Club. The genesis of "Runaway" started in his hometown, Coopersville, and then followed a long and twisted path.

THE EMERGENCE OF DEL SHANNON

When Del Shannon emerged as a rock and roll story, he was one of many performers who had a first hit. "Runaway" was different from other hits; it had a unique sound. When oldies radio began it was one of the lasting tunes on that format. As an individual performer, Shannon had an electric presence. He took the rock and roll world by storm. The attempts to turn him into a teen idol faded quickly. The reason was a simple one. Shannon was a broader and more complex performer than **16 Magazine** and the few other teen publications who interviewed him realized this during the early days of rock music. Few people knew that Shannon loved country music, particularly Hank Williams, or that he was an avid jazz fan. No one knew that he was five years older than Embee Productions birth date of 1939 indicated in their early publicity releases. When the media interviewed Shannon they often commented on his maturity, his intellect and his ability to talk about any type of music.

Everyone was amazed that he had such a wide ranging musical style. His manager, Irving Micahnik, often hollered: "God damn it, Del quit all that shit with the jazz, the country and all that pop music crap. You're a rock and roller." This frustrated Shannon but he was ready to accept the restrictions of being a rock music star.

The typical teen idol of the early 1960s had good looks, an average voice, nice clothes, and he had little worldly experience. Del Shannon was a smart businessman, a consummate songwriter and he attended to the little things that kept a person in the business.

It was Shannon's talent that intrigued people. "I couldn't believe how sophisticated he was compared to the typical teen idol," Dick Clark remarked. Del used his falsetto voice, but he could also shift into a moody pop vocal. These early exercises in musical expression gave an indication of Westover's future. He would write and sing songs in such an unusual manner that he was destined for stardom.

Westover also needed someone to prod him as well as to listen to his ideas. Once he married Shirley Nash, he found his soul mate. Over the years Chuck continued to write original tunes and practice his guitar. He was obsessed with music and the entertainment business.

THE GESTATION OF "RUNAWAY"

By the time that Chuck wrote "Runaway," in late 1960, he had practiced and played his music for more than a decade. "Runaway" may have been written on the spur of the moment, but it was the culmination of a decade of hard work. But for the drummer, Dick Parker, the song came quickly and didn't involve a great deal of effort.

Dick Parker remembered, "We practiced two or three times a week to bring new songs into the group. One day we came in before our show to jam and Max started his organ riff, Del came in on guitar, I began playing my drums and Dugger hit the slapping bass. We played the song that became 'Runaway' and I even think we played it that night. It was not as complicated as people think. It just came together. I think Chuck had to rewrite the words but the tune came quickly. It was somewhere between one and three days to get the song together. We didn't labor on 'Runaway,' the basic song was there, it wasn't much of an evolution."

What was interesting about "Runaway" is that it had an organ sound through an instrument known as the musitron. That musical sound soon turned up in England as the Merseyside sound. While most of Del's music influenced the Merseyside beat, it was "Little Town Flirt" which contained the instrumental bridge identifying this English sound. In American the impact of "Runaway," along with other early hits of Shannon were ignored in the emergence of United Kingdom groups. The Beatles, Gerry and the Pacemakers, the Searchers, and Billy J. Kramer and the Dakotas, among others were readying the Merseyside sound to invade the American marketplace. These groups listened to the first half dozen Del Shannon 45s while crafting the Merseyside sound.

"I remember Del Shannon's records being played at sock hops and the boys (the Beatles) listened to those records regularly," Sam Leach, an early Beatle booker recalled. Brian Kelly, another small-time booking agent, remembered the Beatles talking about Shannon's musical direction. "I think that the early Beatles played their music with Del Shannon's records in mind." Bob Wooler, the Cavern disc jockey, added his reminiscences, "The Beatles took Shannon's instrumental sound and crafted their words around it."

In the midst of writing and recording "Runaway," there was a great deal of stress in Shannon's life. His mother, Leone, had just sold their Coopersville house and was living in a rented room. His dad, Bert, was in a nursing home. Del was married and had a family, and he had his own financial strain. He worked by day at Peter Vice's carpet shop and by night he was Charlie Johnson leading the band at the Hi Lo Club. The pressures on Shannon to write and record were enormous and he made his way into the record business despite the enormous distractions around him.

THE ROAD TO "RUNAWAY": PHASE ONE

"I don't think that Charles ever stopped writing," his mother Leone remembered. Initially, however, he was a musical genius who couldn't find an outlet for his songs. That problem was solved by what many consider a most unlikely source— Charles Westover's high school principal.

Russell Conran, the principal at Coopersville High School, recognized this obsessive-compulsive desire to create original music and he nurtured Chuck's drive. It was Conran who first suggested that he write about things that would allow him to produce his music. "Runaway" was the perfect theme for Charles because in Coopersville and later in Battle Creek he saw two small towns, which stifled his creative flow.

The contradiction in Westover's early view of these towns was that in later years as Del Shannon, he looked back nostalgically and realized that both Coopersville and Battle Creek had a strong impact not only upon his character but his song writing.

"Chuck was always writing songs," Max Crook recalled. There was a drive to succeed in the music business. This prompted him to work daily on his song writing and performing art. Charles Westover was ambitious musically, and he wouldn't rest until he wrote a hit song. "He used to come in the carpet shop and talk about those Italian boys, he loved that Dion," Peter Vice remarked. "I knew that it was only a matter of time until he had his own hit record."

The carpet shop that Vice owned in Battle Creek was an important source for Westover's musical inspiration. Chuck was an unusually astute observer of people and many of the themes behind his early songs were built on accidental occurrences and observances of the customers. "I always knew that Chuck could take everyday incidents and make them into songs," Vice concluded.

Del Shannon: Rock Star In The Making

During his spare time, Chuck spent an inordinate amount of time listening to the radio and analyzing the song themes behind hit records. When Chuck heard Jimmy Jones' million selling "Handy Man," in 1960, he found a style and type of song that would bring him to the forefront of the rock and roll industry.

"I knew that I could write better and sound just as good as the hit record guys with a falsetto," Chuck told Darwin Farr. Soon Charlie was blending a number of styles. The falsetto in Jimmy Jones' and later Roy Orbison's records intrigued Westover and he began to experiment with his own range. He loved Orbison's haunting ballads. So he used his band, backed by Max Crook's musitron, to create a soaring vocal falsetto that blended with the eerie sounding musitron. Without realizing it, Chuck was setting up the formula, which created "Runaway."

When Charles listened to Chuck Berry, he recognized the need to tell a story. Although he seldom acknowledged Berry's influence, Westover played "Sweet Little Sixteen," "Johnny B. Goode" and "Rock and Roll Music" at the Hi Lo Club. It was early rock and roll pioneers like Berry who helped Westover to craft his act. And it was Jimmy Jones falsetto style that intrigued him. He spent a lot of time mastering this style and it eventually became a trademark of his records.

There are many stories about how "Runaway" was made, but one of the best recollections of the record comes from musitron inventor and cowriter of the song, Max Crook.

ABOUT "RUNAWAY"
BY MAX CROOK

The idea for the song "Runaway" was conceived at the Hi Lo Club in Battle Creek, Michigan. Charlie's band, L.D. Dugger on bass, Dick Parker on drums and Max Crook on piano and musitron, was practicing one afternoon at the club when Charlie came up with chords, arrangement and instrumental bridge to this new, incomplete song. Charles took the song idea with him to work at Peter Vice's carpet shop. He completed the verses and wording while working his day job. The next night, the band began trying to play the song. During the next several weeks there were a number of versions of "Runaway" played at the Hi Lo Club.

I contacted disc jockey Ollie McLaughlin about Charlie's song "Runaway" and then brought in a tape recorder to tape many of Charlie's other original songs (some of which were cowritten by me). Interestingly, "Runaway" got buried on my tape. I recorded a number of other songs but just a brief bit of "Runaway." Unknowingly, I taped over most of "Runaway." I thought that "Little Oscar" was also a good tune. Ollie heard the little bit of "Runaway" and was instantly interested. Then Ollie asked us to get together and make another recording of "Runaway."

Ollie took these songs to Big Top Records in Detroit and met with Irving Micahnik and Harry Balk who listened to the tape. They chose "I'll Climb The Mountain High" and no other song for Charlie's first recording session. Charlie was not satisfied with the recordings. Ollie argued strongly to record "Runaway." Arrangements were made for a New York recording session.

Charles, his wife, Shirley, and my wife, Joann, and I traveled to New York to record in the nation's first commercial multiple-track recording studio, Bell Sound. On January 21, 1961, I brought in specialized microphones, echo and vibrato equipment then new to the recording industry and the musitron. This was a pre-electronic age synthesizer which helped characterize the unique sound in "Runaway."

Before "Runaway" was completely mixed and mastered, distributors were allowed to hear a rough mix of it. This was done via a special telephone hookup in Bell Sound's control room. The distributors, located in strategic geographical areas, were very excited and orders poured in by the thousand. The earliest sign was that "Runaway" would be a million-selling record. We weren't surprised, we had the same reception at the Hi Lo Club.

Charles adopted the name Del Shannon and soon left the Hi Lo Club to begin his personal appearances as a touring rock and roll performer. A new singer, Mayf Nutter, stepped in and took over the leadership of the band. I continued to play with Dugger and Parker and the Hi Lo Club operated with another excellent band. Del Shannon was a star and 'Runaway' was a hit record. We were all happy for Charles.

Max Crook

Del Shannon: Relaxing With the Kids

PRACTICING AT THE HI LO CLUB:
THE EARLY SONGS LEADING TO "RUNAWAY"

It was while working at the Hi Lo Club, fronting the Charlie Johnson Band, that Westover began to perform "Handy Man" and other cover songs that used his gifted falsetto. He reasoned that by practicing this sound on "Handy Man," he would be training for future stardom.

Just before Dick Parker introduced Max Crook to Westover, Dick remarked, "Chuck, we aren't going anywhere with our sound. We need something different. I know a guy who is an electronic genius." With that, Chuck invited Max down for an audition and the band began to form a new sound.

With the addition of Crook, the Charlie Johnson Band began to practice in the afternoon at the Hi Lo Club or on non-playing days at Max Crook's house. They were doing everything to create original tunes. Chuck used the slapping bass of L.D. Dugger to try out his country-type songs. An older man with a penchant for country and rockabilly music, Dugger looked like a grandfather, drank heavily and went to work every day in a local tire store. He seemed to sleep on the bandstand, but when Dugger came awake, his slap bass added a great deal to Westover's sound. In many respects Dugger's contribution has been ignored, but he constantly told Chuck about the best in new country music. Dugger liked the honky tonk country sound that was just a step away from rock and roll music and much of Chuck's early musical education was due to Dugger's persistent slapping bass influence.

With a number of influences surrounding him, Westover eventually combined them into a series of pre-Del Shannon songs that still bear his song writing stamp. One day in a conversation with Chuck Marsh, Westover remarked: "I feel like the invisible songwriter." This was a reference to some early songs that he wrote at the Hi Lo Club and played for the locals. When he became Del Shannon he refused to record or release these tunes. The surviving tapes from the Hi Lo Club indicate that they were some of his finest tunes.

One of Charlie's earliest song writing efforts, "Honey Bee," was supposed to feature Dugger's bass, but Dugger was drinking and not available. So Chuck was forced to improvise with a saxophone and Crook's musitron. When "Honey Bee" was played one night at the Hi Lo Club, the song featured a sizzling saxophone instrumental break and then the next night Crook's musitron took on the instrumental break. "Honey Bee" remains an unreleased Del Shannon song which sounds every bit as good a tune as "Runaway." The only copy remains with Max Crook who played both versions at his home for us as we wrote the book.

MAX CROOK AND DICK PARKER MAKE THE CHARLIE JOHNSON BAND SWING

At the Hi Lo Club, the Charlie Johnson Band swung due to its drummer and organ player. They were the key ingredients in the band. The organ that Max Crook played was perfect to practice rock and roll type original tunes. Dick Parker's drums added to the rock and roll mystique. They could also play jazz and on a song that was a Hi Lo Club favorite, "This Feeling That I'll Call Love," there was a modern, contemporary jazz sound. There were so many different musical styles in the band that Chuck wondered if it would work.

"I used to look at Dugger and that old bastard didn't look like he could walk," Westover remarked to Chuck Marsh, "then the music would start and he would play like a 20-year-old." It was Westover's musical partnership with Crook which created the original sound which punctuated "Runaway."

Chuck Westover remembered, "Max would experiment with the organ and make it sound like another instrument. There was no doubt that Max Crook was a musical genius, he didn't want that organ to sound like an organ." Westover was also complimentary about his drummer. "Dick Parker was not only a steady drummer but his drum fills fit perfectly behind my voice. Parker was my cue and I couldn't have done the early music without him," Del Shannon remarked a decade later.

Shannon's song-writing skills were developing rapidly at the Hi Lo Club. But Max Crook also used this time to develop his own sound. He cut a wonderful version of "Caravan" in 1959 which was a demo circulated to record companies under the name, Maximilian. Eventually, when Del Shannon became a star, Maximilian was signed by Big Top and Twirl and released three well-received 45s.

The bond between Westover and Crook was demonstrated on these singles. The most popular of the Maximilian releases: "The Snake" backed with "The Wanderer" and "The Twistin' Ghost" b/w "The Breeze and I and Theme From Peter Gun" on Big Top Records had Shannon's full support. Another great Crook instrumental was "Bumble Boogie" with Del on the guitar. Crook also wrote "Mr. Lonely" for Johnny and the

Hurricanes. It was this early song writing and production of acetate dubs with Crook which helped Chuck Westover evolve into Del Shannon.

Del Shannon: Composing the String of Hits

Max and Del were a team. They played off one another and they were both superb songwriters, both had great production skills and loved to perform. The Hi Lo Club gave them this venue but they were as different as night and day personally. At the break Max was in the back room drinking his Kool Aid and eating the cookies his wife Joanne had packed. Charlie was in the parking lot having a few drinks and raising a little hell. Charlie only needed a few hours sleep before he left for Peter Vice's carpet shop. Despite the differences between Chuck and Max, they meshed on stage and in the studio.

The afternoons often were given to practice sessions. Both Max and Chuck loved to experiment with the music. It was during an unusually cold and overcast October 1960 afternoon that they first put together the tune which would become the mammoth hit "Runaway."

"RUNAWAY":
THE EARLY PHASES OF A MILLION SELLING HIT RECORDS

For more than a year Chuck experimented with his music at the Hi Lo Club or he went over to his friend Max Crook's house to cut demos. For Del Shannon, Max was an alter ego and a constant source of inspiration. They worked together as a team and the quiet, self-effacing Crook seldom took credit for his work with Shannon.

From the time that Crook joined the Charlie Johnson Band he was held by band members in reverential awe as a musical genius. "I never saw anyone like Max Crook," drummer Dick Parker remarked. "He could do anything you wanted electronically."

When Max walked into the Hi Lo and plugged in his newly constructed custom-built keyboard he called a musitron and played its eerie sounds, the entire audience took note. "Hell, I thought that it was some kind of machine that played every instrument in the band," Shannon later remarked to a British journalist. Max made the musitron sound like violins, flutes, saxophones, a piano or an organ. He could get almost any sound he wanted out of the musitron. So the Charlie Johnson Band spent an inordinate amount of time featuring Max's instrumental breaks. They recorded a series of demo songs. Among these, "Little Oscar" stands out as an example of Shannon's craftsman-like song writing and production skill. He was always writing songs but most of them were not yet commercially acceptable ones. Max Crook would cut these demos in his living room and file them away in a cabinet. There is material for a Del Shannon album from the Hi Lo Club days that has not been released.

DICK PARKER, MAX CROOK AND THE WHITE BUCKS AND HOW THEY CAME TO THE CHARLIE JOHNSON BAND

One day as the Doug DeMott Band was falling apart, Westover learned about a young kid who was a fantastic drummer. So Chuck drove to nearby Kalamazoo and pulled his wife's rusty Saab into Dick Parker's front yard. It was a cold morning and suddenly Parker was facing a smallish guy with a pompadour who offered him a job playing in his band at the Hi Lo Club. Parker readily accepted. Another early member of the group, Dick Pace, was hired from Kalamazoo but he left the band after a brief time. Pace already had a large family and he moved to California to play show tunes at Knott's Berry Farm. L. D. Dugger stayed on and guitarist, Bob Popenhagen, was following the Doug DeMott path by playing in the country bars. Then after playing with the Charlie Johnson Band, Parker told Chuck about Max Crook.

Max Crook had his own band when he was in college. So prior to playing with the Charlie Johnson Band, Crook's group the White Bucks recorded a number of songs. A single on Dot Records for the White Bucks in February 1959 indicated that Crook knew his way around the recording studio. Chuck recognized this and spent an inordinate amount of time in Crook's home studio or at the Hi Lo Club. The Dot release impressed Westover and he realized that Max had a technical skill which would help him in his quest for a hit record.

The people who frequented the Hi Lo Club remember that the Charlie Johnson Band worked for almost a year on their music before they wrote "Runaway" in a few days. They also worked on other demos and sent these to Crook's friend, Ollie McLaughlin, who was a disc jockey in Ann Arbor, Michigan. McLaughlin was connected with a number of Detroit record labels and frequently shopped demos in the Motor City. As an Ann Arbor disc jockey he was in a position to influence the release of a popular record. But it would be some time before McLaughlin found a tune that he believed had commercial possibilities. Yet, McLaughlin encouraged Westover's song writing.

Dick Parker remembered that "Chuck was always writing songs and looking for a hit sound." The Hi Lo Club was a dive and a dangerous place. On December 31, 1959, Parker walked out into the alley behind the Hi Lo and was waiting for Dick Pace to come out to give him a ride home. Suddenly, a gorgeous young girl came out the back door. She smiled at Parker. Then a car burst down the alley and a man got out with a shotgun. It was his girlfriend and they had an argument. When Pace showed up he remarked: "You ready to go home Dick." Parker looked astonished and said: "Jesus." He got into the car shaking. This was one of the reasons that Chuck never brought his wife Shirley to the Hi Lo. Shirley came to the club once with one of her brothers, Victor Nash, and his wife Margaret who were visiting from Coopersville.

When he worked nights at the Hi Lo, Chuck was Charlie Johnson and then he came home and was Chuck Westover. The two lives that he led began a pattern which influenced his behavior until his tragic death. There were many people in the club who thought he had a nihilistic attitude toward life. One close friend described Westover as "suicidal" at this early stage of his life. He was a driven man that people worried about during his Battle Creek days. "Chuck always had a dark side to him," Dick Parker recalled, "but he also had a bright side, one which drove him to succeed."

It was this artistic drive to write songs and create commercial music which drove Chuck day and night. Eventually, Ollie McLaughlin, sat around during the after-hours sessions at the Hi Lo Club and recognized the Charlie Johnson Band's commercial appeal. This talent, McLaughlin reasoned, was largely due to Westover's writing and arranging, but his vocal style was so unique that McLaughlin began touting his skills as a solo performer.

The Charlie Johnson Band was never able to move beyond the Hi Lo Club. This is a tragedy because their acetates and recorded shows made them a highly commercial band. The irony is that "Runaway" broke up the band. Max Crook continued as a solo act, Dick Parker began working and raising a family, L. D. Dugger retired. Bob Popenhagen continued to perform in country bands and Dick Pace left for California. For almost a year the Charlie Johnson Band truly was the Little Big Band which rocked Battle Creek.

THE SONGS THAT WORKED IN THE HI LO CLUB AND LED TO THE EMERGENCE OF DEL SHANNON

"Runaway" worked as a song in the Hi Lo Club. Would it be a hit on record? No one was sure. The roaring falsetto in Shannon's voice had made the tune a hit at the Hi Lo. Max Crook's organ solo on the musitron blended so well with Del's falsetto that it made the song commercially unique. The club patrons couldn't get enough of the tune. So Charlie knew that Max had to record the tune with him, because they had cowritten it.

"The idea for the song 'Runaway' was conceived at the Hi Lo Club in Battle Creek," Max Crook remembered. After Max came up with the chord arrangements and instrumental bride, Charlie wrote the lyrics and the band began performing the tune. Once the inspiration for "Runaway" took place the Charlie Johnson Band realized that they had a unique and potential hit sound.

There were other songs. While he performed at the Hi Lo Club, Chuck also wrote and sang "Happiness." This song was cowritten with Jim Ellis who was a regular at the Hi Lo. It was eventually a cut on Shannon's **Little Town Flirt** album. One of the problems with Del's early career is that little care was given to song selection and "Happiness" should have been released early in his career as a potential hit single.

There were a number of people who recognized Chuck's talent. One of them, Charlie Marsh, a local disc jockey known as Charlie O. He talked about Westover's original songs all over town. Marsh was a drinking buddy of Chuck's who spent more time talking about girls than music. They were the perfect pair, the disc jockey who knew the music and had a local following, and the king of Battle Creek bar bands. They toured the bars, went to the local hamburger joints and hung out at the record store. They had a local level of stardom, but both of them wanted national exposure. Eventually, Chuck became Del Shannon with a number one hit record "Runaway," while Charlie Marsh went to work for a small radio station in Douglas, Arizona and had a bit part in a Lee Marvin movie. "I remember that 'Runaway' worked and it was a hell of a song. I knew it would go national," Marsh remembered.

In the late 1950s, Charlie Marsh was a legend in and around Battle Creek. Although he was only in his early twenties, Marsh understood the frenetic energy and lure of rock and roll music. "I was doing things that no disc jockey would," Marsh recalled, "and it earned me a large local following." He hollered and hooted on local radio at the same time that Wolfman Jack adopted the same technique at XERB in Del Rio, Texas. But, as Marsh pointed out, he had the technique long before the Wolfman. "I felt the music, it had a hold on me and my generation." Charlie Marsh remarked from his home in Kalamazoo. "Hell, I kept rock and roll alive in Battle Creek and Chuck Westover was with me every step of the way."

As the Hi Lo Club filled with people to hear the unreleased version of "Runaway" they were surprised by the band members. The band was made of an old bass player, a drummer who looked more like a high school kid and the musitron keyboardist looked and acted like a college professor. The lead singer couldn't figure out if he liked country, jazz, rock or pop music. But when the Charlie Johnson Band began playing, all doubts were assuaged. It was Michigan's finest bar band.

One of the most unlikely influences upon Shannon's song writing and musical direction was the slap-bass player, L.D. Dugger. Although he appeared to be falling asleep and he looked like an old man in rumpled clothes, Dugger was a strong musician. He had a sense of timing that helped Charles develop his own sense of a song.

According to Max Crook and Dick Parker, the Charlie Johnson Band reworked "Runaway" only a few times. "'Runaway' came together quickly," drummer Dick Parker recalled. The musical genius of Max Crook was obvious as he brought in sophisticated chord arrangements and an instrumental bridge using the musitron to create a feeling of instant energy. But Parker's drums also gave the original "Runaway" a special energy. "Charlie did rework the words some," Parker remembered, "but we all seemed to get into it." Then after a few weeks, Charlie completed the lyrics and when the band starting playing the tune for the Hi Lo Club regulars it was infectious. From the moment "Runaway" debuted at the Hi Lo Club, the band had to play it two or three times a night.

While he was writing and polishing what would turn into his first million selling record, Chuck Westover continued to work at Peter Vice's carpet shop. When Charlie showed up each morning with the words and music to "Runaway" in a little briefcase, Vice would listen and offer him encouragement. "He must have worked on that damned song for a long time," Vice chuckled. "At lunch I would loan him a quarter and he would walk across the street to buy a can of tuna fish. He would sit there and eat the tuna fish with no pickles, no onions, nothing." Even in these early days Charlie Johnson fought a weight problem.

There were some secrets that Charlie Johnson kept, one of them was a small little beer joint known as Daisy Mae's at Gun Lake. Charlie would play country music there on Sunday nights. The military people stationed nearby loved to come to Daisy Mae's and listen to the country music and fight between sets. The gizzards and chicken wings were considered the best in Michigan. "I never knew that Chuck played there," Dick Parker remarked. Chuck loved Buck Owens' music and talked at length about Don Rich's guitar playing. He also remained an avid Hank Williams fan. The Daisy Mae gigs on Sunday night allowed Del to play the Williams' songs that he loved while experimenting with Red Foley, Hank Thompson and Jim Reeves songs.

If there was one significant influence upon Chuck Westover it was the 29-year-old Don Rich from the Buck Owens band. Although Don had just joined the Owens band, he supplied the tenor harmony vocals which helped Charlie shape his own sound on "Runaway" and other early original tunes. Owens' "Under Your Spell Again" was a Charlie Johnson favorite as was "Above and Beyond." Charlie was quiet about his infatuation with country music because his drive was to become a rock and roll star. Charlie listened to and adapted many of Owens' musical ideas while performing at local Battle Creek clubs.

The Hi Lo Club was a perfect place to perfect "Runaway" and Max Crook's home studio was the ideal spot to cut a demo. When the demo of "Runaway" was finished it was sent to Mercury Records at 35 Wacker Drive in Chicago. The Windy City based record label seemed the perfect place of Shannon's falsetto with such artists as Dee Clark and others who had a similar sound. The demo came back from Mercury with a resounding no and this led to Harry Balk and Irving Micahnik's Embee Productions becoming the conduit for "Runaway."

THE ROAD TO RECORDING "RUNAWAY": HARRY BALK AND EMBEE PRODUCTIONS

The road to the New York recording studio was a long and arduous one. When the Charlie Johnson band performed "Runaway," there were often visitors who talked about the unique original songs performed in this raucous Battle Creek club.

Charlie Marsh claimed that he had one of the earliest tapes of "Runaway," and he did his best to send it around to the record labels. "I was the major disc jockey in

Battle Creek," Marsh remarked. "Not only was I his first manager but I tried to get his music off the ground." Marsh sent a tape to Ollie McLaughlin in Ann Arbor who forwarded it to Harry Balk at Embee Productions in Detroit.

After work Peter Vice and Chuck Westover would go out for a few beers. The future Del Shannon talked about his rock and roll dreams as they rode around in Vice's brand new White Cadillac. The Charlie Johnson band didn't need to worry, because the word was out that they were a killer group. "Hell, I told him he was already a local star, why go to New York," Vice remarked.

It was difficult for Chuck to balance his time between his daytime job and his night music life. They placed him in two worlds and he lived two lives. His wife, Shirley, worried about the long hours he kept. Her fears were well grounded because Charles Westover was possessed with the music business. He would hone his song writing and performing talents. Darwin "Darr" Farr remembers going to Chuck's house. "I think even then he had a vision of his musical future."

When he came over to Chuck's house to play music in the front yard, Farr recalled that they played a lot of the oldies. "Chuck knew his music and did it his way," Farr remarked. Like many in Battle Creek, Farr recalled that Chuck had a manic quest for stardom. "He was a perfectionist and driven to make his music," Farr concluded.

The regulars who hung out at the Hi Lo Club remembered how Chuck created a strong sense of his own musical sound. The Charlie Johnson Band could take a hit record and perform it in their own way. In other words it was unique. "I remember when I introduced Charlie to Max Crook," drummer Dick Parker recalled. "He knew right away that he could work with Max. That was Chuck, he had a sense of his band's sound."

Sue White was the sister of a guy who wanted to be a wrestler. Her brother, who used the name, Mark Shannon, was a professional wrestler and he is credited with giving Chuck the name Del Shannon. "I loved seeing Chuck play," Sue recalled. "He was so special and we were all so young and crazy."

After they closed the doors at the Hi Lo Club, Charlie and other musicians would meet at the Ringside Bar where the owner, Jackie Saltenwich, would allow them to set up and play into the night. The Ringside was located on Capital Avenue and it was part of the after-hours drinking circuit. The bar was also famous because Squirrelly Shirley was the singing barmaid and everyone loved her ribald sense of humor. It was after 2:30 a.m. when Charlie Johnson and other local musicians would play. Sometimes Max Crook was at these sessions, but more often he was on his way home to Kalamazoo.

Crook realized that the band needed more than just a reputation. So he called a disc jockey, Ollie McLaughlin, and asked him to bring a tape recorder to one of their practice sessions. Max and Ollie laughed as they recalled the days when a much younger Crook would show up late at night at WHRV in Ann Arbor to watch McLaughlin's radio show. It was appropriately dubbed Ollie's Caravan and every teenager in that part of Michigan listened to it. This Ann Arbor rock and roll show had not only made Ollie McLaughlin a household name among radio rock and roll aficionados but he had also acquired a reputation as a talent scout.

Because he was an African-American, McLaughlin was nervous about hanging out at the Hi Lo Club. It had a reputation as a hillbilly, redneck spot. Since its early days when the cereal factories were established and controlled local politics, a black side of town emerged. As a result, he came in for the afternoon or after-hours rehearsals. Ollie got to know Chuck and the band very well and realized that they had a hit-record potential.

Before McLaughlin came to Battle Creek, he had talked at length with Crook about the Charlie Johnson Band. Max had told Ollie that they possessed a different or unique sound. One that would make it easy for their records, if they could ever find a label, to sell in the fickle rock and roll marketplace. Initially, McLaughlin was skeptical.

When Ollie arrived in Battle Creek, he went down to the Grotto and saw some of his friends. Then, when he left, he told his friends at this black nightclub that he was in Battle Creek to see if Max Crook's buddy, Charlie Johnson, could cut it in the recording industry. Surprisingly, the patrons at the Grotto had heard about the Charlie Johnson Band. But McLaughlin dismissed this observation.

McLaughlin later admitted that he was stunned by Shannon's enormous talent. "I couldn't believe his sound, it was so original," McLaughlin remarked to local disc jockey Charlie Marsh. As he watched the Charlie Johnson Band practice, McLaughlin realized that he had a potential hit act.

So he hauled out his tape recorder and made a copy of two songs, "I'll Always Love You" and "The Search." Both songs were eventually included on Del Shannon's first Big Top album **Runaway** (Big Top 1303). But the tape that Ollie made this day was a flawed one. So it took some time for McLaughlin to get the right demo tape.

THE ATMOSPHERE IN AND AROUND BATTLE CREEK ON THE EVE OF "RUNAWAY"

Since there was still such a strong atmosphere of segregation in Battle Creek, McLaughlin arrived at the late afternoon practice session intending to stay only a few minutes. He wound up going out to dinner, then sitting in the Bellman and Waiter's Club and coming back for the Hi Lo's after-hours party. "I couldn't believe it!" McLaughlin observed, "They were still serving drinks at 2:30 a.m." Pa Gilbert always had trouble reading the clock.

McLaughlin couldn't believe it when he recorded Shannon's music. He tried to call Harry Balk at Embee Productions. But then he remembered that Balk's phone was the pay phone in the hall of his office. Embee Productions was still attempting to turn a profit, but they would listen to any new sound.

By then McLaughlin realized that his tape was a faulty one. He had trouble with his machine and only caught a small part of "Runaway." Undaunted, he took the tape back to Kalamazoo where he prepared it for the trip to Embee Productions. McLaughlin had never heard anything so original.

The road to stardom for Chuck Westover began with the record people. Harry Balk produced his records for Embee Productions. Irving Micahnik was the promotional businessman. Balk was an excellent producer and a tough-as-nails businessman. Micahnik was a great promoter but he was an inveterate party goer. Despite Micahnik's erratic behavior, Embee Productions was one of Detroit's most important independent production companies. They knew how to make rock and roll hits and soon Chuck Westover was on his way to stardom. When Harry Balk heard the tape of the Charlie Johnson Band, he realized that the lead singer would need work on his vocals. "I decided after hearing Charlie's voice that we would speed up his recorded product and this would help him achieve a higher level of commercial appeal for his vocal tracks," Balk recalled. From the first day he listened to Chuck, Harry Balk had the ability to redirect and refine his talent. Balk was one of the major reasons for the emergence of Del Shannon as a rock and roll star.

Another reason for Harry Balk's success was that he recorded his acts at New York's state of the art Bell Sound Studios for Big Top Records. The label was successful in a minor league manner, but Harry had negotiated a distribution deal with Hill and Range. So his acts were getting national exposure and they had a number of hit records including the Johnny and the Hurricanes' **Billboard** hits.

But it was the technology, recording equipment and session musicians at Bell Sound Studios that was at least partially responsible for the unique Del Shannon sound. The loose studio atmosphere allowed Max Crook to bring in his black box and set up the musitron. Seasoned studio musicians like Al Caiola realized that there was something special about "Runaway's" sound.

Before Charlie and Max could travel to New York, they had to prepare for their recording session. At the same time they continued their four nights a week at the Hi Lo Club. For the next two weeks, "Runaway" was tested before the Battle Creek audience. Even Pa Gilbert, the Hi Lo Club's owner, told Charlie one night to play the song again. Rufus Wines, who was too busy looking for someone to throw out of the club, even stood at ease to listen to "Runaway." At the instrumental bridge, Rufus would dance at the door. Everyone stood in awe because Rufus normally didn't dance.

The Charlie Johnson band remembered that battles flew around the club when they played "Runaway." After perfecting the song, Charlie and Max drove with McLaughlin to Detroit where they talked at length with Harry and Irv at Embee Productions. After listening to tapes of "Runaway," Harry and Irv remarked that they thought it was three songs. But they liked the instrumental bridge and the falsetto vocal. A deal was made to meet Charlie and Max in New York and cut the record at Bell Sound.

TO NEW YORK, BELL SOUND AND THE "RUNAWAY" SESSION

Returning home to Battle Creek, the Charlie Johnson band put some final touches on "Runaway." Because Embee Productions didn't have any funds for travel, Chuck was forced to drive his car, a 1957 Plymouth, with a heater that didn't work. Charlie and Max, with their wives, left Battle Creek for the long car trip to New York.

"I don't know how we made it," Max Crook remembered, "and we were nervous about going into Bell Studios." The Bell Sound Studio was the only four-track studio in

America. They also had one of the most expensive and sweetest sounding Steinway pianos. The staff almost passed out when Max announced that he was going to make some electronic modifications to the Steinway. When Max and Charlie began to set up their equipment, the studio people stood around in awe as Max nailed chords to the floor and set up his musitron. Most people were intrigued by Max's little black box. It was one of many inventions that Crook had produced over the years and it was designed to augment the piano sound. The little black box contained a multihead tape machine and Max used this commonplace recording device to control the speech, echo and feedback during the recording process. "I could bend the notes with my little black box," Crook remembered, "and in this way we could blend the vocal with the instrumental accompaniment."

Del's vocals were always slow ones which had to be adjusted. Harry Balk realized that if Del was to have a hit record, something had to be done to speed up the vocal tracks. Max's little black box would help that process and allow for the soaring feeling to "Runaway." When he walked into Bell Sound with two suitcases full of mikes, chords and sound equipment, Max surprised the session musicians. They all had an open mind. The session saxophone player, Bill Ramal, acted as the producer for the first session. He encouraged Max to take his time getting the sound right. Guitar legend, Al Caiola, was brought in for the guitar parts and he found Crook's preparation interesting. They were both studio veterans and smart enough to realize that what Max was doing was important to the sound.

BILL RAMAL: SAX PLAYER AS HISTORICAL OBSERVER

During the "Runaway" session, producer Balk brought in a number of well-known session musicians. The intent was a simple one. He wanted the strongest musical accompaniment. The saxophone player, Bill Ramal, provided an important window into Shannon's creative process. Who was Bill Ramal?

Ramal was a young man from New Jersey with a penchant for fine clothing, smooth jazz, oriented saxophone solos and an eye for the ladies. He was the ultimate in musical cool and he was one of the finest local session players.

The education that Ramal received first was three years at the Julliard School of Music and later four years at Columbia University which made him not only musically sound but one of the most articulate observers of the musical scene. He believed that "Runaway" was a sure hit because of how other musicians in the studio reacted to the session.

When Ramal began his professional career he was playing for weddings, bar mitzvahs and at cocktail lounge dance joints. "Then I was married and I happened to get a job playing a rock 'n' roll thing," Ramal continued. "I found it very stimulating...I found that when I was working with the group, I'd lose all my inhibitions and just think about having fun." What Ramal had discovered was the essence of rock and roll music. He also found out that Del Shannon and Max Crook had the same feeling. The "Runaway" session validated Ramal's belief that rock music offered total artistic freedom.

One of his talents was arranging. When Ramal walked into Bell Sound in New York to work on "Runaway," he immediately came away with some arranging ideas. Ramal was also impressed with Shannon. He realized that Shannon had a unique sound. Ramal was intrigued by Max Crook's musitron but he understood that Shannon's falsetto delivery was an essential part of his sound. Ramal urged Del and Max to relax and make their music just like they did at the Hi Lo Club.

Ramal remarked about "Runaway" that there "was an unusual rhythmical figure running through the tune." What Ramal remembered about the tune was that Max Crook's organ created the instrumental break necessary in making it a hit. Much of the magic of "Runaway" came from the unique blend of Balk and Ramal's production skills. They had a way in the studio which created hit records and Del Shannon benefited from this production team.

RECORDING "RUNAWAY": THE TECHNICAL SIDE OF A HIT RECORD

The January 19, 1961 recording date began when Max warmed up on the organ and put Del into the proper mood to record. He was nervous in the studio and found it difficult to unwind. An earlier recording session had failed to produce a hit record, and this experience haunted Del.

After two sessions at the Bell Sound studio, Shannon still sounded flat. The producer, Harry Balk, was worried about Del's slow paced and slightly out of key vocals. "I talked to Del at length about relaxing and just doing the song," producer Balk remarked. "It took a lot of time to get him in the groove that we wanted."

Initially, "Runaway" was too slow and didn't sound inspired. So Balk sat down on a chair in the Bell studio and lit a Cuban cigar. He puffed smoke up to the ceiling and thought about Del's sound. He also thought about the other hits that he produced and he couldn't help but feel that Max Crook's musitron was the key to the sound. It was so upbeat. Then it hit Balk, he had the solution to his problem.

"I took the 'Runaway' tape down to the mixing room," Balk remembered, "and they told me there was nothing that they could do." The production people said that the song would have to be recut in a more uptempo manner. Balk had other plans.

The reason that Harry didn't accept this explanation was that he had engineered other hit tunes and he knew that it was only a matter of reworking Del's vocals. Then Balk increased the speed on "Runaway" and the hit sound emerged. "We finally got Del on key through a little tape magic," Balk chuckled.

While Chuck and Max were recording "Runaway," their wives, Shirley and Joanne, were walking around the television studios in Manhattan. For two young girls, recently married, from small Michigan towns, it was exciting in New York. They walked up to the ticket window for a popular quiz show, Beat The Clock, and found out that there were audience tickets available. They walked in and sat down and suddenly Joann was picked to go on stage. She appeared on national television and won some prizes. "I knew that we had at least one star in the family," Max remarked to Charlie that night.

"That night was magic for Shirley and myself," Joann Crook remembered. "It was ironic that we both had babies nine months after the night that Del recorded 'Runaway,'" she concluded.

The "Runaway" session had gone so well that guitarist Al Caiola offered to purchase a piece of the song. "We knew that we had a night," Max remarked, "now it was up to Harry to promote it." Although Harry Balk was the producer, he realized that he had to prod Irving Micahnik to promote "Runaway."

The marketing of "Runaway" was immediate. The reality was that Balk and Micahnik had a winning song and there was no need for extensive publicity. Yet, Harry and Irv were pros and they took up their duties to promote "Runaway" with a missionary zeal.

BACK TO DETROIT AND THE MARKETING OF "RUNAWAY"

Balk flew back to Detroit to his Embee Production office with his tape. To save money Harry and his partner, Irving Micahnik, had listed their number as a pay phone in the hall of their office building. While they made money, the precarious state of the music business prompted them to cut corners whenever possible.

After playing the master of "Runaway," Harry was satisfied with the final mix. Then he called Del and Ollie McLaughlin and asked them to come to his office. When they arrived Harry Balk was smoking a cigar, had a bottle of champagne handy with three glasses and a big smile adorned his face. "Well, guys," he remarked, "sit down and listen to a number one hit." Then Harry pushed a button on the tape recorder and the new and improved version of "Runaway" filled the room. Ollie smiled. Del looked astonished. Harry waited. Then Shannon started clapping and broke into a smile. "You're right Harry," Del remarked, "we got ourselves a hit." At that point Shannon broke down and almost started to cry. The agony over "Runaway" and the lengthy production had taken its toll.

After Harry Balk finished mixing the final cut of "Runaway," Big Top Records prepared its release. Finally, on February 27, 1961, "Runaway" backed with "Jody," (Big Top 3067) was released. The b-side "Jody" was written for a girl at the Hi Lo Club. Later, Del named his daughter Jody and created the fictional tale that the song was named for her. "It was written before Jody was conceived," Shirley Westover remarked. The slow ballad was accompanied by a rippling piano and an intense vocal with an alto sax backing.

"Runaway's" immediate success helped Harry Balk to maneuver Del Shannon's career into a commercial direction. The early concert appearances after "Runaway" hit the charts proved that Shannon had learned his craft well.

In April 1961, Shannon made his New York debut at the Brooklyn Theater appearing with famed disc jockey Murray the K on a bill featuring a dozen acts. Ray Peterson came in with a $50 pair of shoes and Del was awed. When he found that he was sharing a dressing room with Dion, Shannon promptly got the doo wop legends autograph. "I wasn't comfortable during that first New York appearance," Shannon complained to his producer Harry Balk. "You'll get used to it, kid," Balk remarked. "We're on our way into the rock and roll world."

During his initial New York concert Del brought along a black suit with a red tie and red socks. Dion looked at him horrified. After the first show, Dion took Del across the street and had him purchase an Italian suit. The tailor was paid extra to peg the pants, a new tie, a matching handkerchief, with shoes and socks added to the ensemble. When he called home Del told everyone that he could barely survive on the road due to the expenses associated with touring.

As Shannon reminisced with his friends about his New York date, he talked at length about his dressing room. It was located in a part of the Paramount Theater where there was no heat. A broken window made the room so cold that Shannon could hardly think about his stage show. Shannon was now a star and his management team was making decisions about his future.

From his Detroit office, Harry was on the phone to booking agents, disc jockeys, distributors and promotion people. One of his first engagements, after "Runaway" started to receive chart action, was in Philadelphia to appear on Dick Clark's American Bandstand. After some negotiations, Balk booked Del Shannon for a Monday, April 10, 1961 debut on American Bandstand. "Runaway" entered the **Billboard** Top 40 on March 27, 1961 and this appearance helped its steady rise to number one. Eventually, "Runaway" remained for 17 weeks on the **Billboard** pop chart, thereby establishing Del Shannon as a major rock and roll artist.

Shannon's second single "Hats Off To Larry" backed with "Don't Gild The Lily, Lily" (Big Top 3075) was another song-writing gem that quickly climbed the **Billboard** pop chart. As a **Billboard** spotlight pick for May 29, 1961, "Hats Off to Larry" immediately received major airplay. It eventually rose to number 12 on **Cash Box** and number five on the **Billboard** pop chart. Although the b-side didn't chart, "Don't Gild The Lily, Lily" was considered an interesting departure with its rock and roll and cha-cha feel. Not surprisingly, in England and Europe it became a cult hit.

With two straight hits, Big Top Records put together a hastily produced album **Runaway With Del Shannon** (Big Top 1303) and by late July it was in the stores. Big Top had so much success with Del that they under estimated the potential sales for the LP. Consequently, they pressed a small number of albums.

Harry Balk was instrumental in getting the English to purchase Shannon's music. Freddy Bienstock's London-based publishing company was hired to publicize "Runaway." The head of promotion, Franklyn Boyd hired Malcolm Forrester to handle the day-to-day publicity. The entire Vicki Music catalogue and the output of Big Top Records was placed with Bienstock's aggressive company. Boyd, who had managed Cliff Richard, knew the ins and outs of the music business.

To make "Runaway" a hit, young Forrester convinced English groups to play "Runaway" on BBC radio shows and this led to Shannon's version rising to number one on the English charts. Radio Caroline, the pirate radio station located on a boat off the English shore, collected envelopes with cash from Irving Micahnik. As Forrester remarked: "'Runaway' did not get into the charts based on radio play." It was a combination of publicity, payola and cajoling bands to cover the song that broke it in the U. K.

RUNAWAY: THE MAKING OF A HIT RECORD

One of the most interesting songs on the album was "His Latest Flame" which predated Elvis Presley's version. In order to put the **Runaway With Del Shannon** LP out, many of the tracks were hastily recorded. Despite the time problems, Del's version of the future Presley hit was a stunner. "The Prom" was another strong tune and later when the Robbs covered it on the Argo label it was a regional hit. In addition to recording, Del had to maintain a constant schedule on the concert circuit.

Shannon's concert schedule was grueling. On August 12, 1961 he was in Rochester, New York with Johnny and the Hurricanes, Bobby Lewis, Marcy Jo and others for a WBBF dance.

The third single released in early September 1961, "So Long Baby," which went Top 40, and "The Answer to Everything" (Big Top 3083) was another pairing of a fast a side with a ballad b side. Once again the September 4, 1961 issue of **Billboard** featured the song as a spotlight pick.

On October 7, 1961 Del Shannon appeared before more than 100,000 people at the WTIX Appreciation Show in New Orleans at Ponchartrain Beach. The free show for local radio listeners included Tony Orlando, Dick and Deedee, Danny and the Juniors, Ray Stevens and local talent Joe Barry and John Fred among others. In a gray suit with a dark tie, Del presented a dashing figure on a raised stage before the massive throng. "Runaway" was a massive hit and he was in the first phase of his hit-making career.

The night that Shannon performed in New Orleans, his daughter Jody was born and Max Crook's wife, Joann, also gave birth to a son, David. For years Max and Del joked about the night they cut "Runaway" in New York.

There was a change in Del Shannon. Suddenly he was in demand on the club circuit. He was booked into the "Stage 7 Club" in Phoenix, Arizona. The November 2, 1961 club date was broken up into three parts. During the first show, Del performed "Runaway," Jerry Lee Lewis' "Great Balls of Fire," Ed Townsend's "For Your Precious Love" and his recent hit "Hats Off To Larry." The second show began with "Whole Lotta Shaking," "When Your Heartaches Begin," "Hats Off To Larry" and concluded with "So Long Baby." The third and last set was a repeat of the first show. The set list was written in Del's own hand and it suggests how important covering Jerry Lee Lewis hits was in his early career.

"Runaway's" success was immediate and the tune dominated the **Billboard** and **Cash Box** charts. It was the type of first record which guarantees an artist lasting power. Soon he was appearing all over America and was booked on the most prestigious TV shows.

It was colder than normal when Del arrived in Philadelphia for his second appearance on Dick Clark's American Bandstand. The year was one of the most grueling in Shannon's life and he wanted to get home to Shirley and the kids for Christmas. He suddenly found that he missed Battle Creek, in fact he talked at length about the Hi Lo Club, Max Crook, Peter Vice, Charlie O, and the gang who hung out to see him play, but he continued to appear everywhere he could to promote his music.

After two hits, "Runaway" and "Hats Off to Larry," Del mentioned to Dick Clark that the hits had to keep coming. Clark smiled and agreed. So on the Wednesday afternoon December 13, 1961 American Bandstand Show, Del performed his latest release, "Hey! Little Girl." As he talked at length with Clark, it was obvious that they developed an early friendship.

Promotional Material for "Hey! Little Girl"

Shortly after the American Bandstand Show, Clark and Shannon decided to have dinner together at a local restaurant. That night Del went to dinner at Bookbinder's Restaurant in Philadelphia and told Clark that he couldn't believe that a year ago he was performing every night at a small club in Battle Creek the Hi Lo. As he dug into his lobster, Shannon remembered the days eating a 25¢ can of tuna fish with Peter Vice in the carpet shop. It seemed like a long time since those days. Dick Clark loved Shannon's tales of the infamous Hi Lo Club and they drank and talked into the night.

The appearance on American Bandstand helped "Hey! Little Girl" to chart and it entered the **Billboard** pop chart on January 6, 1962, eventually rising to number 38 during its two-week stint on the Top 40.

In 1961, Del Shannon experienced the fairy-tale life of an artist with two major hit records. The next three years continued to be productive ones before the cycle of failed record releases, changing musical styles and personal problems placed Shannon into another part of his career. As 1962 dawned, Del Shannon was a major rock and roll star ready to enter the second phase of his hit-making career.

Del Shannon and Wayne Carter, 1961

"When I started, people in the music business would tell me that I had four or five years of a pop-star career left," Shannon remarked to Todd Everett in 1986. For much of his life Shannon was plagued by these comments. In 1986 when he appeared with Little Anthony, Frankie Ford, the Crystals and the Del-Vikings as part of the "Good Time Rockin' Roll Revue," he lamented to Frankie Ford the burdens of the rock and roll lifestyle.

When Del Shannon left the Hi Lo Club, he was replaced by Mayf Nutter, who was a singer and guitarist. In 1961, Nutter was only 21 years old and he came out of a northern West Virginia country music background. He was perfect for the Hi Lo Club. Each night Nutter played the best of country music, but the old days were gone. Soon the Hi Lo Club introduced go-go dancers and by the early 1970s there were topless nights. The old days of the Charlie Johnson Band were a faint memory.

DEL SHANNON'S 1961 TORRENTIAL ROUTE TO STARDOM

Once "Runaway" was released, it began climbing the charts, Del Shannon was on his way to stardom. "It was a torrential route," the always glib Chuck Marsh remarked, "it was almost as if Del was on a roller coaster and it was a hell of a ride."

From February through late May 1961, Del Shannon was on the road. The most prestigious of the early gigs was a March 31, show at New York's Paramount Theater with Dion DiMucci, Rosie and the Originals, and Bobby Vee among others. As Del performed in New York he found that he was not only busy but had new demands on his time and money. In a letter home, Del wrote his feelings about stardom. The letter —which was undated—came from The Towers Hotel at Twenty-Five Clark Street in Brooklyn.

> Hi All,
>
> Just got back from the last show. I got there at 10:00 a.m. and left at 11:00 p.m., five shows a day. I just signed a movie contract. The show I'm in is going to be made into a movie, I guess. I wish I could help Mom out, but first I've got a lot of bills of my own plus the T-Bird, plus mainly taxes. I have to have at least ten or more suits and so far I only have three, so it will take more time and hit records before I can afford to help Mom and Dad out. I hope everyone understands. Also, Shirley's mom needs a little help. But my taxes will take half of what I make plus 20 percent to my manager, also you need so many little things. Hotel bills are a fortune, cleaning, oh man there's a million things.
>
> Well I'll let you in on what I'm doing. I'm staying at a nice hotel in Brooklyn with Bobby Vee (Rubber Ball and Devil or Angel) and Dion, who was with the Belmonts. I also see Rosie all the time. What an idiot. She goes around all day squirting her throat with vicks and eats cough drops, she tries to get me to take them. Boy want an ass! Well I'm meeting a lot of stars and they are all very nice to me. Well I hope I get one more hit, it could mean about $500 to $600 more dollars a week. See you all soon, say hi to everyone and the party that was with you at Gun Lake.
>
> **Love, Del Shannon**

As Shannon appeared in concert, "Runaway" steadily rose to the top of the **Billboard** pop chart. It reached the coveted number one position in May and remained in the top 10 for six weeks. A gold record was assured and Shannon was busy with daily concerts.

On May 1, Del returned for a few days with his family. Battle Creek was proud of its adopted son and Shannon hung out at the Hi Lo Club and Greens. It was good to be back with the old gang. The only people who didn't realize that he was famous were the Wines. They thought that they were the most important people in Battle Creek because they could beat up anyone.

After a week at home, Del left for a mid-western tour. On May 6, he was scheduled to begin a tour with The String-Alongs and Rocky Hart. Del was the headliner. Before he left for the tour, Del talked at length about his new record "Hat's Off To Larry" to a local newspaper. He was sure it would be as big as "Runaway."

The **Battle Creek Inquirer** presented a full profile on Shannon, even commenting that his father, Bert, was in a rest home in Marne. The article ended with Del hopping into his 1961 Thunderbird and leaving for a fishing trip. It was time for a brief rest. There wouldn't be many in the future. For the next four years the hits kept coming and Shannon's life was now in the mainstream of the rock and roll music world. It was a long way from Peter Vice's Carpet Shop and the Hi Lo Club.

In July 1961, as Del drove his Thunderbird back home, there is a picture of the neighborhood kids standing in front of Brown's Trailer Park on Avenue A in Battle Creek. It is an eerie sight. Shannon had a number one hit and didn't have the money to move out of the trailer park. That was an omen of things to come. He would continue to have great commercial success on the charts. Del began to handle his money well and soon his family had the best of everything.

BIBLIOGRAPHICAL SOURCES

Interviews with Max Crook, Dick Parker, Charlie Marsh and Bob Popenhagen, Jr., who helped to clarify the origins of "Runaway." Harry Balk was important in reconstructing the recording version of the song. Peter Vice provided hours of material on the carpet store he owned, the Battle Creek music scene and Charlie Johnson's personal life. Dan Bourgoise was instrumental in recalling Del's comments in these early days. Ollie McLaughlin was instrumental in recounting the atmosphere in the Michigan music industry. Rufus Wines gave out a short interview about his days as a bouncer and generally disagreeable bully. He remains that to the present day. On Shannon's influence on the Merseyside scene, Sam Leach, Brian Kelly, Bob Wooler, Joe Flannery, and Clive Epstein provided important material. In Germany, Tony Sheridan, Horst Fascher, Tony Bramwell, and Tom Shaka added material to Shannon's influence upon the Beatles.

Sue Gooch, Sue White, Darwin "Darr" Farr, Ginny Gibbs, Jim Hazel, Don Rodgers, John Anglin, Dick Schlatter, and former mayor of Battle Creek, Albert Bobrofsky, helped to recreate the atmosphere of the Hi Lo Club.

Del's mother, Leone Westover, recalled his early musical days and suggested many of the key influences upon his music and his wife, Shirley Westover, was helpful in recreating the atmosphere around the creation of the hit "Runaway."

"About Runaway," an unpublished manuscript by Max Crook, was used in preparation of this chapter. Also see Todd Everett, "Del Shannon Has Never Run Away," **Los Angeles Herald Examiner**, October 3, 1986, p. 32 for comments from Shannon about the influences of "Runaway" and Battle Creek upon Shannon's career.

See **Billboard**, May 29, 1961 and September 24, 1961 for their pick descriptions of Shannon's second and third record releases. Also see, the **New Orleans Times Picayune**, October 7, 1961 for Shannon's fan appreciation appearance. An interview with long time New Orleans rhythm and blues legend, Eddie Bo helped to place Shannon's New Orleans appearance in perspective.

An excellent collection of materials on the "Runaway" period is reprinted in **And The Music Plays On: Del Shannon Magazine**, Issue number 1, Fall, 1994 and this material is continued and built upon in **And The Music Plays On: Del Shannon Magazine**, Issue number 7, Spring, 1996. For the same period see **The Rock Marketplace**, September, 1972, pp. 3-7, 15. Also see, Howard A. DeWitt and Dennis M. DeWitt, "The Recording of Runaway," **Rock 'N' Blues News**, April-May, 2000, pp. 5-12.

For American Bandstand see, Michael Shore with Dick Clark, **The History of American Bandstand: From The 50s To The 80s** (New York, 1985). A brief interview with Dick Clark in San Francisco while on a book tour helped to clarify "Runaway's" appeal and where Shannon fit into the teen idol syndrome.

For Del's return to Battle Creek after "Runaway's" success see, for example, **Battle Creek Enquirer**, March 29, 1961 and May 28, 1961.

The chart action on "Runaway" is explained in Fred Bronson, **The Billboard Book of Number One Hits** (New York, 1992, 3rd. edition); Fred Bronson, **Billboard's Hottest Hot 100 Hits** (New York, 1995); Paul Gambaccini, Tim Rice and Jonathan Rice, **British Hit Albums** (New York, 1992); Paul Gambaccini, Tim Rice and Jonathan Rice, **British Hit Singles** (New York, 1991, 8th edition); Frank Hoffman and George Albert, **The Cash Box Album Charts, 1955-1974** (Boulder, 1994); Dave McAleer, **The All Music Book of Hit Albums: The Top 10 U. S. and U. K. Albums Charts From 1960 To The Present** (San Francisco, 1995); Craig Rosen, **The Billboard Book of Number One Albums: The Inside Story Behind Pop Music's Blockbuster Records** (New York, 1996); Joel Whitburn, **The Billboard Book of Top 40 Albums** (New York, 1995); Joel Whitburn, **Albums, 1955-1992** (Menomonee Falls, Wisconsin 1993) and Joel Whitburn, **The Billboard Book of Top 40 Hits** (New York, 1996, 6th edition).

A useful chronology in piecing together key events in rock and roll and Paul De Noyer, consulting editor, **The Story of Rock 'N' Roll: The Year-by-Year Illustrated Chronicle** (Miami, 1995) and John Tobler, **This Day In Rock: Day By Day Record of Rock's Biggest Stories** (New York, 1993). Also see Norman N. Nite, **The First Four Decades of Rock 'N' Roll** (New York, 1992, 2nd. edition) for another chart action book. Michael Uslan and Bruce Solomon, **Dick Clark's First 25 Years of Rock & Roll** (New York, 1981) is a brief look at 125 rock music figures.

For key facts and biographical data on rock and roll people and events see, for example, Michael Bane, **Who's Who In Rock** (New York, 1981); Donald Clarke, editor, **The Penguin Encyclopedia of Popular Music** (New York, 1989); Mike Clifford, **The Harmony Illustrated Encyclopedia of Rock** (New York, l992, 7th edition); Colin Larkin, **The Guinness Who's Who of Sixties Music** (New York, 1994); Ed Naha, **Lilian Roxon's Rock Encyclopedia** (New York, 1978); Patricia Romanowski and Holly George-Warren, **The New Rolling Stone Encyclopedia of Rock & Roll** (New York, 1995); Arnold Shaw, **Dictionary of American Pop Rock** (New York, 1982); Irwin Stambler, **The Encyclopedia Pop, Rock and Soul** (New York, 1989) and William York, **Who's Who In Rock Music** (New York, 1982).

The rock and roll atmosphere surrounding the early 1960s and the creation of "Runaway" was recreated through a number of excellent books. See, for example,

Michael Bane, **White Boys Singing The Blues** (New York, 1982); Nik Cohn, **Awopbopaloobopalopbamboom** (London, 1969); Lee Cotten, **All Shook Up: Elvis Day-By-Day, 1954-1977** (Ann Arbor, 1993); Charlie Gillett, **The Sound of the City** (London, 1971); Phil Hardy and Dave Laing, editors, **The Encyclopedia of Rock, Volume 1: The Age of Rock 'n' Roll** (London, 1976); D. Laing, K. Denselow, and R. Shelton, **The Electric Muse: The Story of Folk Into Rock** (London, 1975); Roger White, **Walk Right Back: The Everly Brothers** (London, 1984) and George White, **Bo Diddley: Living Legend** (London, 1993).

On the production side of a hit record, blues legend Jimmy McCracklin provided hours of instruction in understanding the recording process.

For Malcolm Forrester's comments on "Runaway," see Andrew Loog Oldham, **Stoned: A Memoir of London in the 1960s** (New York, 2000), p. 262.

The CD "Runaway" released by the Canadian based Unidisc Music, Inc. with extensive liner notes by Brian Young includes the original tracks and a bonus mono "Runaway" version. It is an excellent rerelease.

5: THOSE HITS JUST KEPT ON COMING: 1961-65

"I didn't know if I would have ever had another hit, then I met Maron McKenzie and we wrote 'Little Town Flirt.' I knew then that the hits would continue," Del Shannon

On July 29, 1961, Del Shannon appeared on the cover of **Cash Box**. This was the second best known rock music magazine in America and the subsequent feature story predicted a bright future for Shannon. Suddenly, the teen press couldn't get enough of Shannon. It made him nervous because he was 27, not 21 or 22 as his various press releases described.

Another problem was that Shannon was famous. Shannon knew that without continued hit records, he could be back in the Hi Lo Club. That prospect frightened Del and he worked non-stop for the next four years to guarantee his continued success.

THE RISE TO FAME AND WHAT IT MEANT

The rapid rise to stardom was a dizzying experience for Del Shannon. He had left the Charlie Johnson Band behind at the Hi Lo Club, but he was still a family man. He loved his wife and kids and came home when he could squeeze in a visit. But fame was a burden.

When he returned to Battle Creek, Del talked at length with his old friend, disc jockey, Chuck Marsh, and he complained at length about the travails of stardom. Shannon was happy with the **Cash Box** interview because it was the first to suggest that he had the prospect of a long and promising career. Del was enthused with the way that **Cash Box** described his future career. In the quiet moments, alone with Marsh, Shannon talked at length about the pressures of the business, but he also let everyone know that he had a potential bevy of new hit records. There was no doubt in Del's mind that the hits would keep coming. He was right, the hits did continue for the next four years.

From 1961 to 1965, Shannon was not only a consistent hit maker but a popular touring act. Although fame wasn't what Del envisioned. He found it difficult to balance his professional and personal life. While visiting Battle Creek, Shannon's close friends noted that he seemed to have two personalities. One night he was happy about the future. The next night he would confide to close friends that he was depressed and uncertain about the future.

Del Shannon Recording at Mira Sound, 1962

Del Shannon's biggest worry was that he wouldn't have a second hit. After the success of "Runaway," he planned the follow up to his first number-one hit with care. Shannon realized that his record releases during the next few years would determine the length of his recording career. Not only did Del envision that he needed a blockbuster follow-up hit, but he was determined to tour to increase his record sales. If you had a hit record you stayed on the road. This attitude would keep Del away from home until the late 1960s when his career began slowing down.

The role of the record producer has always been an integral in the rise of rock musicians. When Harry Balk produced "Runaway," he tinkered with the sound by increasing the speed of the record. As a result, Balk provided the driving energy behind "Runaway's" hit sound. After Balk purposely sped up the tape, Shannon had a hit. Del protested, "It doesn't sound anything like me." Harry held his ground and Del's sound emerged. For the next four years, Balk continued to use his production genius to sustain and nurture Shannon's career. He also gave him a great deal of advice about touring, song writing and dealing with the pressure of the rock music world.

HARRY BALK: THE CONTINUED PRODUCTION GENIUS BEHIND DEL SHANNON

Harry Balk was not only the production genius behind Shannon's early hits, he was a good friend who had Del's best interest at heart. In the music industry, there have been many sinister tales about Balk and Micahnik and the Embee Production business tactics. They weren't angels, but Harry Balk explained the industry in great detail. "We signed Del to the standard contract," Harry remarked, "No one held a gun to his head. It was a take it-or-leave-it deal." Over the years Shannon bitched about the two per cent royalty rate. He didn't talk to Harry for more than a decade. So their parting was acrimonious. In time, they reconciled and became good friends, but in the heated moments of the early 1960s they did business in a hostile atmosphere.

Balk defended his business practices. "It was tough to continually make a profit in the music business." Balk continued, "Look at all the companies that went bankrupt." It was the early 1960s and record companies and musical entrepreneurs like Balk and Micahnik, who owned Embee Productions, could be swallowed up in a moment. As Balk pointed out, hard business decisions had to be made. "Sure we made mistakes," Balk continued, "but we never made Del sign a contract, we weren't gangsters." Since he entered the music business managing and producing Little Willie John, Balk had the ability to recognize a hit song. He could also produce hits. Balk was a producer whose ear was tuned to the marketplace. This was one of the reasons that Shannon continued to have hits.

With his long experience in the business, Balk recognized when an artist was reaching the end of the line. "I saw Del's song writing slow down and knew we had to do something about it," Balk concluded.

It was Balk who suggested that Del seek a song writing partner. In long discussions with Shannon, Balk lectured him about the difficulty of touring, recording and writing. It was too much for one person and Balk hoped to conserve and extend Shannon's talent.

When Shannon began writing his hit records, he paid close attention to other Michigan bands. Del loved garage music and when James Coe and the Gigolo's or Dick and the Teen Beats played around Michigan, he was there to see them. Not only was Shannon looking for fresh music and ideas, he was also unhappy with the direction of American rock and roll music.

The hit years with Embee Productions created bad feelings for Shannon, because he was a skilled businessman who knew how to invest his money. No matter what Balk and Micahnik said, Del believed that he should have received increased royalties. This feeling persisted until he founded his own record label, Berlee.

"HATS OFF TO LARRY": THE TALE OF A HIT SONG

Shannon wrote songs that reflected his vision of American music. A number of Del's close friends remarked that he wrote his second hit, "Hats Off To Larry," before he composed "Runaway." Shirley Westover pointed out that the songs original title was "Hats Off To Harry," as a tribute to producer Balk. At the Hi Lo Club, Larry Gilbert, now living in Pennsylvania, claims that the song was written as a tribute to him. Shirley's version is the correct one. It was common for Del to write songs day and night. There is no way of knowing how many of his early hits were written prior to "Runaway's" rapid rise to the number one spot on the **Billboard** Hot 100.

When Shannon finally recorded "Hats Off To Larry," he was shy and tentative about having another hit. The pressure of the rock music business was already getting to Del.

In June 1961, "Hats Off To Larry" backed with "Don't Gild the Lily, Lily" (Big Top 3075) continued the string of hits. It proved that Shannon was no fluke on the **Billboard** Hot 100 as he reached the number five position.

Del Shannon In Australia, 1962

Big Top Records placed an ad in the June 5, 1961 **Billboard** featuring "Hats Off To Larry" while also promoting Ray Peterson's "You Thrill Me" (Dunes 2006), Curtis Lee's "Pretty Little Angel Eyes" (Dunes 2007) and Johnny and the Hurricanes "Old Smokie" (Big Top 3076). "Hats Off To Larry" was labeled by **Billboard** as "a driving rocker...."and it was also one of the magazine's spotlight picks.

A second hit made touring a guaranteed proposition. Since his first appearance at the Brooklyn Paramount Theater in 1961, Del had written numerous letters to his parents, his wife Shirley and to close friends complaining about the emotional drain of being a rock and roll star. In a letter to his parents he suggested that he needed "ten suits to maintain his rock star image." Del continued: "I have to tip the bellhops, the taxi and at the restaurants where I eat." He wrote his parents in March 1961 suggesting that the money he made was being put right back into his career. The clothing, the daily living expenses and the nights out as a rock and roll star ate up Shannon's income.

His father, Bert, was having health problems and the family needed money. "We didn't mention a thing to Charles," Del's mother Leone remarked, "he would have sent us what we needed and done without on the road." However, Del did send money and was aware of his father's problems. This created more pressure and he never complained about supporting two families.

THE CRITICS AND THE TOURS: THE HITS CONTINUE

The years from 1961 through 1965 were a whirlwind that saw Shannon never stop to catch his breath. He continually turned out chart hits, but the toll on his personal life was a serious one. He had seized the brass ring of stardom but was having trouble hanging onto it.

Del Shannon: Happy in England, 1963

During the 1960s and 1970s, Del gave some revealing interviews. In 1973, for example, he told an Australian radio disc jockey that he had rewritten "Hats Off To Larry," shortly after "Runaway" hit the charts. "I learned some things about hooks, timing and production from 'Runaway,'" Del told the Australian interviewer, "and I realized that Harry Balk was one of the keys to my success." From his earliest song writing and production days, Shannon was a technician who carefully crafted his hit sound. He also liked to answer the critics.

While he was on tour in August 1961 with Bobby Lewis, Marcy Jo and Johnny and the Hurricanes, Del continued to write songs. But he was shy about his song writing and kept it to himself.

He had worked too long in the Hi Lo Club to let his hit making potential decline. Shannon was having trouble with the touring schedule, trying to balance his family life and somehow convince America that he was a rock and roll star. "I think that Charlie was feeling the pressure right after 'Runaway,'" Peter Vice remembered. "He didn't seem to be himself."

During visits home to Battle Creek, Del would visit Vice and they would drink themselves into a stupor and long for the good old days. They reminisced while staying out half the night and still coming to work. Del could unwind at home in Battle Creek. When he was on the road it was all business and often it was boring and depressing.

The touring from 1961 through 1965 was non-stop. During this period the fans became close to Shannon and he developed a solid record-buying base. His live shows were excellent ones. The press paid close attention to his music but there was no real rock and roll journalism. So Shannon had to endure four years of inane media questions. He did so with a professionalism that belied his years.

One of the primary changes in Del's stage was to get rid of his guitar. Harry Balk insisted that Shannon appear on stage in a good-looking suit and use his sultry good looks and stage moves to excite the crowd. In England, Shannon appeared in concert with his guitar but used it as a security blanket.

DEL RETURNS TO THE HI LO CLUB, FALL 1962

In the midst of making hit records, Del Shannon often returned to the Hi Lo Club. The good memories, the great music and the luscious young girls drew Shannon back. In the fall of 1962, Karl Palmer and his band were playing a Saturday night at the Gilbert Lounge. The old Hi Lo Club's reputation for wild and raucous behavior prompted Ma and Pa Gilbert to remold the club image.

It was still the same old Hi Lo Club. The bar was knee deep in drinkers, there was a raucous atmosphere and Karl Palmer and his group tore up the place musically. The patrons tore it up every other way.

"You could hear a buzz all over the club," Karl Palmer recalled. "Then Charlie came through the club wearing a flashy new suit and smoking a huge cigar. Suddenly it was like old times."

For some reason Del wouldn't get on stage and perform with the band. Finally, at 1:15 a.m. he walked up and did 45 minutes. Michigan liquor laws demanded a 2:00 a.m. closing and Pa Gilbert got up on stage and shut off the music.

The next Tuesday, Del walked into the Gilbert Lounge and performed "Runaway" and "Hats Off to Larry." All the local bar flys, male and female alike, made the show and Del spent a night with his old friends. Shirley was at home in their new Southfield, Michigan home, but she was happy to see her husband enjoy himself. This set a pattern that lasted until Shannon's untimely death.

At least once a year, Del would walk into the Gilbert Lounge hang out and then get up and play with the band. He would also drive his rent-a-car to Green's to see his old country western buddies. Battle Creek had a lure that Shannon could not escape. Even as the hits kept on coming, he returned to his musical roots. Battle Creek was a safe place from the refuges of the rock and roll world.

HANGING OUT WITH DION AND TALKING BOB DYLAN

The price of fame was a heavy one. Del often had little time and even less privacy. Shannon did make some life-long friends in the music business. Dion DiMucci became a close friend. Shannon told XXXY radio in Australia in 1973 that few people could get along with Dion, Del remained a staunch friend.

A Serious Del Shannon in England, 1962

95

In 1962, Del decided to fly to New York and see Dion. They sat in his house and talked music. Then Dion went to put a tape on, Del asked: "Who the hell is that?" Dion replied, "His name is Bob Dylan." When he went home to Southfield, Michigan all Shannon could talk about was Dylan 's music. He had something special and Shannon knew it.

That weekend Del and Dion ate in local Italian restaurants and talked about future hit records. It was a good time for Del as he had found a like-minded music friend. Much of their time was spent listening to Dylan's Greenwich Village tapes. Del still needed to hit the road. His singles were continuing to chart and he needed to get back to the concert grind.

This was a tough personal time for Dion, and Shannon spent hours with him talking about the rigors of the rock and roll world. With Del touring constantly, these little weekends would become less frequent.

THE THIRD DEL SHANNON SINGLE: "SO LONG BABY"

Just as Del Shannon was beginning a tour in Rochester, New York, his third Big Top single "So Long Baby" received a heavy push from Embee Productions. Both Balk and Micahnik realized that with a third 45 hit, Shannon would be a permanent fixture on rock and roll radio.

With that in mind, Micahnik arranged an interview with Rochester, New York disc jockey, Jack Palvino, on WBBF. Palvino interviewed Shannon backstage. The result was one of the most literate interviews in rock and roll history.

During the interview with Shannon, Palvino questioned him at length about his hits. What was surprising was that Shannon mildly complained about the rigors of the rock and roll lifestyle. Irving glared from outside the control booth. Then Shannon quickly reverted back to the good interview person. Then Del stated that his next single "So Long Baby" would be even bigger than "Runaway." Palvino cautioned Shannon about expecting two monster hits so close, but they both agreed that the new record was a great one.

Then Micahnik took the disc jockey out for dinner and slipped him some spending money. The payola rat race was still in place and Irving greased the wheel to guarantee radio play.

Shannon never enjoyed the interviews because he often agreed with disc jockeys who had little, if any, knowledge about the future of rock music. In private, Del would rant and rave about the state of rock journalism. However, it was important to play the public relations game and Shannon was always his charming self. The pressure and deception he felt in the business took its toll over time. He never was able to handle the pressures of the rock music business very well and it ate away at his soul.

Because "So Long Baby" didn't climb to the top of the charts, Del was depressed and talked about going back to the Hi Lo Club. This was just bluster, because he was sold on being a rock star.

During the sessions when Shannon recorded "So Long Baby," Max Crook developed a grunting, growling sound with the musitron which sounded more like a saxophone. With Del playing a kazoo for the instrumental break the song simply didn't sound like a pop hit. Consequently, "So Long Baby" was a Top 40 hit but not a

Del Shannon: At Home In Southfield, Michigan, 1964

When Del's third American single, "So Long Baby," backed with "The Answer To Everything" (Big Top 3083) reached the number 28 position on the **Billboard** Hot 100, it peaked but then quickly slipped off the chart.

With his obsessive-compulsive nature, Del found it difficult to accept the lack of chart success. He knew that it was a great song. Harry Balk also saw it as a sure hit. "So Long Baby" was a better song than its chart position," Balk recalled. He was right about the tune in England. It reached the Top Ten on England's **New Musical Express** chart. "The Merseyside bands were keen on Del Shannon," Ray Coleman who wrote for **Melody Maker**, **Disc** and the **New Musical Express** commented. Del had no way of knowing his influence upon British bands, but he would find out shortly.

It was in England that Shannon became an influence upon a new generation of rock and roll hit makers. As the Merseyside sound grew up around Liverpool, it was the unique sounds of Del Shannon's words and music which created a part of the English rock sound.

INTRODUCING THE ROBBS

As Del Shannon created his early hits, his career became intertwined with a Wisconsin band known as the Robbs. In 1959, the Robb brothers, Dee, Joe and Bruce, as well as their cousin, Craig, organized a group known as Dee and the Starliners. The leader, Dee Robb, was cut in the teen-idol mold. But he was different than the one-dimensional singers who emerged in the late 1950s and early 1960s. Dee was a studio wizard. He had a knowledge of recording equipment and techniques bordering on the phenomenal.

Eventually, Dick Clark noticed the Robbs. They were hired as a band to backup the stars who played on Clark's Caravan of Stars. Soon they were on the road with Brian Hyland, Dion DiMucci, Gene Pitney, Bobby Lewis, Bobby Vinton and Del Shannon among others. On the road, the Robbs were young, crazy musicians who loved to party. Joe Robb remembered, "It seems like only yesterday that Del and his roadie, Wayne Carter, were drinking on the road with us. Those were good times." It was these early tours which helped Shannon and the Robbs to form a life-long friendship.

Musically, the Robbs were ahead of their time. They blended country and rock music. Joe Robb had a lap steel guitar as a kid and Dee played an acoustic guitar. They not only experimented with songs but liked to blend divergent styles.

The first time that the Robbs met Del they let him know that his record, "The Prom," was one of their favorites. They cut a version of it for the Chicago Argo label in 1962 and this brought Del and the Robbs together in a production sense.

One of Shannon's favorite guys in the Robbs was their road manager, Con Merten. He not only handled publicity, but he had a knack for getting the band recognition.

As Del and the Robbs talked, they realized they had more in common than girls, booze and good times. They were producers who would in time enter into a working relationship at the Robbs' Cherokee Studio, but in these early years, they were little more than a backing band.

The Robbs have gone on to become studio giants. From their Hollywood headquarters they have provided the sound for rock and roll million sellers like Rod Stewart and the sound for movies by top directors like John Carpenter.

CHARTING IN ENGLAND AND
THE ROBB'S EMERGE AS MUSICAL PARTNERS

With three Top 30 American hits, Del Shannon was a strong commercial act. The September 4, 1961 **Billboard** made "So Long Baby" a spotlight pick and described the song as: "an impressive disc...." So the lack of Top 10 success puzzled everyone. "I think that we couldn't get past the American Bandstand Philadelphia kids," Harry Balk remarked.

Hanging Out With English Rockers Peter and Gordon, 1964

In England, however, "So Long Baby" was a massive hit. It reached number three in the United Kingdom and charted on the **Melody Maker**, **New Music Express** and **Disc** charts. Clearly there was a downside to Shannon's hit records. The more success he had, the more he was frustrated by the record business.

One day Del approached Irving Micahnik and asked him if it was possible to stay out of the limelight and still be a star. Irving smiled and said, "I have booked you on American Bandstand. Here's a hundred bucks buy a suit." Irving lit a cigar and walked away.

Del Shannon's early success brought him a great deal of television exposure. On December 13, 1961, he appeared on the Dick Clark American Bandstand show. The appearance on Clark's Philadelphia show helped to popularize Del's music.

As other artists recognized Del's song-writing talent, they began covering his songs. In 1962, when the Robbs' released "The Prom" (Argo 5439), this teen heartthrob group had a hit with this early Shannon tune. Ironically, "The Prom" was recorded in Nashville. The Jordanaires were on the original acetate and the production brought a new dimension to Shannon's music. When Dee Robb was asked where he got the song, he remarked: "Right off the first Del Shannon album, the guy was one hell of a songwriter."

Although not a household word in the history of rock and roll, the Robbs were legitimate teen idols in the mid-1960s. They wore matching outfits, had cute Beatle haircuts and were extremely talented singer songwriters. In addition, Dee Robb was one of the guys that the girls screamed about in concert. After Dick Clark saw them, he hired them on the spot. They became featured performers on the afternoon television show, Where The Action Is. Paul Revere and the Raiders was the other band that the Robbs dueled on this afternoon sun in the fun, surf show.

There was more to the Robbs than just being teen idols, they had a genius studio quality. They could record a hit sound and soon were in demand as producers. Later, in the 1970s, the Robbs opened Cherokee Studios in Los Angeles and backed Shannon on his **In Concert** album.

The Robbs became life-long musical partners. They were also close personal friends and there was many a night that the Robbs and Del consumed enough liquor to float a canoe. After Del moved to the San Fernando Valley and later to Newhall, the Robbs saw him weekly. They hung out at Shannon's house or at their recording ranch, Cherokee Studio. Until the day Del Shannon died, the Robbs were an integral part of his life.

THE FOURTH DEL SHANNON SINGLE: "HEY! LITTLE GIRL"

Because he had so much success with Shannon, Balk quickly recorded and released the fourth 1961 single. "Hey! Little Girl" backed with "I Don't Care Anymore" (Big Top 3083). This song was an attempt to keep Shannon's original hit sound alive. By mid-November 1961, one trade magazine wrote: "Shannon who's been a chart-maker every time out since bowing on Big Top...can do it again with this one."

Father's Day, 1965, Daughter Kym, Dan Bourgoise and Del

"Hey! Little Girl" was an up-tempo tune reminiscent of "Runaway" and it contained the falsetto that was Shannon's trademark. With syrupy strings and a hard driving pop arrangement, it seemed like a sure hit. Why it only reached number 38 in its eight weeks on the **Billboard** pop chart remains a mystery. The b side "I Don't Care Anymore" had a maudlin country western tone to it. The song was one of Del's favorites and he loved the string arrangement that Balk used. The old days at Daisy Mae's country-western bar come through as Shannon sounded like he could cross over into the country market.

When "Hey Little Girl" didn't go to the top of the charts, Shannon was once again frustrated. He took his music seriously and couldn't understand why all the records didn't sell well. The reason was a simple one—Marketing.

Unfortunately, Shannon was marketed as a teen idol. He had shaved five years off his age, was supposedly single, well dressed and a great interview. The magazines lined up to feature the good-looking Michigan singer.

Del Shannon's early success as a teen idol was reflected in a January 1962 issue of the teen magazine **16**. Del was featured in an article entitled: "Meet U.S. Bonds and Del Shannon." He sat through an entire day with magazine staffers to ensure good media coverage. When he left **16** and walked down to a local bar for a beer, Shannon was both thrilled and tired. He had to keep his thoughts on **16** to himself. The magazine asked innocuous and vapid questions but, as Irving Micahnik remarked, "there was no such thing as bad publicity."

While at the offices of **16**, he met and became friendly with Gloria Stavers. She was not only the editor of the trendy teen magazine but she took an immediate liking to Del Shannon. The importance of **16 Magazine** did not escape Harry Balk. Since more than two thirds of all 45s and half of all LPs were purchased by girls from 12 to 17, **16 Magazine** was important to Shannon's career.

The editor at **16 Magazine**, Gloria Stavers not only made a pass at Del but she let him know that her magazine could help his career. He just laughed at the whole incident. Stavers was famed for chasing young rock stars into the bedroom but Shannon wisely ignored her without offending this teen idol maker. They remained good friends and Stavers admired Shannon for his integrity as well as his talent.

Because of the close personal relationship that Del developed with Stavers, he was treated well by **16 Magazine** staffers. He was featured regularly in the magazine, but, because he was older, there were often drawings rather than pictures of him.

One of the assets of Shannon's early career was the fine records that Harry Balk produced for the Big Top label. Not only were Del's songs highly commercial but they had a lasting quality. A list of the early Big Top 45 indicates that Shannon would be around for a long time. The word oldies but goodies hadn't been coined, but the output from Big Top guaranteed Shannon's touring future.

The Big Top record releases provided a steady stream of hits. The material was strong and Del's partnership with producer Harry Balk was a healthy one. It was in England that Shannon soon found that he had a new market for his material.

Del Shannon's 1961-1962 Big Top Record Releases

45 Record Releases

Runaway/Jody (Big Top 3066)
Hats Off To Larry/ Don't Gild The Lily, Lily (Big Top 3075)
So Long Baby/Answer To Everything (Big Top 3063)
Hey! Little Girl/I Don't Cry Anymore (Big Top 3091)
Ginny In The Mirror/I Won't Be There (Big Top 3098)
Cry Myself To Sleep/I'm Gonna Move On (Big Top 3112)
Swiss Maid/You Never Talked About Me (Big Top 3117)
Little Town Flirt/The Wamboo (Big Town 3131)

Long Playing Albums

Runaway With Del Shannon (Big Top 1303)

DEL SHANNON: ENGLISH HIT ARTIST

It was Harry Balk who first realized that Shannon's American record sales were declining. As a result, he began looking to other markets. Because he was busy as a producer, he didn't have time to travel abroad. So Balk began plotting the sound that Del needed to succeed in other markets.

One day, Irving Micahnik came into Balk's office and they began discussing the English touring market. Harry and Irv decided that they would get Del an English record deal and they would release Shannon's records in the United Kingdom to support his tours. They told Del that there were expenses involved in promoting him in the English market and so a contract for a one percent royalty was executed. This turned out to be one of Balk's shrewdest moves as it guaranteed Shannon a spot in English rock and roll until his untimely death. It also made sure that Balk and Micahnik would split most of the royalties.

England was an important place for American-roots rockers. Since Bill Haley and the Comets toured the United Kingdom in the mid-1950s, followed by Eddie Cochran and Gene Vincent, there was a strong demand for American-roots rockers. So Balk began negotiating to release Shannon's records in England and Europe.

In England, "Hats Off To Larry" hit the **New Musical Express** Top 30 on September 16, 1961 and eventually rose to number eight during its nine weeks on the British pop chart. In fact, "Hats Off To Larry" sold so well that Harry Balk immediately got Shannon into the studio for a follow up.

DEL SHANNON'S 'HATS OFF TO LARRY AND THE BRITISH CHARTS

	NME	RM
September 15, 1961	10	-
September 22, 1961	9	9
September 29, 1961	9	-
October 6, 1961	9	9
October 13, 1961	8	-
October 20, 1961	9	-

NME=NEW MUSICAL EXPRESS   RM=RECORD MIRROR

The next British 45 was "So Long Baby." It was a marvelous song and when it was released it early December, 1961 it shot to number 10 on the **New Musical Express** Top 30. When "So Long Baby" remained for a long period on the **New Musical Express** chart and vacillated from the 10th to 25th position, Balk knew he had a permanent U. K. hit maker.

THOSE HITS JUST KEPT ON COMING

While he was in England in 1962, Del appeared in a rock and roll movie, "It's Trad Dad." In this movie Shannon sang "You Never Talked About Me." It was released in black and white in the U. S. as "Ring-A-Ding Rhythm" and featured Chubby Checker, Gary U. S. Bonds, Gene Vincent, Helen Shapiro, Craig Douglas, Gene McDaniels and the Brook Brothers. The director, Richard Lester, who went on to direct the Beatles' film debut "A Hard Day's Night" combined traditional jazz and rock in this musical exploitation film.

Del Shannon

HANGING OUT WITH TOMMY BOYCE: 1962

His movie-star story is one of the tales that Del loved to tell his friends. One night he announced to his wife, Shirley, that they were going to a three-movie bill at the local drive-in. Shirley was skeptical because Del didn't like to sit for that long. What Del didn't tell his wife is that the English movie, **It's Trad Dad**, was the third feature. After sitting through two terrible movies, the management announced that the theater was closing. Del and Shirley were the only people remaining in the cold, outdoor movie theater. There weren't enough people to see **It's Trad Dad**. Shannon never saw the movie and joked about the story for years.

By 1962, American rock and roll was in the doldrums, and Del Shannon was writing some of the best music of his career. After having multiple hits in 1961 and watching "Runaway" sell a million copies, Shannon was ready to continue his success. Just as his American career was taking off Del became a star in England.

While touring in 1962, Del met Tommy Boyce. At the time, Boyce was an unknown singer songwriter living in New York. Exactly where and when Del met Tommy is not known. What is important is that they became close, life-long friends.

Del Shannon: Relaxing With Jody and Kym

In 1962, Del's wife, Shirley, went to New York with him and they hung out with Tommy and his girlfriend Susan. Susan was living in a small New York apartment. She was a college professor at New York University. "She wanted to marry Tommy but she ended up marrying some record executive." She had a daughter named Shannon born in the 1970s. "Tommy and Del were like brothers," Dan Bourgoise remarked.

Tommy Boyce remained an important influence on Shannon. He was the consummate songwriter and he had hooks and story lines which were guaranteed hits. They both liked country music and talked at length about moving away from rock and roll music. Del's producer, Harry Balk, was arranging for some country sessions.

SHANNON'S 1962 NASHVILLE SESSIONS: THE GENIUS OF PRODUCER HARRY BALK

In May 1962, Harry Balk flew to Nashville with his wife and sister-in-law to arrange for Del to cut some country tunes. "We wanted to mend our fences with Del," Balk remarked. "For a long time, Del had wanted to record in Nashville and create some country music. We wanted him to pursue his dream." This session also helped to alleviate Del's bitterness over his low royalty payments. There was a spontaneous genius to Balk's creativity and he believed that Shannon could stretch beyond the confines of the rock music world. If only he could get Del to forget about money.

Since their first meeting Del had told Harry about his interest in and dedication to country music. Now it was time to see if Shannon could make a country record.

**DEL SHANNON'S UNRELEASED COUNTRY AND WESTERN ALBUM,
BERLEE RECORDS, 1963**

Wrong Day, Wrong Way
Table Reserved For the Blues
Pardon Me (I Guess I'm In The Way)
Queen of the Honky Tonk
Three Cheers To Johnny
Loafing
The Nearness of You
I'll Remember April
I Can Tell
The Snap of His Fingers
Standing on the Corner
I've Been Working On The Railroad/Hey Baby

All songs recorded at United Sound Studios, Detroit, Michigan

---

For years, Shannon had talked about making an album of Hank Williams' tunes. Balk agreed that it was a good idea. Privately, Balk admitted in later years, that he was simply indulging Del. When arrangements were completed for Shannon's country record, Balk decided it was too expensive to cut in Nashville. So he decided to fly Del back to Detroit to cut the album at United Sound. The Nashville trip was productive because Del and Harry found a country hit for Shannon. Harry wanted Del in the proper mindset because he desperately needed another hit single. So Harry searched around Nashville for songwriters. He and Del spent two days going from door to door and listening to song pluggers. None of their songs fit Shannon.

They were about to go home when Harry put the word out that they were looking for tunes. It didn't take long for the army of songwriters who lived in and around Nashville to find Shannon.

A country songwriter, Rober Miller, who was working as a janitor approached Balk, and they talked at length about Shannon's country sound. Miller played a new song, "Swiss Maid," and Balk knew that he had found his country single.

By the time Shannon went into the studio to cut "Swiss Maid," Miller came over with a better song but he was too busy to spend anymore time. So he simply gave up and flew off to New York when Balk was too busy to talk to him.

Another outcome of the Nashville trip was to record an album of Hank Williams' tunes. The country album was cut in Detroit. As producer Balk suggested there was a tradition of country music greatness in Michigan. So why record it in Nashville? Since his earliest days in Coopersville, Del had played the country classics associated with Williams' career. While playing at Battle Creek's Hi Lo Club or performing Sunday nights at Daisy Mae's at Gun Lake, Shannon had played all of the key Williams' tunes.

When Shannon cut the songs for the Hank Williams album at the United Sound Studios at 5840 Second Avenue., it took only two days. Since the Hank Williams LP had been in the planning stage for some time, it was easy to record. Del took the Hi Lo Club drummer, Marcus Terry, and he left to cut the country album in Detroit's United Sound Studio. The album entitled, **Del Shannon Sings Hank Williams: Your Cheatin' Heart**, saw Shannon use Bob "Babbit" Kreinar on bass and Dennis Coffey and Bill Knight on guitars.

Shannon was intimately familiar with Williams' music and recorded the album in record time. Because of his strong feeling for Williams music, Del wrote the liner notes. The selection of songs featured "Your Cheatin' Heart," "Kaw-Liga," "I Can't Help Myself," "You Win Again" and "Cold, Cold Heart" among the 12 Williams' classics.

There were three unreleased songs left out of the album, "Wrong Day, Wrong Way," "Table Reserved For the Blues" and "Queen of the Honky Tonks" remain unreleased. The location of these songs remains a mystery. Del did record in Nashville cutting "The Swiss Maid," "Cry Myself To Sleep," "I'm Gonna Move On" and "She Thinks I Still Care" with the Jordanaires backing him up while Ray Stevens played organ.

When the **Del Shannon Sings Hank Williams: Your Cheatin' Heart** (Amy 8004) was released in 1964, it failed to make a chart appearance. No Amy singles featuring Hank Williams' tunes were released and both Harry Balk and Amy Records viewed the LP as a sop to Shannon's ego. This was a mistake because the tunes were uniformly strong. However, in the 1960s, rock and roll artists didn't cross over into the country field.

Harry Balk's production was outstanding on the Williams' LP and he allowed Del to give his own interpretation of such Williams' tunes as "Long Gone Lonesome Blues" and "I Can't Help It." "I think Del could have been a country music star in another time," Balk recalled. Shannon's fans were perplexed and the album didn't sell well.

"I think Del thought that he was singing for the rough, drinking crowd at Daisy Mae's," Chuck Marsh recalled. "His ability to cover Hank Williams was eerie."

In 1990, Rhino Records rereleased the Hank Williams album and it remains a strong statement of Shannon's multi-talented abilities. He was as much at home with a country tune as a ballad or a rock song. One of the reasons that Del Shannon's country music was ignored was his worldwide popularity. Irving Micahnik, the businessman behind Embee Productions, believed that Shannon was a rock and pop star and he had little time to promote a country music album.

One day Micahnik told Del that the Australian market was another place for his music. They talked at length about taking a trip to Australia and with surprising speed, Micahnik bought airline tickets. Del wondered if there was a casino down under. There was and Irving had a good time. There were also business contracts to execute and Micahnik was a pro. He established Shannon as an Australian star. Not only was Del's music popular but London Records promoted it with unflagging interest.

DEL SHANNON'S BILLBOARD TOP 40 HITS

Runaway, No. 1, 12 weeks, 1961
Hats Off To Larry, No. 5, 11 weeks, 1961
So Long Baby, No. 28, 5 weeks, 1961
Hey! Little Girl, No. 38, 2 weeks, 1962
Little Town Flirt, No. 12, 7 weeks, 1963
Handy Man, No. 22, 7 weeks, 1964
Keep Searchin' (We'll Follow The Sun), No. 9, 10 weeks, 1964
Stranger In Town, No. 30, 4 weeks, 1965
Sea of Love, No. 33, 4 weeks, 1982

THE AUSTRALIAN AND ENGLISH MARKETS: FOREIGN HOMES FOR DEL SHANNON

In February 1962, Del Shannon flew to Australia. Like the United Kingdom, the country down under proved to be another important foreign market. While he was in Sydney, Del met with Kevin Ritchie, the promotional manager for E.M.I. Records and Ken Sparkes, a disc jockey with 2GB radio and they held a very public press conference announcing the release of Shannon's records in Australia.

The Australian trips continued. In 1964, Shannon appeared at the Sydney Stadium on a tour which included the Searchers, Peter and Gordon, Dinah Lee and Eden Kane. Del's version of "Runaway" was the most applauded song at the Sydney Stadium show and he received two standing ovations. "When the Searchers came on to close the October 1 show, Shannon had stolen their thunder.

It was during this show that Del showed Peter and Gordon his song, "I Go To Pieces." They loved it, recorded it and the results was a top ten hit. Gordon Waller recalled that Del was "unassuming, just another bloke to have a beer with." Recalling his time with Del in Australia, during an interview at the 2000 Beatlefest in Los Angeles, Waller praised Shannon for his showmanship and professional approach to the music. "He had an eye on the business side and most of us just wanted a good time," Waller recalled.

Harry M. Miller Promotions, who dubbed the tour "Starlift '64," was ecstatic with Shannon's drawing power. The Festival Hall was filled with "Runaway" fans and for the remainder of his career, Shannon was a major Australian star. From 1961 to 1964 the London label released seven Australian singles, two EPs and six albums. They all sold well.

The English market was always a lucrative one. In September 1962, Del toured the U. K. with Dion and Buzz Clifford. At this point, "Runaway" had already been an English smash, and Shannon's seven singles released by the London label in 1961-1962 were U. K. chart busters. By the time that he toured England, "The Swiss Maid" and "You Never Talked About Me" were best sellers. When Del arrived in London "Cry Myself To Sleep" was number 29 in England. During his tour the English embraced "The Swiss Maid" and it quickly rose to number 2. By late 1962, Del had six British hit singles. His American hits numbered only two with "Runaway" and "Hats Off To Larry." It was this fact which prompted Shannon to consider founding his own record label.

The lure of the U. K. market was a strong one. After "Runaway" hit the British charts, Shannon had nine other hits in 1961-1963. "Hats Off To Larry" charted at number 6 in the fall of 1961, and then Del had three hits in 1962, "Hey Little Girl," "Cry Myself to Sleep" and "The Swiss Maid." They were all Top 30 English hits.

Irving Micahnik was the architect of some other hit releases. When "Two Kinds of Teardrops" rose to number 5 on the British charts, Micahnik and road manager Mike Risposi went for a weekend to Selsdon Park in Surrey, England and flipped a coin over whether to release "Two Silhouettes" or "My Wild One" for Del's next U. K. release. Fortunately, they chose "Two Silhouettes" and it promptly rose to number 23 in the United Kingdom.

THE BERLEE RECORD YEARS: DEL SHANNON'S LABEL AND INDEPENDENT PRODUCTION

Del Shannon parted ways with producer Harry Balk and promoter Irving Micahnik in 1963. He was furious with a record deal that paid him poorly and he couldn't stand Irving and Harry's meddling in his music. In conversations with Dion DiMucci and Bobby Vee, Del found out that his two percent royalty payment was half of their royalty deal. In the foreign markets Shannon's royalty was a paltry one per cent. He had simmered with anger over this since 1961. Then Micahnik's financial problems began to allegedly take money from Del's pocket. At least this is what Del told his close friends.

One night Del came home and announced to his wife Shirley that he was going to set up his own record label. Mercury Records had turned down Shannon's request for a recording contract. He blamed Balk and Micahnik and he believed that Embee Productions had blackballed him. In the basement of Shannon's Southfield, Michigan home, Berlee records was born. The name came from his dad, Bert, and his mother, Leone.

After he filed a lawsuit against Balk and Micahnik, Del formally went into business for himself. It was the fall of 1963 when Berlee began doing business. From its inception, Berlee was a good idea that had trouble getting off the ground. Part of the reason for Del's record company having problems can be traced to the music industry. He could never convince the major distributors that his label was a legitimate one.

There were only two releases on the Berlee label, but they made Shannon's point. He could produce himself and he needed more freedom in the studio. The experiment with Berlee was an important one. The first single in October 1963, "Sue's Gotta Be Mine" backed with "Now She's Gone" (Berlee B-501,) was an excellent single.

"Sue's Gotta Be Mine" charted at number 77 in America and in England, London Records released it to excellent sales. The second Berlee single released in March 1964, "That's The Way Love Is," bubbled under on **Billboard** at 117, and backed with "Time of Day" (Berlee B-502), it was an excellent record.

"That's The Way Love Is" provided an example of Del's song-writing genius. He sat down and wrote the song in an hour. Shannon always worked best under pressure and he often had ideas that he instantly translated into song. There were also many rarities that Shannon wrote and recorded, but these songs barely saw the light of day.

"Time of Day" is the key rarity on the Berlee label. It was a straight-ahead rock ballad which should have been a chart song. Del's use of violins gave the song a special feel and it was just right for the times. Berlee had neither money nor influence on the **Billboard** or **Cashbox** charts, so it wasn't immediately released.

All four tracks were cut at the same session at New York's Bell Studio. Shannon was the producer and Bill Ramal played saxophone and arranged the tracks. This led to strained feelings between Del's former producer, Harry Balk, and Ramal. Harry quickly forgot about it and used Ramal for future Embee Productions sessions. The Berlee singles were then pressed in New York and distributed by Diamond Records.

The work associated with a record label, even a small one, was enormous and Shannon began looking around for a record deal. He had made his point. Del could produce himself and distribute his own records. Shannon realized that if he was to remain a creative artist, he had to sign with an established record label.

It was Shannon's problems with Embee Productions that doomed the Berlee label. The lawsuits and counter suits between Del and Balk and Micahnik ended when Shannon signed with Amy Records. It was a subsidiary of Bell Records and in time would become the Arista label. "I went to Amy," Del told Charlie Marsh, "and it is a depressing story. I had to sign with Embee to get my career back on track."

THE AMY RECORD YEARS

In 1964, Del Shannon signed with Amy Records and he wasn't happy about it. After having formed his own record label, Berlee, Shannon lost a lawsuit to Embee Productions. Since he had a binding contract with Balk and Micahnik, Shannon wasn't free to continue to release material on his own label. So after he lost the lawsuit, Del reluctantly returned to Balk's label to complete his contract.

Del had written his best material with Embee Productions and he wanted to recapture this creative process. When he returned to Amy, Del's writing was at its peak. He not only composed some of his best songs, but he was once again in a hit-record frame of mind. The English Invasion had inspired Shannon. He watched with interest as American television embraced the Beatles. Del realized that he had a similar writing and recording style. Not for one moment did Del take credit for the Beatles' Merseyside sound but he remarked to close friends that the English had adopted part of his sound. So he was not unhappy because Del could write songs that sold well in the United Kingdom.

Shannon was pleased that Amy had cut a deal with the United Kingdom's Stateside label and his material would be readily available in the English market. As Del stressed, he had had more hits in the U. K. than at home. Amy did provide solid entries into the English marketplace but there was still a contentious relationship between Shannon and Embee Productions.

Over time Del's attitude toward Balk softened. Not only was he a skilled producer, Harry was one of the few people who would challenge Del. "I told him we had to speed up his voice on 'Runaway,'" Balk remarked, "and then I got him a great song writing partner in Maron McKenzie." So the thought of returning to work with Balk was not an entirely unpleasant one.

At Amy, Del was reunited with songwriter Maron McKenzie. Shannon's first Amy single, "Mary Jane," was a tribute to Hank Ballard and the Midnighters and to Dion DiMucci. The b side, "Stains on My Letter," was a Shannon tune which returned the old song writing magic.

The United Kingdom market continued to be a vibrant one. In England, Del had two singles released in the same day. "That's The Way Love Is" was a Berlee single released on the London label and "Mary Jane" was an Amy tune put out on the Stateside label.

After Del had released the cover version of the Beatles "From Me To You," he completed his contract with Big Top Records. What Del didn't realize is that his contract with Embee Productions gave them the right to select his next label. So this is the reason that he had to sign with Amy.

While not a major label, on the surface Amy seemed to offer some creative freedom. Del was still young and he believed that the force of his song-writing and production skills would keep him in the Top 40.

There were eight singles released on the Amy label and three albums. The Amy Record years were important ones for Shannon as he matured and grew as a songwriter and recording artist.

One reason that Del signed with Amy Records was because it was located in Detroit near his home in Southfield, Michigan. The first Amy album, **Handy Man** (Amy 8003 M) attempted to cash in on Shannon's cover version of the Jimmy Jones hit. The album and the hit song were the work of Harry Balk. He not only matched Jones' style and voice to Del's but he provided the type of production which made the song a hit. While he recorded for Amy, Del used the Royaltones as his backup band. They were on such hits as "Handy Man," "Do You Want to Dance" and "Keep Searchin' (We'll Follow the Sun)." Other great Royaltones' cuts included "Move It On Over" and "Break Up." Del told everyone that the Royaltones were the only band who could back him in the studio.

"I met Del about the time that he cut 'Handy Man," Dan Bourgoise continued. "So I watched all the Amy material come together, and in some cases was a part of that, but I never went with Del to the New York sessions." Young Bourgoise worked in a record shop and had befriended Shannon. "I was kind of like a little brother to Del," Bourgoise remarked. "Eventually I moved to California where I lived with him and Shirley for a time."

During the controversy over his contract with Embee Productions and the Amy recordings, Del was unhappy about losing a potential recording contract with Mercury Records. After listening to some of Shannon's demos, the Chicago-based firm talked at length about signing Shannon, but they backed off because of his legal dispute with Embee Productions.

Shannon was depressed. He was with a new label but back with the old management firm. No one seemed to understand it. Micahnik and Balk were silent. No one knew that they had an iron clad contract with Shannon.

THOSE HITS JUST KEPT ON COMING

At Amy Records, Shannon's biggest hit "Keep Searchin'" rose to number 4 in England and charted at number 9 on the **Billboard** Hot 100. When Del wrote "Keep Searchin'" it was originally entitled: "We Will Follow The Sun." The music featured the minor chords like those in "Runaway" and Steve Monahan sang the harmony parts. All this was done in Del's basement and then it was taken to the producer. There is no doubt that Balk's production techniques remained strong as "Keep Searchin' (We'll Follow The Sun)" charted in the Top 10. At this point, Harry and Del got along fine but business problems threatened to disrupt their relationship.

"Keep Searchin' (We'll Follow The Sun)" was a popular cover tune. Gary Lewis and the Playboys cut it and an Argentina group, The Shakers, had a Latin American hit with it. It was at this time that Del wrote "I Go To Pieces" and developed a strong reputation as a U. K. songwriter.

Some years later Del looked back on "Keep Searchin' (We'll Follow The Sun)." He recalled that the writing process was a quick one. "I was in the basement of my house in Detroit, and a couple friends of mine were there. They said, 'You ought to write another song in the minors.' Minors meaning chords. I said, 'Nah, I don't think we should do that.' Well, they kept giving me another jug, and I wrote 'If we gotta keep on the run, we'll follow the sun." Then Del recalled that he worked from about one to five in the morning, took a short nap and got out of bed and finished the song from seven to eight in the morning. The theme behind "Keep Searchin' (We'll Follow The Sun)" was a perfect reflection of Shannon's drive to write hit records.

There were other chart songs, but also a number of records that for some unexplainable reason never charted. A cover of Bobby Freeman's "Do You Wanna Dance" charted at number 43 in the U. S. but failed to register on the United Kingdom charts. "Broken Promises," the b side to "Keep Searchin' (We'll Follow The Sun)," was a strong tune which deserved promotion. Shannon and the Royaltones cut enough material for an album. Some of these tunes were not released. These included covers of Roy Orbison's "Crying," Chuck Berry's "Memphis, Tennessee" Dion's "Ruby Baby" and there were originals like "I'll Be Lonely Tomorrow," written with Maron McKenzie and "I Can't Fool Around Anymore" written with two members of the Royaltones.

Dan Bourgoise remembered, "I was there for the writing of 'Keep Searchin' Steve Monahan and I were there with Del in his basement in Southfield....Del first had this phrase, 'if we gotta keep on the run, we'll follow the sun." Then Steve Monahan came up with the "wee-oos" that distinguish "Keep Searchin'." How fair was Shannon with his split of the royalties with co songwriters? "Del was always generous in splitting song writer's credit with others," Bourgoise remarked.

Bourgoise believed that much of Shannon's song writing success was due to people who could intellectually stimulate him, thereby pushing Del into new creative directions. "To keep challenging him to come up with a better lyric or melody was my role," Bourgoise concluded.

One of the unsolved mysteries of the Amy Record years is a rumor that Shannon recorded a jazz album. It was an LP tentatively entitled: **Del Shannon Sings and Plays Jazz**. The album never surfaced and there is no record of a song list. Yet, some former executives at Amy remember such a project. The obvious conclusion is that Micahnik took the tapes and lost them. Shannon had to retain his sense of humor considering the events surrounding the Amy Record years. Some years later, the lost tapes were rumored to be at a car dealership in Detroit

While at Amy Records, Del recorded the weakest song of his career. In 1966, just as Shannon was entering his deal with Liberty, Amy released "I Can't Believe My Ears" backed with "I Wish I Wasn't Me Tonight" (Amy 947). "I hated that record," Del recalled. The reason was a simple one. The same songwriter who turned out "Don't Gild the Lily, Lily" wrote "I Can't Believe My Ears". While Del never said he hated that song, it was not one of his favorites. "Don't Gild the Lily, Lily" was a hit," Shannon remarked. "So I never said a word." It was Irving Micahnik who loved and sought out these songs. Harry Balk thought that they were too schmaltzy for Del but he deferred for some reason to Micahnik. All this frustrated Shannon.

There is another reason that "I Can't Believe My Ears" was a disappointment. It was the eighth and final single that Shannon owed Embee Productions. He wanted out of his deal with Irving Micahnik and the single didn't matter.

The reason that Shannon cut "I Can't Believe My Ears" is that he didn't want to write any more songs for Embee Productions. The dispute over publishing rights caused Shannon to explode periodically. So he told Micahnik to pick his last single. At the time Dan Bourgoise, his young friend from Michigan he met in a local record store, was in the Naval Reserve. When Dan heard the song on the radio, he thought: "Del, what's the deal?"

While it appeared that Balk was deferring to Micahnik, the truth was that the partnership was dissolving. The strains of expenditures and difficulties in balancing the books brought an end to Embee Productions.

It was while he was with Amy Records that Del continued his friendship with a group of young musicians, the Robbs. From 1961 they had been on the road with Del sporadically and remained his good friends until the day he died.

BACK TO THE AMERICAN MARKET: ENTER THE ROBBS ONCE AGAIN IN THE MIDST OF THE AMY YEARS

In 1961 while on tour in Wisconsin, Del originally had met the Robbs. They had a large teen following in and around Wisconsin, Minnesota, Michigan and Illinois. After Shannon met the Robbs, he became a fan because they had cut Shannon's "The Prom" (Argo 5439) and made it a regional hit. The Robbs' musical skill impressed Shannon and when he could, he took them on the road. "The Prom" was an obscure song from Shannon's **Runaway** album and the Robbs let Del know that they were big fans. When he listened to the Robbs play, Del realized that he didn't have to put up with the pick -up bands that were driving him crazy on tour.

For a time the Robbs became Del Shannon's backup band, but they were musically so advanced that they were signed to Mercury Records in the mid-1960s. However, the Robbs remained an integral part of Del's music and life until the day he died.

During the period of Del's hits from 1961 to 1965, the Robbs were signed to the Chicago-based Chess label. Leonard Chess saw the Robbs as his signature white act and he put some money and energy behind their records. Dale Hawkins had just left Chess and the Robbs were considered his replacement.

In 1962, it was in the Chess studios that the Robbs discovered their knack for production. Because of his penchant for saving money, Chess didn't hire professional engineers on a full-time basis. Willie Dixon handled much of the production load, so the Robbs were able to use the studio for long periods of time. This became an apprenticeship which in later years made their Cherokee recording studio a hit factory.

During the British Invasion, the Robbs backed Chad and Jeremy, and Freddy and the Dreamers in a series of American concerts. They also began saving money for a move to Los Angeles. Finally, in 1967, they relocated to California to pursue television appearances, recording freedom and a new career direction.

DEL SHANNON AMY RECORDS PART TWO: MUSIC PUBLISHER, SONG WRITER AND BOB SEGER

In 1964, Del Shannon formed a publishing company, Shidel Music, and set up a recording studio in the basement of his Southfield, Michigan home. Del could spot talent. He soon found a young kid and listened to him play his guitar and sing his original tunes. "The kid sounded like Bob Dylan, but with a better voice," Del told Peter Vice. "I knew he had it." The young kid was 16-year-old Bob Seger. The equipment in Shannon's basement was average but the zeal of local rock and rollers quickly brought in some great talent.

Eventually, Shannon signed Doug Brown and Bob Seger to contracts as song writers. They turned out a number of songs. Some were commercial and others were simply amateurish works. Doug Brown and the Omens recorded a radio spot for the Northwest lounge. Another local entertainment venue, the Club Guy Haven featured Jamie Coe's band and Del loved to hang out there. The Sounds Inc. was another house band and Shannon worked with them on new songs.

The Shannon home studio was responsible for a number of demos. Doug Brown and Steve Monahan cut "I Don't Mind," in May 1964, and Seger and Brown recorded "Alone In the Crowd" which was Bob Seger's first recording with Del Shannon singing background. Doug Brown and Dan Monahan cut "Until I Saw You Cry" and "Tell Bobby Not to Cry." Then Seger and Brown recorded "Too Good to be True" with a Del Shannon falsetto.

It was during this period that Shannon cut the demo version of "I Go To Pieces," that Peter and Gordon made into a top 10 hit. Del also cut a Doug Brown song in an attempt to get a demo into Elvis Presley's hand. Colonel Tom Parker wrote Shannon and let him know that "Just You" wouldn't be cut by Presley unless Shidel Music sold the rights to it. Shannon politely informed the Colonel that he wasn't selling out his own publishing company.

Dan Bourgoise remembered, "Del wanted to do something like a Jerry Butler record. He wrote 'I Go To Pieces' originally in that rhythm and blues style of Lloyd Brown, who was a black Grand Rapids lounge singer." Bourgoise continued, "I believe Del produced the song, and he shopped it to Mercury. He never thought of the song originally for himself. He did write songs for others back then, many of which never got released. When Del went to Australia he played Lloyd's demo version for Peter and Gordon backstage on the Australian package tour."

During 1964, Del was a featured performer on the night time national rock and roll shows. He appeared on both Shindig and Hullabaloo. Prior to these appearances his only significant rock and roll television appearance was on Dick Clark's daytime American Bandstand show.

It was the fifth Amy single "Stranger In Town," released in February 1965, which had a semblance of the old Del Shannon sound. It contained a full rock-band sound and Balk slammed two by four wooden blocks together to create an eerie echo effect. Rock critic, Dave Marsh, selected this song as one of the one hundred best songs of all time. The last Amy single, "Break Up," charted at number 95 on the **Billboard** Hot 100.

1965 AND THE HITS STOP COMING

In late September 1965, the English single "Move It On Over" backed with "She Still Remembers Tony" (Stateside SS 452) was released to generally favorable reviews. The London-based **Record Mirror**, remarked in its September 21, 1965 issue that Shannon's sound was a bit dated, but the record was generally a good one. Although it bubbled under at number 128 on **Billboard**, the general consensus in the industry was that Shannon's song writing talent was once again on track.

As the "Move It On Over" single was released, Del was preparing for the move to California. He was under a great deal of pressure to continue his hit-record run. From his house on Robert Street in Southfield, Michigan, he would drive to a summer cottage he owned at Cobb Lake. It was a place to relax and reflect on his work. As the frustration grew in Shannon's life, he took hundreds of "Move It On Over" 45s out to the lake and threw them in the water. "Del thought that 'Move It On Over' was a sizzling, crunchy rocker that was a sure hit," Dan Bourgoise continued, "Keep Searchin' has just brought him back to the top of the charts and 'I Go To Pieces' and 'Stranger in Town' had some success. Personally, I think to this day that 'Move It On Over' is one of his best all-time greatest records—it was a song that captured all of Del's anger at the time." Bourgoise continued, "I asked Del what he was going to do after he moved to California. He told me that he was going to cut some country records." Then Dan was surprised when Shannon said: "Who cares, it's all over." The pressure to have another hit was once again causing Shannon problems.

"Stranger in Town" is the closest song to a personal anthem for Shannon. It had a dark, eerie mood to it. Dave Marsh's book, **The Heart of Rock & Soul: The 1001 Greatest Singles Ever Made**, described Shannon as "its leading paranoid." This is a harsh judgment, but there is an element of truth to it. The theme in "Stranger in Town" is that some stark individual looking for revenge is pursuing the singer. The images in Shannon's music quickly caught the attention of television producers.

In the 1980s, Michael Mann's television police drama, "Crime Story," used a re-recorded version of "Runaway" as its theme. There is an element of fear in the tune and it suggests Shannon's disenchantment with the rock and roll lifestyle.

DEL SHANNON'S UNRELEASED FOURTH ALBUM FOR AMY, 1965
Game of Love
She Still Remembers Tony
No One Knows
I Can't Believe My Ears
Just You
Break Up
Tired of Waiting For You

My Love Has Gone
Tell Her No
I Wish I Wasn't Me Tonight
This Is All I Have To Give
Move It On Over

This album was recorded at New York's Bell Sound Studio

When Dan and Del pulled up two lawn chairs at Cobb Lake it was a strange sight. Here was one of America's top recording stars pitching his 45s into the cold water. Del had a cabin at Cobb Lake and when he went into the house and pulled out the box of 45s, Bourgoise was horrified. Dan hollered: "I'm telling ya, the record is great." Del smiled and he began throwing records like saucers or frisbees into the lake. At this point Del commented that he was going to retire from rock and roll and began recording country music.

Some time after this incident, Del left to do a California television show. Then he called Dan and told him that he had purchased a home in Van Nuys, California. This upscale Los Angeles suburb was the perfect location to record for Liberty Records and revive his career. Del's career was far from over.

The English music magazines kept a closer eye on Shannon's career than did their American counterparts. The January 23, 1965 issue of **Record Mirror** praised Shannon's Hank Williams album and had positive comments about his recent English hit, "Keep Searchin." In a lengthy conversation with Norman Jopling, Shannon complained that fame had changed his friends. "They just don't behave as they used to toward me," Shannon remarked. The strain of four years of stardom, making hit records and touring had taken its toll on Del. He needed to get off the road and take a vacation. Unfortunately, his career was still in high gear and it would be some time before he could relax. Yet, he vowed to spend more time in the recording studio and less time on the road.

Del finished the interview with Norman Jopling by remarking that he had his own record company and had signed Lloyd Brown to a contract. "I wrote 'I Go To Pieces' for Brown," Shannon remarked, "but then Peter and Gordon had a hit with it." Shannon closed the interview by remarking that he would spend more time in the recording studio and working with other artists.

As 1965 came to an end, Shannon had spent the better part of the year recording an album that Irving Micahnik had entitled **Move On Over**, but Del fell apart when it had been discovered that the master tapes had been lost. It seems that the tapes had actually not been lost. Rather they had been confiscated in lieu of payment when Embee Productions was unable to pay off the studio time . The masters were seized by a local automobile dealor and then taken to a New York City warehouse. The car dealor who owned the warehouse alledgedlythrew out the tapes.

There were other problems with Shannon's career. He was often booked on shows that had little impact upon the rock and roll world. The low point in Del's early career came in 1965 when he appeared on the Detroit based Soupy Sales Show. Neither Shannon nor the comedian warmed up to each other and the result was a disaster. Del needed something to alleviate his fears.

So in 1965, Shannon purchased a new Cadillac, but it had a rattle in it so he drove his old 1961 Corvair around Los Angeles. "I think that Del wanted to keep that Cadillac new," his wife Shirley remarked, "He sure took good care of his money." Del Shannon realized that the hits would not be coming forever and he told his old friend, Michigan disc jockey, Charlie Marsh, that he was saving his money for "a rainy day."

During this time Del was upset that many of his best songs never saw the light of day. He had a large amount of material that Embee Productions either couldn't or wouldn't release. The songs were uniformly excellent.

THE DEL SHANNON PEPSI COLA COMMERCIALS

In 1965, Shannon's string of hits made him a hot commodity. This fact was not lost on commercial advertisers. The Pepsi-Cola Co. signed Del to three contracts and he recorded two one-minute commercial spots and a 30 second segment. The Royaltones were his backing band. Somehow in the recording process, four different versions of the three commercials emerged.

The Pepsi people decided to take one of the 60 second versions and make it into two ads. The first has an instrumental break and the second 60 second spot has an added verse. Then Pepsi took all of its advertising jingle and put them on a novelty record.

In 1996, Vox Records released two of the four versions of the Pepsi commercial in a CD entitled, **Great Cola Commercials, Volume 2**. Then the Australian Raven Corporation included a segment from the Pepsi commercials on their box set. For the pure Shannon collector, these tracks are undiscovered gems.

What makes Del's commercial special is that he used the song "Handy Man" as the vehicle to sell Pepsi. With lyrics that shout in a falsetto "Come alive-come alive, you're in the Pepsi generation," Shannon had one of the best commercials of the day.

The Pepsi Cola commercials are another example of Shannon's business genius. He realized that the commercials would help to sell his records. Over time these brief radio segments not only became collector items but they defined this type of advertisement for the rock and roll marketplace.

UNRELEASED DEL SHANNON STUDIO CUTS, 1962-1965

This Feeling Called Love, Mira Sound, N. Y., 1962
Sandy (aka Little Sandy), West End Sound, London, 1963
Walk Like An Angel, West End sound, London, 1963
I Go To Pieces, Bell Sound, N. Y, 1964
Just You, United Sound, Detroit, 1964
Torture (version 1), United Sound, Detroit, 1964
Torture (version 2), United Sound, Detroit, 1964
Froggy (with son, Craig), United Sound, Detroit, 1964
Nothin' (with the Teenbeats), United Sound, 1964
Instrumental (untitled), United Sound, 1964

My Love Has Gone, Bell Sound, 1965
Game of Love, Bell Sound, 1965
No One Knows, Bell Sound, 1965
Tired of Waiting For You, Bell Sound, 1965
Tell Her No, Bell Sound, New York, 1965

Note: Over time some of these tracks have been released.

OF WRITS AND ROYALTIES AND CHART SUCCESS:
A CONCLUSION

From 1961 through 1965, Del Shannon was a continual hit-making act. He would continue this success into 1966 and then vanish from the **Billboard** charts until 1982 when the single "Sea of Love" and the album **Drop Down and Get Me** brought him back.

The royalties from Shannon's songs began showing up in some strange places. In France, Eddy Mitchell cut "Little Town Flirt" as "Si Tu Penses (If You Think)," Frank Alamo recorded "Hey! Little Girl" as "Ma Mere (My Mother)," Sylvia Vartan released "So Long Baby" as "Avec Toi (Without You)" and Danny Logan and the Pirates recorded two Shannon tunes "Cry Myself To Sleep" as "Je Pleure Aussi (I'll Cry Too)" and "Oublie Larry (Forget Larry)" in a tribute to "Hats Off to Larry." In Japan, "Runaway" was cut by Venus, the Irish charts in 1974 featured "Runaway" by the Snakehips which rose to number 13 on the national hit listing. Strangely enough only one Shannon single was released in Ireland. This took place in 1966 when Liberty put out "The Big Hurt."

One of the strangest foreign releases took place in South Africa. It was there that "Runaway" came out on a 78. In 1962, when Lawrence Welk released "Runaway" in the American market, it contained the real name of the composer, Charles Westover.

DEL SHANNON: CASH BOX HITS 1961-1965

Runaway, No. 1, 16 weeks, 1961
Hats Off To Larry, No. 2, 13 weeks, 1961
So Long Baby, No. 38, 10 weeks, 1961
Hey! Little Girl, No. 47, 10 weeks, 1961
The Swiss Maid, No. 76, 8 weeks, 1962
Little Town Flirt, No. 11, 15 weeks, 1962
Two Kinds of Teardrops, No. 55, 7 weeks, 1963
From Me To You, No. 67, 4 weeks, 1963
Sue's Gotta Be Mine, No. 68, 5 weeks, 1963
Handy Man, No. 19, 11 weeks, 1964
Do You Want To Dance, No. 45, 6 weeks, 1964
Keep Searchin' (We'll Follow The Sun), No. 8, 15 weeks, 1964
Stranger In Town, No. 33, 6 weeks, 1965
Break Up, No. 83, 3 weeks, 1965

The royalties for "Runaway" and the other early hits often got lost in the corporate shuffle. Then, in 1975, when Dan Bourgoise founded Bug Music things changed. The result was that Del not only got paid, but his early records were once again leased for commercial purposes and repackaging. Because of his royalty difficulties, Del became angry with Balk and Micahnik.

There was a soap opera quality to Shannon's relationship with Embee Productions. He left the company to form his own label, Berlee, but he found difficulty distributing his material. Consequently, he resigned with Balk and Micahnik after losing a bitter law suit. Then when "Keep Searchin' (We'll Follow The Sun)" became a hit, Del once again complained about a lack of royalty payments. He left Embee Productions and signed with Liberty Records. What this did was to create financial and personal chaos until the late 1970s when Irving Micahnik died and Dan Bourgoise settled the financial differences. Bourgoise also gave Del's song writing rights to him.

THE NEW DEL SHANNON: 1965

In 1965, Del Shannon underwent some personal changes. He began combing his hair forward because of a receding hairline, Shannon was always sensitive about his hair style. With the advent of the Beatles, he could comb his hair forward to affect the Merseyside mod look.

It was in clothing that Del changed dramatically. He had always worn sharp suits that cost a lot of money. Suddenly, he was buying flowered shirts, wearing beads and loud colors. It was the mid-1960s and all the elements of fashion changed. Shannon was right in the midst of this cultural explosion. The psychedelic Del Shannon was about to emerge.

BIBLIOGRAPHICAL ESSAY

For the Beatles and Del Shannon see Howard A. DeWitt, **The Beatles: Untold Tales** (Fremont, 1985). Bob Wooler, the Cavern disc jockey, viewed some of Del Shannon's 1963 English tour shows and offered his observations. Also, the Granada Tour Program for May 1963, which sold for one shilling, was used to reconstruct the English tour. The early chapters in Howard A. DeWitt, **Paul McCartney: From Liverpool To Let It Be** (Fremont, 1992) were a major source for this chapter. Also see, Howard A. DeWitt, **Chuck Berry: Rock 'N' Roll Music** (Ann Arbor, 1985) and Howard A. DeWitt, **Sun Elvis: Presley in the 1950s** (Ann Arbor, 1993) for an indication of how roots American rock influenced Del Shannon and his early hit records.

The files of **Melody Maker, Disc, Record Mirror** and the **New Musical Express** were examined in detail at the Collindale Library in London, England. The British music press was an important source in determining his initial U.K. and European popularity. The comments of author Steve Turner on the British music scene were also valuable ones. A series of interviews with the Robbs at their Cherokee Studio established many previously unknown parts of Shannon's life. Peter Vice, Dan Bourgoise and Shirley Westover provided excellent interviews for this chapter. Harry Balk provided some comments on these years. Brief interviews with Delbert McClinton clarified his relationship to John Lennon and the Beatles. Also, Clive Epstein, Joe Flannery, Tony Sheridan, Ray Coleman, Horst Fascher, Alistair Taylor, Eddie Hoover, Kingsize Taylor, Billy J. Kramer and Sam Leach provided information on Del Shannon's appearances in England and Germany. Johnny Tillotson provided some anecdotes on the problems of fame and money and Shannon's adjustment to post stardom fame. Karl Palmer was unusually helpful in reconstructing Shannon's return to the Hi Lo Club. The Popenhagen family also recalled vignettes about Del's life. Dick Schlatter provided some important insights into the new Hi Lo Club reputation.

For comments on "Daytona Beach Weekend," see Marshall Crenshaw, **Hollywood Rock: A Guide To Rock N Roll In The Movies** (New York, 1994). See **Billboard** and **Cash Box** for ads and comments on Del's releases from 1961 to 1965. Also, see **And The Music Plays On: Del Shannon Magazine**, Issue 1, Fall, 1994, pp. 2-6 for a reprint of many record reviews from this period. For the attempt to place Del Shannon in the teen idol role see, **16 Magazine**, January, 1962, p. 35 for a Del Shannon-Gary U.S. Bonds comparative feature. This is an interesting piece intended for the teen market and suggests some of the pressures that Shannon faced in his early teen-idol mold.

The English music newspapers were helpful, see Norman Jopling's articles in **Record Mirror**, January 23, 1965 and February 13, 1965 for excellent pieces on Del Shannon. On Shannon's country music roots comments by producer Harry Balk and long time friend of Shannon, Charlie Marsh helped to sort out this material. Also see, **Del Shannon Sings Hank Williams: Your Cheatin' Heart** (Rhino R2 70982) for a reissue of this classic material. Del's original liner notes are reprinted.

For Shannon's early success see, for example, **The Cash Box**, July 19, 1961 and **Billboard**, February 10, 1962, February 24, 1962 August 18, 1962, October 6, 1962 and December 8, 1962.

Also, see, Howard A. DeWitt and Dennis M. DeWitt, "The Recording of Runaway," **Rock & Blues News**, April-May, 2000, pp. 5-12.

For some key rarities in this period of Shannon's career see Mark Dillman, "Del Shannon's Coolest Rarities: My Idea For a Box Set," **And The Music Plays On: Del Shannon Magazine**, Issue 4, Summer, 1995, pp. 28-30.

Brian Young, "Dan Bourgoise Interview Notes," 20 pages in possession of the author. These notes cast a great deal of light upon the relationship between Shannon and Amy Records.

See Dave Peckett's liner notes to **Live In England/And The Music Plays On** (Beat Goes On Records-BGOCED-280,); Ken Barnes' liner notes to **Del Shannon: 1961-1990, A Complete Career Anthology** (Raven CD-RVCD-51); Adam Komorowski's liner notes to **Del Shannon: The Definitive Collection** (Charly Records-CPCD-8315-2) and Adam Komorowski's liner notes to **Del Shannon: The EP Collection** (See For Miles Records-SEECD 677).

For an excellent rating of Del's singles see, Dave Marsh, **The Heart of Rock & Soul: The 1001 Greatest Singles Ever Made** (New York, 1989, revised edition, 1999).

Brian Young, "Notes on Berlee and Amy Records," four-page research manuscript in the possession of the author. An interview with Gordon Waller at the 1999 Beatlefest in Los Angeles helped to clarify material for this chapter. Interviews with a number of other musicians who had hits in the late 1950s and early 1960s or were on the music scene including Hank Ballard, Gary Troxel of the Fleetwoods, Dale Hawkins, Gene Summers, Jimmy McCracklin, Don Wilson, Nokie Edwards and Bob Bogle of the Ventures, Glen Glenn and Lowell Fulson helped to add depths and dimension to this chapter. Ron Peterson of the Seattle band, the Frantics, helped to clarify some historical points about the recording business.

Interviews with Bill Griggs, America's foremost Buddy Holly expert, helped to clarify many issues surrounding this chapter. Maria Elena Holly's comments were also useful.

See, Bob Fisher, "Writs and Royalties," reprinted in **And The Music Plays On: Del Shannon Magazine,** Issue 1, Fall, 1994, p. 16 for an excellent discussion of royalties. For the Australian XXXY radio interview see the transcript in **And The Music Plays On: Del Shannon Magazine,** Issue 6, Winter, 1995, pp. 12-15.

For the role of Gene Vincent in Shannon's career see, Britt Hagarty, **The Day The World Turned Blue: A Biography of Gene Vincent** (Vancouver, 1983). A recent and well written and researched book on Vincent is Susan Vanhecke, **Race With The Devil: Gene Vincent's Life In The Fast Lane** (New York, 2000). A series of interviews with Melody Jean Vincent helped to ferret out material comparing her dad, Gene Vincent, to the problems that Del Shannon faced in the music business. Donnie Brooks was also helpful in recalled key events in the early 1960s. Hank Ballard added some material on the rockers who followed his lead.

Other important sources on the early 1960s include, Steve Chapple and Reebee Garorfalo, **Rock 'n' Roll Is Here To Pay** (Chicago, 1977); Johnny Stuart, **Rockers** (London, 1987) and Nick Tosches, **Hellfire: The Jerry Lee Lewis Story** (New York, 1982, reprint edition 1992). A highly unreliable look at the early 1960s with poor scholarship and insipid writing is Colin Escott's, **Good Rockin' Tonight: Sun Records and the Birth of Rock 'n' Roll** (New York, 1991).

For London in the 1960s see, Andrew Loog Oldham, **Stoned: A Memoir of London in the 1960s** (New York, 2000).

On Bob Dylan see Howard Sounes, **Down The Highway: The Life of Bob Dylan** (New York, 2001); Clinton Heylin, **Dylan: Behind The Shades** (New York, 1991); Robert Shelton, **No Direction Home: The Life and Music of Bob Dylan** (New York, 1986); Bob Spitz, **Dylan: The Biography** (New York, 1989) and Paul Williams, **Bob Dylan: Performing Artist, Book One, 1960-1973** (London, 1990).

See the Canadian based firm Unidisc Music Inc. re-releases of **Little Town Flirt** amd **Handy Man** for this period. The extensive liner notes by Brian Young were important to this study.

6: DAN BOURGOISE: THE BUG MUSIC STORY AND DEL'S ROYALTIES

"I met Del Shannon when I was just a 20-year-old kid. It was awesome and then we became best friends for life," Dan Bourgoise

In March, 2000 Bug Music held an invitation only party to celebrate its 25th anniversary. The star-studded Hollywood gathering feted a company that has collected song writing and publishing royalties for a quarter of a century for some of the biggest and smallest names in the music industry. This has always been Bug Music's secret; they represented everybody like they were family. What makes Bug Music stand out is that they serve the artist. One of the more shameful aspects of the music business is the tendency to not pay a fair royalty to blues artists. The litany of stories about artists not being treated fairly is well known. A good example is Jimmy McCracklin whose royalties for song writing and publishing for the **Billboard** Top 10 hit, "The Walk," were delayed for more than 20 years. Then McCracklin signed with Bug and the money started rolling into the bank.

Del Shannon, Dan Bourgoise and Fontaine Brown

Over the years, blues legend John Lee Hooker, tried to collect his substantial song writing and publishing royalties without success. Then Dan and Fred Bourgoise a t Bug Music signed on to represent Hooker and he became an instant millionaire.

When Bug Music began its operation, many singer-songwriters abandoned traditional music publishers. The reason was a simple one. They weren't getting paid. The business of handling copyrights was left to lawyers and accountants. This proved to be a mistake for many artists. There were also common practices in the industry which hurt the artist.

It was commonplace for song writers to sell their product. Little Richard and John Fogarty are two examples of people who sold copyrights not realizing that they were a lifelong asset. Other lesser known acts like Arthur Alexander found their royalties due to Bug Music. An obscure Southern soul performer and songwriter, Alexander's signature tunes "You Better Move On" and "Anna (Go To Him)" were recorded by the Rolling Stones and Beatles respectively. "Arthur sold or signed away his publishing which was typical in those days," Garry Velletri of the Nashville Bug office remarked. In Alexander's case Bug Music was able to regain the original songwriter's royalties.

When Bourgoise began Bug Music, the industry took notice and there was a new attitude toward paying song writing, publishing and mechanical royalties. Long before Dan had a fancy office in Hollywood, he was making inroads into the music business.

YOUNG DAN BOURGOISE: MEETING A KID ON A BIKE, A FAKE ID AND A MUSIC STORE

Dan Bourgoise was born on February 18, 1944 in Detroit, Michigan. There were influences from the Detroit years which matured and became an integral part of Bourgoise's personality. The earliest influence was roots rock and roll. Like many kids his age, Dan listened to the radio, bought the current 45 hit records and watched the rising rock and roll and country acts on local television. He was also a typical kid and one day this led him to meet another rock and roller.

Before he was a rock and roll fanatic, Bourgoise was riding his tricycle one day on the sidewalk in front of his house. He was only seven years old when he met another kid on Appoline Street, who lived five doors down. He introduced himself as Steve Monahan. It was ironic because eventually they would both enter the record business. Monahan would record and Bourgoise would manage him. As they grew up rock and roll consumed their lives.

By the time Dan and Steve were in high school, they had a serious commitment to rock and roll. Like many young kids, Dan grew up watching the Ed Sullivan Show. It was Elvis Presley and other early rock and roll artists like Fats Domino, Little Richard, Buddy Holly and Chuck Berry who enthralled young Bourgoise. Then the Beatles took over the American music scene and the 20-year old rock and roller saw his future in the music business.

Steve Monahan, Del Shannon and Dan Bourgoise: Holding Buck Owens LPs

Bourgoise was also a fan. Dan developed an early case of the vinyl disease. Record collecting and the intricacies of the music business intrigued him. By the time that Bourgoise graduated high school in 1962, he was so enamored with music that he hoped to make it a career. How to create his spot in the music business wasn't yet apparent to 18-year-old Bourgoise. So, like many young men of his generation, he began to think of furthering his education.

DAN BOURGOISE

He started college at the Henry Ford Junior College in Detroit. Although the music bug kept getting in the way of his education, he was a diligent economics student. He simply couldn't escape the call of the rock and roll world.

While in college, Bourgoise worked at a small vinyl record store in Detroit-Joyline Records. It was at this shop that he developed his encyclopedic knowledge of rock and roll. "I knew every song on the **Billboard** list," Bourgoise commented. "I thought it was my job." Pretty soon young Dan's encyclopedic knowledge began attracting attention. When he ordered records from the one-stop wholesalers, they often asked Bourgoise for his opinion on which records might be future hits.

What became readily apparent was that Dan could predict future hits. He had the ear and the feel for a hit. But he was also concerned about his future, so he did pay some attention to his studies. In 1964 Dan Bourgoise had finished his two-year program at Henry Ford Junior College in Southfield, Michigan. He had a decision to make. Should he transfer to a major university? His grades were fine but he had little interest in college. He was shy about articulating his unhappiness with school.

How could Dan tell anyone that he thought college was a waste of time? Boring subjects. Pompous professors. Disinterested students. Poorly written books. He yearned for the real world. The course of study at Henry Ford Junior College did little to interest Bourgoise but he dutifully trotted off to class. He wasn't sure why.

Dan had many interests but none were as important as music. When he was behind the counter at Joyline Records, he was in his element. Soon it became apparent that Bourgoise was a savvy marketer. However, he was also a 20-year-old kid. So it took some time to be taken seriously. Yet, at Joyline Records, Dan showed the signs of being a serious entrepreneur.

The lessons that Dan learned at Joyline Records were lifelong ones. He established a rack at the store for the top 10 hits. He was a whiz at special ordering for customers. He stocked a wide variety of records. In later years, these early experiences would help him in the publishing business.

THE BIRTH OF BUG MUSIC

Dan Bourgoise founded the Bug Music Company in 1975 with a $1000 loan from his friend, rock star Del Shannon. Along with his brother, Fred, who joined the firm in late 1977, Bourgoise had a vision. It was to collect royalties for artists, protect song writers and provide an honest and efficient service for collecting mechanical royalties. Within a decade, Bug Music was one of the largest, most prestigious and integrity-filled music publishing company operating out of Hollywood. Bug became so successful that it established offices in Nashville in 1985, London in 1992, New York in 1996, and Munich in 1999.

Over the years, Bug Music has been a small, family affair. It is essentially Dan and Fred who run the company. Fred was experienced in the music business when he joined his brother. He was a singles buyer and manager for Tower Records. What drove the Bourgoise brothers was the belief that a small company that not only cared about the artists, but served them honestly, could make a difference in the music business. The word of mouth in the music industry was immediate and artists rushed to Bug to avail themselves of their services.

By late 1977, when Fred Bourgoise joined his brother Dan at Bug Music, they occupied a building near Musso and Frank's Grill. This landmark Hollywood luncheon spot had been since the 1920s where the best deals were made in the entertainment business. Early in his career, Dan was too busy getting Bug Music running to enjoy this famous lunch spot. For the first few years it was a struggle. There is an incestuous attitude in the music industry and the record companies are wary of new and small companies. Bug Music persisted and became successful.

Dan Bourgoise, Del and Al Coury of Network Records

With a roster of recording stars that is amongst the largest in the music business, Bourgoise now oversees a multi-million-dollar royalty collection and licensing firm. **Cashbox** editorialized that Bug Music was "the best place to collect your royalties."

From the day that Dan met the Michigan rock and roll sensation, Del Shannon, they became fast friends. Over the years Bourgoise was not only Shannon's closest friend and confidant, he was a business partner. They shared the same interest in rock and roll music and were like-minded businessmen. While he was still in his thirties, Bourgoise secured the rights to Shannon's old songs. This brought in millions of dollars for Shannon.

Over the years, Dan evolved from a fan of Shannon's into an adviser, a business partner and eventually the administrator of his music catalog. He also produced some of Shannon's music in the late 1960s. After Del's tragic death, Bourgoise licensed his material in good taste and secured the estate a fair share of royalties. Dan has single-handedly put most of the bootleggers out of business. "Protecting Del's product has always been my goal," Bourgoise remarked. This was a long way from Bourgoise's humble beginnings in Detroit, Michigan.

THE DAN BOURGOISE STORY: THE ELEMENTS OF SUCCESS

The elements of success in Dan's life began long before Bug Music became a major force in the music business. "I realized early that people bought out of habit or because they liked a particular artist," Bourgoise remarked. What Dan came to believe was that niche marketing was important. Even the lesser-known artists had a place in the music business. So at Joyline Records, he also stocked the obscure and often the unknown.

In the early 1960s, he began a personal career direction that allowed him to drive a brand new Jaguar, live in the Hollywood Hills with a beautiful wife who is also a recording artist and become one of the prime movers in the music business. The success of Bug Music is such that the major music trade magazines call it the most aggressive, artist-oriented company on the music scene."

A typical comment came from **Billboard** magazine which labeled Bug Music as the company with the highest degree of integrity in an industry when the artist has trouble collecting his or her royalties.

TALES OF BUG ARTISTS

Among Bug Music's earliest clients were blues performers who had never received their fair share of royalties. Such blues luminaries as John Lee Hooker, Jimmy McCracklin, Willie Dixon, Johnny Otis and the estate of Muddy Waters gave Bug Music a vote of confidence.

In the early 1990s when Willie Dixon came to Oakland, California for a school harmonica clinic, I interviewed him with Scott Cameron and Jimmy McCracklin present in his Holiday Inn room. Dixon was enthusiastic about Bug Music. "I'm finally getting the money that is due me," Dixon remarked, "I had never been able to collect it." Soon word of mouth brought in hundreds of other songwriters.

Dixon had good reason to be happy. Led Zeppelin's monster million-selling hit, "Whole Lotta Love," was credited to Led Zeppelin's Jimmy Page and Robert Plant. The truth was that they had ripped it off. It was a Willie Dixon song. A company that Bug Music worked with, the Scott Cameron Organization, stepped in and collected Dixon's royalties. Dan worked closely with Scott and watched this settlement in which the court records were sealed. There was a settlement, but neither Bourgoise nor Cameron will discuss it. With the money, Dixon established the Blues Heaven Foundation, an organization to educate performers about publishing. It also grants funds to artists in need and provides scholarships to inner city youth with musical promise.

Other Bug artists have sold their songs for commercials due to Bug Music. Etta James sings "I Just Wanna Make Love To You" is in a Coca-Cola commercial. Iggy Pop is perhaps the strangest commercial phenomena. With his band Iggy and the Stooges and later as a solo act, he was a cult figure. Now Iggy Pop's music is all over national television. He has sold a large number of tunes to national advertisers due to Bug Music's expertise. "I always ask and get top dollar for commercial tunes," Dan remarked. "These artists deserve both financial and artistic respect."

The elements of success for Bourgoise evolved around his business acumen. He has served some of the lesser known but artistically recognized clients in the business, including John Hiatt, John Prine, T-Bone Burnett, Los Lobos, Nanci Griffith and Robert Earl Keen. In the country music field such acts as Johnny Cash and the Dixie Chicks, among others, have added to Bug Music's growing Nashville office.

Within the industry Bug Music receives the praise of key figures. When Bug opened a Nashville office, Tony Brown, an MCA executive, called Bourgoise's company "a nice little jewel on Music Row."

The specter of Del Shannon has always loomed over Bug Music. He was like a big brother who gave his blessing to the company. Shannon was also an important early influence upon Bourgoise. Musically speaking, Del established the initial base for Bug Music's operation.

DEL SHANNON AS AN EARLY INFLUENCE ON DAN BOURGOISE

"I had never been a real big country music fan," Dan Bourgoise recalled. "I was more into pop and Motown and rock and roll while growing up near Detroit." It was Del Shannon who turned Bourgoise on to country sounds. "I used to go over to Del's house and he would play Faron Young, Buck Owens and Hank Williams," Bourgoise continued, "and I went bonkers over that stuff."

When Buck Owens and the Buckaroos came through town at the Michigan State Fair in August 1964, Del, Steve Monahan and Dan went to see them.

Bourgoise remembered: "Del was playing on a stage where he did three shows a day. He was doing shows at 2 p.m., 4 p.m. and 7 p.m. The stages would rotate and so they had a lot of time to kill. On one of the other stages, Buck Owens and the Buckaroos were playing to large crowds. At a nearby stage, Little Stevie was mesmerizing audiences. So the three of us hung out for some time with Buck Owens and then we got together with Little Stevie Wonder. When Del showed up, Little Stevie Wonder talked to him-it was obvious that he knew Del's music. When we knew that Buck Owens was going to be on, we all got excited because Del had turned us on to his music. We had this picture of us holding up all his records and we gave it to Buck. We wanted to show him we were real fans."

But there was more to Shannon's influence. In the saner moments, Bourgoise watched as Del, a consummate businessman in the music industry, negotiated with booking agents, the recording people and the promotion departments. Since Dan was privy to Del's confidence, he learned about a good and a bad business deal. Shannon had both types in his career.

Perhaps the strongest impression that Del made upon Dan was the need to nurture and protect talent. Bourgoise has never said when he got the idea for Bug Music but he remembered, "When I was a kid, other kids used to take my last name Bourgoise, and they'd call me Bug Eyes." Dan continued. "The first BMI company that I had was Bug Eyes Music. And then I noted that a lot of the famous media companies were three letter ones-NBC, CBS, ABC, MCA, RCA, EMI and BMI. So I decided to shorten it." It was one thing to have a company, it was another to make money. From the time that he was 18, Bourgoise had a knack for marketing. He also had a feel for the music industry.

THE GREENING OF DAN BOURGOISE: THE EARLY YEARS

When Del Shannon got to know Dan Bourgoise, he remarked to a close friend that "the kid knows how to make money." From his earliest days, Dan was not only able to market and merchandise rock and roll music, but he often saw the trends emerging in the business.

When Dan installed a rack to sell 45 records and LPs at Joyline Records he was a couple of years ahead of the rack jobbers. The rack was an instant hit and its contents vanished quickly. He found that customers liked a spot where they could pull out the latest hits and purchase them. Then he realized that local bands needed a slot. Marketing was clearly an early interest. The selections, all of which Dan picked, were the hottest sellers in the local area. Soon distributors, disc jockeys and music industry people began talking about the rack at Joyline Records. It seemed as though he knew what people wanted. Dan was in the music business, if at the lowest level, and he became an instant expert who helped others select their music.

"I was successful in an odd sort of way," Bourgoise continued. "I had **Billboard** calling me for the position of records in the Detroit area. It was heady for a kid. I had my foot in the show-business door."

Thirty years later, blues legend Jimmy McCracklin, would lavish praise about Bourgoise. "I like the way Bug Music goes after those European royalties that are hard to collect," McCracklin noted, "and I get my money in a timely fashion." The estate of Oakland song writing legend Bob Geddins, feels the same way. One of the songs Geddins owned was used in a Chevrolet commercial and Bob Geddins, Jr., was presented with a

$35,000 check. It was Jimmy McCracklin who suggested to Geddins, prior to is death, that he consider having Bourgoise collect this royalties.

He not only collects the money for McCracklin's song writing and publishing, he was the first person to find all of the money and collect it. McCracklin hesitated to say that Bourgoise is the only honest publishing company representative. "Let me just say that Mr. Bourgoise found money from my song writing that no one else could, he is an artist's dream," McCracklin concluded.

He also had known a like-minded musical maniac. One who had grown up five doors from his house. His name was Steve Monahan and they had been friends since they met on their bicycles as kids. Now Steve was also into the music business. When he heard Monahan sing, Bourgoise searched around for a musical contract for his young friend. Soon, with Dan's help, Steve signed a deal with the Chicago-based Vee Jay Record company. Dan Bourgoise was only 17 when he negotiated the deal for Steve Monahan with Vee Jay. Dan was convinced that this was where he would get his first million. "We went to Chicago and recorded 'The Leaves of Fall' by Steve Monahan and this is what brought me into the business. Then, of course, the first of many disappointments resulted. It was pure innocence on my part. This was it, I have done it. I am the manager of a star. When that turned out not to be the case, I learned some valuable lessons about the industry," Dan remembered.

Bourgoise continued: "I really saw myself getting into the music business at a top level, it was a tonic for my soul. I knew that I had talent." At this stage in his life, Dan wondered which talent was his calling. As a producer, Bourgoise has a feel for a hit song. He was also a good public relations person. He had a flair for booking and management. He had a publishing firm. It took some time for Bourgoise to find his direction and his job at Joyline Records helped him to mature into a music publisher. When the British invasion took place in 1964, Dan spent a lot of time analyzing the changes in musical trends. He came to realize that he could benefit from understanding the mercurial tastes of record buyers.

He watched the **Meet The Beatles** album climb to the top of the American charts. Dan was now the key employee of Joyline Records, but it was owned by other people. It was both a record and hobby shop. It was Bourgoise who ran the record side of it. His mother, Eleanore, and 12-year-old brother Fred, were also working in the store and things were going well. But Dan found that there was room for more profits. He responded by purchasing the entire local wholesale stock of the Beatles' first album. For a time, Dan's store was the only place to purchase the Beatle record. Not only did the store make a huge profit, but Bourgoise became a local legend. Once again, **Billboard** was on the phone asking him to predict the next batch of hit records.

Joyline Records was a vehicle for Bourgoise that brought him into the local clubs. The number of local bands playing in bowling alleys, small clubs, the cocktail lounges and the teen dances was voluminous. If Bourgoise was to take in the music scene, he needed a fake ID. Once this was accomplished, Dan haunted the local clubs and continued to educate himself. He saw in the garage bands the future of American song writing.

DAN BOURGOISE

SUCCESS: ENTERING ANOTHER MUSICAL WORLD
AND DEL SHANNON'S LIFE

"I think the key to my success in those years," Bourgoise remarked, "was the fake ID that got me into all the bars. It was another way of learning about the music." Then Del met the man who would change his life.

When Bourgoise met Del Shannon it was something of an accident. "I met Del through a writer known then as Doug Brown, but who is now known as Fontaine Brown," Bourgoise remarked. It seems that Brown was in a bowling alley with a nightclub attached to it and Del's wife, Shirley, was bowling in a league there. It was after the bowling league introduction that Dan and Del's friendship flourished, but Fontaine Brown was also an influence.

Del Shannon , the 1970s

At Joyline Music, Dan and Fontaine would close the shop. They would get a six pack of beer and listen to all the new records. "I had all the new singles and we would play the recent Jimmy Reed, Howlin' Wolf and Muddy Waters singles. What I think I

134

learned from Fontaine was about the blues, Del taught me country music, but Fontaine knew his blues. He turned me on to all kinds of great blues. The bowling alley had a cocktail lounge where they all went in and had a drink. Without the fake ID Dan might not have been able to talk at length with Del.

Bourgoise was already something of a local mover. He had founded a small publishing company with Doug Brown. The song publishing unit was known as Two Souls Music. It was established in 1963 to handle the publishing from Brown's prolific pen. Not only was Brown a song writer par excellence, but he was a performer. There were also many Detroit area groups and individual singers who were clamoring for a publishing deal.

Shannon was impressed when he heard young Bourgoise talk at length about the business end of the music industry. This was a subject dear to Del's heart and he was interested in getting to know young Bourgoise.

When Shannon talked publishing with Bourgoise, it was to learn anything he could to benefit his own publishing firm. "Del already had his own publishing company, Shidel Music," Bourgoise remarked, "and this became a topic that we talked a lot about during the early stages of our friendship."

While he was living in Southfield, Michigan, Del regularly invited Dan over to his house. In Shannon's basement he called his work room-the Mole Hole-he was in the midst of writing songs with an African American song writer, Maron McKenzie. After they had talked for a while, Del suggested that they enter into a joint business venture to push their songs and those of other artists. Bourgoise and Shannon agreed that they could make some money if Del took their songs on the road and exposed them to the general public.

During this time a 17-year-old kid, Bob Seger, showed up with his tunes. They were all young and eager to enter the music business. Del became the leader to them. The first time that Bob Seger went into a recording studio, Del paid for the time. It was another good friend, Fontaine Brown, who began crafting Seger's career. So not only was Del a recording artist, but he was a guru to fledgling local musicians. Del liked to have fun and this was as important as the music.

So another reason for hanging out with Bourgoise was his fun-loving attitude. He had a full head of dark hair, wore stylish clothes and loved to have fun. Definitely Del Shannon's kind of friend.

DEL AND DAN: THE EARLY FRIENDSHIP AND THE MUSICAL MOVE TO LOS ANGELES

It was surprising to Bourgoise that after his interest in Del Shannon as a fan, he quickly became a good friend. "I couldn't believe how fortunate I was to know Del," Bourgoise remembered. He had no idea that he would also become involved in Shannon's song writing and publishing or that he would act as his manager and convince Del to increase his booking fees. In 1964, Dan was happy simply to hang out with Shannon.

The Shannon residence in Southfield, Michigan quickly became Bourgoise's second home. He sat in awe at the feet of a recording genius who had had a number-one hit with his first record. "It was a heady experience," Bourgoise recalled. Shannon had just moved to Southfield, Michigan. This predominantly Jewish suburb was not only up scale, but one where Shannon could work without interruption. At first Dan was in awe of Del, and their friendship was one that reflected hero worship. Then, as their friendship blossomed, Dan was forced to join the U.S. Navy Reserves and spend six months in the service.

Eventually, Bourgoise decided to move to Los Angeles with the Shannon family. It was a fortuitous journey which began by taking Dan to the pinnacle of the music publishing business. "It was 1966," Bourgoise recalled, "Del was getting ready to sign with Liberty."

THE PARTNERSHIP WITH BERNIE YESZIN

While living in Los Angeles, Bourgoise represented the Monkees official photographer, Bernie Yeszin. Bernie had been the art director in Detroit for Motown. He had shot all of the major Motown album covers, and he was a recognized industry figure. Then, about 1966, Bernie went to Los Angeles. He ended up at Liberty Records and it was there that Dan met him. When Dan found out that Bernie was from Detroit, they became fast friends.

Bourgoise remembered: "One night Del and I went over to see Tommy Boyce and Bobby Hart and they had been working on the Monkees project for TV. We were both skeptical about the proposed show. We had seen some of the sessions, the idea of a TV show that is kind of Beatle-like is destined to flop we thought. Both Boyce and Hart had been working hard on the stuff and the songs were strong. One night they said come over with us, we are going to Don Kirschner's house. This home had been Douglas Fairbanks mansion and it had a projection room. We went to see a screening of the debut episode of the Monkees show. After it ended we knew that it would be a hit. The music was first rate, the characters were carefully acted and the writing was excellent. Overall we knew the Monkees show was a winner." With this screening, Bourgoise's education in the music business intensified. He realized how to approach major recording corporations about selling album art.

Dan continued: "I went into business with Bernie and I approached Colgems, a new label, and I got him the contract for the album art. Then Dan began selling the art to the LP covers. With his 15 per cent fee, Dan was in business. "We got $450 for the album cover shots and $250 for other covers. We sold photos for $300 or $400 from the Monkee shows. I was selling all these photos quickly. There is a picture of Del and I and Mickey Dolenz and when I went with Del to Europe, I sold that picture to all of the British music trade magazines. As the Monkee thing expanded, I went to record companies with Bernie's stuff." As a result, Dan went to UNI when it started and represented Bernie who designed the first UNI label as well as the Stax and Volt logos. Along the way, Bernie shot covers for Otis Redding and Carla Thomas and then the

Count 5 and Brenton Wood. As a result of his partnership with Bourgoise, Yeszin went to work for Del Shannon.

The Further Adventures of Charles Westover cover was shot by Bernie. Bernie was also something of a player in the music business. He was the person who brought Fontaine Brown to the Motown songwriting system. It was Dan who introduced Brown to Yeszin. Bernie introduced Brown to Mickey Stevenson, the Motown producer, who wrote "Stubborn Kind of Fella." Soon Bourgoise was hanging out with other Motown music types who were forsaking the cold Detroit winters for the sunny Southern California climate. Clarence Paul was another Motown writer and producer who came to LA. Then a renegade group of ex-Motown producers led by Tom Nixon, the head engineer at Motown, founded Venture Records. This company was bankrolled by MGM with the hope of making it Motown West. They dumped a great deal of money into the company but had no hits.

THE ROYALTIES AND DEL SHANNON

As Bourgoise watched the Monkees musical adventure, he realized that there were probably missing royalties. Then as Dan investigated, he was amazed by the level of uncollected royalties. The revelations was an easy one to decide. When he began his career in the music business, Dan worked as a song plugger for folk singer Buffy Saint Marie. Consequently, he honed his eye not only for new talent but continued to use his song plugging talents.

This experience led to a new job. By the early 1970s, Bourgoise was working in the A & R department at United Artists Records. He quickly signed the progressive bluegrass band, Country Gazette, and then he inked Ray Benson's country aggregation Asleep At The Wheel to a long-term agreement. These signing's earned Bourgoise a reputation as a knowledgeable talent scout.

Bourgoise funded this project and Tommy Allsup produced the album that was designed to help Bob Wills' wife, Betty. She was to receive $5000 to care for her sick husband. The December 3-4, 1973 recording sessions, which produced the Wills' album, was made without the full support of the label. United Artists' commented that they had more Bob Wills' records than they could sell. When they found out that Capitol country music superstar, Merle Haggard, would sing the vocals, they changed their mind. What Bourgoise demonstrated in the Wills' album was that he would not be controlled by the corporate big wigs. As a result, United Artists prepared a budget which was minimal at best.

Bourgoise still completed the project. He produced the album for only $11,000 and this included the $5000 to Wills' wife, Betty. The tale of the Wills' LP helped Bourgoise to earn the respect of most everyone in the industry. After he finished this task for United Artists, one of his bosses called Dan in and delivered some bad news. He was fired. The reason was that UA believed that Bourgoise had scammed the company by producing an album that had little, if anything, to do with Wills. Bourgoise couldn't believe this level of corporate stupidity. He left the office with a resolve to open his own firm.

Dan was angered by the corporate structure at United Artists and this went a long way into influencing his decision to go into the publishing business. "After that," Bourgoise remembered, "I decided no more working for record companies. I'll just start my own and do what I want, and will not have to be second-guessed." But the problem was finding the money to create the business. So Dan turned to what he knew best for a short time; he became Del Shannon's full-time manager. He immediately secured a recording contract with Island Records. It was at this point that Del mentioned that he had not received any royalties in a decade. The hit movie, "American Graffiti" featured "Runaway" and Bourgoise realized that it was a source of instant royalties.

As Del and Dan talked about the music business, it was obvious that there were missing royalties. The question was how to collect them. The answer, as Dan envisioned it, was his own company.

THE GENESIS OF BUG MUSIC AND
THE LOST DEL SHANNON TAPES

The genesis of Bug Music was a strange one. It began almost accidentally when Bourgoise told Shannon that he would try to get his copyrights back. It was 1975 when Bourgoise went after the copyrights. Much of the material was improperly filed, lost or simply deemed insignificant by the record labels.

The actual opening of Bug Music took place in March 1975 with Shannon as their only client. But what a song writing talent. Del had not been paid adequate royalties during his career and his European, Far Eastern and Australian royalties were virtually impossible to calculate. Collecting them was also a problem. This began a two- year journey which was ultimately successful and profitable.

The problem was to find someone in the music business who could help Bourgoise negotiate the royalty battlefield. Dan was good friends with Detroit producer, Harry Balk. It was Balk who had produced "Runaway" and Shannon's other early hits. He was not only a legendary producer but well thought of in the music industry. Balk was the only white producer hired at Motown and his work with Johnny and the Hurricanes that took an average bar band and made them into a hit act. Balk's partner at Embee Productions, Irving Micahnik, had died recently so he wasn't able to offer his opinions. Balk was only too happy to help Dan and in the process this would help Harry to repair his relationship with Shannon.

The problem was to find the masters to Shannon's old tunes. Micahnik had misplaced some of the tapes. Bourgoise found this incredulous. So it was up to him to talk to Harry and negotiate with Micahnik's estate and find out about the Shannon songs. It didn't take long for Bourgoise to reacquire the song rights.

In the process Bourgoise located many of the lost tapes. He also came to realize that Balk's role in Shannon's career was a seminal one. Over time Dan developed a great deal of respect for Balk. He believes that, as a producer, Balk's contributions have never been fully recognized. So they not only became fast friends, but Dan learned that he and Harry had many of the same interests. Harry, like Del, was owed back royalties. So they worked together in an informal business arrangement. This helped

Del to get his royalties back as Balk was the producer and helped Bourgoise locate many of the missing tapes. In the process Bug Music became a major player in the music industry.

When Balk's partner at Embee Productions, Irving Micahnik, died in 1978, Del and Dan acquired the copyrights to the Embee Productions and Twirl Records catalog. Except for the Johnny and the Hurricanes material, Bourgoise secured the rights to a publishing goldmine. Micahnik, as was his practice, had the last laugh. There were no master tapes. So when it came time for Bourgoise to license Shannon's material, he had to go to record collectors. Many of the early re releases were reproduced from clean records. After Bourgoise and Balk secured mint records, they were remastered for commercial release. "The stereo albums that we put out with Rhino," Bourgoise reflected, "and had it not been for a collector in Florida, we could not have released the material."

The original copyrights were in the hands of an equity firm, Omega, and this company had no idea what the copyrights were or why they were continually earning money. When Bourgoise offered to purchase the copyrights for $10,000, Omega executives jumped at the deal. Omega viewed the copyrights as little more than a nuisance.

It took three years to collect some of the bigger royalties. While Del was in rehabilitation in 1978, Bourgoise called him with the news that he had collected $160,000. These royalties were coming to Bug Music from England, Bourgoise explained, and the money was only from Big Top royalties. Both Dan and Del realized that they had collected only a small sum of the money owed.

A shrewd businessman, Bourgoise not only purchased the rights to the Twirl Record catalog but he began looking into licensing this material for reissue. With this purchase, Bug Music secured the rights to Bobbi Smith and the Dreamgirls, the Royaltones, Johnny and the Hurricanes and Del Shannon.

From the earliest days there were problems finding the master song tapes. "We didn't know what Irving had done with the masters," Bourgoise recalled. Then Bill Inglot let Bourgoise know that some of the tapes were from the Bell Sound days. They were mixed in with a lot of Roulette Record materials. Surprisingly, these tapes were stored in an auto dealership in Queens, New York. The auto dealer, who was getting ready to retire to Florida, he had the master tapes for two Del Shannon albums, **Del Shannon Sings Hank Williams** and **Little Town Flirt**. Inglot explained that many of the attic tapes had been thrown away. So it may have contained other Shannon masters. The lost jazz album was rumored to have been in this pile.

This forced Bourgoise to find clean discs and use them to master Del's reissues. The reason for the lost discs surfaced. At first it was a rumor that Micahnik owed money to Bell Studios. Then it was confirmed that Micahnik had put up the tapes as security for a debt. When Micahnik died, Dan went to his business and told his partner that Del had received the copyright on his songs. If Micahnik's organization didn't stop licensing the tapes, Bourgoise would have to file a cease and desist order. The conversation was friendly and Dan asked what they were using for master tapes. Astonished, Bourgoise looked at a quarter-inch tape that Irving had made and the songs were coming off this poorly recorded copy.

Micahnik had taken a $20-dollar tape recorder and cut a series of inexpensive tapes. It was from this material that Del Shannon's re releases were being issued. What was incredible was that Micahnik licensed Shannon's work using nothing more than crude tapes from a recorder that he had purchased on sale at Sears. No one in the industry complained or questioned Micahnik's tapes.

One of the fundamental truth of Irving Micahnik's career is that he spent little money on his artists. He reasoned: why spend money on production, the consumer would purchase the record no matter how it sounded. There were some industry people who couldn't believe Micahnik's audacity.

One of these skeptics was Craig Leon who produced Del Shannon's LP, **The Vintage Years**. He recalled that when he dealt with Micahnik and asked for the master tapes, he received a shock. Irving came by one afternoon with a grocery shopping bag full of 45s. They were mint records and Micahnik explained that the tapes were lost. Leon realized that Micahnik didn't have copies of the Shannon's masters. "They were probably at Bell Sound," Leon told Bourgoise. Micahnik's attitude was why pay all that money to get the tapes when the records produce the same sound. This accounts for the inferior quality of many of Shannon's reissues. The lack of controls over Shannon's material frustrated Shannon. During his life time he squirmed when he heard his old records.

As a result, he made a disastrous decision. He decided to re record some of his early hits. These records were quick and inferior ones. They besmirched the sound and the quality of Del's early hits. This led to the low point in releasing Shannon's material when K Tel and Gusto offered Del a thousand dollars a song to re-record his old songs. The companies would also pay all studio costs. Shannon believed that this was an instant moneymaker. Every time that he thought about his early hits, Del became angry. He wasn't receiving royalties and he would do anything to stop Micahnik from releasing his 1960s hits.

Shannon's original band mate, Max Crook, was brought in with his musitron for the K Tel sessions. Del hoped to recreate his original hit sound but things didn't work out for them in the studio. Harry Balk wasn't present as a producer and this hurt the sessions. After cutting four songs and going home with $10,000, Shannon felt better. When he listened to his re-recorded songs he knew that he had made a mistake. Once again the industry had defeated him.

WHAT DAN BOURGOISE LEARNED FROM THE EARLY YEARS IN THE MUSIC BUSINESS

Bourgoise learned a great deal from his experiences with Shannon and Balk. He realized that the money was in the songwriting, mechanical royalty and licensing the material for future use.

It was the type of experiences that Dan had with Del that helped him to attract the cream of the song-writing talent. When artists talked to Bourgoise, they realized that he not only understood the industry but was an honest man who could collect their money. As a result, Bug Music soon signed a following of disgruntled writers who wanted to be paid their fair share of royalties. What attracted such clients as T-Bone Burnett, Jimmy McCracklin, Lowell Fulson, John Lee Hooker, John Prine and Townes Van Zandt among others is that Bug Music was a publishing administrator. Put in simple terms, they would collect your song writing royalties, handle your licensing and search out those who didn't pay royalties. Soon Bug Music had trouble keeping up with the demand for their services.

This was only part of Bourgoise's training. He was still first and foremost a music guy. The record collector in Dan's soul never wavered and he spent an inordinate amount of time talking music with Shannon.

DAN AND DEL TALK MUSIC

During their friendship, Dan and Del continually talked about music. These conversations provide a window into Shannon's musical psyche and a good look at how Bourgoise educated himself for success in the music business. Another important result of these conversations is that Shannon explained his live concert strategy.

In concert Del usually performed four or five of his hits. There were songs that he seldom sang. "Hey! Little Girl" was rarely performed in live shows. It seems that Shannon was uncomfortable performing this tune. He also didn't like to sing some of his more obscure tunes. Consequently, Bourgoise attempted to get Shannon to perform many of the tunes which were not hits. It was Dan who realized that the serious fans loved the b-sides. Del would simply reply: "Nah, Nah." There were parts of his career that Shannon ignored or simply forgot.

Eventually, Shannon came to realize that b sides and collectable records were an integral part of the music business. In time, Dan educated Shannon on the intricacies of the collector. Bourgoise was also an influence upon Shannon's performing. He convinced him to expand his repertoire.

When they talked, Dan was insistent that Del vary his shows. Shannon had a tendency to come out and ask how everyone was doing and then go into a patterned set featuring "Runaway," "Hats Off To Larry," "Little Town Flirt" and "Keep Searchin' (I'll Follow The Sun)." "I told Del that there were a lot of people who had favorites which weren't hits," Bourgoise remarked. "Move It On Over" was a tune that Bourgoise pushed Shannon to do in live shows. It is a great song and a potential crowd pleaser. Finally, Del listened and during the **Drop Down And Get Me** album tour, "Move It On Over" became a crowd favorite. Both Mike Campbell and Dennis Coffey, who co wrote the song, urged Shannon to use it in concert. "Dennis Coffey's guitar licks are really superb on the song," Bourgoise remarked.

By the last decade of his career, Shannon was a consummate performer who had expanded his repertoire. This was thanks to Dan Bourgoise. Throughout Shannon's lengthy career he depended upon Bourgoise' opinion. The result was that Del had a built-in critic who not only helped him mold his stage shows but retain a current sound.

BUG MUSIC: PHASE TWO THE NASHVILLE OFFICE

The Nashville music market is one of the most difficult to crack. The local establishment is an ingrained aristocracy that defines the country sound. Many publishers had attempted to break into Nashville's music row with limited success. So Dan sent his brother to crack this difficult market.

Fred Bourgoise would fly to Nashville, check into the Hall of Fame Motor Inn on Music Row, and he would begin the process of trying to sell Asleep at the Wheel's music. Local publishers were interested and Fred's mellow, non-salesman approach, made Bug Music an immediate Nashville presence. Soon they had enough business to open a local office. Even though the Bourgoise's wanted to open a Nashville office, they needed the right person to run it.

They found Garry Velletri, who on the surface looked like the last person to run a country music office. Velletri was a post punk Yankee from New York who headed up Faulty Products, a New York Indie company which distributed the Dead Kennedys, the Circle Jerks, the Police, and the Bangles. When the Bangles had a top 10 hit, Faulty Products went bankrupt because they could not meet the demand for their product. Suddenly, Velletri was without a job. After going to work for EMI, Velletri came to Nashville to work with Jason and the Scorchers. He was burnt out on the New York music scene and moved permanently to Nashville. He was in the right place at the right time.

He approached Bug Music about a job. They hired him to open the Nashville office. In the spring of 1985, when Bug Music opened a small arm of the California corporation in Nashville, Tennessee, few people took the West Coast publishing firm seriously. Bourgoise remembered that it was more like "a tiny attic" than an office. The office that Velletri had was a dream for him and he was given the title, senior vice president. He remarked: "it was just me and a telephone and a desk." Bug Music quickly became a big hitter in Nashville. This roster of prime talent attracted interest in the country music capitol. They sent some of their business to Nashville. Soon Velletri had Waylon Jennings, Rosanne Cash, John Stewart, John Prine and John Hiatt among others, and business boomed.

Soon Bug Music also signed some fresh writing talent including Nanci Griffith, Fred Koller, and Robert Earl Keen to publishing deals. With its reputation for honesty and integrity Bug Music prompted MCA executive Tony Brown to suggest that Bug was "a nice jewel here on Music Row." Then Brown escorted Wynonna Judd down to Nashville's Bug Music where she selected two Jesse Winchester records from their vast catalog. "I went there specially thinking that we would find something," Brown remembered. Not only did Wynonna love Bug Music, the environment, the people and the feeling for country music, but she began talking about it. As a result, Bug Music was in a position to sign a wealth of new talent.

In Nashville, Bug Music attracted the same attention as in Hollywood. They continued to collect royalties for artists who had given up. They also peddled songs, helped both new and old artists with recording contracts and hired song pluggers to sell their product. There was an excitement and vitality within Bug Music. This is what prompted Bug Music to evolve into one of the major royalty collecting agencies. It had been a long and hard journey from Michigan but Dan had made it.

DAN BOURGOISE AS PRODUCER AND COLLECTOR OF UNRELEASED GEMS

During his years in the music business, Bourgoise has achieved a great deal. One of his unrecognized talents is as a producer. Along with Fontaine Brown, he produced Brian Hyland's "Delila." The critically acclaimed solo LP by Steve Monahan was another Bourgoise production gem. He also wrote two songs with Shannon, "Silently" and "The Music Plays On."

The Steve Monahan LP, **City Of Windows** (Kapp 835) was released in the summer of 1967 and charted at number 78 for four weeks on the **Cashbox** album chart. It is not surprising that Monahan's record sounded a bit like **The Further Adventures of Charles Westover**. A single from the LP, "City of Windows," charted for four weeks but other cuts from the LP failed to garner airplay. It was a fine LP that was lost in the midst of changing musical tastes.

For a time Monahan, Hyland and Bourgoise shared a house in the Hollywood Hills. It looked as though Dan would become a record producer. He had the talent and the feel for record production but Bourgoise was first and foremost a businessman; one who could collect song-writing royalties.

Even though he was an excellent producer, Shannon often had trouble collecting royalties. This is where Dan Bourgoise came in and he also began assembling and cataloguing Shannon's unreleased tunes. The 1960s provided some real gems. Just after he cut "Runaway," Shannon laid down tracks at Detroit's United Sound, these tunes included "Wrong Day, Wrong Way," "Queen of the Honky Tonks" and "Table Reserved For The Blues." These were three excellent songs that no one was willing to release. In February 1962 along with the Johnny Howard Band, Del performed "So Long Baby" on the London based One O'Clock Jump show. The intent was to release it as a live single. This marvelous version was doomed unacceptable for commercial release. Dan believed in these songs and to this day champions them.

In May 1963 when Shannon cut a cover of the Beatles' "From Me To You" in England, he also recorded a tune known as "Little Sandy" or "Sandy" as well as "Walk Like An Angel." These weren't released at the time because the convention wisdom was that they didn't fit into the current rock and roll market.

This end of the business frustrated Shannon and he often turned to Bourgoise for advice on his songs and his career. So Dan became the specialist in finding the missing and the unreleased Shannon material.

Dan Bourgoise is like a pit bull when it comes to protecting Del Shannon's recordings. When Charly Records in England released **Del Shannon: The Definitive Collection**, Bourgoise took legal action to protect Del's estate. As the licensing agent for Shannon, Bug Music makes sure that everything is carefully and fairly controlled. Apart from the reissues, Bourgoise's biggest cache of material is the unreleased Del Shannon cuts.

DAN BOURGOISE

What is intriguing about Charly is that they often license material knowing that it is a bootleg. Many of the record companies overlook these releases because it costs more money to keep them off the market than the royalties they produce. This didn't matter to Bug Music. They would keep bootlegs off the market no matter the cost. In the European Economic Community there is a clause that allows legal bootlegs. But Bug Music challenges these releases and prevents them from flooding the market.

Bourgoise also became something of an archivist. He collected unreleased songs, rarities and even bootlegged materials. Bug Music is literally a Del Shannon archive. In a series of lengthy interviews with Brian Young, the editor of the Del Shannon fanzine, **And The Music Plays On: Del Shannon Magazine**, the wealth of material became apparent. As Dan and Brian talked they discussed the depth of unreleased Shannon songs. There is enough unreleased Shannon for at least two CDs and maybe more. The songs are uniformly strong and suggest Del's musical diversity.

"You know, it's interesting how there's no way that the things on the obscure or odd labels are preserved for reissue," Bourgoise continued. "All the people are out of business and the masters got lost." In this lengthy interview Bourgoise talked about what was missing from the Shannon collection. Surprisingly, the first Big Top album, **Runaway**, is not available in stereo. As Bourgoise explained, "The Search' and 'I'll Always Love You' have a basic two-track sound with Del on one side and the music on the other." These cuts are not available anywhere, they were lost. Once again Irving Micahnik can be blamed for this fiasco. Bourgoise continued, "the remaining ten tracks on the album were done with three-track equipment. Five of these, 'Misery,' 'Day Dreams,' 'His Latest Flame,' 'The Prom' and 'He Doesn't Care' have the musitron on one channel and the other instruments on the second track with Del's voice on the third track." This incredible mix is also missing.

"The **Runaway** LP in stereo is one of record collecting's true gems," Bourgoise continued, "with documented sales in the $250 and upward range. The **Little Town Flirt** album is probably just as rare in stereo, but if you look for one marked 'stereo,' you may never find one." Bourgoise went on to explain that the jackets of both the stereo and mono versions were the same. To save money Big Top people neglected to tell which was stereo and which was mono.

Bourgoise continued, "When Del went to Amy his first two albums **Handy Man** and **Del Shannon Sings Hank Williams**, were mono releases, although the material was probably recorded in stereo." Then when Shannon signed with Liberty and he began cutting material for them, there were some unique releases. The most interesting item was an album produced by Rolling Stones' mentor, Andrew Loog Oldham, **Home and Away**. Unfortunately, this LP wasn't released. Although a portion of this LP was issued in the singles market, the majority of the material was never heard by the general public. Eventually, in 1978 **Home and Away** was issued in England.

"After Del left Liberty he became a rock and roll wanderer," Bourgoise observed. "A couple of singles for Dunhill, a live LP for UA in 1973, two singles for Island in 1975, and finally a single and LP for the Network label in 1981." When asked about the re channeled stereo that was released on Del, Bourgoise made it known that Shannon disapproved. Yet, as Dan pointed out, there were some important songs that had trouble finding the marketplace.

DAN BOURGOISE

In the late 1960s, when the album **The Further Adventures of Charles Westover** languished in the cut out bins, someone asked Dan if there were any unreleased tracks from it. "Only 'The Letter,'" he replied, "as far as I know." What this comment suggests is that Shannon was a studio rat. But few people knew what he recorded in his own facility, known as the Mole Hole or at Liberty's recording facility.

Some of the gems discussed were a 1970s album that Del cut at Dublin Sound in Ireland. This LP, which was never released contained "Till I Found You," "Raylene," "Black Is Black," "Oh, Pretty Woman" "One Track Mind," "Amanda," "Another Lonely Night," "Love Don't Come Easy," "Best Days of My Life," "Love Letters" and "Today I Started Loving You Again." At the time this LP was cut, Del was touring Europe and he took his road band into the studio. It was Bourgoise's job to take these songs around to the record companies. Although it was good material, Don remarked that the usual response was, "Oh, another Del Shannon album. What does that mean? He's a 60s guy. This is the 70s." Bourgoise knew that he was fighting a losing battle, but he diligently approached every record company. "They just weren't interested," Dan concluded.

In 1978 when the **And The Music Plays On** LP came out, there were unreleased cuts of "In My Arms Again" and "Distant Ghost." At about the same time there were multiple versions of "In My Arms Again," "Distant Ghost" and "And The Music Plays On." Bourgoise remembered, "There were so many versions of these songs because Del was going into the studio all the time."

One day, Pat Pipolo of Island Records asked Del what he had in the can. When Del told him all of the tunes, Island signed him to a contract. On February 7, 1979, Del cut versions of "Amanda" and "Take Me Back" which were not released. This track was cut with the assistance of Steve Smith who produced former Traffic sideman Jim Capaldi. The tragedy of Del's brief sojourn with Island is that the master tapes he cut are missing. So whatever he did musically is lost. No one seems to know what happened to them. The prevailing feeling was after all he's a "60s guy so why keep the tapes." In a letter to the Australian based Raven label, Island confessed that they were having trouble finding all the tapes that Del recorded.

"I'm definitely going to get as much of the unreleased material out as possible and in the best sound quality," Bourgoise reflected. "That's why it's taking such a long time. Everything needs to be transferred to DAT." Bourgoise let it be known that only the skilled production techniques of Dee Robb or Bill Inglot would handle this delicate task. "They're the only ones that I trust with the master tapes," Bourgoise continued, "and Dee Robb was there for most of it, so he knew what Del wanted as far as sound, and so Dee will mix it the way that Del would have wanted it."

In a reflective mood, Bourgoise talked about the highlights of the time that Del spent working with Brian Hyland. For a time Brian lived with Del and Shirley and it was therapeutic for both of them. "Lady Liz and the Three Piece Jug Band" is one of 15 or 20 songs that Del and Brian wrote together that has never been released. "I've got an acetate of Del actually singing 'On The East Side' which Brian originally recorded," Dan continued. "They were both signed as staff songwriters for the Trousdale Publishing Company." The song-writing partnership between Shannon and Hyland was a winner. They worked diligently and turned out a large number of songs.

When they finished working on their material it was snapped up. Waylon Jennings cut "I've Got Eyes For You," Beth Moore recorded "Go Go Girl" on Capitol, and Barbara Lewis' "How Can I Tell" was produced by Ollie McLaughlin. In the industry, the Shannon-Hyland song-writing duo attracted a great deal of positive attention.

"Brian Hyland moved in with Del for a couple of years and literally what they would do was get up every morning and start writing songs," Bourgoise continued. "They were like a song factory. It was a good exercise for Del because by that time, he hadn't really written anything for a few years. And it was good for Brian, because he never wrote very much prior to hooking up with Del. All of Hyland's hits were written by other artists. And I'm sure that bothered Brian. He wanted desperately to emerge as a songwriter."

Shirley Westover remarked: "Brian Hyland was like a family member, our son, Craig, used to call him the brother he never had and Chuck called him a little brother. Every night we sat down to dinner and it was a wonderful time. Those who wrote that Chuck and Brian squabbled were journalists or jealous family members."

However, before time and circumstances ruined their working relationship they had success. What happened to the Shannon-Hyland musical partnership? It was Brian's wife, Rosemary, who believed that her husband was too close to Del. Rosemary liked Bobby Hart and she wanted him to produce Hyland's music. Before Brian and Rosemary got married, Brian had always told Del that he would be the best man. When the marriage took place at a justice of the peace's office in Santa Monica, Bobby Hart was the best man. The marriage ended their friendship because Rosemary was jealous of Shannon's family life. She was also a 1960s musical groupie who wanted to recraft Hyland's career along the lines of Native American music. "Rosemary wanted Hyland to become a 60s rocker called 'Wild Buffalo," one of Del's friends remarked. "She didn't have a clue about the music industry."

Despite the personal differences, Del continued to love Brian. After his marriage, Hyland went his own commercial way. The Shannon-Hyland song writing and production partnership was one of pure magic. Part of their song writing magic was due to communication. Del and Brian talked at length about their song writing direction. They also had production ideas which were significant ones. The remake of Curtis Mayfield's "Gypsy Woman" stands as the highpoint of their collaboration. They wanted to be remembered like Leiber and Stoller, Boyce and Hart and Pomus and Shuman. As staff writers for Trousdale Music they were part of the ABC/Dunhill Publishing Corporation. It was one of the most productive in the 1970s.

While the Shannon and Hyland team mainly composed their own songs, Del still arranged and recorded cover versions of highly commercial songs. A demo of Wayne Fontana and the Mindbenders "Game of Love" was completed but not released at the time. It remains one of Shannon's best unreleased tunes. One of Shannon's Mole Hole characteristics was to cut demos of cover tunes and to file them for future use. As a result, there is a wealth of material available for release.

The question of lost master tapes remained a vexing problem. When Del founded Berlee Records he was casual about his master tapes. Consequently, many were misplaced or lost. Irving Micahnik has lost a number of the Del tapes or couldn't get them from the studio because he owed them money. When Dan began his project to get

Del back the song writing and publishing rights to his songs he faced a monumental task. The stereo masters to Del's Berlee recordings were also missing. When the various labels finished with a tape often they didn't file it in a coherent manner. So Bourgoise began the Bug Archives which houses everything available by Del Shannon.

There are some mystery songs remaining. "Little Oscar" which Del cut at the Hi Lo Club is in Max Crook's possession and deserves a commercial release. "It's A Lie" is a song which sounds as though it was from the **Drop Down And Get Me** album and it has not been released.

To make sure that Shannon's music is available and rare tunes do not escape notice, Bourgoise hired Bill Inglot to search out this material. Although Bill Inglot lives in Los Angeles, he travels to England and Europe and is authorized by Bourgoise to take any masters in any record company vault. Not only is Inglot a master at his job but he has a knack for uncovering previously ignored material. So, over the years, Bourgoise has not only built up an impressive archive of Shannon material but he has licensed it with good taste and an eye to production quality. As a result, the Del Shannon posthumous releases are some of the best in the 1990s.

WHAT THE INDUSTRY HAS TO SAY ABOUT BUG MUSIC

By 1992, Bug Music had been in business for seven years. The Los Angeles office now has 15 employees, there are five in Nashville and two in the London office. "Some independent companies are built to be sold," Fred Bourgoise continued, "and that's a whole different concept than we we're about." What Fred suggested is the core of Bug Music. They are a family-owned business with a great track record in the industry. "We've watched all these independent companies get gobbled up, chimed in his brother Dan. The lesson is that Bug Music does not fit into the typical corporate music slot. They have a wide range of acts, often promote new song writers and dance to their own business beat. The industry has responded by recognizing Bug Music as the premier independent music publishing firm.

"We're probably the Cleveland Indians of publishing," Dan joked, "but for our business that makes sense." What Bug Music has refused to do is to get into bidding wars. They do deals that make sense. They specialize in the singer-song writer who has a vast catalogue. Due to their commitment to the music, there are often deals made with fledgling artists. There are few rules at Bug. Ultimate success seems to be the only tried and true business practice.

When writers for the various music magazine tour the Bug Music offices in Hollywood they find a down-home type of employee and a casual atmosphere. They also notice that Bug takes the extra step for its clients. "We tend to be old-line publishers," Fred remarked. "We still think of the old Brill building style." This is a reference to the New York song-writing factory that turned out many of the early rock and roll hits. What this reference suggests is that Bug maintains a creative atmosphere and pays royalties fairly and timely. In the music business, this has not often been the case.

Bug Music's ultimate compliment is that its writers come from other artists. They also sign writers who have not recorded. Leo Kottke brought John Hiatt in to play some demos for Dan and Fred. After hearing Hiatt's songs they signed him to a publishing deal. He hadn't recorded a song, but Bug Music fixed that by negotiating Hiatt's first record contract.

The September 21, 1996 issue of **Billboard** featured a story which suggested that while Bug Music had its share of roots rockers like Dave Alvin and Dale Watson, it was now going in a more commercial direction. The Astro Puppees CD **You Win the Brides** was hailed as a blend or roots and pop music. This was also the direction that Bug Music took as it expanded its formidable list of artists.

THE PAIN OF DEL SHANNON'S DEATH

When Del Shannon died Dan Bourgoise was devastated. He had not seen Del very much in the last year. Their friendship, however, remained a strong one. When Dan's mother was involved in a serious automobile accident in the late 1980s, Del dropped all of his concert dates and rushed to Detroit to comfort Dan and his mother. After Dan's mother recovered from this hit and run accident the friendship remained strong although they saw less of each other.

For years Bourgoise booked Del and was responsible for the rising booking fee which had enabled Shannon to earn a nice living. But then something happened, Del decided to book himself.

Ironically, Dan was with Fontaine Brown at a record release party the night that Del died. They were celebrating a new Dave Edmunds record. Fontaine had written "Closer To The Flame" and "Sincerely" for the new Edmunds LP and it was a night of good times. Then Dan received a phone call from LeAnne with the devastating news. A chain of events unfolded which depressed Bourgoise. He had trouble finding out the circumstances behind Del's untimely death. He also thought back at how Shannon had taken over his own bookings and perhaps he had spent too much time on his career.

It was Bourgoise who called Shirley at 11:30 p.m. "I couldn't handle the thought of Del's death and I asked Dan if he would call the kids. He agreed." Shirley was devastated and wondered what had gone wrong. She didn't sleep that night and stayed in bed the next day. "I was physically ill and spent hours thinking about my former husband. What had gone wrong?" Shirley was never able to answer that question. But she told me that she had a good idea what went wrong.

Whatever the reason for Del's suicide, Dan and other close friends had trouble understanding it. At this point in his career, Del was making more money than ever and his life appeared to be a pleasant one. Dan and other friends had not seen Shannon for some time. He was spending time trying to get his third new house in as many years in order while balancing an increasingly productive and trying concert schedule. No one could figure out why Del was booking himself. It was putting him into a position of extreme exhaustion.

It was during this phase of his career that Del began booking his own shows. While this was a job that Dan had handled for years, Bourgoise's duties at Bug Music were so cumbersome that it was probably a relief for him to be relieved of this task. So Dan parted with these duties on friendly terms with Del, but he was worried about his old friend. Shannon was in a precarious emotional state and after a thirty-eight year friendship, Bourgoise knew something was wrong.

Two weeks before Del died, there were signs of trouble. Kym, Shirley's oldest daughter, called her mother and told her that she thought her father was dying. "I made a U-turn and walked up to my dad's car, it was stopped, he looked terrible, he looked like he was dying." Kym urged her mother to call Del. "I didn't call him right away and I called the Monday before he died and left a message. He never called me back. Tuesday I called him back again. This time his machine came on, when he heard my voice he finally picked up the phone. I told him that I was worried about him. He told me that he just had a sinus infection. She asked him if he was seeing a doctor and he said he was okay. I said let's have lunch and he said ok in a couple of weeks when I feel better."

The pain of Del's death engulfed Bourgoise. There were many memories that Bourgoise recalled over the years. Some were tragic. Dan remembered that Del found a young kid who committed suicide on a beach in Wales. In this picturesque part of England, Del viewed the body of a young boy laying on the rocks. Dan and Del came down and saw that the boy had jumped off a nearby cliff. This was in 1969 and they were both horrified. Then in the mid-1970s Del came across a body in the desert. It was another suicide. Now Del had taken his life. It was a tragic reminder of people's tragic nature.

In the six years after Shannon's death, Bug Music prospered. Suddenly Dan Bourgoise was a wealthy and influential part of the music business. However, he remained as sincere and honest as he had been while working at Joyline Records. A happy marriage, a home in the Hollywood Hills and a Jaguar did little, if anything, to change Bourgoise. Still a kid at heart he continued to search out new music.

FROM THE ASTRO PUPPEES TO THE MILLENNIUM

In September 1996, Bug Music announced that one of his acts, the Astro Puppees had singed with Oakland's roots-based High Tone label. The Astro Puppees album, **You Win The Bride**, turned into an indie favorite. The groups lead singer, Kelly Ryan, teamed with Maureen Serrao to write all of the tunes except for a cover of Stealers Wheel's "Stuck In The Middle With You." With this signing, Bug Music entered a new musical direction. The Astro Puppees were a contemporary radio group. Larry Sloven, the president of High Tone, suggested that the group was helping his label branch out into new directions.

Both Kelly and Maureen were former Bug Music employees. Their engineer, Don Dixon, was also a Bug Music employee. "I was the original Kelly Girl at Bug," Ryan remarked, "I wrote the newsletter, made the tapes, sent out pictures, but I was more and more in the closet as a songwriter since there where so many great writers at Bug...." After years of playing solo in local Los Angeles clubs, Ryan began selling her songs to established acts. The Shoes released "It's Not Christmas" in 1991, but the hopes of stardom faded. Ryan then went to cooking school in Ireland where she took her guitar and continued to write songs. Then she returned to Los Angeles with one hundred tapes of new songs. As a result, the lead song on her CD, **You Win The Bride**, became a college radio play list favorite. The song, "Underdog," became a regular on KFJC at Foothill College in northern California. The Austin, Texas music scene was the next place where Ryan's music was played extensively and she did a well-received show there. What Bourgoise recognized was a song-writing direction which would create a future for the Astro Puppees. It was an indication that Bug Music was going in some new directions. They hadn't abandoned the roots rockers, but the company was delving into new types of music.

One of the signs that Bug Music was going to be around for a long time emerged in the mid-1990s when their frenetic song pluggers began selling tunes in a broader market. Wynonna Judd looked to Bug Music for her new tunes. Then, Rosanne Cash and Waylon Jennings recorded hits written by Los Lobos and John Hiatt. This cross pollination between country and Los Angeles music would have been impossible without Bug song pluggers. One of the hottest country acts today, the Dixie Chicks, are part of the Bug Music empire. There is no categorizing acts with so many of the top indie artists, like Jay Farrar of Son Volt, who are also with the Bug organization.

With his glasses, soft smile and easy going manner, Dan Bourgoise is the antithesis of the cigar chewing, shiny suit, suede-shoe-wearing recording mogul. But in matters of business, Bourgoise is a tiger. When a Coca-Cola company representative asked for a Willie Dixon song for a commercial, Bourgoise demanded top dollar. The agent balked and said: "Well, after all, it's not Neil Diamond." When Dan pushed her and asked if she had heard the song. She responded, "No." He had her listen to it and made the deal.

By 1995 when Bug Music celebrated its 20th anniversary with a party of Hollywood's famed Brown Derby, the Bourgoise brothers were doing $15 million worth of business a year. Two years later, Bug Music was instrumental in helping to win a landmark English court decision in which legendary producer, Phil Spector, had his copyright to his first hit, "To Know Him Is To Love Him," returned to his song-writing domain.

The aggressive stance that Bug Music has taken for song writers reached its nadir in 1997 when Senator Strom Thurmond, a South Carolina Republican and Jesse Helms, a North Carolina Republican, introduced a bill in Congress they labeled "The Fairness in Musical Licensing Act." Bug Music was in the forefront of a campaign which exposed this bill as one that would exempt most commercial establishments from paying royalties on music used for less than 60 seconds. This would not only drastically reduce the income of writers, but also take away their controls. This bill would allow TV, radio, satellite and cable companies to use songs at their discretion with no thought to proper royalty payments. The Bourgoise brothers spearheaded a drive to educate legislators and the general public.

During the 1997 Super Bowl Oakland song writer, Bob Geddins, and his partner K. C. Douglas, both deceased, had their tune "Mercury Blues" featured at the half time show. This song was part of a campaign for Ford Trucks and the estates for both writers received a hefty check. The $35,000 check that Bourgoise handed to Bob Geddins Jr. was a pleasant task.

Del Shannon: Back On Top

In October 1997, Willie Dixon's wife, Marie, and his daughter, Shirley, celebrated the grand opening of the Blue Heaven Foundation at 2120 S. Michigan Ave. This was an irony as Dixon and the Leonard Chess made a fortune in the building. Unfortunately, Dixon didn't receive his share of the fortune until he hired Bug Music.

New Day Dawning, the 1999 Wynonna Judd CD, had three Bug Music songs and this was considered a task that a small publishing house couldn't accomplish. So it dawned on everyone in the industry that Bug Music was now a major player.

In May 2000, Bug Music announced that one of their writers, Erik Hickenlooper and Jim Funk, had written the number one country hit, "Buy Me A Rose" for Kenny Rogers. The frequent publicity releases from Bug suggest that the company maintained its position in a number of markets.

By 2000, the 56-year-old Bourgoise was recognized as a major figure in the Los Angeles music business. His brother Fred, now 49, continued to work hand in hand with Dan in a business that had grown so rapidly that it now collected song writing royalties for Beavis and Butthead.

The staff at Bug Music has grown from one person administrating 20 copyrights to 40 people, in liaison with two lawyers, who handle more than seventy-thousand copyrights. When one walks into Bug Music, Johnny Cash, Iggy Pop or Buddy Guy might be drinking a cup of coffee. Bug is looking to the future. With Internet and digital music as an anticipated source of revenue, Dan and Fred are looking into new frontiers. One day when you call up new music on something like rock n roll.com, Dan and Fred will be there to collect the royalties due the guitar player.

The ultimate compliment comes from former Blaster, Dave Alvin: "I haven't had to work a day job in 20 years, and I owe a lot of that to Bug." Need anyone say more?

BIBLIOGRAPHICAL SOURCES

This chapter is based on eight separate interviews with Dan Bourgoise. Also interviewed were Fontaine Brown, Shirley Westover, Stephen Monahan, Brian Young, Harry Balk, Max Crook, Lowell Fulson, Willie Dixon, Jimmy McCracklin, Dee Robb, Craig Westover, Jody Westover and Kym Westover.

Willie Dixon was interviewed at length about his problems collecting royalties and he provided a number of significant insights into Dan Bourgoise and Bug Music's success. Lowell Fulson and Johnny Otis also provided in depth interviews on the publishing end of the industry. Etta James was interviewed about her commercials via phone calls to her Riverside, California home.

Brian Young, "Dan Bourgoise Interview Notes," twenty pages in possession of the author. Internal publicity items from Bug Music helped in shaping this chapter. An interview by Dennis DeWitt was also instrumental in recreating the Bug Music experience. See, for example, Dennis DeWitt, "Notes on Interviews with Dan Bourgoise," in possession of the author.

"Del Shannon's New Mystery: The Case of the Missing Tapes," **And The Music Plays On: Del Shannon Magazine**, Issue 11, Spring, 1997, pp. 31-39.

For the expansion of Bug Music into there markets, see, for example, Jim Bessman, "Astro Puppees Launched on High Tone With Debut Set, 'You Win The Bride," **Billboard**, September 21, 1996. Also see, "Publisher Profile: Dan and Fred Bourgoise," **Music Connection**, October 26-November 8, 1992 for a brief profile of the key figures in Bug Music.

Two excellent stories on Bug Music's alternative approach are Sabrina Kaleta, "Triumph of the Underdogs," **Los Angeles New Times**, March 9-15, 2000 and Natalie Nichols, "Brothers Build Loyal Clientele With Scrappy Publishing Firm," **Los Angeles Times**, March 26, 2000. See a Bug Music publication, Daniel Cooper, "Off The Beaten Path," for a story of Bug Music (Hollywood, 2000). Also see Dave Konjoyan, "The Discrete Charm of the Bourgoises," **Hits**, October 16, 1985 and David Hirshland, "Spector Case Provides Crucial Precedent," **Billboard**, May 17, 1997.

On the music industry see, for example, Frederic Dannen, **Hit Men** (New York, 1990) and Joe Smith, **Off The Record: An Oral History of Popular Music** (New York, 1989).

On Bug's 25th anniversary see, Fetzer Mills, "Bug Music Celebrates 25th," **Goldmine**, May 5, 2000, p. 10.

For the influence of Motown see, Suzanne E. Smith, **Dancing In The Street: Motown and the Cultural Politics of Detroit** (Cambridge, 1999) and Nelson George, **The Death of Rhythm and Blues** (New York, 1988). For information on the blues and independent labels, see Charlie Gillett, **The Sound of the City: The Rise of Rock and Roll** (New York, 1983) and Lars Bjorn, "From Hastings Street to the Bluebird: The Blues and Jazz Traditions in Detroit," **Michigan Quarterly Review**, number 25, issue 2 (Spring, 1986), pp. 257-267.

For Arthur Alexander's partnership with Bug Music see, Richard Younger, **Gotta Shot of Rhythm and Blues: The Arthur Alexander Story** (Tuscaloosa, 2000), pp. 72, 174, 181. Also see the classic and well written study of one-hit wonders, Wayne Jancik's, **Billboard Book of One Hit Wonders** (New York, 1990).

7: DEL SHANNON'S MISSING SECOND ALBUM AND THE ENGLISH MARKET

"Why my second album was never released in the U.S. remains a mystery to me," Del Shannon in a BBC radio interview

The success of "Runaway" made Del Shannon a prime time rock and roll star. But he was more than an American musical act. In 1961-1962, 13 singles were released by the Big Top, London and Helidor labels in the U.S., U. K., Germany and Australia. Shannon was truly an international star.

The earliest indication of this success was the formation of fan clubs or appreciation societies. In England, there was a concern that the Beatles and the rise of what would become known as the English invasion would eclipse American roots rock. So in the U.K., Del Shannon fans were intent upon maintaining his popularity. The same feeling was true internationally.

Del Shannon: The 1960s

In Australia, a Shannon fan club was formed to compliment the Del Shannon Appreciation Society which evolved in the United Kingdom. The demand for Shannon's records were so strong that his management firm was having trouble coping due to his success.

Embee Productions pushed Del overseas because his contract called for only a one per cent royalty. In this way profits could be maximized. This strategy also posed some problems.

One of the problems that Embee Productions faced was how to handle the demand for Shannon's music outside of the United States. Irving Micahnik decided to face this problem head-on by shifting much of the marketing to England.

As Harry Balk's partner in Embee Productions, Micahnik's job was promotion. Harry Balk told Micahnik that the key to the English strategy was to sell records while maintaining a busy concert schedule. Unfortunately,

While Shannon was conquering the English marketplace, an album tentatively entitled, **Hats Off To Del Shannon**, was prepared for release. It was intended to be the second Shannon album, but it was lost amid the machinations of making Del an English star. It also serves as one of the earliest frustrations that Shannon experienced in the music business.

IRVING MICAHNIK AND THE U.K. STRATEGY

At home in Detroit—as Micahnik found—Shannon's record label, Big Top, was having trouble getting paid from its larger distributors. In just a few years Big Top would go bankrupt. At this point, everyone was predicting success. Embee Productions was blinded by Shannon's record sales. The problem was getting their money from Big Top. Balk and Micahnik were frustrated by the lack of money coming into their company. In turn this created friction with Shannon. He couldn't understand why his royalties were not being paid promptly.

While this was a common problem in the recording business, it didn't help Micahnik who found himself increasingly short of cash. The music business was filled with unscrupulous characters and none were worse than the one-stop record distributors. As a result, the money that Embee Productions put out in support of Shannon's career often didn't translate into royalty payments.

Although Micahnik did collect the money for song writing, even these payments were late or slightly short when Shannon received them. Over the years, Del became increasingly belligerent toward Micahnik and producer Harry Balk. It was a nasty situation that soon burst into open confrontation and prompted Del to leave Embee Productions.

In 1961-1962, Shannon was at the forefront of the rock and roll marketplace and everything was fine. For the moment, everything appeared rosy. Trouble was lurking in the shadows and when the hits stopped, so did the working agreement between Del and Harry and Irving

THE DEL SHANNON SHOW

GRANADA MAY 1963   program one shilling

Del Shannon: An English Program Cover, May 1963

There were a number of business decisions which Micahnik made which were hard to understand. Even though "Runaway" had the appearance of a blockbuster hit, Micahnik would not commit company funds to advertise and he advised Big Top to press only a small quantity of the first album. After dozens of phone calls between Micahnik and New York's Big Top executives, a strange decision was made on the number of albums pressed.

Del Shannon's first release, **Runaway (Big Top 1303)** had a one thousand album pressing in stereo and this had made it a much sought-after collectable. After the LP was pressed, Irving Micahnik misplaced the tapes. There were also some disparities with the recordings, two of the cuts on the LP were completed on a two-track system and the remaining 10 on three-track equipment. The reason for this was a simple one. The technology changed dramatically from 1960 to 1961.

The reason for the two-track recordings was that Bell Sound was merely a two- track recording studio in 1960, but it was still considered a state-of-the-art recording facility. The next year when he recorded the remainder of his first albums tunes, Bell Sound was a state-of-the-art three track recording system.

157

DEL SHANNON'S MISSING SECOND ALBUM

As a result of the problems with the industry, Irving Micahnik made the decision not to immediately release a second Del Shannon album in the American market. He reasoned that England, or perhaps Australia, was the place to release a second Shannon album. This decision hurt Del's career and created what one critic called "the lost second album controversy."

One of Micahnik's problems was that he didn't always consult his business partner, producer Harry Balk. So when Irv made the decision to wait until 1963 and then release a second Del Shannon album in England, there was trouble at Embee Productions. Not only was Del unhappy, but Balk realized that he had irreconcilable differences with his partner.

The legacy of bickering and recrimination was held in check by Del's phenomenal commercial success in the American market. Although Shannon was a popular English touring act, his U. K. sales were often mixed. This was surprising considering Shannon's phenomenal record sales.

Finally, Del went to Irving and complained about his business practices. Shannon was unhappy about the U. K. promotional plan. When Shannon's "Runaway" album was released in the United Kingdom it failed to reach the top 20. The London label, which had licensed "Runaway," did little, if anything to advertise the album and it was issued long after the "Runaway" single dropped off the British charts. Ray Coleman, one of England's best-known journalists, remarked, "Del Shannon was caught between an inept promotion, and a disinterested record label, London, and this was hardly the road to commercial success."

It seems no one was in charge of promoting and publicizing Shannon's music. Despite these problems, Shannon did have success in the English market. It was the up and down commercial cycle that frustrated him.

KEEPING SHANNON'S HITS AFLOAT

In 1961-1962, as Del Shannon was crafted into a musical act who was able to sell his tunes in the United States, England and Australia, he found a sound that influenced a large number of future rock and roll stars. He was a quasi-international star but in America there was no mention in the press of his worldwide popularity. By the mid-1960s, Del seemed like any other rock star with a couple hits. There was much more to him than that and much of his declining fame can be traced to the decision to remove him from the American marketplace.

Del In England, 1967

When producer Harry Balk and Embee production magnate Irving Micahnik went to work they did so with zeal; they had a product to sell and they were masters at it. They represented a lot of acts and recorded a large number of artists. So they didn't always pay close attention to the ingredients necessary in maintaining Shannon's hit record sales. There was one missing ingredient in the Del Shannon mix. It was impossible to guarantee that he would continue to write hit records. The hit-record business was a precarious one and an artist was only as popular as his last hit.

"I worried about the songs," Micahnik remarked to more than one person as Del's music sold all over the world. They knew it wouldn't last forever, but both Micahnik and producer Balk believed that Shannon had a song-writing direction which would last. They weren't wrong as the magic continued for more than two years.

The success of Shannon's **Runaway** album made it difficult for Micahnik to meet the demand for the product. Micahnik's personal life was coming apart and he was not ready for this degree of success. The success of the first album had turned the process into a nightmare. Micahnik decided to merchandise Shannon's music through the English and Australian marketplace. "I think we need to escape the sharks in America," Micahnik told one distributor. "We got a hit record and we can't get paid."

One of the problems with the English marketplace was that it was in transition. What this suggests is that there was the rising tide of new U. K. music groups. Despite all the problems with Embee Productions, Del Shannon was still an English star. It was a long and tortured road, but it bore the fruits of stardom.

THE ROAD TO ENGLISH STARDOM AND ITS FRUITS

In 1962 as Micahnik-with the help of Balk-concentrated on the English marketplace, there were signs of success. What is ironic is that the touring income far exceeded record royalties. London Records paid a fair royalty, but somewhere in the process, Del didn't receive the share he had expected.This angered him and bred resentment. On the surface, however, the signs of success were everywhere.

In 1962, the prestigious British record magazine, the **New Musical Express**, named Shannon as the fifth most popular world male artist. This honor guaranteed heavy English record sales and continuous concerts. Embee Productions lost no time in taking advantage of the marketplace.

A barrage of English 45s were released and three of Shannon's songs charted, "So Long Baby," peaking at number 10, "Hey! Little Girl," rising to number 4 and "Cry Myself to Sleep" coming in at number 28 in two brief weeks on the charts.

The English press reacted positively in 1962 to Shannon's work. One London-based music publication called "Cry Myself To Sleep" a new and welcome direction for Shannon's music. It seemed that everything he did, the English bought and embraced. This fact was not lost on Micahnik who reasoned that he could sell an English LP with greater profit than an American release.

Del Catching A Nap, 1963

By late 1962, Del had charted six English 45 releases with "Runaway" reaching number 1 in 1961 and "Swiss Maid" ending the streak by peaking at number 2 during its fourteen weeks on the **New Musical Express** chart. "I think it was absolutely incredible that Del Shannon had so much chart success in the U.K.," Ray

Coleman continued. "We were promoting our own and ignoring the Americans, so you can see that Shannon's music hit a special chord with the English."

London Records placed a great deal of emphasis on Shannon's music. They released an advertisement appearing in most British newspapers and music magazines proclaiming "This is Del Shannon." The ad not only promoted the **Runaway** album but publicized the EP not surprisingly entitled **Runaway** (London 1312) containing the title song as well as "Hats Off To Larry," "Lies" and "His Latest Flame." This ad also contained a plug for Del's newest London single "Cry Myself to Sleep" backed with "I'm Gonna Move" (HLX 9587). It was only a matter of time until the hits started coming in England.

THE HITS COME IN ENGLAND FOR SHANNON: 1963

As the hits continued in the English marketplace in 1963, there was talk about how Shannon's music had influenced the Mersey sound. This was a reference to the hundreds of bands in and around Liverpool.

Since the Beatles had emerged in the English rock music marketplace in 1962, when "Love Me Do" hit the charts, virtually every British band out of or near Liverpool had signed a recording contract. There was no doubt that most had listened to "Runaway" and most of Del's other music with more than just a passing interest. Del Shannon had helped to create the Merseyside sound with his early records.

The sale of Shannon's English LP was brisk and his singles had an equally strong run. Since a band was being formed on every street corner in England, there was a strong demand for the American product. This is not surprising, considering how heavily Shannon toured in the U. K.

During the early 1960s, as Shannon toured England, he often appeared with the rising British bands. The Beatles were one band that favored Del's music, although they didn't cover any of his hits. John Lennon once remarked that Del had the musical background that allowed the Merseyside bands to develop their sound.

On February 22, 1963, the **New Musical Express** reported that promoter Tito Burns announced a Del Shannon-Johnny Tillotson English tour. That show would take place in mid-April, the press release stated, and it would be followed with a full-fledged English tour. The dates were impressive ones and included a BBC show at the Royal Albert Concert Hall. Not only was this London's premier concert venue, but the April 18, 1963 concert featured the Beatles as well as the Springfields with Dusty Springfield and the popular Vernon Girls. The BBC show at the Royal Albert Concert Hall was a venue designed to expose every pop and rock group in England. The Beatles manager, Brian Epstein, used his managerial clout to book such popular English acts as John Leyton and the Bachelors, pop crooner Matt Monro, teen idol Shane Fenton and the Fentones, and jazzman Chris Barber.

The April 18, Royal Albert Concert Hall Show was an unqualified success. Del received the type of applause and adulation accorded most American acts. It also provided immediate bookings. Irving Micahnik had brought Del back to England to tour in the small towns outside of London. The early 1963 tour was intended to expand Del in the U.K. marketplace. It turned into an unqualified success and guaranteed Shannon continual work in the United Kingdom. From this point on his career was a continuous one in the small clubs and suburban concert sites in the major cities as well as the English countryside.

DEL SHANNON'S ENGLISH TOUR, APRIL-MAY, 1963

April 18, Royal Albert Hall with the Beatles, the Springfields, the Vernon Girls, Shane Fenton, Matt Monro, Julie Grant, and Chris Barber among others

April 20, Winter Gardens, Bournemouth
April 21, De Montfort, Leicester
April 22, Theater Royal, Norwich
April 23, Town Hall, Birmingham
April 24 , Rialto, York
April 25, Odeon, Manchester
April 26, Odeon, Newcastle
April 27, Gaumont, Bradford
April 28, Empire, Liverpool
April 29 Essoldo, Stoke-On-Trent
April 30, Hammersmith, Odeon,
London
May 2, Civic Auditorium, Wolvershampton
May 3, "Go Man Go" BBC radio show
May 5, Granadas at Kingston, Tooting, Walthamstow
May 7, Bedord
May 12, Colston, Bristol

Other dates without specific nights included:

Wooldwich

Essoldo, Brighton

Guildhall, Portsmouth

Sophia Gardens, Cardiff

WHAT WAS THE PRICE OF DEL SHANNON'S ENGLISH SUCCESS?

As Del Shannon and Irving Micahnik prepared to attack the English marketplace, Del turned to Irving and asked: "What's the price for my English success?" Irving chewed on a cigar and looked cagily at Del: "The price of success is instant record sales. We don't need the U.S. market, it's done, you can make it here."

Del shuttered and wondered what was going on. He had just had a number one **Billboard** hit and now Big Top was concentrating upon the English record market which was brimming with new, local talent like the Beatles, the Rolling Stones, the Yardbirds and numerous others. Irving told him to mind his own business. They were going to concentrate upon the U. K. and Australia. Shannon thought it was a mistake. On the other hand, record sales indicated that, for the moment, Micahnik was right. Shannon was a big English pop star. "Your first three English albums are the biggest in this country for an American artist," Irv gloated.

When the first Shannon LP was released in England with the title **Runaway With Del Shannon** (London HA-X 2402), it was followed in 1963 by two more LPs **Hats Off To Larry** (London HA-X 8071) and **Little Town Flirt** (London HA-X 8091).

On March 8, 1963 the **New Musical Express** devoted a brief column to Shannon's Royal Albert Hall concert and announced that "Del Shannon will be the first American rock artist to star in a BBC Albert Hall Concert." Not a bad tribute to Micahnik's booking skills. The primary reason for Shannon's appearance on these shows was his ability to write songs that attracted the rising English musicians. No group was more enthralled with Shannon than the Beatles, in particular the Beatles co-chief songwriter, John Lennon, had a penchant for the pop ditties that Shannon made a staple of his music.

What was significant about Shannon's early LPs, according to Charlie Lennon, is that John remarked to his friends and to a number of magazines that he listened to Shannon's music while writing songs. The chief song writing Beatle never said what Shannon songs influenced him. The reason for this was a simple one. Lennon and the other Beatles paid as much attention to Shannon's music as his lyrics. The Merseyside shuffle was little more than a recreation of the music that Shannon had made at the Hi Lo Club in Battle Creek and then had carried into the studio while recording his early albums.

WHAT GIVES DEL SHANNON HIS STAYING POWER?

Some critics were surprised at Shannon's staying power in the British marketplace. When "Swiss Maid" made its appearance for four weeks on the **New Musical Express** chart and peaked at number 3, the staff at **Disc** and **Melody Maker** held special meetings to report on Shannon's career. "The English rock music press didn't like to miss anything," Ray Coleman recalled, "and they were more than intrigued by Shannon's successes."

While "Little Town Flirt" was on the **NME** chart for nine weeks peaking at number 4, "Two Silhouettes" was briefly on the charts for three weeks reaching number 20 and these two records ended Shannon's string of 1963 British hits. For the rest of his life, Del could depend upon the English for strong record sales and a rabid concert following. What was obvious was that Del was special in the United Kingdom. It was his combination of uptempo songs with a falsetto, his ballads and the pop tunes which made him a British icon.

In the American market, Shannon had five releases in 1963, and his records continued to sell well. The figures for Del's record sales were never released. Embee Productions had too many irons in the fire to keep accurate sales records. There were also money problems at Embee Productions.

For Harry Balk and Irving Micahnik, however, times were difficult. Del was increasingly upset with his contracts. As a consummate businessman, Shannon believed that he had signed agreements which were loaded in favor of his label. It was difficult for Irv and Harry to deal with him and things did not go smoothly.

Success in England confused everyone. His American booking agents couldn't understand the reason for some of his U. K. hits. "Swiss Maid" didn't receive airplay in the United States but in the U.K. it was not only a huge hit but continued as a cult song long after it left the charts. Other Shannon tunes that failed to receive notice in America, notably "The Answer To Everything" became a staple on Radio Caroline, the pirate radio station operating off the English coast. Also, "Cry Myself to Sleep" was a British hit. Other tunes, notably "Don't Gild The Lily, Lily" and "I Won't Be There" received heavy U.K. airplay and continued to be played into the 1990s.

The English love affair with Del Shannon's music was a permanent one. It began with his hits records in the early 1960s. Then he toured England constantly. This helped him to create international stardom while maintaining a market for his records in the U. K. The key to Shannon's popularity in England was due to the small venues that he played. The fans identified with him and he spent an inordinate amount of time signing autographs and hanging out with the fans.

HATS OFF TO DEL SHANNON: THE LOST ALBUM

In America, Del Shannon's second album was never released. In England in 1963, the LP **Hats Off To Del Shannon** was put out on the London label with notes by Tony Barrow. Del was described as one who "smokes cigars, writes songs, plays football, drinks milk, collects model trains, enjoys jazz, plays piano, impersonates Johnny Ray." Shannon was embarrassed by the notes. Barrow went on to write that Del almost became a professional football player. The misinformation continued with a description of Shannon's two years in the service. The reality is that he had two hitches in the army. Then Barrow suggested that Del almost went into real estate, then police work and eventually became a singer.

The **Hats Off To Del Shannon** album, despite the pompous and highly inaccurate liner notes, was a gem. It included two rare Shannon American b-sides "I Won't Be There," complete with its violin crescendo and "I Don't Care Anymore," with a Bobby Vee influenced vocal, which had not been released in the U. K. The tracks on this album included the English hit "The Swiss Maid," a Roger Miller song which reached number 2 in England but was considered inappropriate for American rock audiences. With its beer barrel polka sound, Big Top executives turned a deaf ear to "The Swiss Maid." In addition to "Hats Off To Larry" and "Hey! Little Girl," number 2 on the English charts, there were other U. K. favorites notably "Ginny In The Mirror," "Don't Gild The Lily Lily," "I Cry Myself To Sleep," a Top 30 chart favorite earlier in 1962, and "So Long Baby."

In England, two singles "So Long Baby" backed with Burt Bacharach's "The Answer To Everything" and the Doc Pumas, Mort Shuman tune "Hey! Little Girl" backed with "You Never Talked About Me," were steady sellers in the U. K. market. The 1962 British movie "It's Trad Dad" featured Shannon's "Hey! Little Girl" with a group known as the Dukes of Dixieland backing Del.

DEL SHANNON'S MISSING SECOND ALBUM

After a successful English tour in the fall of 1962, the **Hats Off To Del Shannon** LP sold very well upon its April 1963 release. It rose to number 9 on the U. K. charts and Del toured England with Johnny Tillotson in support of the album. In concert the plaintive "Cry Myself To Sleep" was a British favorite. The up-tempo "Ginny In The Mirror" was another in concert favorite.

For some unexplainable reason, this album wasn't considered for the U. S. marketplace. This is strange considering the level of Shannon's hit making potential. But in England, Del was an even bigger act. "The Answer To Everything" hit the British charts but it couldn't garner even local airplay around Detroit. Other songs like "Cry Myself to Sleep," "I Won't Be There" and "Don't Gild The Lily Lily" sold well and were popular radio songs. In the American market these songs didn't make a ripple.

Big Top Records was the culprit in this situation. They had only pressed a thousand of the **Runaway** album, and they wanted to release a hit U. S. LP. When "Runaway" began rising up the charts, Big Top brought Shannon in to hastily record an LP. Del wasn't ready with a series of original songs. So while the **Runaway** LP remains a fan favorite, it has an uneven quality to it. Part of the problem was the industry. Shannon's enormous talent was sacrificed to immediate sales. In England, most of his songs were somewhere on the charts, but in the American market. Big Top paid no attention to the so called non-hit songs. As a result they had a disinterested opinion on much of Del's early music.

They didn't view **Hats Off To Del Shannon** as a hit vehicle. The Big Top brass felt that it needed more potential hits. They talked to Embee Productions and made their feelings known. Their main argument was that "Hats Off to Larry" hadn't been included on the **Runaway** album and, as a result, they could abandon the **Runaway** LP and issue a strong second album. They didn't believe that LP was the English released **Hats Off To Del Shannon**.

When Irving Micahnik made the decision not to release the **Hats Off To Del Shannon** LP, he reasoned that it would hurt the sales of the **Runaway** album and any subsequent LP. The other factor was the emergence of "Little Town Flirt" as a major hit. The moguls at Big Top wanted to release an album using the title song of Del's new hit. After a bit of discussion, Big Top records decided to issue a "Little Town Flirt" album and include "Hats Off To Larry" and "Hey! Little Girl" on the new LP. It would be a mini greatest hits album, the Big Top executives argued, and so there was no need for **Hats Off To Del Shannon** in the American marketplace.

At this point in his career, Micahnik was having fun and his mind wasn't on the music business. He loved to travel to England for the casinos and while this didn't have a drastic impact upon Del's touring income, it would have helped had Irving promoted the records with more diligence. While Shannon was popular with many hits, he could have been an even bigger star.

Had Micahnik taken the time to listen to the **Hats Off To Del Shannon** album he would have realized that his business partner, producer Harry Balk, had taken some of Shannon's most commercial material and put it on record.

Del Shannon was frustrated when the LP was not released in the U.S. because he had spent an inordinate amount of time writing songs. These would be used on later albums. The cover records were what made **Hats Off To Del Shannon** so interesting, with songs written by Doc Pomus, Mort Shuman, Burt Bacharach and Roger Miller. The **Hats Off To Del Shannon** album is a pure rock and roll LP. It contains the most commercial material of Del's early years. Consequently, many view this LP as a greatest hits package. It wasn't because Del was simply on his way up the charts.

The frustration that Shannon endured with the **Hats Off To Del Shannon** LP, combined with disputes over royalties, prompted him to form his own record company Berlee. So the controversy over the missing or lost second LP was a catalyst to Shannon's next level of creativity.

DEL SHANNON IN THE AMERICAN MARKETPLACE: 1963

In 1963, Del Shannon reached a critical juncture in his American recording and performing career. He had three singles released on the Big Top label and began to consider forming his own record company. In the American market place, Del believed that Embee Productions weren't doing their job.

Balk and Micahnik's Embee Productions had a good reputation for turning out hit records and this prompted the business-minded Shannon to delay his departure. Balk and Micahnik also owned Artists, Inc. of Detroit, Michigan which managed Shannon as well as Johnny and the Hurricanes.

The bad blood which had been building since 1961 took a turn for the worse when Shannon complained that the royalties paid to the song writing company, Vicki Music, wound up mostly in Balk and Micahnik's pockets. The multi-talented song writing skills which Shannon exhibited also produced a strong sense of his own destiny. Eventually, this led to a demand for control of his product. A demand that Balk and Micahnik were not about to meet. So the tensions continued to poison an otherwise strong artistic-business relationship.

In 1963, the hits were not as strong. Although he had three chart records, "Two Kinds of Teardrops," a number 50 hit and a cover of the Beatles, "From Me To You" which reached number 77, Shannon was unhappy with his management. So he formed the Berlee label and released "Sue's Gotta Be Mine" which peaked at number 71 in late 1963. The question was how would Shannon survive the British Invasion. The Beatles were coming to America and everything in the music business would change.

Had the **Hats Off To Del Shannon** LP been released in the U. S. it may have helped Del's career. However, Irving Micahnik-in collaboration with Big Top records- prevented the album from seeing the light of day. The result was that Shannon went his own way and organized his own record label.

BIBLIOGRAPHICAL SOURCES

Extensive interviews with Harry Balk, Maron McKenzie, Dan Bourgoise, Shirley Westover, Max Crook, Chuck Marsh, Fontaine Brown and the Robbs helped to shape this chapter.

In England, Joe Flannery, Ray Coleman, Bob Wooler, Alistair Taylor, Sam Leach, Brian Kelly, Tony Bramwell and Clive Epstein graciously talked at length about Del's English career. In Germany, Tony Sheridan, Tom Shaka and Horst Fascher helped to flush out caveats of Shannon's influence and success. Dave Williams provided background to English rock and roll which helped place Shannon's career in perspective.

DEL SHANNON'S MISSING SECOND ALBUM

Recent CD releases contain excellent liner notes see, for example, **Del Shannon-Runaway With Del Shannon/ Hats Off To Del Shannon** (BMG BGOCD467) with liner notes by Lazell and **Del Shannon: The Definitive Collection** (Charly CPCD8315-2) with excellent liner notes by noted British writer Adam Komorowski. The Charly release was unauthorized and because the estate wasn't consulted Bug Music took legal action. It was withdrawn from the market and is now a priceless collectors item.

For an excellent historical bootleg see **Del Shannon: Let The Good Times Roll (**Big Top BCD 017890).

The liner notes form the English LP **Hats Off To Del Shannon** written by Tony Barrow were a valuable source.

A brief interview with Dick Clark during a book signing at San Francisco's Macy's in the 1980s helped to place this period in perspective. Also see the inclusive article by Dan Bourgoise and Brian Young, "The Missing Second Album: Hats Off To Del Shannon," **And The Music Plays On: Del Shannon Magazine**, Issue 11 (Spring, 1997), p. 23.

For English rock and roll in the early 1960s see, for example, Howard A. DeWitt, **The Beatles: Untold Tales** (Fremont, 1985); Philip Norman, **Shout: The Beatles In Their Generation** (New York, 1982). For the role of personal managers in the United Kingdom see, Johnny Rogan, **Starmakers and Svengalis** (London, 1988).

Interviews with Mervyn, Dorothy and Phil Solomon helped to establish the course of the English music industry at this time. The Solomon Organization was the best booking agency in the U. K. and the three participants shared a vast number of tales about the business.

For Del's lost album see the Canadian based firm Unidisc Music Inc. rerelease of "Hats Off To Del Shannon" with Brian Young's excellent liner notes.

Del Shannon: Rock Star In The Making

8: DEL SHANNON AND THE BEATLES: INFLUENCING THE MERSEY SOUND, 1962-1965

"We would sit around and use some of Del Shannon's chords and his sound to achieve our own musical direction. 'Runaway,' and 'Little Town Flirt' helped us to create the Mersey sound." John Lennon in a conversation with Charlie Lennon, 1969

When "Runaway" hit the British charts in 1961, Del Shannon's influence was undeniable. While American rock and roll had been an integral part of the British rock music scene since the 1950s, few artists had the impact upon United Kingdom bands that Del did during his career. His musical sound, as well as his vocals, were so distinct that they became the basis for the Mersey sound, this was the musical direction which came from Liverpool and featured the Beatles. Such Shannon classics as "Little Town Flirt" and "Two Kinds of Teardrops" had the musical direction that fledgling British bands loved. Wittingly or unwittingly, these tunes became a major influence upon developing British rock and roll. Pete Best, the original Beatles' drummer, remarked: "Without Del Shannon, the Merseyside sound would have been much less distinct." There were others in Liverpool who echoed these sentiments. "I remember how popular Del Shannon's records were," Bob Wooler, the compere at the Cavern Club, remarked. As the Beatles moved into the British charts, Shannon was aware of them. He was the first American artist to record and release a Beatle song, "From Me To You," in the United States and he toured England as the initial strains of Beatlemania changed the direction of rock and roll music.

What is interesting is that Shannon cut "From Me To You" in England. When it was released in 1963 on the Big Top label in American, the Heliodor imprint in Germany and the London label in the U. K. virtually gave it no airplay. Yet, when the Beatles invaded America in 1964, Shannon's version of "From Me To You" had strong regional airplay in the Middle West and New England states. Not surprisingly, despite his English popularity, it wasn't a big U. K. favorite.

A brief tour of England in 1962 was the main reason that Shannon was so influential upon the rising British rock and roll bands. After he arrived back home the English based Del Shannon Fan Club put out volume II, number 1 of "Shannon Small Talk." From his greeting to the fans, "My record hit number 15 the first week and it looked like it will be in the top ten next week," Shannon gushed about his English tour. The British bands were also a big influence upon him as he wrote songs with a decided English rock flair. "I think that Del was on the precipice of change after he came back from these early English tours," Charlie Marsh, an old friend from Battle Creek, remarked.

DEL SHANNON IN 1962-1963: ON THE PRECIPICE OF CHANGE

In 1962-1963, as Beatlemania was preparing to engulf America, Del Shannon's American television appearances on Shindig, Hullabaloo, Dick Clark's American Bandstand and the Lloyd Thaxton Show helped to sell his early hits. The Beatles and other bands during the British Invasion had made heavy inroads into the market, but Shannon survived it.

The "Shannon Small Talk" newsletter had a message from Del: "After 'Keep Searchin,' I have another tune ready for release called 'Stranger In Town," Del wrote. "I think it's much stronger than 'Searchin." Then Shannon went on to discuss his new album which included such cover tunes as Roy Orbison's "Runnin' Scared," Jay and the Americans', "She Cried" and the Four Seasons' "Rag Doll." The album also included six original tunes. In "Shannon Small Talk," a publication of the Del Shannon Fan Club, volume II, number l, Shannon felt obliged to point out that he had written "I Go To Pieces" for Peter and Gordon which was included as a cover tune on the album. This publication also publicized the **Del Shannon Sings Hank Williams** album which had just appeared.

After he toured England, Del once again wrote out a brief statement for the "Shannon Small Talk," volume II, number 2. Shannon remarked that his month in England was a big success. "Keep Searchin' (We'll Follow The Sun)" went to number 3 in England," Shannon wrote. The truth is that it rose to number 4 on the **New Musical Express** chart. When he returned to New York, Shannon appeared on the Hullabaloo Show.

When Shannon taped the Hullabaloo show for a March 22, 1963 release, he spent an inordinate amount of time in the studio. Paul Anka, Chubby Checker and Rita Pavona appeared with him. Then Shannon took off for an April 15 through June 2, tour with Dick Clark.

The constant touring put Del in touch with a host of creative people. While touring Scotland, Shannon met a songwriter, Ross Watson, and told his fans in the "Shannon Small Talk" newsletter to expect some songs from Watson's pen. "I cut one of his tunes," Shannon wrote. "It is sort of a folk number. I'm sure I'll use it as my next single."

LIVERPOOL AND THE BEATLES

By 1963, the Beatles and every other Merseyside band had the shuffling beat that Shannon employed in "Little Town Flirt" and they had taken this musical direction to the bank.

The rock and roll explosion hit the small, quaint town of Liverpool in the autumn of 1961. The economy was in horrible condition, a young man could become a soccer star or a rock musician. Work on the docks had given out and many were on the dole. There was little else to do in Liverpool. "We didn't know where our next meal was coming from, so a little good music and beer helped," Eddie Porter recalled. He also remembered how everyone talked about the new music.

Beatles' Ringo Starr and Paul McCartney Hang out With Del Shannon, 1964

When Bob Wooler wrote articles in the Liverpool music newspaper, the **Mersey Beat**, he never wrote about Del Shannon's records. "We all took it for granted that everyone knew everything about 'Runaway' and the man behind it," Wooler stated. What the Liverpool bands did was to take Del's soaring musical sound and add their own lyrics to it.

One British musician, Gerry Marsden, initially was hostile to Del Shannon. Once he got to know him, however, Marsden became a close friend. The "Ferry Across the Mersey" star forged a friendship with Del based on music and respect. Their relationship goes a long way to explain the key elements of Shannon's influence upon the subsequent English Invasion.

GERRY MARSDEN AND DEL SHANNON: A FRIENDSHIP FORGED IN MUSIC

In the late 1980s, Del Shannon was recounting the time that Gerry Marsden of Gerry of the Pacemakers had forced him out of his hotel room to have a drink. "You know," Del remarked, "I wish I could have had the fun that those guys had." Then Del speculated on his influence. "You know I would sit around my hotel room and they would listen to me sing new and old songs." It was Gerry Marsden who spent a lot of time with Del, but he was joined periodically by John Lennon and Paul McCartney.

As Gerry Marsden began his career, he was on a number of package tours with Del Shannon. It was Shannon's musical direction which encouraged Marsden to write and record some of his biggest hits. The shuffling Merseybeat sound was so identifiable in Shannon's early music and a part of his act long before Marsden finished his string of hits.

Del, Dion and Joe Brown in England, 1962

Marsden recalled his first tour with Del: "Shannon enjoyed big hits with 'Runaway,' 'Swiss Maid' and 'Hats Off To Larry," Marsden recalled, "and we thought he was a bit snooty and big headed." This attitude ended when Marsden and his band persuaded Del to have some drinks with them in a London hotel.

Marsden tricked Shannon into coming out of his hotel room in his shorts to receive a bogus telegram. Del then went downstairs and drank with Marsden and the Pacemakers in his bathrobe. From that point on they were fast friends and Gerry Marsden and the Pacemakers toured with Shannon in England over the years.

Marsden recalled that Shannon's records were required listening. They were like an instructional manual for fledgling British bands. During the winter of 1962-1963, a quiet revolution created hundreds of British rock and roll bands. Their sound was a pop-oriented and highly commercial-type of rock music which bore the distinct imprint of Del Shannon's early hits.

Bob Wooler, the disc jockey at Liverpool's Cavern Club, remembers: "John loved to play Del Shannon's records and he borrowed every one that I owned. I couldn't play 'Runaway' because Lennon refused to give it back." In a lengthy interview, Wooler talked about the popularity of Shannon's London label releases. "They seemed to be everywhere and had a direction quite different from the Frankie Avalon, Bobby Darin and Fabian music that dominated the American market." With a wink of his eye, Wooler suggested that Shannon was undeniably a key influence upon the Merseyside sound.

CREATING THE MERSEYSIDE SOUND FROM DEL SHANNON'S RECORDS

How did Shannon's music influence the Beatles? The answer is a simple one. His English label, London Records, packaged the remainders or left over singles and placed them in the bargain bins with other records. "John Lennon and Paul McCartney found Shannon's records in these bargain bins," Joe Flannery, a close friend of Brian Epstein's, remembered. "When I managed my brother's group, Lee Curtis and the All Stars, every Merseyside group practiced to 'Runaway."

Allan Williams, the Beatles first manager, sat in his Jacaranda Club and complained that the Beatles wore out the juke box playing "Runaway." "Those blokes just loved Shannon's instrumental breaks', hell it sounded just like the music that they were doing," Williams concluded.

Sam Leach, a local prompter, suggested: "Del Shannon provided chords for the boys to write their songs. He had a spirited, free-form type of shuffling music."

Brian Kelly, another Liverpool promoter who booked the Beatles, had similar observations. On December 27, 1960 the Beatles played for Kelly at the Litherland Town Hall. This began a two-year friendship in which Kelly was close to the boys. "It was a year later when I heard John Lennon talking about Del Shannon's music," Kelly recalled. "Then I took a listen and it was obvious that this American had a strong influence upon the boys."

Clive Epstein remembered "My brother would get in a Del Shannon record and one of the Beatles or another Merseyside musician would buy it up. We were intrigued by their interest in this obscure American." These comments were echoed time and time again by most everyone involved in the Merseyside music scene.

If Shannon had any influences upon the Beatles and other Merseyside bands, they also helped his popularity to cross over into the English and European markets.

DEL SHANNON: ENGLAND, SOME UNLIKELY HITS AND INFLUENCING THE BEATLES

Until his death, Shannon could depend upon English and Scottish tours and during the low points in his career he flew to London and toured with a pickup band. The early English hits for Del Shannon were not always in line with the American hits and this helped to expand his sales and popularity. A case in point is a cover of Roger Miller's "Little Swiss Maid" which Shannon cut in Nashville. Considered too corny for American audiences, it was a monster English and European hit.

In 1961, as the Merseyside sound formed, Del hit the charts in England in July when "Runaway" sold half-a-million copies in a 90-day period. Then in October, "Hats Off To Larry" hit number 6 on the U. K. charts.

The hits continued in January 1962 when "So Long Baby" charted at number 10 in the U. K. In Ma, 1962 "Hey! Little Girl" rose to number two on the British charts, followed by "Cry Myself To Sleep" at number 29 in September 1962, and the following month a cover version of Roger Miller's obscure tune "The Swiss Maid" gave Del another number 2 hit. Only Frank Ifield's "Lovesick Blues" kept it from being number one.

It was the minor hits and the obscure tunes which brought the chord changes, the musical breaks and the direction that characterized the Merseyside sound. The cutting edge to Shannon's music, particularly Max Crook's musitron sound, intrigued the Beatles, and they quickly found out that they could not mimic Del's style. John Lennon remarked that Little Willie John's "Leave My Kitten Alone" was easy to cover but Shannon's "Runaway," "Hats Off To Larry" and "Little Town Flirt" were rock and roll originals which defied the cover artist.

Because of the success of "Runaway," Del toured England in September 1962 with Dion, as he established a niche in Great Britain which allowed him to expand his career in Europe. When he returned to the United States, Shannon realized that the Beatles were destined for international stardom. So he made it a point to cover one of their songs.

On October 2, 1962, **Cash Box** featured a picture of Del Shannon in London with his manager Irving Micahnik and Geoff Milne of Decca. They were celebrating the success of "The Swiss Maid" on the English charts.

For the remainder of 1962, Irving Micahnik spent a great deal of time in London, promoting Del Shannon's career. But Micahnik also did some fine tuning for Shannon's career. It was ironic that for all of Micahnik's faults, the difficulties in paying studio costs, the inability to always take care of business and the long absences from daily duties, he was still able to do a great deal for Shannon. Micahnik remains one of the major contradictions in rock and roll history.

DEL SHANNON IN ENGLAND: 1963 AND THE TRIUMPH OF A NEW ENGLISH SOUND

In 1963, Del was headlining a show at London's palatial Royal Albert Hall, and the Beatles did one show with him. "The place was jammed and the Beatles were really hot," Del recalled to Ray Coleman. "They had something like three number one hits in a row at the time." As Del completed his show with the Beatles, he recognized their innate song writing talents. He realized that he could cover one of their songs and perhaps have an American hit with it. But first he had to understand their music.

Shannon spent much of that show talking to John Lennon. "I told him that "From Me To You" has got a little bit of a falsetto in it. So I'm going to record it," Del recalled. When Shannon saw Lennon about four months later, John remarked: "Ah, you did it, didn't you." Lennon smiled and grinned in approval. This made Del feel good and he was aware of the impact that the Beatles and the British Invasion would have on American music. "I could see the changes coming when I toured England in 1963," Del later told the English newspaper **Disc**. His keen interest in new types of music was one of the traits which kept Shannon's career going until his untimely death.

To get the right sound on "From Me To You," Del cut it in England. He used musicians who could combine the Beatle sound with his own musical direction. Del was happy with "From Me To You," because it did hit number 77 on the **Billboard** Hot 100, becoming the first Lennon-McCartney song in the American market.

The British hits made Del a hot touring act in the U. K. On April 20, 1963 Shannon opened a tour with Johnny Tillotson in Bournemouth. This Saturday night show featured the Springfields with future pop star Dusty Springfield leading the folk group. Most all the talk was about Liverpool's favorite sons, the Beatles. The Fab Four's success eclipsed every other act in the music business. One Beatle in particular interested Shannon, John Lennon.

DEL SHANNON AND JOHN LENNON: AN AMERICAN SINGER-SONGWRITER INFLUENCES A BEATLE

There were many American influences upon Lennon's song writing. As a writer Lennon was able to borrow material from other singers like Shannon and incorporate them into his own classics.

"When I was researching my John Lennon biography," Ray Coleman remarked, "there was a tendency for the Beatles to down play Shannon's influence. They were told by their manager, Brian Epstein, to try to avoid being tied in with an American oldies act. All a person has to do is look at all the pictures of Del with the Beatles to understand that they were friends and he influenced them."

In Liverpool and later in London, Lennon spent hours going through the discount bins of local record stores. He purchased everything that he could find by Del Shannon. Before he became a famous Beatle, Lennon bought records from local seamen at the Liverpool port, borrowed records from Bob Wooler, purchased a few 45s from Brian Epstein's store and often borrowed records that he forgot to return.

DEL SHANNON AND THE BEATLES

When the Beatles signed their contract with Parlophone Records and began to write their own songs, there was enormous pressure upon Lennon to turn out hit records. Like many songwriters, he studied the American charts and was aware of the type of tunes which were popular on the **Billboard Hot 100**.

This process prompted Lennon to spend a lot of time listening to American rock and roll. He was an unadulterated rock music fanatic and kept up with the American charts. Anything that was new intrigued him. When "Runaway" hit the American charts in early 1961 and quickly found its way to England and Europe, Lennon was playing in Hamburg. He told Horst Fascher: "That organ sound on 'Runaway' is wonderful."

Lennon chatting with Ray Coleman told him that he first heard "Runaway" on Radio Luxembourg. It was one of the new songs from the U.S. and Lennon still preferred the music of Buddy Holly, Jerry Lee Lewis, Gene Vincent, Little Richard, Chuck Berry, Arthur Alexander, Eddie Cochran and Larry Williams. "I don't think I could ever do a song like Del Shannon," Lennon remarked to Coleman in an interview later in the 1960s.

After crafting his early music around American roots rockers, Lennon picked up on the shuffle in Shannon's songs. In particular, John spent hours listening to "Two Kinds of Teardrops" and "Little Town Flirt." John was not the only one to adapt to Shannon's music. Some of the more obscure Liverpool groups, notably Kingsize Taylor and the Dominoes, Lee Curtis and the All Stars, Rory Storm and the Hurricanes and Gerry and the Pacemakers, used Shannon's music to develop their own unique sound.

The ability to write songs from American rock originals was one of Lennon's gifts. He used a version of Elvis Presley's "Baby Let's Play House" to write "Run For Your Life." After listening to half a dozen of Shannon's single, Lennon sat down and wrote "I'll Be Back" from this sampling of Del's songs. When Lennon composed "Do You Want to Know A Secret," he used a line from Snow White and the Seven Dwarfs. "I think John only needed a small spark from others," Ray Coleman remarked, "and then he was off and writing a song."

By chance, Shannon and Lennon got together in 1963. On Sunday, April 14, Shannon headlined the Beatles third appearance on the television program "Thank Your Lucky Stars." This show broadcast from the Teddington Studio Center, Teddington was taped and scheduled for Saturday, April 20 on the ITV network.

The Beatles arrived in Teddington after a morning rehearsal. They decided to perform "From Me To You" and Shannon was amazed at the depth of the song. He talked for half an hour with John and Paul about the tune. Del wondered if he should let them know that he wanted to record it. Irving Micahnik whispered in Del's ear that they had to get into a local studio and record it.

The "Thank Your Lucky Stars" TV show was important for both Del and the Beatles because they influenced each other. They all talked to him at length about his music. Del was able to see other acts, notably the Dave Clark Five, the Vernon Girls and Bert Weedon. When he met Weedon, Del joked that this was his middle name.

After the taping, Shannon joined the Beatles for a few beers at a local bar. The conversation turned to songs and Irving told the Beatles he loved "From Me To You." It was Del who first recognized the commercial possibilities of "From Me to You" in the American marketplace. He saw the Beatles as a future American hit act. A few nights later, Irving and Del went to dinner and talked late into the night over cigars and brandy about the Beatles. This cemented the deal to cut "From Me To You."

What was reprehensible about Micahnik is that he took credit in the press for Shannon recording "From Me To You." Del simply ignored him and concentrated upon his English concert schedule.

But Del still had one more concert with the Beatles. On Thursday, April 18, 1963 he performed at London's Royal Albert Hall. Located in the Kensington Gore area, the Royal Albert Hall is one of London's most prestigious concert venues. The show that Shannon appeared on with the Beatles was entitled "Swinging Sound 63." It was a broadcast featuring the Springfields, Lance Percival, Rolf Harris, the Vernon Girls, Kenny Lynch, Shane Fenton and the Fentones, and George Melly.

That night the Beatles performed "From Me To You" and it brought down the house. It didn't take Del a minute to decide to cut the tune. Later, in 1964, Lennon would admit to Shannon that his song, "I'll Be Back," was a reworking of one of Del's tunes. This show was one which was a strange concert because of Melly's addition to the bill. He was a Liverpool jazz singer and art critic who was added to the bill to introduce the Beatles. "The Beatles were worried that Del Shannon would be a tough act to compete with," Clive Epstein remembered, "so my brother brought in George to ease the tensions." There were also copious amounts of food and alcohol as this television show turned into a recording marathon. "I think Brian was worried that his boys would get swallowed up by the more experienced American singer," Cavern club disc jockey Bob Wooler continued. "But what I saw was an extraordinary amount of respect for the Beatles by Del Shannon and he seemed to be doing everything he could to help them."

This concert was difficult to record and the BBC had a rather complicated production schedule. The first half of the show was from 8:00 to 8:50 p.m. and the second was from 9:10 to 10:15 p.m.. What made this concert strange is that the first half was never broadcast over BBC radio. It was essentially a Beatle concert for Royal Albert patrons.

Shannon watched as the Beatles performed their first concert at the Royal Albert Hall. He turned to Irving Micahnik and remarked: "These guys are on their way."

After spending all day with the Beatles at the Royal Albert Hall, Shannon came to realize not only their talent but their professionalism. After Del performed "Runaway" and "Little Town Flirt," he joined the Beatles on stage for the finale. All the acts came out and joined in on a rousing instrumental version of "Mack The Knife." It was typical British television, some of the hottest rock acts of the decade were forced to close with a German Cabaret song. The Royal Albert Hall appearance provided Shannon with some new material. Irving Micahnik booked some studio time and Del prepared to record in London.

It was at the April 18, 1963 Beatle concert that Shannon first heard "From Me To You." He loved the song. Micahnik was equally impressed with its commercial potential. They had the same thought. It would be a hit in the American market. So they made plans to record it.

Finally, on May 1, 1963, Del walked into the West-End Studio in London and prepared to cut "From Me To You." An arranger, Ivor Raymond, was hired and English studio musicians were brought in to record four songs.

The final version of "From Me To You," was followed by "Sandy," a song borrowed from Johnny Fortune, a Shannon original "Walk Like An Angel," and a cover version of Linda Scott's "Town Crier." The only song released at the time from this session was "From Me To You." No one has ever figured out why the other three songs remained unreleased.

Del was about to leave Embee Productions. He was unhappy with Micahnik and Shannon was ready to set up his own label. Shortly after this English tour, Berlee Records was founded and Shannon went off into a new direction.

When Del Shannon left England after this 1963 appearance with the Beatles, he was not only a strong influence upon their music but a close friend. John Lennon frequently mentioned Shannon's mentor role but Del's music went beyond the Beatles. He had a strong impact upon the entire British music marketplace. When the Beatles arrived in America and Del Shannon was in the vicinity he was in their hotel room drinking, talking and having fun.

THE BEATLES IN 1963:
WAS DEL SHANNON THE MAIN INFLUENCE?

Sitting in the Grapes Pub in 1983, Bob Wooler, the former Cavern disc jockey, looked up and asked: "Was Del Shannon the main influence upon the Beatles?" Wooler then went into a lengthy story about the first year of English Beatlemania.

"You know 1963 was special and I can't help but think that the boys learned something from Shannon," Wooler remarked. He continued by suggesting that their song writing borrowed a great deal from Shannon's early hits and that much of the Merseyside sound owed a debt to Del. Mark Herstgaard argued that "Please Please Me," "was a 100 percent John Lennon composition inspired by Roy Orbison's 'Only The Lonely,'" but Bob Wooler disputes this and suggests that the song and most other early Beatle tunes owed their unique sound to Shannon's musical direction. "Listen to the original version of 'Please Please Me," Wooler continued, "and you will see that it's slow, quite unlike the hit. It's pure Del Shannon," he concluded.

"Another important point is that John Lennon spent a lot of time with Del Shannon talking song writing," Wooler continued. "He wanted to learn how to write while on the road."

As John Lennon and Paul McCartney churned out songs in 1963, they mentioned Shannon but only in passing. They preferred to invoke the names of the earlier legends of American rock and roll. So when they were asked how they got the inspiration to write "From Me To You," Paul diplomatically gave credit to a local British rock music newspaper. There was a column of letters in one of the British rock newspapers called "From You To Us." Paul claims the Beatles purloined the title. All the better to build Beatle publicity and record sales. The truth was a bit more complicated.

"From Me To You" was written to test a song writing theory that the words "me" and "you" were the ones most frequently used in hit songs. The Beatles wrote "From Me To You" in the back of a van they used to travel around England. It was composed just five days before the March 5, 1963 recording session. The following month, Del appeared with the Beatles on British TV and they discussed the song.

Del told John that the perfect harmonies on "From Me To You" reminded him of the old days at the Hi Lo Club in Battle Creek, Michigan. When John asked, "What is the Hi Lo Club?" Del explained about Doug DeMott and the boys in his first band. John was mesmerized with the story. Shannon and Lennon then spent much of an evening comparing the ferocious bouncers at the Hi Lo with those in Hamburg. But much of the evening was spent on music. "I think that Del Shannon was an unwitting influence upon the Beatles," Clive Epstein remarked. "He had that sound that they liked."

It was Brian Epstein who continually told the Beatles to mention the big names in American rock and roll when citing influences. "I don't think many have heard of Del Shannon," he told the Beatles, "and he may just be a passing artist."

"John Lennon took exception to Brian Epstein continually demanding that the boys invoke certain rock and rollers as influences," Brian Kelly, a local Liverpool promoter recalled. "I think some early American songwriters were not mentioned," Sam Leach, another promoter, concluded.

DEL SHANNON AND THE ENGLISH SONG WRITING MARKET

In October 1963, Del's second English album, the British version of the **Little Town Flirt** LP, was released in the United Kingdom and rose to number 15 on the chart in mid-November, 1963. This album was a follow up to Del's first English LP **Hats Off To Del Shannon** which had peaked at number 9 on the British charts.

Shannon's song writing also attracted British acts. When Peter and Gordon covered Del's "I Go To Pieces" it was the result of an accident. Del was touring Australia and he played the song for Peter Asher. Throughout his career Shannon had many songs covered by other artists and Asher remarked that "Del was the most commercial songwriter in America."

The **Little Town Flirt** album contained 12 songs in its U. S. release and it was a magnificent reflection of Shannon's talent. The U. K. version of **Little Town Flirt** also included "My Wild One" and sold very well in the English market. In addition to his big hit, "Little Town Flirt," written with Maron McKenzie, Shannon also had minor chart hits with "Two Kinds of Tear Drops" and "From Me To You." He also covered his good friend Dion DiMucci's "Runaround Sue," Roy Orbison's "Dream Baby" and Bruce Channel's "Hey Baby."

When Delbert McClinton toured England as Channel's harmonica player for the "Hey Baby" tour, he found that Del Shannon's music was everywhere. "Del had more hits in England than in America," McClinton concluded. But Shannon's hits were world wide ones.

Once he returned from England, Del told his wife Shirley that he could play England anytime he felt like it. "Chuck was one of the U.K.'s biggest stars," Shirley Westover continued, "and he loved going to London." One of his favorite London venues was Dingwall's. It was a club located in the midst of the Camden Town Market and Del loved to walk into the club and watch himself on their TV screen when he wasn't playing this venue.

The Beatles and Del Shannon were seldom linked musically but there was a strong connection. One that helped to shape the English invasion of America and the course of rock and roll music. There is no doubt that Del was a strong influence upon the Mersey sound but he also provided advice on song writing and the music business that had a dramatic impact upon John Lennon. Paul McCartney, on the other hand, paid little attention to Shannon's advice, but the Beatles song writing genius still owed an enormous debt to his influence. Del Shannon was a songwriter par excellence and the Beatles debt to him was an overwhelming one.

THE BEATLES CONTINUE TO BE AN INFLUENCE

Del Shannon had an enormous impact upon the Beatles. But the Fab Four were also amongst Shannon's biggest fans. In 1965, Del was seen hanging around the Beatles hotel room. Whenever the Beatles were around they went to see Del perform. When Del appeared with Chuck Berry at London's Saville Theater on February 19, 1967, John Lennon and Ringo Starr showed up to cheer Del on.

In 1975, when Shannon released **The Vintage Years** album, he used a photo with Paul McCartney and Ringo Starr in their Florida hotel room to publicize his place in the Merseyside sound. It was an LP that sold in respectable numbers and helped to revive Shannon's sagging career. This 1964 picture was only one of many that Del collected over the years. Like most contemporary musical artists, Del wanted to use his connection with the Beatles for commercial purposes.

When Robert Stigwood's movie **Sgt. Pepper's Lonely Hearts Club Band** was in production in 1978, Shannon made a brief cameo appearance. The Beatles were often a presence in Del's music, if somewhat of an unseen one. When Del cut the **Drop Down And Get Me** album with Tom Petty, he recorded a cover version of the Beatles' "I Should Have Known Better." It was left out of the LP.

"Hot Love" was one of Del's songs cut in May 1988 which was completed with the help of Beatle George Harrison. Throughout his lengthy career, Del was close to the Beatles. He flew to Miami to be with them when they prepared their television appearance on the Ed Sullivan Show in 1964. There is no doubt that Shannon influenced the Beatles and other Mersey beat groups. He was also a good friend. But in his own quiet manner, Del never tried to take advantage of his friendship with the Fab Four. He was simply content to know them.

BIBLIOGRAPHICAL SOURCES

Interviews with Charlie Lennon, Joe Flannery, Clive Epstein, Bob Wooler, Allan Williams, Alistair Taylor, Kingsize Taylor, Horst Fascher, Eddie Hoover, Gerry Marsden, Ray Coleman, Eddie Porter and Tony Sheridan helped to establish Del Shannon's influence on the Merseyside sound. Sam Leach and Brian Kelly provided in- depth interviews about early Beatle concerts that they promoted in Liverpool and how Del Shannon's musical influence was evident in their early career. Billy J. Kramer was interviewed at a Beatlefest and he provided additional information on Shannon's influence. In Albuquerque, New Mexico, Jack Good was tracked down and he gave out some excellent information on Shannon's British television and radio appearances. Eddie Porter had important insights into the birth of Liverpool rock and roll.

Perhaps the most valuable interview was with the late British blues legend, Alexis Koerner, who had a deep understanding of the musical changes coming over England and its relationship to American music. This interview was conducted during the early stages of my Chuck Berry research and Del's name came up in conversation.

Tom Shaka, an American blues artist now popular in Germany, provided two extensive interviews on Del Shannon's European influences.

Shirley Westover recalled the triumphs of the English trips. Kym, Jody and Craig Westover graciously shared their memories of traveling with their dad.

For Del's influence upon the Beatles, see Howard A. DeWitt, **The Beatles: Untold Tales** (Fremont, 1985), pp. 219-222 and Philip Norman, **Shout: The Beatles In Their Generation** (New York, 1981), Chapters 9-11.

The story of B.B.C. Shannon broadcasts is hinted at in Kevin Howlett, **The Beatles At The BEEB** (London, 1982). For Beatle appearances see Mark Lewisohn, **The Beatles Live! The Ultimate Reference Book** (News York, 1986).

Ray Coleman's, **Lennon** (New York, 1984), chapters 6-14 helped to shape this chapter. A lengthy interview with Ray Coleman at a Los Angeles Beatlefest prompted him to include anecdotes about Del Shannon that he had left out of his Lennon biography. Also see, Howard A. DeWitt, **Paul McCartney: From Liverpool To Let It Be** (Fremont, 1992), passim.

For the Beatles in 1963 see Allan Kozin, **The Beatles** (London, 1995), chapter 3; Hunter Davies, **The Beatles** (2nd edition, New York, 1996), chapters 20-22 and Mark Hertsgaard, **A Day In The Life: The Music and Artistry of the Beatles** (New York, 1995), chapters 3-5.

An interesting look at Del Shannon's influence is contained in Gerry Marsden, with Ray Coleman, **I'll Never Walk Alone: An Autobiography** (London, 1993), passim.

Publications of the Del Shannon Fan Club, "Shannon Small Talk," Volume I, number 1 and Volume II, number 2 were important to this chapter.

For an excellent encyclopedic look at Shannon's career, see Dafydd Rees and Luke Crampton, **VH 1's Music First Rock Stars Encyclopedia** (New York, 1996), pp. 898-899. Also see, H. V. Fulpen, **The Beatles: An Illustrated Diary** (New York, 1982).

Other useful Beatle titles include, Nicholas Schaffner, **The Beatles Forever** (New York, 1977); Gareth Powloski, **How They Became The Beatles: A Definitive History of the Early Years** (New York, 1990); Alan Kozinn, **The Beatles** (London, 1995); Tim Riley, **Tell Me Why: A Beatles Commentary** (New York, 1988); Steve

DEL SHANNON AND THE BEATLES

Turner, **A Hard Day's Write: The Story Behind Every Beatles Song** (London, 1994) and Ian McDonald, **Revolution In The Head: The Beatles Records and the Sixties** (New York, 1994).

Kristofer Engelhardt, **Beatles Undercover** (Burlington, Ontairo, 1998) is an excellent look at how Del covered the Beatles.

Interviews with Mervyn, Phil and Dorothy Solomon added a great deal to our knowledge of the Beatles and Shannon's English popularity.

9: THE LIBERTY YEARS: 1966 TO 1968

"Going to Los Angeles was exciting for all of us. The hippie movement had begun and we partook," Dan Bourgoise, President and Founder of Bug Music

In late 1965, Del moved to Los Angeles and the following year signed with Liberty Records. The relocation to the West Coast was a calculated attempt to revive his early hit-making years. The hits had stopped once the British invasion took America by storm.

"Liberty offered me a lot of money," Shannon told Mike McDowell, "I sold my home in Michigan and bought a boring home on Cobb Lake." This was a rural area outside Grand Rapids and Shannon soon tired of the area. This accelerated his decision to move to California.

Del Shannon: A Liberty Records Promo Picture

Del was so bored that he threw most of the unsold copies of his recent single, "Move It On Over," into Cobb Lake. "I became lazy," Shannon recalled. "The only club around there was the one about two miles away that I used to work in on Sunday nights." Shannon was unhappy but couldn't do anything about it. Then he called Tommy Boyce for advice.

"What are you doing at Cobb Lake?" Boyce asked. "Get your ass out here to Los Angeles. It's where all the recording activity takes place. Dot Records wants to sign you."

With that advice Del found it surprisingly easy to negotiate a recording contract with Liberty Records. "Del was surprised that Liberty would offer him a monthly salary," Shirley Westover remarked. "He was determined to take advantage of the time to write, record and produce other acts." Before he signed with Liberty, Shannon talked to Columbia and sought Dick Clark's advice. Columbia would not meet Shannon's financial demands and Liberty was only too happy to sign him to a guaranteed salary contract. Dot Records quickly vanished from the scene. They simply didn't have the money to sign Shannon. The business atmosphere at Dot reminded Del of the years with Embee Productions. "I'm not going through the humiliation of dealing with Irving again," Del told his old friend Battle Creek disc jockey, Charlie Marsh. The frustration of dealing with Irving Micahnik and his financial problems were a reminder of past unhappy business dealings.

The only bright spot in Shannon's dealing with Liberty Records was his relationship with its president, Hal Bennett. It was Bennett who marketed Shannon in the Philippines and the Far East. He also supported Del's English recording ventures. Unfortunately, Bennett did not overrule corporate decisions to have Del cut cover tunes. As he arrived in Los Angeles, Shannon was happy about his new contract. In three years he left Liberty bitter and disillusioned. The main reason for Del's joy was his friendship with Tommy Boyce.

CALIFORNIA IS THE ANSWER TO THE DOWNTURN IN HIT RECORDS

California was the answer to all of Shannon's frustration. When he arrived in Los Angeles, Del stayed with Boyce.

The reason that Shannon was in Los Angeles was to appear on Dick Clark's popular television program "Where The Action Is." While Del stayed with Boyce and his friend Bobby Hart, they talked at length about the future of the music business. Del liked the California weather and it was as a result of this trip that he moved to Los Angeles.

But there were also serious matters to consider. Del realized that Liberty had staff writers, a strong production team and was willing to pay a monthly salary. So Shannon began looking around for a house.

Shannon's three-year deal with Liberty was negotiated through Snuff Garrett who wanted to produce Del's music. With the money, Shannon bought some property and put a sign on it that read: "Ghost Road." Always the consummate investor, Del hung onto the land until it appreciated in value. He would often take the Robbs on drunken rides out to Ghost Road and they would play tapes, drink whiskey and have a good time. The California years proved to be both a tonic to Del and a curse. He had some of the best and the worst times of his life.

Del believed that the creative energy in the music business was no longer centered in New York. Consequently, he searched out musicians, songwriters and producers in and around Los Angeles. From the studio in his home he called the Mole Hole, Shannon tried to find a second set of hit records under the California sunshine.

Del Shannon, 1966

The move from Michigan did a great deal to enhance Del's creativity. He continued to write new songs but was just as interested in production. Country music continued to fascinate him. He would drive down to North Hollywood's Palomino Club and bring home people for a midnight dinner. "I would get a call," Shirley remarked, "and I would have to run out at midnight to the market to get a full spread of food." Del would take his newfound friends into the Mole Hole and they would make music until the wee hours of the morning.

CHANGES IN THE MUSIC BUSINESS AND
DEL SHANNON'S CAREER

The arrival of the Beatles, the subsequent commercial success of the English invasion and the inevitable changes in musical styles made Del Shannon an oldies act. Rock and roll is music designed to exploit fads and current trends. The hits for some artists are short-lived and except for a few superstars, the successes of stardom quickly fade for most early rock and roll performers. It was no different for Del Shannon. He had his hits and then had to face how to survive in the rock and roll marketplace.

Del Shannon's incredible hit-making period from 1961 through 1965 faded in the early glow of psychedelic music. After the experiment with his own record company, Berlee, Del was ready to learn about West Coast rock and roll. The deal with Liberty was arranged because they believed that Del could fit into the same successful market as Bobby Vee and Gary Lewis and have the same success during the mid-1960s.

In 1961, when Shannon had appeared with Bobby Vee and Dion on a New York rock and roll show, he talked at length with them about the music business. Vee's advice was to move to Los Angeles where the best recording facilities, the ablest producers and the more rock and roll oriented record companies operated. Del took Vee's advice and began planning the move to Los Angeles. However, it took him four years to finalize the moves.

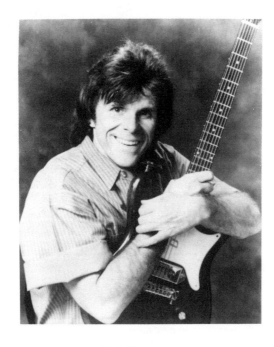

Del Shannon

GOSSIP, RUMOR AND DEL'S RECORDS

As Del prepared to move to Los Angeles, the Del Shannon Appreciation Society began publicizing a forthcoming album. The Fan Club publicity releases suggested that in 1965 a new LP would include "Tired of Waiting" and "Game of Love" as well as "Can't Believe My Ears." These were singles that had been released in the English and Australian markets. Del shed some light on these recordings in a 1965 article "Shannon Small Talk." Because his singles "Break Up" and "Move It On Over" were both commercial failures, the album never saw the light of day.

When he did move to California, Shannon spent an inordinate amount of time watching the hit TV show "Batman" and toyed with the idea of trying to write television music.

By the mid-1960s, "Runaway" had been recorded by acts as diverse as Lawrence Welk and the Shirelles. Instrumental versions by the Ventures and Chantays made Shannon's classic tune a favorite with surfers.

As he moved out to Los Angeles, Shannon believed that he could extend his creativity. He wanted to do a number of select covers but also to continue to produce himself. The Liberty years turned out to be one of the more disastrous parts of his career. He had a producer who didn't know how to record him, a company that forced him into songs that Liberty owned and a promotion department who treated him like an oldies act before his time.

Del and Shirley In Los Angeles, 1968

The late 1960s turned out to be a time of change and a test of Shannon's artistic integrity. He survived the years with Liberty Records but it almost killed his creativity and career. It was also a period which brought enormous changes to his personal life.

DEL SHANNON: THE SCOUTING TRIP TO LOS ANGELES AND THE FINAL MOVE

When Del called Shirley and told her to prepare for the final move to California, she was surprised. Del had purchased a house on 5821 Lemona in Van Nuys. It was a small two-bedroom house in a nice neighborhood and was typical of Del's parsimonious ways in that it was the smallest but nicest house in the area.

After loading up their cars with everything from clothes to guitars, Shirley left their cabin to drive to Los Angeles. Dan Bourgoise drove Del's Cadillac to California because he couldn't drive a stick shift. So Shirley had to drive the Corvair. Dan was embarrassed that Shirley had to drive the little car.

When he arrived in Los Angeles, Shannon had little knowledge of the City of the Angels. Like most people, he went to Hollywood and looked around. Then Del simply drove around the valleys that blanked Los Angeles and Hollywood. It didn't take him long to find a tree-shaded suburb with modestly priced homes.

In the San Fernando Valley there were a great many homes. The home at 5821 Lemona was simply too small. Shirley told Del to buy a house at the same price and so he paid in excess of $100,000 for the home. Dan Bourgoise and Steve Monahan lived for a brief period with Del and Shirley, and the move to California was a happy time.

Across the street, Wanda and Al Tyson lived with their young daughter, LeAnne. The two families quickly became close friends.

THE LIBERTY RECORD EXPERIMENT WITH DEL SHANNON

When he arrived in Los Angeles and signed with Liberty Records, Del was assigned to work with legendary producer Tommy "Snuff" Garrett. To guarantee a new string of hits, Liberty told Del that they were bringing in Leon Russell and Nick DeCaro to arrange his singles. A veteran of the rock and roll wars, Russell had a innate commercial sense. But for Del Shannon it was the wrong advice. Russell believed that Del's falsetto tone could be used to bring back some old pop hits.

After some discussion, Shannon reluctantly agreed with Russell and told him that he would love to cover Toni Fisher's 1959 hit, "The Big Hurt." When Del mentioned his original tunes, Russell and DeCaro ignored him. They had their own ideas. It would be best, they argued, to recycle some of the old hits. Pop music always had a way of coming back, and they believed that proper song selection would guarantee a new string of hits.

Some years later, Mike McDowell asked Shannon why he recorded "The Big Hurt." "I always liked that song," Shannon stated. "That phasing effect in her version always knocked me out." What Del referred to was the process of recording the song in mono but mixing it on two separate tracks.

The inspiration to record "The Big Hurt" came one day while Shannon stood on a small mountain he owned near Los Angeles. This was the road where he had put up the sign "Ghost Road" and it was the source of some of his best ideas.

A Promotional Piece From Liberty Records for Billboard Magazine

"So I went to Snuff Garrett," Shannon continued, "and I said let's go into Goldstar Studios where she cut it and do the same thing." Garrett loved the idea.

In May 1966, Shannon went into the Liberty studio with Garrett and they talked at length about how to properly record "The Big Hurt." They decided to recreate the phasing technique because it is an attention-grabbing device. It helped Toni Fisher produce a unique sound and have a hit record. They reasoned it would do the same for Shannon.

After playing the record for Garrett, Shannon went on to explain how he wanted his record to sound. At that point Del knew that organizationally Liberty Records would be unable to adapt itself to his recording ideas and in particular his Vision for "The Big Hurt".

Del was also upset that Garrett used the phasing technique in producing Bobby Vee's "Look At Me Girl." What bothered Shannon was that phasing was used on the Vee record to cover up a hissing vocal over the guitar intro. "I should have complained about Garrett, but I thought we could work it out," Shannon remarked one night to Bob Popenhagen at Green's Tavern in Battle Creek. It was only when he returned to the Hi Lo or Green's that Del would vent his displeasure with the Liberty years.

Shannon was too eager to have Liberty Records promote his material, so he never challenged Garrett's production techniques. The results were disastrous as Garrett and Liberty proved that they had little idea what to do with Shannon's unique talent. "I couldn't understand Del's obsession with 'The Big Hurt,' Garrett remarked to Leon Russell. What Garrett didn't realize is that obsession was a key part of Shannon's personality.

The obsession with "The Big Hurt" also offers another important insight in Shannon's personality. When he recorded for Big Top in 1961-1962, Del met Toni Fisher when she was in the studio cutting "West of The Wall" (Big Top 3097) which went to number 37 in its 11 weeks on the **Billboard** pop chart. Shannon spent hours with her and he picked up the phasing technique. When he tried to get Snuff Garrett to adopt it, Shannon was treated like the village idiot. He finally just gave up and went along with Garrett's production ideas. The legendary producer demonstrated in working with Shannon that his reputation was greater than the substance of his records.

BONES HOWE: THE ENGINEER WHO TURNED THE LIBERTY YEARS INTO A DISASTER

When Del Shannon came aboard at Liberty Records, Dayone "Bones" Howe was the engineer and producer of many of their hits. A tall, thin, extremely hard-working young man who was born in Minneapolis in 1933, and saw his role as that of a hit maker. His track record indicated that he was a gifted sound engineer.

After hitting the charts with the Turtles, the Grass Roots, the Association, Johnny Rivers and the Fifth Dimension, Howe acquired a reputation which exceeded his abilities. Howe was first and foremost an engineer, but the tendency in the industry was to marry the engineering with the production. He was first and foremost a soundman. He had successfully handled sound at the Monterey Pop Festival in June 1967,

In Del Shannon's years with Liberty, it unwittingly ended Del's commercial impulse. The selection of cover songs which Shannon cut and the inability to translate into recordings Del's experimental vision killed Shannon's commercial future. Unbeknownst to Del, he entered the Liberty Record deal with a strike against him. Liberty could not bring the quality of material for Del that Harry Balk had done earlier in the 1960's

DEL SHANNON'S BIG HURT: A ONE-MAN BAND IN A CORPORATE STRUCTURE

The Liberty Record years found Shannon to be a one-man band in a corporate structure. He was constantly writing new tunes and fiddling with studio production techniques. "Del Shannon was so full of creativity, it frightened some people," a former Liberty executive remarked.

Unfortunately, there was tension in the recording studio. Del was used to his home studio, a small recording oasis in an informal atmosphere. None of this existed at Liberty as studio time was booked to the precise minute, the musicians were contracted for a block of time and the recording atmosphere was so preplanned that it virtually strangled his creativity.

"I don't think that Del Shannon was ready for assembly line record production," Maron McKenzie remarked. "When we worked on 'Little Town Flirt' it was experimentation, a jovial atmosphere and a few drinks that kept us going." None of this existed at Liberty Records and Snuff Garrett was too taken with his own persona to change the assembly line production technique.

What Del Shannon missed was the sure hand of producer Harry Balk. Despite Del's complaints over his contract with Embee Productions, he had a very special place in his heart for Balk. It was Balk who accelerated the speed on "Runaway" to make it a hit. It was Balk who encouraged Shannon's early song writing. It was Balk who brought in Maron McKenzie to help him write songs.

Yet, despite the atmosphere, Del was filled with ideas for new songs. Snuff Garrett went to the top brass at Liberty and urged them to have a talk with Shannon. He had to accept studio direction. Del was hurt. He agreed to go along with Garrett's musical ideas. This turned out to be a monumental mistake.

During this time Del made a series of phone calls to his old friend and band mate Max Crook. As Shannon wailed and moaned about the problems he had with Liberty Records, Crook had only one piece of advice. "Cut the records, Chuck," Crook remarked. Then Del and Max talked at length about the California lifestyle. Unwittingly, as a result of these phone calls, Crook moved to the Los Angeles area and went to work as a fireman. From time to time he would appear with Shannon in concert. It was Crook's advice and unfailing friendship that persuaded Shannon to honor his Liberty contract. Before he recorded his first tune for Liberty, Shannon had considered getting out of the deal, but it was a big company and he decided to give it a try.

On his first single, "The Big Hurt," Del discovered that it was mixed improperly. The noisy organ background was an attempt to recreate Max Crook's musitron sound and a trio that backed up Del often drowned out his vocals. It wasn't until the 18th take that Del announced that the record was acceptable. Then Snuff Garrett mixed down what he considered some slow and unproductive areas in the record. The result was that the sound wasn't Del Shannon. When Del heard the final cut, he was upset. This led to a minor confrontation between Garrett and Shannon. After bitter words were exchanged and acrimonious feelings built up, Garrett and Liberty Records gave in and allowed Del to master his product. After long discussions with Garrett, Del was given some freedom in the studio.

THE FAILURE OF "THE BIG HURT" AND THE REEMERGENCE OF SHANNON'S SONG-WRITING SKILLS

When "The Big Hurt" was released in March 1966, it limped onto the **Billboard Hot 100** at number 94 and quickly faded into obscurity. So Liberty decided to dust off Del's song-writing skills. He had argued with Garrett and studio brass for months about his original tunes. If Shannon wanted to write some new hits tunes, Liberty executives reasoned, then he would be given a chance.

As a result, Liberty decided to release a single containing Shannon originals "For A Little While" backed with "Hey Little Star," but this 45 failed to chart. Then Liberty released "Show Me" backed with "Never Thought I Could," and while it was one of Shannon's strongest records, it also failed to make the charts. Dan Bourgoise remembered: "Del wrote 'Show Me' which was really a strong piece for him and then when it failed, it put Del in this sort of a funk." Shannon was also surprised that his cover of Toni Fisher's "The Big Hurt" failed to chart. He couldn't figure out why these tunes didn't sell. In fact, after "The Big Hurt" promotion, Del stopped going out on the road and remained home. He took any suggestion that Liberty made about releasing records and this led to a chain of dismal covers. Such songs as the Cyrkles' "Red Rubber Ball" and Bobby Hebbs' "Sunny" were not typical Shannon tunes.

Part of the reason for Shannon's lack of commercial success was changing tastes in the music industry. As it was in this case, Liberty didn't promote Shannon's new material. Studio executives reasoned that his legion of fans from the early hit record days would continue to purchase Shannon's new 45s and LPs.

Not only were Liberty executives lazy when it came to Shannon's music but "Never Thought I Could" had already appeared as the b-side on "The Big Hurt." When it was released on the Toni Fisher cover 45 it was called "I Got It Bad." For Shannon's fans this was an unforgivable omission. Obviously, Liberty executives looked upon Shannon's material as filler.

WHAT WENT WRONG AT LIBERTY RECORDS

The Liberty Record contract was a fiasco. Del realized this, Liberty was of the same opinion. Liberty believed that Del's sound was dated. What went wrong? The answer is a complicated one. First, neither Snuff Garrett nor Leon Russell had a window into Del's song-writing mind or production direction. They were producing acts like Gary Lewis and the Playboys and this made it difficult for them to turn Shannon's music into a commercial direction.

Liberty used house producers and this gave the music a production-line quality. They didn't spend the extra money or the time to make the records tight. In contrast, Harry Balk was a careful, hit-tuned producer who spent both time and money to guarantee the proper sound.

The session musicians at Liberty were excellent ones. However, they couldn't hold a candle to the Detroit-based Royaltones. The Dennis Coffey band was not only a tight unit but had a handle on Shannon's music. The fact that Del didn't have one hit with Liberty suggests that promotional money was another problem. The Liberty brain thrust defended themselves by saying that he was through having hits. They were wrong as Shannon continued to chart sporadically after leaving Liberty.

Del With The Monkees, 1968

The real problem at Liberty was concept. Del had used background vocalists successfully on his records. Liberty refused to hire the expensive, but necessary, vocalists and instead they double tracked Del's voice. This turned out to be a huge mistake. The double tracking had Del singing on one track while the second track found him singing harmony with himself. It simply didn't work. Although Liberty allowed Del to rearrange the cover records, he seldom took the time to do so.

On the other hand, Del continued to write. The songs he composed during the Liberty years were not hits. Was it due to Shannon's declining song-writing skills? Was it due to Liberty Records' ineptitude? The answer is obvious. Liberty didn't have the production commitment to make some excellent songs, notably, "She" and "Show Me," hits.

The lack of promotion and the failure to hire a tight studio band doomed Shannon's recording efforts. "She," which was written by Tommy Boyce and Bobby Hart, was ready for the hit market, but it was quickly recorded by the Monkees who were the group of promotional choice.

At Liberty the problem was management. When the Rolling Stones' manager, Andrew Loog Oldham, cut a Del Shannon album, **Home And Away**, the executives in charge decided it wasn't suitable for the market. In June 1967, the Monterey Pop Festival had made the suits at Liberty into instant music critics. They wanted someone with a psychedelic sound, a more fashionable set of clothes, a more Beatle-like haircut and a more contemporary sound. This kind of attitude killed any chance for **Home And Away** to be released.

It was this type of thinking which prompted Del to cut a psychedelic LP, **The Further Adventures of Charles Westover**, the result was a commercial bomb. However, like many failures, this album turned into a cult item. Over the years with excessive bells and whistles in the LP, to quote Dan Bourgoise, it turned out to be the forerunner of a new type of music. Shannon demonstrated the personal touch in this LP and broke new boundaries. Unfortunately, it was 20 years before critics began recognizing the genius behind **The Further Adventures of Charles Westover**.

ON TOUR BUT ONLY FOR A MOMENT: THE CHANGES IN SHANNON'S LIFE

There was one positive aspect of the Liberty Record contract. It gave Shannon a degree of financial freedom. Del had never received a salary from a record company. Now he had one. So it was no longer necessary to tour incessantly. But there were still some lucrative package tours.

In May and June 1966, Del was part of a Dick Clark Caravan of Stars. It was a grueling 60-day tour and Steve Monahan was brought along as much for friendship as musical support. At this point in his career, Del didn't have a manager and he made his own decisions on concerts. His good friend Dan Bourgoise was in the service for six months and Del was tired of the concert trail.

As Del cut his Liberty Records, he spent more time performing in and around Southern California. His life was changing as he looked more toward producing his own material. Liberty had other ideas. Consequently, when he left Liberty, Del spent two years producing himself and other acts.

This period as a producer suggested that Shannon was much more than a performing act. He was a singer-songwriter who could produce hit records. The nature of the music business at that time was geared not to recognize Shannon's talents. "He didn't listen to other music when he was writing," Shirley Westover remarked. "He believed that it would hurt his creative process." As his wife Shirley watched Del agonize over the Liberty years, she did everything she could to bolster his confidence.

THIS IS MY BAG OR IS IT?

After a number of sessions, Liberty released an album, **This Is My Bag** (Liberty 3453) which featured mostly cover records. The album's liner notes described Del Shannon as having "the right sound and feeling to a song." The back cover silhouetted Shannon leaning against a tree. The shot was taken in the San Fernando Valley close to where Shannon lived. Liberty spent very little money recording the album. Producer, Snuff Garrett, failed to understand that American rock and roll music was going through a period of teen-oriented rockers who appealed to the bubble gum crowd. Del wasn't Bobby Vee and this was the type of artist that Garrett could produce successfully.

When Shannon's fans bought the **This Is My Bag** album, "The Big Hurt" was in rechanneled stereo and some fans wrote to Liberty complaining about this process. The cover on the **This Is My Bag** album had a picture of Del in a green corduroy coat with a matching green T-shirt. His hair was short, he looked thin and relatively happy. The songs were an odd assortment of tunes with Snuff Garrett's production and they included cover versions of Gary Lewis and the Playboys' "Everybody Loves A Clown," Lou Christie's "Lightnin' Strikes," Paul Revere and the Raiders' "Kicks," Freddy Cannon's, "Action," Bobby Goldsboro's "It's Too Late," Bob Kuban and the In Men's, "The Cheater," Roy Orbison's "Oh Pretty Woman" and a Jackie DeShannon original, "When You Walk In The Room."

Looking back on the **This Is My Bag** album, Del told Dan Bourgoise that he didn't care very much for "Action" even though it was cowritten by his good friend Tommy Boyce. Del didn't want to record the song and he didn't want it used on Dick Clark's TV show "Where The Action Is." Shannon did like some of the songs on his next album, **Total Commitment**. His cover of the Rolling Stones' "Under My Thumb" was one of his favorites. Later, as Bourgoise suggested, Del regretted not allowing Clark to use Del's version of the "Action" theme for his show.

The DeShannon song was originally recorded by the Searchers and had a distinct folk-rock quality to it. Del used the Searchers arrangement and the song was a solid one. One of the problems with the **This Is My Bag** LP was the production direction. The album sounded like the Dave Clark 5 met Del in an alley.

There were only three original songs that Shannon wrote for **This Is My Bag** but they were strong ones. "For A Little While," "Never Thought I Could," and "Hey! Little Star" were indications that Shannon's song-writing skills were still intact. Leon Russell was consulted not only on the production but the marketing of the **This Is My Bag** album and he suggested that Dick Clark's television program "Where The Action Is" was the perfect place to market the new Del Shannon. This technique failed miserably and the LP sank into the cutout bins. One day Del walked into a Northridge shopping center and saw the **This Is My Bag** album with a 99 cent sticker on it.

Because he was no longer a hit-making machine Liberty Records quickly soured on Del Shannon. They also began questioning his musical interests. After **This Is My Bag** failed to sell, Shannon produced his next single. Liberty Records sent him some memos questioning his choice of material. This was because Del covered the Rolling Stones' "Under My Thumb" and the flip side was a Shannon original, cowritten with Roy Neviett, "She Was Mine." Both tunes were commercially in line with musical tastes in the mid 1960s. Once again Liberty Records didn't feel that they had "the teen feeling."

TOTAL COMMITMENT: THE SECOND LIBERTY LP

Liberty Records prepared to release another LP, but they were uncertain of how to market Del Shannon. This time Del convinced the moguls at Liberty Records that he was capable of producing his own material. The corporate mentality at Liberty wasn't so sure, so a compromise was reached. Dallas Smith was brought in to coproduce the new album. The second Liberty album **Total Commitment** (Liberty 3479) was released in

September 1966 with Del and Smith producing an excellent LP. This album was filled with cover songs and the Liberty publicity department ignored his work.

The liner notes for **Total Commitment** were written by Del's long-time friend, manager and business partner, Dan Bourgoise. Since he had been with Shannon from the earliest days of his career, Bourgoise's notes captured the essence of the new Del Shannon. He was an artist trying to find another niche in the rapidly changing world of rock and roll music. Liberty didn't help this attempt to create a new Shannon by designing an album cover with a shadowy picture of Shannon in a white sweater with small circular lines running around the cover. On the top the LP title **Total Commitment** was offset by Shannon's name in red letters. The album proclaimed that the hits were "Under My Thumb," "Summer In The City," "The Pied Piper," "Time Won't Let Me," "Red Rubber Ball" and "Sunny." Once again, Liberty Records hadn't learned its lesson. A bevy of cover records which had recently been hits by other artists were mixed with four Shannon originals "She Was Mine," "Show Me," "What Makes You Run" and "I Can't Be True." These tunes were strong and interesting, but Liberty didn't believe that they were right for the times.

In November 1966, in an attempt to revive his old hit making days, Del went into the studio with Tommy Boyce and Bobby Hart who were then the hottest song writing and production team in the business. The only problem is that they were hot with the Monkees, and this sound hardly translated to Shannon's music. But Shannon agreed to work with Boyce and Hart, because Boyce had always been eager to produce Del. So Shannon gave his good friend a chance.

The Boyce and Hart Sessions prompted Liberty to release a single with the a side being a Boyce and Hart tune, "She," and it was backed with a Shannon original

"What Makes You Run." The song received immediate airplay but vanished from the scene when the Monkees released their own version.

The Liberty "She" session was a strange one. Max Crook was brought into the studio for his last studio recording date with Del. The airlines lost Crook's musitron and so Liberty delayed the session. For some unexplained reason the musitron ended up in LaGuardia in New York. Finally, it was sent to Los Angeles and the recording session took place. Del told Max, "Liberty can't seem to get anything right, but I love the paycheck."

As Crook looked back on the "She" session, he was proud of their collaboration. Unfortunately, it was the last recorded song that Max appeared on, along with "Stand Up" and "The House Where Nobody Lives," all recorded at the same session on Max Crook's 30th birthday. When Del Shannon released his "Live in England" album in 1973, Crook was dubbed on it.

Del and Shirley (far right) Relaxing at a Wedding Reception, 1967

When he arrived in England with his good friend Dan Bourgoise in tow, Del went onto a number of TV and radio shows to promote "She." Many of his close friends thought that the tune was being overexposed. It was during the promotion to try to make "She" a hit that a bearded young man showed up. He announced that he was Andrew Loog Oldham. "He told us that he was a big fan," Dan Bourgoise remarked. "He asked us if we wanted to come out to the car. He said that he had the new Beatle single in the trunk. He let us know that it hadn't been released. It turned out to be "Penny Lane" and "Strawberry Fields Forever." As Bourgoise and Shannon sat in Oldham's Rolls Royce listening to the new Beatle single, they prepared for the coming round of media interviews.

THE LIBERTY YEARS

In an interview with English journalist, Peter Jones, Shannon remembered that Boyce and Hart came to him with "She" as the perfect Del Shannon song. Boyce and Shannon had been friends for years and Del talked at length about his new sound, his new records and his new career direction. Shannon also lamented that his career was in trouble. The hits were over, his song writing was not as skilled and he was floundering personally. Del Shannon was unhappy after half a decade of stardom.

Despite these problems, the Boyce and Hart sessions were excellent ones. They produced two great Shannon tunes "Stand Up" and "The House Where Nobody Lives." However, Liberty refused to release these songs. It took Del 22 takes to get "Stand Up" into the can. For some reason Liberty decided that it was not a strong tune and made the same decision for "The House Where Nobody Lives." It wasn't until the CD **Del Shannon: The Liberty Years** (EMI CDP 95842-2) was released that these tunes became available to the general public. Then it was discovered that someone had failed to rewind the master tapes properly and when Liberty began preparing the CD they had difficulty restoring "Stand Up."

Yet, there were other parts of the Liberty Years which helped Shannon's talents to grow. He worked with Brian Hyland of "Itsy Bitsy, Teenie Weenie Yellow Polka Dot Bikini" fame. One day Brian Hyland came over to Del's house to write some songs with him. He slept on the couch, and six months later was still living with Shirley and Del. Shannon wrote "You Don't Love Me" and "Leaving You Behind" with Hyland, but, once again, there was no interest in promoting these songs from Liberty. Other people have recognized the Hyland-Shannon song-writing magic. When Barbara Lewis cut "How Can I Tell," she called them a dream-song team.

During his years with Liberty Records, Shannon met Andrew Loog Oldham, the Rolling Stones producer, and they talked at length about making a record. While attending a BBC show, Shannon and Oldham found that they had mutual musical interests. Oldham has just founded the Immediate label and courted Del to record for him.   Dan Bourgoise remembered, "Oldham wanted to do an album, starting out with some singles. So those sessions had Mick Jagger stopping by, John Paul Jones and Nicky Hopkins were in the studio, it was the cream of what was going on in London and suddenly we were right in the middle of it."

Andrew Loog Oldham booked studio time and began hiring musicians. He found that many of London's top musicians were interested in working with Shannon. The code name, "the England Album," was given to Shannon's new project. Led Zeppelin's John Paul Jones was brought in to play bass, Nicky Hopkins signed on as the piano player, and the backup singers were two studio veterans, P.P. Arnold and Madeline Bell.

An obscure English band, Twice As Much, had three songs that they wanted Shannon to record and they brought them to his hotel room. Oldham had put this band together as his version of Peter and Gordon. The tunes "It's My Feeling," "Life Is But Nothing" and "Easy To Say" were excellent ones, but not in Shannon's style. "It's My Feeling " was written after Twice As Much members, Andy Rose and David Skinner, had listened to American folk-rockers Spanky and Our Gang. On "Life Is But Nothing" they borrowed the horn riffs from Dusty Springfield's "Wishin' and Hoppin," and a backup chorus repeatedly chanted "You're Stoned" on "Easy To Say." It was the first time that Shannon felt like a rock and roll dinosaur. The result was three disastrous tunes which lost the Del Shannon sound in the early sea of psychedelic nonsense. If there was a plus to this time it was that Del thought that it was hip to record with Oldham.

The Immediate staff had even weaker songs. Another songwriter associated with Andrew Loog Oldham's management team, Billy Nicholls, contributed three tunes for Del. These songs, "Friendly With You," "Cut and Come Again" and "Led Along" sound like they were written for Brian Wilson and the Beach Boys. Nicholls was obviously influenced by Wilson's "Pet Sounds." Despite his problems, Del discovered that Liberty hadn't given up on him.

In 1967, after five failed singles, Liberty Records decided to make another attempt to break Shannon. They spent an unusual amount of time producing "Led Along" and backed it with "I Can't Be True" (Liberty 55961) but, once again, this record failed to chart. But the English market remained a lucrative one.

Shannon's strong following continued in the United Kingdom. Since his 1963 English tour, Shannon had been a mainstream act and Liberty prepared a 45 for this market. The English single, "Mind Over Matter" backed with "Led Along" (Liberty 10277) was hailed by **Disc, Melody Maker** and the **New Musical Express** as vintage Del Shannon. In England, Del's appeal and popularity never waned and he found himself in demand for concerts and television appearances.

When these tunes failed to chart, Liberty Records reached an all-time low in its creative approach to Shannon's career. They decided to re-record "Runaway." In a moment of corporate desperation, a suggestion was made to slow down "Runaway" and rename it "Runaway 67." To add insult to injury, Liberty added phony applause and released it with "He Cheated" (Liberty 55993). Not surprisingly, "Runaway 67" sold well in England and Europe but failed to make a dent at home. "Del wrote 'Silently' as kind of a protest to the attempt to make 'Runaway 67' a hit," Dan Bourgoise recalled. It was Oldham who pushed Shannon into re cutting "Runaway 67."

While touring England in January-February 1967, Del promoted his new single "She" while playing a series of concerts. On January 28, 1967 the **Record Mirror** called "She" a song with "a flair and commercial feel to it." One of the memorable Shannon concerts in England took place at London's Saville Theater when Brian Epstein, the Beatles' manager, booked Chuck Berry and Del Shannon for a show. As Del came out on stage he noticed the Beatles sitting in a box on his right and the Rolling Stones ensconced in a private booth on his right. Then Shannon went into one of the most energetic performances of his career.

During that February tour of England, Del appeared on the BBC's lunchtime show "Pop Inn." It was filmed on Lower Regent Street in London and was hosted by disc jockey, Keith Fordyce. With a full noon-time audience, Del came out with a Beatles style haircut, he was wearing a polka-dot shirt with an open neck and a nicely tailored waistcoat. Then Del lip-synced to his latest record, "She." After the show, Del stood outside the studio and signed autographs for an hour. It was his willingness to do as many shows as possible and sign for the fans that was half of his popularity. The other half of course was his musical genius.

When Shannon's LP **Total Commitment** was released the London-based **Record Mirror** wrote: "Shannon's rock-slanted heavy pop style comes across better on this LP than his last, 'This Is My Bag.'" The publicity tour of England and the concerts were a success. When Del Shannon and Chuck Berry appeared together at the Seville Theater, a picture in the February 25, 1967 **New Musical Express** shows a smiling and obviously happy Shannon adjusting Berry's tie.

During his years at Liberty there was a programmed schedule for 45s. There was a 90-day window between singles. The choices of cover records were strange ones. Dee Clark's "Raindrops" was not the type of cover that Del's fans would purchase. The Rolling Stones' "Under My Thumb" was as far from Shannon's style as any tune he cut in his career, but it had a great feel with Del producing the single. In Oklahoma, Washington D. C. and Baltimore, Shannon's "Under My Thumb" was a regional hit. Given a chance nationally, it might have charted.

The remake of "Runaway" lacked energy and sounded like a pale imitation of the original. "She" was a potentially great single, but Liberty failed to promote it. Surprisingly, to Liberty executives, these singles sold very well outside the United States. It wasn't just in England that Del was a star. Suddenly, he began having hits in the Far East.

THE LIBERTY SINGLES

The Big Hurt/I Got It Bad, 1966
For A Little While/Hey! Little Star, 1966
Show Me/Never Thought I Would, 1966
Under My Thumb/ She Was Mine, 1966
She/What Makes You Run, 1967
Led Along/I Can't Be True, 1967
Mind Over Matter/Led Along, 1967
Runaway '67/He Cheated, 1967
Runaway '67/Show Me, 1967
Thinkin' It Over/Runnin' On Back, 1968
Gemini/Magical Music Box, 1968
Raindrops/You Don't Love Me, 1968

DEL SHANNON IN THE PHILIPPINES:
THE BIRTH OF A NEW TYPE OF STARDOM

In the Philippines, Shannon's 45 "The Letter" backed with the b side "Silently" (Liberty 20376) became a hit with the b side "Silently" also reaching the Philippine Top 10. "The Letter" was produced by Del's old friend, Fontaine Brown, and it was a perfect cover with Del's vocal style adding a special touch. There were five singles released in the Philippines and "Sunny" went to number one at the same time that Bobby Hebbs' version reached the number two position on the **Billboard** listing.

"Strangely enough, soon after the second Liberty album was released, somebody booked me on a tour of the Philippines. When the plane landed, I got up to get off," Shannon continued. "I looked outside and there was a huge mob of people there." The reception surprised Del, he didn't know that he was a star in the Philippines. He checked into his hotel and then got set for his concert. When he went on stage there was a huge brass band. This puzzled Shannon because his music didn't feature horns. Then somebody said he had a number one hit with his cover of Bobby Hebb's "Sunny." "I told Shirley that I would take a number one hit anywhere, I didn't care what it was," Del remarked to his wife.

"The Box Tops had a hit with 'The Letter,'" Shannon continued. "So I cut the song and released it in the Philippines." The tune quickly went to number one and Shannon was all over Philippine radio plugging his latest release. "I was really unhappy that Liberty wouldn't release 'The Letter' in America," Shannon remarked to Mike McDowell.

Del Shannon In The Philippines, 1967

To support his new Philippine hits, Del Shannon toured the archipelago and was amazed at the reception to his cover records. In 1965, the Stateside Record label released a cover of Frankie Valli and the Four Seasons' "Rag Doll" backed with "Over You" (Stateside 805) and it became a staple of Philippine Top 40 radio. Suddenly, Del had hit records in the Philippines. "When I arrived there," Shannon remarked, "I had six hits in the top 10. It was amazing." Among Del's most popular Philippine releases was a Rolling Stones' set of cover tunes released in 1966 "Time Won't Let Me" backed with "Under My Thumb." (Liberty 20352). Lou Christie's "Lightnin' Strikes" backed with a Shannon original "Hey! Little Star" was also a Top 10 Philippine hit.

The fans who turned out to greet him in a 1967 tour were rabid ones. When he performed before 35,000 people a night at Rizal Stadium in Manila, the crowds asked for b-sides as well as the hits. This largely scale football stadium was the perfect venue for Del Shannon because it could accommodate his legion of Filipino fans. After performing for four nights, Shannon had drawn more than 250,000 rock fans. Among his admirers was Imelda Marcos, the wife of the President Fernando Marcos, and she went backstage and had three albums signed. In her apartment in Makati hangs a picture of her with Shannon. The only problem was that Shannon didn't always know the words to his cover records. "I had them hold up the words," Shannon remembered. "I certainly was going to take advantage of these new hits." Del also performed his American hits and came away a major star in the Philippines. Soon his records were selling all over the Far East and it became a venue that he could tour anytime he desired. The money was excellent and the respect that he received as a major American recording artist was a healing salve to Shannon's wounded ego. He simply could not buy a hit in America. So the Far East, England and Australia salvaged his career in the mid-1960s and momentarily alleviated his periodic depression.

In 1968, after cutting "Runaway '67," Del flew into Sydney, Australia for a series of concerts. The local newspapers remarked that he had a new hairdo. It was much like a Beatle haircut. He played at the Chequers Night Club high on a hill overlooking Sydney harbor. It was an engagement that Del had taken on short notice—as the regular act, Gail Martin, was sick. A well-publicized opening by American singer Buddy Greco at the Chevron Silver Slipper threatened to eclipse Shannon's show. But this was not to be the case.

When Shannon took the stage he was an instant hit. The sold-out crowds greeted Del like he was royalty. One newspaper columnist described Shannon's Chequers' concert as: "a guy standing perfectly still, slapping a guitar and rolling out songs which hit the customers like a powerhouse charge." In America he was an oldies act, but in Australia, Shannon was a reigning star. When the Chequers' crowd requested the new "Runaway '67," Del apologized for not doing it. He needed violins, he explained. As one Sydney newspaper wrote: "His thing is to stand there, guitar in hand, and with a rapid motion and finger action build up a tremendous momentum in his high, twangy voice with its country-and-western overtones."

Del loved working Chequers and remarked to a group of Australian reporters why he preferred the night club. "This is my third trip to Australia," Shannon continued. "During my first concert at the Sydney stadium the stage revolved and I almost fell off it." Then Shannon talked about the kindness of Lee Gordon during his first visit to Australia for a series of big stadium shows and he also had kind words for his second promoter, Harry M. Miller." Joe Veitch, a local Australian reporter, was impressed with Shannon's candor and spent a great deal of time extolling Del's showmanship.

Back home in the U. S., Shannon was equally forthcoming. Looking back on this part of his career, Shannon realized that he could sell a lot of cover records. "The reason I went back and did 'The Letter,'" Del told American journalists Steve Kolanjian and David Dasch, "was because I said I might as well capitalize on these cover jobs." But Shannon readily admitted that except for "Rag Doll," he didn't care for the Philippine cover records. Part of the problem was Liberty Records inept production. Shannon angrily remarked that "The Letter" couldn't be released because it was recorded in an inferior mono mix. There was a multi-track master that Liberty lost or misplaced and no one at the Hollywood Liberty offices had any idea where to find Shannon's masters.

The time in the Philippines was a positive one for Del and his wife, Shirley. They had what amounted to a second honeymoon. But with 20,000 rabid fans meeting them at the Manila airport, the trip was more a coronation of Shannon's talent. He was considered a star of such magnitude that Ferdinand Marcos, the President of the Philippines, sent a note congratulating him on his success.

LIBERTY RECORDS AND HAVING YOUR OWN PRODUCTION CREW

"When we arrived in California," Dan Bourgoise recalled, "most of the record executives wore three-piece suits. A little more than a year later they were wearing their hair long, sported psychedelic clothes and were telling you to produce yourself." The change from the staid days of 1966 into the Summer of Love and the Monterey Pop Festival of 1967 had a dramatic impact upon Shannon's career.

His recent records with Andrew Loog Oldham were considered too pop and somewhat passe by the Monterey Pop people. They told Del that he had to find his own voice. The result was that he began thinking about a psychedelic album. This was the genesis of **The Further Adventures of Charles Westover**. While this LP was still a year away, it had its gestation in the Monterey Pop Festival era.

In an attempt to make up for their past mistakes, the Liberty Records executives who now wore paisley clothes with wild colors , decided to let Shannon bring in his own production crew. This was partially due to Liberty management's inability to record Del with commercial success. He was once again a hot item in world record sales.

With English, European, Japanese and Philippine record sales doing well, Liberty Records planned another Del Shannon album. It was tentatively entitled **Home and Away**, but it was never completed and released. Looking back on the **Home and Away** LP, Shannon recalled that Andrew Loog Oldham was simply too busy to complete it.

Because of his international popularity, Del toured Japan in 1967. As a result of his popularity there, Toshihiko Uchida formed a local Del Shannon Fan club. The Japanese continued to buy Shannon's music in large numbers. They loved the covers. So Liberty intensified its pressure to have Shannon sing other people's songs.

It set a pattern of covers. This wasn't what Del intended. As always Shannon included autobiographical songs. His favorite was patterned after the Shields' 1958 hit, but retitled "He Cheated." It was not surprising that the song confessed some of his personal indiscretions.

Despite these creative spurts, by late 1968 Liberty Records had soured on Shannon. The full-blown psychedelic music revolution made him appear like an old has-been. In a monumental blow to his ego, Garrett informed Shannon he was through in the business. Nothing was further from the truth. Then just as Liberty Records and Snuff Garrett wrote off Shannon, the English came to his rescue.

Del went to London and recorded some tracks for a new English single and potentially an album. He also revived his first hit "Runaway." The prestigious English music magazine, the **Record Mirror**, wrote that Del's 1967 re-recording of "Runaway" was a smash. "If you switched on your transistor/wireless and heard someone singing a peculiar version of Del Shannon's big hit 'Runaway,' switched it off again because you bought the original, then you must be wondering who was singing it." In gleeful editorial tones the **Record Mirror** announced it was Del. The article went on to praise Andrew Loog Oldham's production and interviewed Shannon at length.

Not only was Andrew Loog Oldham the Rolling Stones producer, but he was one of the most respected people in the recording industry. As he gushed over Shannon's talent to the British press, the hurt of the Liberty years vanished. But when he went to England to record with Oldham, Del found it virtually impossible to get an album completed.

During the interview with **Record Mirror**, Del was unhappy with Oldham's busy schedule. "We never seem to get together for a long recording session," Del lamented. Shannon showed a great deal of confidence in his new songs. "About a year ago...I wasn't writing good songs," Shannon remarked. Surprisingly, Del observed that after listening to the Beatles, the Bee Gees and the Vanilla Fudge, he came up with a new song direction. "The new songs are still me, I've just changed direction," Del remarked.

Then Shannon launched into a lengthy discussion of recording studios and suggested that Olympic Studio in Hollywood was his favorite. Ever the diplomat, he needlessly praised Liberty Records for their diligence in allowing him to pursue a new musical direction. Foremost in Del's thoughts was the resurgence of his career.

THE FURTHER ADVENTURES OF CHARLES WESTOVER

To revive his sagging career, Del brought his old friend Dan Bourgoise and another friend from the Southfield, Michigan days, Fontaine Brown, and they began to work on the album which became **The Further Adventures of Charles Westover** (Liberty 7539). During the last few months of 1967 the album was prepared for a February 1968 release.

Dan Bourgoise remembered this LP, "We had a lot of fun making it and I think there were some great songs on it. But I think that we were doing what the record company wanted us to do...." Looking back on **The Further Adventures of Charles Westover**, Del remarked: "That wasn't me at all. The real Del Shannon is me when I was doing Keep Searchin'...." Despite his disclaimer, Del's attempt to create a psychedelic album made it a cult success. It wasn't a commercial LP and soon was found in the dollar cut-out bins.

The **Further Adventures of Charles Westover** is an album which defines Shannon's studio genius. The single from this album, "Thinking It Over" backed with "Runnin' On Back" (Liberty 56018) sank from sight amidst the glow of psychedelic hits. The liner notes for **The Further Adventures of Charles Westover** were written by Ron Koslow who later went on to become one of the creative forces behind Beauty and the Beast. In the late 1960s, Koslow was a freelance writer who specialized in the Los Angeles pop scene.

The forces surrounding San Francisco's Haight Ashbury and the general influence of psychedelic music had an impact upon Shannon. He hoped that **The Further Adventures of Charles Westover** would be recognized as a creative concept LP along the lines of the Beatles' **Sgt. Pepper** album. In April 1968, a second single, appropriately titled, "Gemini" backed with "Magical Musical Box" (Liberty 56036) was as advanced as the Beatles' "Sgt. Pepper's Lonely Hearts Club Band" or Brian Wilson's "Smile" songs. But Del Shannon was remembered as the singer who recorded "Runaway," "Little Town Flirt" and "Hats Off To Larry." The industry and the general public didn't accept a psychedelic Shannon.

The summer of 1968 was another of many turning points in Shannon's career. The brass at Liberty once again reversed their field on putting out Del Shannon records. Now they decided that the old Del should turn out records. What this meant is that he was brought into the studio to cut a remake of Dee Clark's classic "Raindrops" and he began writing songs with Brian Hyland.

After he came to California, Hyland showed up at Del's house to write songs and didn't leave for six months. The results were some amazing tunes showcasing Hyland and Shannon's song writing skills. The Hyland-Shannon tunes included "You Don't Love Me" and "Leaving Me Behind." But the 45 "Raindrops" backed with "You Don't Love Me" (Liberty 56070) failed to chart and Shannon was ready to give up on Liberty Records.

After writing songs with Brian Hyland, Del decided to produce his blonde-haired, teen-idol friend. The pairing of Shannon and Hyland was an instant hit as Del's production of Hyland's "Gypsy Woman" released on the Uni label went to number three on the **Billboard** pop chart during its 13 weeks in 1970. This was the beginning of another career for Del Shannon. He went on to discover Smith and help them take "Baby It's You" into the top 10. Shannon was far from through as a performer, songwriter and producer. However, he was finished with Liberty Records. It was an experiment gone awry.

Looking back on **The Further Adventures of Charles Westover**, Dan Bourgoise summed it up the best, "We threw in too many kitchen sinks on this album." Despite the problem of not having an abundance of hit records, the Liberty years were important ones in Shannon's career. He demonstrated that he could still make hit records. In the studio it was obvious to everyone that Shannon was a producer. He cut through the essentials which was necessary for good production. With this in mind, Del decided to take a few years off from the touring business to become a producer.

THE LIBERTY YEARS YIELD SOME STRANGE INFLUENCES

The Liberty years were strange ones. Yet, they yielded some interesting music and extraordinary influences. When the Swedish group, the Shanes, appeared on Norwegian television in 1966 performing "Never Thought I Could" and "The Big Hurt" became a Top 10 Australian hit. Del was an international star. The Liberty years were ones where Del realized that he had to retain his sense of creative independence. During the next two decades, Shannon would have peaks and valleys of song writing success but because of the arbitrary manner in which Liberty executives treated him he retained his sense of independence.

BIBLIOGRAPHICAL SOURCES

The liner notes by Steve Kolanjian and David Dasch to **Del Shannon: The Liberty Years**, EMI Legends of Rock N Roll Series, CD P-7-95842-2 is a useful introduction to the early Liberty Record years. While performing in San Francisco in the course of an interview, Dennis Diken of the Smithereens suggested that Del's Liberty Records had an enormous impact upon his band. In 1987, Del went into the studio with the Smithereens and found that they had played his Liberty Records when they began their recording career. An excellent review of this CD is Dawn Eden's in **Goldmine**, July 12, 1991, p. 114.

A double CD rerelease **Del Shannon, This Is My Bag/ Total Commitment**, Beat Goes On Records 1996, contains two albums. The liner notes by Roger Dopson are first rate and Dan Bourgoise adds an interesting after word. This CD also contains some rare photos and reproduces some key articles. The re-mastering of the original material makes this one of Shannon's best rereleases.

Mike McDowell, "The Del Shannon Story, Part 2: The Further Adventures of Charles Westover," **Blitz**, number 42, March-April, 1982, pp. 16-18 was important to this chapter.

An article by Norman Jopling in **Record Mirror**, October 21, 1967 contained some revealing Shannon quotes. Other **Record Mirror** stories on Shannon appeared on January 28, 1967 and February 11, 1967. Also see the **Newcastle Journal**, February 8, 1967 for an article on Shannon's appearance in that English town. The **New Musical Express** on February 4 and 25, 1967 had short stories on Shannon's new album.

A brief interview with Leon Russell while he was waiting to perform in Chino, California in 1997 helped to clarify much of the early Liberty years. Max Crook, Dan Bourgoise, Shirley Westover, Jody Westover, Kym Wilkerson, Craig Westover, Brian Young and Fontaine Brown added material to clarify this period in Shannon's life.

Publications of the Del Shannon Appreciation Society from 1971 to 1977 facilitated the completion of this chapter.

Brian Young, "Dan Bourgoise Interview Notes," manuscript in possession of the author was a key source.

See the "Del Shannon Follower," a British fanzine, for information on Del in this period. David Ritchie of Sydney, Australia, provided an undated scrapbook of newspaper clippings helpful to this chapter. Brian Young, "My Thoughts on Years at Liberty Records," four-page manuscript in possession of author, was a major source in analyzing why the Liberty years were both a musical success and an commercial failure.

For Bones Howe see, Eric Olsen, Paul Verna and Carlo Wolff, **The Encyclopedia of Record Producers** (New York, 1999), pp. 333-335.

On Chuck Berry's influence see, Howard A. DeWitt, **Chuck Berry: Rock 'n' Roll Music** (Ann Arbor, 1985), Chapters 5-7.

The Robbs with Dan Bourgoise

10: LOST IN THE MUSICAL OZONE, 1971-1977

'I got tired of the rock star life. It was hard to write songs. I needed some time off. So I got lost in the musical ozone of the mid-1970s" Del Shannon

In the early and mid-1970s Del Shannon was lost in the musical ozone. "I don't think that Del took the changes very well in the music industry,"Andrew Loog Oldham, the Rolling Stones' producer remarked. Shannon was searching for a hit record as the industry became increasingly oriented to heavier sounds and a disco beat. The concept record had been around for a time and Del had failed to chart with his concept LP, **The Further Adventures of Charles Westover**. It was not Del Shannon's style. "I felt like I was on Mars in the mid-1970s," Del told his old friend Charlie Marsh, "but I knew the changes were temporary."

When he signed with Liberty Records, Del envisioned the old hit magic returning and he was confident that his sound would once again dominate the airwaves. But this was not to be the case. The mercurial nature of the music business thrust Shannon into the background. Suddenly, he was an oldies but goodies artist. There was still a lot of excellent new music in Shannon, but it would take some time to come out.

CHANGING STYLES AND TASTES: THE ENGLISH VERSION

Changing styles, new musical tastes and the inability of Liberty Records to properly record and market his music created a career crisis. The old Del Shannon sound had vanished in America, at least in the hit record sense. In England and Australia, Shannon remained an important musical act. When Del arrived in London, the greeting from his fans was rabid.

"We rented a house in Manchester for six weeks and the whole family got to see that part of England," Shirley Westover remarked. "It was a special time for the family and we really enjoyed the countryside." Shirley and her children, Craig, Kym and Jody spent some idyllic times in the United Kingdom in the 1970s. Since he was relaxed and at ease with his family, Del's shows were superb ones.

When he toured England his performances at Dingwall's, a club in the London suburb of Camden Town, Del was treated like rock and roll royalty. The English music newspapers, the **New Musical Express**, **Disc** and **Melody Maker**, wrote effusively about

Shannon's pioneering sound. Shannon remained a proven songwriter, a respected producer and a fine performer. Eventually, in 1972, Del signed with United Artists in England and the English arm of UA was eager to pair Del with local artists.

Del Shannon in England

There were a number of English artists who hoped to produce Shannon and write songs with him. Del recorded three tracks with Electric Light Orchestra, co-founder, Jeff Lynne. The first time Del went into the studio for a lengthy recording session with Lynne on December 27, 1973, they completed some songs, which they referred to as "the dead set." This was a take off on the use of dead and deadly in song titles.

But the cuts were not ready for release. Only one was released in the U. K. and the rest were deemed unsuitable for commercial purposes. These tracks included "Broken Down Angel," "The Deadly Game," "Alive But Dead" and "The Ghost." They weren't typical Del Shannon songs and United Artists wasn't sure what to do with them. "The Ghost" was released in Australia as the b-side to Shannon's cover version of the Shades of Blue hit, "Oh How Happy" (Interfusion K5439). Although the United Artist period was one of commercial stagnation, Shannon continued his musical growth. His old friend Steve Monahan was working as a producer on these songs along with Jeff Lynne of the Electric Light Orchestra. Part of his resurgence was due to a new backup band, the Robbs.

DEL SHANNON 1971 ENGLISH TOUR
October 25, Del arrives at London's airport at 10:30 a.m.
The Leo Clayment Agency, 112 Hounsditch, London promoted this tour

October 25-30, Del rehearses and does press interviews.

October 31-November 6, Wookey Hollow, 33 Belmont Rd., Liverpool and also appearances at Allison's. This private English club charged twenty-five pence for a table reservation and fifty pence for a membership. Admission was between thirty and fifty pence.

November 7-13, Top Hat, Spennymoor. At this club Del was contracted to perform a late show and the promoter had lined up seven different clubs for the early show.

November 15-21, Excel Bowl, Middlesborough and Stockton Fiesta. The Excel Bowl charged sixty to ninety pence with a free table booking if you arrived before 8:30 p. m. Del went on stage at 9:30 p.m. The Fiesta Club had a cover, which varied from thirty five to ninety five pence. Del took the stage at 11:30 p.m.

November 22, The Jimmy Young Show, BBC Radio 1. An announcement from the Del Shannon Appreciation Society suggested that many other radio shows were in the works. However, none were specifically identified.

November 24-27, Uncle Tom's Cabin, School Street, Darwen, Lancashire. Del took the stage at 11:30 p.m. There was a sliding admission of thirty to sixty pence with no membership required.

November 28, Tudor House, Maidstone, Kent.

November 29, Del boarded the plane for New York.

During this phase of Shannon's career he hooked up with a young band, the Robbs, who had the looks and the sound of the Monkees. They were young, good-looking, and musically adept and Dee Robb was a natural engineer as far as knowing what Del wanted in sound.

The tours that Del Shannon undertook in the 1970s were financially lucrative because he didn't carry a backup band. He used pickup musicians and still was able to please his British audiences. The London-based Harry Sellers Agency booked Del into clubs, which sold out, to his legion of British fans. The John Maxflare Band backed Shannon on the 1972 tour and they played his hits with skill. Henry Sellers did an excellent job of promoting the tour and he booked Shannon into venues where he made a good wage. There were other indications that Del was speaking to a broader audience.

One of the signs that Shannon's music was being taken seriously took place when the movie "Dusty and Sweets McGee" came out in 1971 with a soundtrack featuring Shannon's "Runaway" as well as Van Morrison's "Into the Mystic" and Little Eva's "Locomotion." This was a semi-documentary on the Los Angeles drug scene and while it never found a mainstream audience, "Dusty and Sweets McGee" became an underground classic.

Del And Shirley, 1983

THE 1972 ENGLISH TOUR

During the 1972 tour, in a note to Graham Gardner, there were comments from Del and Shirley about how much they loved England. What Del told Gardner was that the British audiences knew all his songs and appreciated some of the more obscure tunes. This tour featured the song "The Answer To Everything" which Del dedicated to his English audiences.

In the midst of the 1972 English tour, Del went into B.B.C.'s Maida Vale Studio in West London to cut some tunes for a radio broadcast. With the Maxflare Band providing excellent backup, Shannon was in exceptionally good voice. He cut "Keep Searchin' (We'll Follow The Sun)," "Hats Off To Larry," "Kelly," and "What's A Matter Baby."

When Del appeared for a week at Birmingham's Barbarella club, a member of the Del Shannon Appreciation Society, Jim Dunscombe, showed up with nine albums. He got them signed and had a long talk with Del. When Dunscombe received an invitation to be Shannon's guest at the Princess club, where he would record tracks for a live album, he was ecstatic.

The last night of the tour at the Princess and Georgian Club in Manchester, Shannon recorded some live cuts for a future album. The crowd stood and cheered "Two Kinds of Teardrops" and Del was able to cut a half a dozen other tunes for future release.

DEL SHANNON 1972 ENGLISH TOUR
October 29-November 4, Allisons and Wooky Hollow Clubs, Liverpool, Lancashire

November 5-November 11, The Sente, Peterlee, County Durham

November 9, B.B.C. Birmingham, Members of Del Shannon Appreciation Society Appear

November 12-November 18, Barbarella's Club, Birmingham, Warwickshire

November 19, The Copperfield Club, Bolton, Lancashire

November 20-November 25, The Talk of the South Club, Southend, Essex

November 26, The Cosmo Club, Carlisle, Cumberland

November 27, A Day Off

November 28, The Thornton and Father Time Clubs, Bradford, Yorkshire

November 29, The Garrick Club, Leigh, Liverpool, Lancashire

November 30, The Viking Club, Goole, Yorkshire and The Aquarius Club, Lincoln Yorkshire

December 1-2, The Princess and Georgian Clubs, Manchester, Lancashire

---

The English often did an excellent job picking out some of Shannon's better music. When Waylon Jennings released "I've Got Eyes For You," few Americans realized that it was a Shannon-Brian Hyland tune. In the 1970s, the die-hard loyalty of the British fans was an important part of Shannon's continued career. He could always depend upon the United Kingdom to receive his music warmly.

Del And Shirley With The Kids, 1978

When Del returned to California for Christmas, he was exhausted. The road was no longer any fun and he was at wits end over his career. "I suppose it will be England once again," Del remarked to Shirley over Christmas dinner. "He longed to have another American hit," Shirley remembered.

One of the highlights of Del's European tour occurred after he left England. On Saturday morning, December 30, 1972, disc jockey Brian McKenzie played "Ginny In The Mirror" and "Don't Gild The Lily, Lily" while wishing Del a happy birthday. "When I heard about Brian's gesture," Shannon remarked to Charlie Marsh," it reinforced how nice the British have been to me and my music." This love affair with England would continue.

One English fan lamented that most of Shannon's concerts were in the north of England. Since 1967, he had appeared in the southwest at Paignton only once. What this suggests is that most of Del's concerts and club dates were in Liverpool, Manchester and Carlisle and these areas brought him national attention.

The Del Shannon Appreciation Society also publicized odd releases. A German United Artists single with "Runaway" on the a-side and a cover of the Cascades' "Rhythm of the Rain" as the flip side was sold in large numbers in the United Kingdom.

IN THE RECORDING STUDIO IN 1972

In 1972, Del went into the Robbs' Cherokee studio and cut "Early In The Morning" backed with "What's A Matter Baby." Both songs were well produced and Del was happy with his voice. There were some other gems. On "I Go To Pieces" Del used a rhythm and blues voice and he wrote on the tape: "10/3/72-a rhythm and blues cut." It was a two-track final mix of the master. Shannon hoped that it would be released as a single. It remains to this day an unreleased track. Shannon never seemed to feel his version of "I Go To Pieces" to be good enough for commercial release. He still struggled with the thought that he gave up a self-penned hit to Peter and Gordon.

Although he had little chart success in 1972, Shannon was once again making good music. The amount of time that Shannon spent in the recording studio was legendary. He continually cut new songs and did his best to build a huge catalog of commercial material. The end result was a cache of unreleased songs that he had trouble peddling to the record labels. This not only frustrated Del but led to frequent arguments with the various record labels.

ENGLAND ONCE AGAIN: THE JUNE, 1973 ENGLISH TOUR

In late May 1973, Del and Shirley arrived in London for a two and a half-month tour. The bookings were so strong that the tour was extended to three months and the guarantees were raised by as much as 25 percent. Shannon's popularity continued unabated in the United Kingdom and there was new fan interest in his music.

Shirley Westover remembered the kindness of the fans. They had a genuine interest in his growing family. She was also impressed with the family atmosphere in northern England. Because he had his children with him, Del rented a house in Manchester. He could travel by car or train an hour and be at most of the clubs he would perform in during the next 10 weeks. Craig was 16 when they went to England. The British newspaper, **Music Week** in its June 23, 1973 issue, made a point of Shannon's family and new-found maturity.

Surprisingly, **Music Week** reported that Shannon was studying to become a ventriloquist. The magazine didn't realize that Del was chiding them for reporting that he was an artist from the 1960s desperately trying to fit into the 1970s. Throughout his life Shannon believed that he was a contemporary artist and he informed the British press that his best songs were still ahead of him.

In the English market United Artists re-released "Kelly" as a single. In Liverpool, Blackpool, Manchester and Birmingham, Del Shannon's records sold well. "Kelly" was a hit in these markets and the popularity of Shannon's b-sides was something of a curse. He wanted to record new music but the old b-sides were discovered and became hits.

One of the strangest English television shows that Del appeared on was "The Old Grey Whistle Test" where on June 19,1973, Del performed "Louise, Louise" and "Kelly" backed up by the Impalas. For years video segments of this program have circulated among fans and the show demonstrates the breadth of Shannon's talent.

Del Shannon: At Home in California

When Shannon played the Lancashire countryside in the summer of 1973 the tours were sold out. The English loved Del's cover versions of Roy Orbison's "Crying" and Jimmy Jones' "Handy Man." This seemed to depress Shannon more than encourage him. He wanted to cut new songs, not sell the old ones. But, as he told Charlie Marsh, it was better to sell something than nothing at all.

Yet, the tours were grueling. British promoter, Henry Sellers, booked Shannon into small venues, which quickly sold out in the countryside and provided Del with excellent press. Del had to work hard each night and travel incessantly. Shannon never complained and did everything in his power to please his British fans. This included full cooperation with a professional fan club that looked out for Del and recorded his every move.

The Del Shannon Appreciation Society was ecstatic about every one of his tours. They released detailed information sheets on Del's concerts, his private life and his future recording activity. A sample from the DSAS read: "Well, here we are, smack bang in the middle of another great tour by Del and what a success this one is turning out to be," the fan club president wrote.

It was not just the fan club which helped Shannon's career. The **New Musical Express, Melody Maker** and **Disc** were the three premier British music newspapers and they were all friendly to his sound. "I think that Del Shannon had a musical integrity that the British press recognized," rock critic Ray Coleman recalled, "and he obviously had a tremendous influence upon the Merseyside sound.

In response to the strong fan interest, an ad in the **New Musical Express** proclaimed June 18-23 Del Shannon Week. U.A. Records and the Del Shannon Appreciation Society-with the hope of selling a lot of records-placed the ad. However, the album was relegated to the cut out bin. This ad led to some television appearances for Shannon. He appeared on the "Old Grey Whistle Test" on BBC 2 TV on June 19, 1973 performing a new song "Louise, Louise" and he also sang his recent single "Kelly." The fan reaction was, as always in England, a strong one. Radio One's "Scene and Heard" program featured "Runaway" to commemorate Shannon's visit to the United Kingdom. The "Old Grey Whistle Test" was a strong show as Del came out with a cowboy hat in great humor and rocked with the backup group, the Impalas.

Del Shannon in England, late 1960s

On June 25, 1973, Del made an appearance on the "Scene and Heard" program for a lengthy interview and spent most of the time plugging the new single "Kelly."

The reviews for Shannon's recent album **Live In England** were positive ones and the sales were superb in the United Kingdom. Much of the material was old songs and Del made it clear in a number of interviews that he was bothered by the oldies concept. He wanted to come back with some new music.

Shannon's family life was at an all-time high during the tour. His wife, Shirley, and the kids, Craig, Kym and Jody, came along on the tour and everyone had a great time. Leone, Del's mother, joined them and the tour turned into a nice family vacation. "I never saw Charles happier than he was in the early 1970s," Leone recalled.

In the midst of this euphoria there were some problems. Shannon agreed to allow the Cotour label to release an album. Then Del had second thoughts about the deal and the Del Shannon Appreciation Society urged its readers to boycott the LP.

DEL SHANNON'S 1973 ENGLISH TOUR

May 27-June 2, Cooperfield Club and Broadway Club, Failsworth

June 3-9, Rosegrove Club, Burnley and Talk of the North Eccles

June 10, TBA

June 14-16, Barbarella's Club, Birmingham

June 17-23, Wookey Hollow and Alisons, Liverpool

June 24-30, Barrick Club Leigh and Fagins Club, Manchester

July 1, 1973 La Dolce Vita Club, Birmingham

July 5-8, Tour of Spain and TV Appearances

July 13-15, U.S. Military Bases, Naples

July 18-22, TBA One Nighters

July 23, Townsman Club, Swansea

July 30-August 4, 1973 Circus Tavern, Purfleet, near Tilbury, Essex

August 5-10, 1973 Fiesta Club, Stockton on Tees

While Shannon was on tour in England in 1973, his record companies began to squabble with each other. As a result there were some strange record releases. When United Artists released "What's The Matter Baby" it was as a result of U.A.'s threat to Del to release some old records. So Shannon went into the studio and cut the tune. United Artists told Del that they wanted to release the record at the same time as the

Live In England album. Then, after Shannon had spent considerable time and was under undue pressure, United Artists released an old record. The 45 "Kelly" backed with "Coopersville Yodel." Shannon was not pleased about it. United Artists showed little concern for his future and were simply trying to take as much money as possible out of the English market.

ANDREW LOOG OLDHAM AND THE ROLLING STONE CONNECTION

There were many English groups eager to work with Shannon and he was flattered when the Rolling Stones' producer Andrew Loog Oldham offered to produce a Shannon album. Oldham was only one of many English musical giants who hoped to bring him back to the mainstream of the rock music marketplace.

By working with Rolling Stones producer, Andrew Loog Oldham, as well as Dave Edmunds, Brinsley Schwartz and Jeff Lynne, Shannon maintained his career despite the cataclysmic changes in the music business. In 1974, Del went to Wales where he recorded at Dave Edmunds' home studio, known as the Rockfield Studio. After laying down the vocal tracks one night at Edmunds recording facility, Shannon left the next day and Dave then placed the instrumental tracks in the appropriate places. The two excellent versions of "The Music Plays On." One was a country flavored tune and the other one was more rock-oriented and commercial. The second cut was the one released in 1978 on the **And The Music Plays On** album.

Throughout the 1970s, Del toured the world and there was an increased demand for his music. He also maintained his lifelong friendship with Max Crook who was working for the Thousand Oaks Fire Department. Max continued to write and record in his home studio. Del would drive out and spend some nights with Max and his wife and this helped him to maintain a steady writing and recording pace during the 1970s.

As a result of the new interest in Del's career, he decided to record a live album. But it wasn't really a live album. It was a pseudo-live LP and Andrew Loog Oldham's idea was to create the original Shannon rock and roll sound. This turned out to be a mistake in judgement. Recalling the experience for Australian radio, XXXY, Del commented about the live LP: "That was his idea (Andrew Loog Oldham). The truth is, after we recorded it and I did the vocals and everything, I went back to Los Angeles. He flew to L. A. later, and played it for me. I asked, 'Where did the clapping come from?' He said (in a British tone) 'Twas the Orchestra." Del was shocked that the orchestra would clap like a live audience. To make the story even stranger, Del had to fly back to London to end the final words to the live LP. He recorded "Thank you." That became the last phrase necessary in completing the album.

In 1973, the oldies centered **Live In England**, a Liberty album, sold well in England and Australia but quickly found its way to the cut out bins in America. Del loved to spend time in the studio and he continued to tape new songs throughout the 1970s.

In December 1973, American rock critic Greg Shaw saw Shannon live at a taping of the television show "In Concert" and he raved about Del's performance. "He was great," Shaw wrote the English fan club. "His whole family was there, wife and daughters, and although the audience wasn't that large, it was an electrifying show." Shaw concluded that he believed that Del would once again become a star.

During the 1970s Del's appearance began changing as he grew a beard, lost weight and became a jogger. He had struggled his entire life with alcohol and depression and during this period he began reassessing his life. Despite his good intentions, Del didn't join AA until 1978.

He also gave a series of very revealing newspaper interviews when he was in England. As Karen and Richard Carpenter took England by storm in a series of highly successful concerts, Shannon was asked his opinion about the best selling American pop duo. "I think that they are one of the biggest draws around and they probably make a lot of money," Shannon remarked to a **Record Mirror** reporter. "Musically, I think they're very clever...but I think 'Jambalaya' is an insult to Hank Williams."

Shortly after this interview, Shannon began a month-long tour of England, interrupted by a five-day vacation in Spain from June 30 through July 4. He toured in some of his favorite spots appearing at Sheffield's "Fiesta Club," Bailey's in Liverpool, Haney and Blackburn, and he also had a large crowd for his Warren Country Club concert in Stockport. These concerts in small clubs were filled to capacity for Shannon's performances.

One of the strangest interviews during 1974 occurred when the Australian magazine **Disc and Tape Review** in its March 1974 issue pressed Del on retirement. He was surprised by the question. "Retire," Shannon responded. "The idea scares me to death." The article continued by describing Shannon's month-long tour of Australia and erroneously the Australian journalist suggested that Shannon had not been touring for the past four years. This article concluded that his recent English tour had led to the **Live In England** LP which they suggested "contains all his hits from the 60s...." The purpose of the article was a mystery but it was press coverage.

The English were in the vanguard of moving Del Shannon's career back into a hit making direction. Not only did the **New Musical Express**, **Melody Maker** and **Disc** rave about his 45s but they supported his tours. For Del it was a mixed blessing. He loved traveling to England. The lifestyle was slower and the fans were adoring. But he found the ritual of playing in small clubs and out of the way venues confining. At least in an artistic sense. Del was happy about the paydays and believed that he could always maintain his career in England.

To his friends and fans throughout the United Kingdom, Shannon confessed that he desperately wanted another hit record. It was frustrating for him to make excellent music and not have it hit the **Billboard Hot 100**. Del was a realist and he knew that changing musical tastes trapped some artists. He vowed to continue on and look for this elusive hit record. Perhaps he could find it in an English tour.

ENGLAND ONCE AGAIN: 1974

In May and June 1974, Shannon toured Great Britain in what seemed to be a never-ending string of small club dates. His English fan club was very active, the pirate radio stations and the B.B.C. all continued to play Del's music and praise his innovative falsetto vocals.

DEL SHANNON ENGLISH CLUB TOUR, 1974

May 31-June 1, Barbarellas, Birmingham

June 2-8, Fiesta Club, Sheffield

June 9-15, Batley Variety Club, Sheffield

June 16-22, Fiesta Club, Stockton

June 23-29, Garrick, Leigh and Fagins, Manchester

June 30-July 4, Holiday in Spain

July 5-6, Edinburgh

July 7-13, Baileys, Liverpool

July 14-20, Baileys, Hanley

July 21, Cooperfields, Bolton

July 24, Willows, Salford

July 25, Warren Country Club, Stockport

July 26-27, Hull and Filey

July 28, Baileys, Blackburn

ON TOUR IN AMERICA, 1971-1975

During the early 1970s, the constant American tours were becoming monotonous. In the early 1970s, the Holiday Inn chain booked Shannon for a series of shows. When he played these concerts, a local band backed him. One of the strangest pairings took place in Newburg, New York, where Jimmy Sturr backed up Shannon, a well-known Grammy winning polka artist. The result was that Del's show had the sound of a polka band.

After this show Del met Dennis Kelemen and his wife and talked at length about the frustration of being constantly on the road. They went to his room and listened to the **Live In England** album. Kelemen loved it but was depressed because Del appeared so lonely. It was obvious that life on the road was not a picnic.

There is no doubt that Shannon missed his family while on the road. He loved to work in his home studio, known affectionately as the Mole Hole, and he had a zeal for family life.

AT HOME WITH DEL SHANNON IN THE 1970s:
A LOOK AT THE FAMILY SIDE

In the early 1970s the house at 10821 Melvin in Northridge was the center of some of Del's most creative music. He had the garage converted to a studio. In the garage there was all the necessary recording equipment. Del's stereo equipment, a desk, a vibrating reclining chair and a couch that made into a bed which allowed him to record day and night.

He called it the Mole Hole because there were no windows in it. Del called the tree outside the Mole Hole the pee tree because he would use it instead of going into the bathroom.

Jody, Del's thirteen-year-old daughter, remembers that the sounds from the studio kept her awake. "Dad," Jody would holler, "can you turn it down? I can't sleep." Del would respond: "It's my job, this is what I have to do for a living."

"During the 1970s, Del would sit in that room for months and create," Shirley remembered. Bobby Hart, Tommy Boyce, Dan Bourgoise, the Robbs, Brian Hyland and his other friends would come to Del's house and they would take Del's tapes and listen to them in the desert. Del loved to ride his motorcycle in the desert and it was here that he often played his new music. Del would call the boys and tell them to come for a jet ride with music. "I was never able to take that jet ride," Shirley recalled. Del's mother, Leone, loved the jet ride and she was often seen on the back of Del's motorcycle riding speedily through the California hills and desert.

While living in Northridge, the Robbs were always at the house. So were Tommy Boyce and Bobby Hart. One night the British stage music giant, Tim Rice, came and they all had dinner. Tim was an admirer of Chuck's and they went out and spent much of the night in the Mole Hole. Dan Bourgoise was there and Steve Monahan. Shirley used Tim Rice's limo to go to Ralph's Supermarket for some food. "Those were wonderful days," Shirley recalled.

Del Shannon in 1975

DEL SHANNON: ON TOUR IN 1975 AND
A RENEWED INTEREST IN THE RECORDING PROCESS

Finally, in 1975 there was renewed interest in Shannon as a recording artist. Island Records, with its strong British management connection, believed that it could once again break Shannon in the record market. Island held lengthy and detailed discussions with Shannon and a decision was made to cover the Zombies' hit "Tell Her No." The finished version was a bland cover; Del didn't seem to have his heart in it. This is strange because Del loved the song and it was his idea to record it. Once again the recording process didn't go his way. But in England, Australia and the Philippines "Tell Her No" backed with "Restless" sold very well. Once again Island, like other record labels, wasn't as interested in Shannon's new and original songs. "I think Island saw me as an oldies artist," Del remarked to a British fan. This not only depressed him but he continued to believe in his talent. Shannon began writing songs with Jeff Lynne and "Cry Baby Cry" backed with "In My Arms Again" brought Shannon's talent back into the spotlight. Unfortunately, record buys ignored the 45 and Island did little to promote it.

Del had his own ideas about cover records. He took an acetate of a cover of Phil Phillips' "Sea of Love" to the Island executives. They listened to it and passed on what they termed "an oldies hit." But Del persisted and the "Sea of Love" cover was recorded at the Muscle Shoals, Alabama studio, with producer Steve Smith. This version was never released and Del re-cut it with Tom Petty six years later and it

226

became a hit. The Muscle Shoals rhythm section backed him and "Amanda" and "Rayleen" were also cut. In 1982, Shannon had the last laugh when "Sea of Love" went to number 33 on the **Billboard** Top 40.

Del Shannon: The Island Record Look

The Muscle Shoals connection was an invigorating one for Shannon. The fabled Music Shoals recording atmosphere blended pop, country, gospel, blues and roots rock and roll. When he toured England, local musicians told Del about Arthur Alexander's "You Better Move On" and how it had defined the Muscle Shoals sound. So when Shannon arrived in the area he was transfixed by its historical image. The Wilson Pickett hits had been recorded there, as were Percy Sledge's hits. Recording in Muscle Shoals seemed like a good idea and this recording atmosphere provided Del's last **Billboard** Top 40 hit.

One of the most interesting songs from this period is "In My Arms Again" which was cut in three different versions in three separate recording studios. What Del was looking for was a different recording atmosphere. One was cut at the Robbs' rural Cherokee Ranch, the second at their Los Angeles based Cherokee Studio and the final version was completed at the Warner Brothers Nashville studio.

Because of the renewed interest in Shannon's career, he was once again in demand for European concert tours. Del preferred to perform for those who had been loyal to him. So in June, 1975, he began one of his usual British and Scottish tours.

Del Shannon June 1975 English-Scottish Tour

June 8, Palace Lido, Douglas, Isle of Man

June 12, Warren Country Club, Stockport

June 13, Coventry Chrysler Club, Coventry

June 14-20, A Week Tour of Scotland

June 24, Garrick Theater, Leigh

June 25, Barbarellas Club, Birmingham

June 26, Morecombe Bowl, Morecombe

June 27, Camelot Club, Taunton, Somerset

June 28, St. Neotts and St. Ives, Cornwall (double club booking)

June 29, Kings Club, Canvey Island, Essex

June 30, Theatre Club, Wakefield

June 6-12, Bunnies Club, Cleethorpes

The 1975 British tour was an unqualified success. Once again Henry Sellers did an excellent job booking Del into clubs that he could sell out and he received an inordinately positive press reception. Ron Clark's Del Shannon News Service helped to popularize the tour and hyped Shannon's Island release of the old Zombie hit "Tell Her No." One piece of bad news from the Del Shannon News Service was that they would no longer sell mail order copies of Shannon's records. Ron Clark offered as an explanation the difficulty of purchasing Del's records for resale. The frequent change in labels and the small number of Shannon discs pressed were cited as reasons for this policy.

TOURING, RECORDING AND FINDING
ANOTHER HIT NICHE, 1976

In 1976 Shannon once again planned a tour which began in a club near his former home in Southfield, Michigan, and after 12 performances in the United States and Canada, he traveled to England for a series of concerts. From March 30 through June 26, 1974, Del played this grueling concert schedule. The high point took place on May 14-15, 1976, when he opened the British tour in Manchester at the Garrick Club.

After just three days performing in England, Del went on B.B.C. radio for a special program. The remainder of the tour was in small clubs and was highly successful. Shannon's personal performing style brought him a legion of new fans. When he finished this tour with four nights at the Batley Variety Club, Shannon was approached to continue his tour of England. He declined as he was tired from constant public appearances.

The first signs of Shannon's fatigue and dissatisfaction with the rock and roll world surfaced in 1976. He was having trouble finding a new hit sound and the wear and tear of the road was taking its toll. Yet, Del continued to sign contracts for lucrative club date tours. In England, he was always assured of a large audience and positive media coverage.

DEL SHANNON'S 1976 AMERICAN AND ENGLISH-SCOTTISH TOUR

March 30-April 4, Golden Spur, Southgate, Michigan
April 5, Fargo Civic Auditorium, Fargo, North Dakota
April 6, Grand Forks Armory, Grand Forks, North Dakota
April 7, Civic Auditorium, Aberdeen, North Dakota
April 8, Huron Auditorium, Huron, North Dakota
April 9, Watertown Auditorium, Watertown, South Dakota
April 12-15, Town and Country Club, Winnipeg, Canada
April 16, Camp Shiloh, Shiloh, Canada
May 13, Flight to London
May 14-15, Garrick Club, Leigh and Valentines
May 16, Kings Country Club, Easbourne
May 17, B.B.C. Radio Appearance
May 19, Kings Club, Ilford, Essex
May 20, Unspecified Club, Lancashire
May 21, Sands Club and Top Hat, Spennymoor (double club booking)
May 23, Haven Club, Whitehaven
May 24, Unspecified Club, Manchester
May 26-29, Blighty's Club, Farnworth
May 30-June 5, One Nighters, Scotland
June 6-12, Bunnies Club, Cloothorpes
June 15-19, Nite Spot Club, Bedford
June 22, U.S.A.F. Base, Bontwaters, Suffolk
June 23-26, Batley Variety Club, Batley

"I Go To Pieces" remained one of Shannon's favorite songs and in 1976 he began working on a new arrangement. He told close friends that it was a tune that he believed would be a hit-done his way. Then Johnny Rivers cut a version of the song that he intended to release as a single. In an interview with British journalist Graham Gardner in May 1978, Del said that he had decided "not to do any of the old songs again." It was the machinations within the music industry over his old songs that frustrated Shannon. So he simply went back on the road to make good music.

During the 1977 English tour, Del was still drinking. Shirley went along with him. She spent her time at the museums and he would perform at night. Shirley loved England but she felt lost with her husband. The drinking had gotten out of hand and she was determined to leave him. The next year, however, Del Shannon would quit drinking and his life took some dramatic turns.

As the 1970s ended, there were two records that recaptured the imagination of Del's fans worldwide. The **Live In England** album on Liberty, combined with a 1975 release on Sire, helped to reignite his popularity. Once again his powerful voice and intricate guitar licks excited the fans. These albums sold very well and there was every indication that Shannon's career was once again on the upsurge.

Del and Carl Perkins in the late 1970s

THE CONTINUED COOPERSVILLE CONNECTION

As Del's tours continued to keep him busy, his connection to Coopersville deepened. Del Shannon was only 16 years old in 1977 but his alter ego Chuck Westover was forty-three. As he entered into his middle age years, Del was pressured by show business demands. So he came to view Coopersville as a respite from the turmoil of his California life style in the midst of the recording industry.

He returned home more frequently and often looked up his buddies. On February 19, 1977, Russell Conran, the retired Coopersville High School principal, wrote Del a letter. It suggested his ties to Coopersville:

Dear Charles:

   If it astonishes you to hear from me twice in such a brief period of time, there is a reason. I wrote you last to thank you for the record you sent me, this time to inform you that we made a trip to Sears Roebuck and purchased a stereo, so we could listen to the record.

   I recall how you began by performing before an audience of a dozen or so admiring students with a few frowning adults lurking in the background, of which I was occasionally one such person, and now I have heard you perform, after a thunderous ovation, before an audience whom I would imagine numbered in the thousands, and with their enthusiastic approval and enjoyment.

   I was surprised by your virtuosity, and I felt the pride that is mine by right of having a dubious part in your inconspicuous beginnings. I admire your success and I admire you for attaining it.

   However, you may be slipping! This time you performed to an audience consisting of two aging persons in the plainness of their living room. But were an admiring duo, which should brace you up as well as indicate you have not lost your appeal. I hope so.

   Really, Charles, my admiration for you is based in the facts that you have handled success with equanimity and good sense. In my humble situation, this raises you to a pinnacle of worth that neither money nor fame could exceed. For this you have my unstinting admiration, even though I doubt that I shall ever develop a similar admiration for rock music. Sorry about that!

                                   Sincerely,
                                   Russell Conran
                                   February 19, 1977

For months Del carried this letter around and showed it to family and friends. All through his life, Conran had given Shannon a personal validation that he could not find in the outside world. It was the memories of Coopersville that kept Del from getting lost in the musical ozone.

Del And Shirley At Home

BIBLIOGRAPHICAL ESSAY

The liner notes to Rhino's compilation CD, **Del Shannon: Greatest Hits**, Rhino CD R2 70977 contains some gems of information about the early and mid-1970s. For reviews of Shannon's music in this period see the, **Torrance California Daily Breeze**, December 16, 1973: Chris Martin's review of **Live In England** in the **Los Angeles Times**, December 23, 1973.

See the Del Shannon News Service publications for this period for tour and personal information. A number of reprints of newspaper articles and other items from **And The Music Lives On: Del Shannon Magazine** helped to shape this chapter. For Shannon's comments on the Carpenters see the **Record Mirror**, April 27, 1974 .

A telephone interview with Greg Shaw, July 1996, helped to establish some important parts of Shannon's 1970s persona. On the Australian tour of 1974, see "Why Del Won't Run-Away," **Disc and Tape Review**, March 1974.

See "Hats Off To Del Shannon," **The Rock Marketplace**, September 1971 for an in-depth look at Shannon's career.

For brief mention of Shannon in the British context see, Derek Johnson, **Beat Music** (London, 1972), pp. 55, 73, 89, 115.

The **New Musical Express**, September 12, 1972 explains Henry Sellers' plans for Del Shannon's tour.

Also see **Music Week**, June 23, 1973 for some incisive comments on Shannon's English appeal and also see the **New Musical Express**, June 2, 1973 for information on Shannon's English tour. Also, the Del Shannon News Service mailed out a series of handouts, which were instrumental in this chapter.

Interviews with Bob Wooler, the Cavern disc jockey, helped to establish the English view of Del Shannon's music.

On Shannon's recording and song selection experiences in Nashville a series of interviews with local session musicians and producers helped to fill in many holes. Many of these people requested anonymity, but their impressions were supported by Eddie Bond, Stan Kesler, Marcus Van Story and Ronald Smith in Memphis. Jim Denson was also unusually helpful about the music scene in Memphis and Nashville.

On the British press, Ray Coleman provided a lengthy interview while appearing at the Los Angeles Beatlefest in the early 1990s. Subsequent interviews were arranged in England. Also, Joe Flannery, Clive Epstein, Brian Kelly, Eddie Hoover, Sam Leach and Alistair Taylor provided excellent comments on the British press and music industry.

Some of the musical trends of the 1970s were discussed with blues artists, Lowell Fulson and Jimmy McCracklin. They helped me to understand the problems of the industry in that time.

A lengthy interview with Russell Conran in Coopersville and the discovery of some of his letters to Del Shannon helped in formulating this chapter.

A wide variety of musicians were interviewed on the subject of surviving in the 1970s and these include bluesmen Lowell Fulson and Johnny Otis, rockabilly legends, Glen Glenn, Gene Summers and Dale Hawkins and Delbert McClinton.

On the movies and Del, see David Ehrenstein and Bill Reed, **Rock On Film** (New York, 1982), Rob Burt, **Rock and Roll In The Movies** (Dorset, 1983); Philip Jenkinson and Alan Werner, **Celluloid Rock: Twenty Years of Movie Rock** (London, 1974) and Marshall Crenshaw, **Hollywood Rock: A Guide To Rock And Role In the Movies** (New York, 1994).

Graham Gardner, "Interview," **And The Music Plays On: Del Shannon Magazine**, number 6, Winter, 1995, pp.8-15 was useful.

Jody Westover was gracious in recalling her life with Shirley and her dad, Chuck Westover.

Del Shannon: A Publicity Shot, 1969-1970

11: DEL IN TRANSITION: 1978-1983

"The career that I had depended on for almost thirty years suddenly was a dead end. I couldn't believe it, but thinking back I wondered if I would have another shot at stardom. But I was tired of being on the road and ambivalent about another round of stardom. I often wondered if I could survive the world of rock and roll." Del Shannon in a conversation with Charlie Marsh

In early 1978, Del Shannon sat in his house complaining about the music industry. "I'm in transition is what the labels are telling me," Del remarked. "What in the hell is in transition?" Shannon's outburst was an indication of his frustration. He hadn't had a major single release since 1975 and no one appeared interested in his music. He was in the middle of a seven-year hit slump and it would be another four years before the Network label released two Shannon singles. He was frustrated, periodically depressed and sick of performing on the oldies circuit.

The rock and roll lifestyle and the general insensitivity to those around him was taking a toll on his marriage. He was often two people. The pliable, easy-going Charles Westover by day and the maniacal rock star, Del Shannon, by night. He continued to write music, record in his private studio and seek out other musicians. The creative juices flowed as well as ever but Del Shannon was entering his mid-40s and uncertain if he had a continued commercial future.

If there was any solace to his life it was at the family home on the outskirts of Newhall. The small ranch house that Shannon purchased-over his wife Shirley's objections-was a country fortress against the vagaries of the rock and roll lifestyle. Located in the area outside of Newhall, the small home was in a rural setting. It was the perfect place to raise a family and unwind from the tensions of the music business.

The changes that the late 1970s brought to Del Shannon's career were reflected in May 1978 when he sat down for an interview with British fan club journalist Graham Gardner. This interview was one of the most in-depth of Shannon's career because he was at ease with one of his staunchest fans.

One of the reasons that Shannon survived artistically and financially in the mid and late 1970s was due to the support he received from his English, European and Australian audiences. They maintained working fan clubs and besieged the record companies with requests for his records.

Del and Shirley, 1982

The English-based Del Shannon Appreciation Society was a boon to Del's career. He loved to tour in the United Kingdom. It was the one place where he felt that he and his music were accepted. Del loved the food, the people, the English countryside and the sense of accomplishment which accompanied his British tours.

During the course of this lengthy interview with Gardner, Del talked about cutting back on touring. He also had no idea about a new record. He was frustrated over the attitudes in the music industry. Shannon would still converse at length about recording some new hits. There was a confused message in Shannon's interview. On one hand he talked of having new records, and a few minutes later, Del would lament the problems of rock and roll stardom. "Being on the road all the time gets confusing," Del remarked, "it's a lonely situation." Shannon hoped to concentrate upon song writing and producing. He told Gardner that after almost 20 years on the road he was ready for a rest.

Del Shannon: Pensive About The Music Business

Not only was Del concerned about his career, all indications were that he would have difficulty getting a good recording contract. Shannon was definitely in transition. His record releases in 1978 were not promising ones. He was paid to cut four songs or K-Tel in Nashville and the remakes of "Keep Searchin' (We'll Follow The Sun)," "Runaway," "Hats Off To Larry" and "Little Town Flirt" were self-acknowledged mistakes. Del was paid $10,000 for his efforts and this was at least a financial balm to his ego.

In the United Kingdom a budget label, Sunset released **And The Music Plays On** (Sunset 50412) album in March 1978, and in America another budget label, put out **Golden Hits: The Best of Del Shannon** (Pickwick 3595).

These albums were an attempt to revive Shannon's flagging recording career. Because they were budget label releases, no one took these LPs seriously. Another problem with the **And The Music Plays On** (Sunset 50412) album was that the material had been turned down earlier by Liberty and word within the industry was that the songs were second rate. Nothing was further from the truth. There are a number of minor Del Shannon masterpieces on this album.

One of the most important changes in Shannon's career occurred was when he went to England, and he was able to work with Rolling Stones' producer Andrew Loog Oldham. This experience was a positive one because Del was able to record with a group of British session musicians which included John Paul Jones, Nicky Hopkins and perhaps an uncredited Jimmy Page on guitar. The English based Immediate record label also provided a songwriter, Billy Nicholls, whose tunes "Friendly With You," "Led Along" and "Cut and Come Again" were excellent songs for Shannon. These tunes had a romantic quality which was made for Shannon's voice.

Other songs which were important contributions to the **And The Music Plays On** (Sunset 50412) album were a remake of Dee Clark's "Raindrops" and "Leaving You Behind." Dan Bourgoise helped Shannon produce these songs. Not only was Bourgoise Shannon's best friend, he understood the direction of his music better than anyone in the industry. His fledgling Bug Music company was also collecting Del's royalties and his financial future looked bright. "Now all we need is another hit record," Del remarked to Bourgoise.

The budget label releases provided a steady income but Shannon was not thrilled with the product. The K-Tel label released a single featuring "Runaway" backed with "Hats Off to Larry." Both songs were re-recordings. Del was paid cash on the spot. At a thousand dollars a song, it was a nice deal. However, the new product was a sub standard recording of the old hits. The same 45 was released in England by the Creole label and in Germany by Polydor Records. Del then leased "Runaway" and "Hats Off To Larry" (Gusto 2035) to the American-based Gusto label. The same record was released under the imprint of the Eric and K-Tel labels and between them they sold more than 50,000 copies.

Del Shannon: Reflecting on The Good Times

"Am I just an oldies act?" Del asked. "I don't think that I will ever come back into the mainstream of the record business," Shannon remarked to Charlie Marsh. Del told his old Michigan friend that he was ready to go into the real estate business full time. He was frustrated with the record business. This was not surprising, because it appeared that Del Shannon's music was destined for the bargain bins.

MEETING TOM PETTY IN 1978

One day, Dan Bourgoise walked into his office at Bug Music and found a phone message from Tom Petty. He called Petty back and found out that he wanted to work with Shannon. Petty told Bourgoise that he was a big Del Shannon fan. Tom not only hoped to produce Del's next album but he wanted to take him on the road. So the three of them got together in Dan's office and talked about Del's music.

It was a fortuitous meeting. Petty's backup band, the Heartbreakers, were the perfect studio group to revitalize Del's career. In November 1978, Petty and the Heartbreakers went into Sound City in Van Nuys to get the feel of playing with Shannon. As Bourgoise remarked, "it was just to mess around." There was also a gig at the Santa Monica Civic Auditorium on New Year's Eve where Shannon was going to join Petty and his group to perform "Runaway."

After the rehearsal at Sound City, Del played a tape of a song called "Drop Down And Get Me," which later became the title cut of Petty's produced LP. There were other songs on the tape. Shannon sang a creditable version of the Beatles' "I Should Have Known Better," "Joker on the Run," "Take Me Back" and "Jamie." Everyone agreed that Del still had it. Now it was time to find a hit. This wasn't an easy time in his career as the disco era had changed musical tastes.

"If Del had walked into a record company with his songs from the late 1970s and was an unknown, he would have been signed on the spot," Dan Bourgoise remarked, "but the industry had a standard and all they saw was the oldies but goodies Del."

DEL'S CAREER PROBLEMS IN THE LATE 1970s

By the late 1970s Shannon was depressed because many of his best produced songs had never been released. Since the early 1970s when Del went into the studio with Brian Hyland, he produced Hyland's "Gypsy Woman" and a cover version of the Drifters' "Up On The Roof." There was some disagreement between Del and Brian, and Bobby Hart was brought into to produce some new songs.

The years that Hyland lived with Del and Shirley were important ones for both artists. But soon time and changing musical directions ended their relationship. "Brian went his way, wanting to produce himself," Del concluded. "I think it was his wife who put Brian up to leaving Del," Charlie Marsh remembered. "He didn't want to be the Brian Hyland of "Itsie Bitsie Teenie Weenie Yellow Polka Dot Bikini," Marsh continued. "He thought he would be a one-man Led Zeppelin." Charlie Marsh may have overstated their differences but for some reason Del and Brian went their separate ways.

The American oldies market was still a lucrative venue for Del Shannon, but he preferred to tour England. Since the early 1960s, he and his music had been accepted in England and he felt at home there.

As he toured England in 1978, Shannon was exhausted. He opened his May-June tour on May 16 at the Jubilee 77 Club in Telford, Salop and the small club was sold out two months in advance of Shannon's appearance. They continued with five concerts in small English venues, including Valentines Club in Manchester, and he followed this with a six day tour of Scotland. On Monday, May 29, Del appeared at the Menwith Hill United States Army base in Harrogate, York, and regaled the audience with tales of his own service in Germany. He had to perform "Runaway" three times for the GI's eager to relive some of the old American rock and roll.

DEL SHANNON MAY-JUNE, 1978 ENGLISH-SCOTTISH TOUR

May 16, 77 Club, Telford, Salop

May 17, Unidentified Club,

May 18, New WMC, Grimsby, Lines

May 19-20, Valentines Club, Manchester

May 22, Crystal Rooms, Hereford

May 23-28, Tour of Scotland

May 29, Menwith Hill U.S. Base, Harrogate, York

May 31, Olympic Variety Club, Stoke-On-Trent

June 1, Windmill, Copford, Essex

June 2, Unannounced Venue

June 3, Whitchurch Leisure Centre, Whitchurch, Salop

June 4, Allen's Cross Social Club, Birmingham

June 5, Railway Club, Rugby

June 6, Mackadown Hotel, Birmingham

June 7, Amery Unionist Club, Wolverhampton

June 8, Sunnyside Hotel, Northhampton

June 9, Labour Club, Bedworth, Warwicks

June 10, Social Club, Willenhall, Coventry.

GRAHAM GARDNER AND THE DEL SHANNON
APPRECIATION SOCIETY HELPS DEL ROLL ON

The Del Shannon Appreciation Society, led by the able British journalist, Graham Gardner, put out a sheet on the 1978 tour. Gardner remarked that Shannon looked trim and fit and appeared to be on the verge of writing some new hits. During this tour, Del plugged the album **And The Music Plays On** (Sunset SLS 50412) and featured the song "Life Is But Nothing." The English fan club suggested that Del's local audience write to United Artists in London and pressure them to release "Life Is But Nothing" backed with "The Ghost" as a single. More than five thousand letters descended upon UA's London office, but nothing came of it. United Artists had no plans to release a Shannon single.

When Del ended the May-June 1978 British tour at the Social Club in Willenhall, Coventry, he was depressed by the small venues. He was making a nice living, but Shannon still yearned for another hit. He hated the concert format where he simply repeated the same set night after night. It was frustrating for a creative artist to be caught in a musical time warp.

He felt guilty for not being able to give the English fans some new songs. "I want to give them new material," he told Gardner, "but I can't give it to them by just coming over and doing it on stage." Del lamented his lack of time. He was trying to write new songs, but he had trouble finding the time. "I got my head together, I got a lot of other things together, and now I know I can get my writing back together," Del concluded.

During the 1960s Shannon wrote hundreds of songs. "I used to write tons of songs in the early days," Shannon reminisced, "and then all of a sudden I just stopped." In an eerie moment, Shannon looked at Gardner and suggested that the rock and roll lifestyle was killing him. "Have a lot of hits, go on the road, make lots of money and die!" Shannon remarked. As he sat with Gardner during the interview, Del was visibly upset. "I've got to discipline myself in other areas of my life," Shannon hollered, "and into my writing and I will do it."

The intense preoccupation to write was evident in Shannon's personal life. He began spending more time in his study. The Mole Hole, as he called it, was the perfect place to create his music. The more Shannon wrote the more intense he became with his songs. While Shannon did take time for himself, frequently he was leaving home in his car to visit his friends the Robbs, at the Cherokee studio. He could also be seen motoring down to Hollywood to see Dan Bourgoise at Bug Music or simply going out to the Palomino Club to check out a new band-Shannon did have an active social life. But music was first and foremost in his mind. Not all of his sessions were in the Mole Hole; he regularly went into professional recording studios.

Del had a plan for his recording sessions. He would usually go into the studio with drums and bass. This would allow him to lay down the initial tracks and later finish the sessions with a full band. After he laid down these studio tracks, Shannon would go home and listen to them in the Mole Hole. "I'll go in the next day," Del recalled, "we'll do the bass guitar and sometimes the piano." With the new technology Shannon spent an inordinate amount of time in the studio experimenting with lead vocals. Jeff Lynne of the Electric Light Orchestra was spending a great deal of time in Hollywood and he would come into the studio to help Del with the final cuts.

On the business side Dan Bourgoise was working on reacquiring the copyrights of all of Del's old songs. This included the material he had recorded for Harry Balk and Irving Micahnik at Twirl Records. But Dan also represented the interests of Don and Juan as well as Max Crook's recordings as Maximilian. These people had a special bond with Bourgoise-one forged by Del Shannon. Dan would do anything to help his old friend. The real gold though was Del's Embee Production material. Over time Bourgoise secured all of these masters. But recording wasn't Shannon's only activity. He was still an active performer.

It was these performances which continued to build and enhance Shannon's performing legacy. In his last decade of performing, Del's fan base grew and his albums continued to sell.

THE SURF BALLROOM AND THE OLDIES BUT GOODIES

On the oldies circuit Del Shannon was a top draw. It was a part of the music business that Shannon had ambivalent feelings about, and he wasn't always comfortable in the oldies format. But some appearances had a special feeling. In February 1979, the first Memorial dance for the late Buddy Holly, Ritchie Valens and J. P. Richardson (the Big Bopper) was held the at the Surf Ballroom in Clear Lake, Iowa. This was the last concert site before the fatal plane crash which killed these rock and roll giants.

As he flew into Clear Lake, Iowa, Del was alternately happy and depressed. He had fond memories of his early days in the business. When the plane carrying Buddy Holly, the Big Bopper and Ritchie Valens had crashed in February 1959, Del was playing at the Hi Lo Club in Battle Creek. Suddenly, he recalled how depressed he had been that day. Soon these memories receded and Del began thinking about his show at the Surf Ballroom.

The two-day concert at the Surf Ballroom and in nearby venues took on the aura of a saintly event. There were hushed conversations about the big three who had died in the tragic plane crash. There was a Friday night sock hop and the next day a concert in the park. But it was the main event at the Surf Ballroom that drew the most attention and all eyes were riveted on Del Shannon. He had the sound, the career and the personality to recreate the good old days of rock and roll.

With Wolfman Jack taking on the master of ceremonies role, the Surf Ballroom presented Jimmy Clanton, the Drifters and concert closer Shannon. Niki Sullivan of the Crickets showed up with his seven-year-old twin sons and the crowd was in a festive mood. The event became so large that a Lubbock, Texas radio station staged a disco dance at the Memorial City Center. A Buddy Holly sound-a-like band was hired and the first Memorial concert took on a circus air. Del watched from the side of the stage and shook his head as someone played disco records.

Bobby Vee, Shirley and Del in Alaska, 1980s

When the show opened, there were almost two thousand fans from 35 states, England, Europe and Japan in the audience. The concert turned into a love fest and lasted more than six hours. With tickets priced at $17.50, the show was not only a sell out, but it began a series of memorial concerts.

Del was depressed with the commercialism surrounding the concert. He believed that the reason for the concert was ignored. Three rock and roll pioneers had died and this seemed forgotten in the celebration. Shannon changed his mind about this when he found out that a street was to be named for Buddy Holly. Maria Elena Holly had similar concerns about the celebration but she graciously withdrew her complaints.

What was ironic is that Shannon's last public appearance would be at a Memorial concert for Buddy Holly in Fargo, North Dakota in 1990. Then five days after this concert, Shannon committed suicide. As he told Charlie Marsh: "The Buddy Holly Memorial concerts were about profit, not the music, not the entertainers, not about that time in history. It is depressing."

THE AA CRUISE: DEL CELEBRATES SOBRIETY WITH SHIRLEY

In 1979 for their 25th anniversary, Del and Shirley took an AA cruise from San Pedro, California down to the Mexican Riviera. "It was one big AA cruise and one meeting after another. It had been a long time since they had been together and both of them looked forward to it.

The cruise was a pleasant vacation. Ted and Fran Sommers were friends who went along and they all enjoyed the time on the seas. Del was eating modestly and exercising vigorously. The old days were behind him and he felt healthy, both mentally and physically.

Before the cruise, Tommy Boyce hung out at Del's house in late 1979. He came over almost every day. In 1965, Boyce had introduced Del to marijuana and they remained friends over the years. By 1979, Del was no longer smoking dope and drinking. He had also given up the pills. Boyce was happy for him.

At the Rafters, the local AA chapter near his home in Newhall, Del became something of a legend for helping his friends. If you slipped you could call Shannon anytime of the day or night for help.

There was a sensitive side to Del when it came to his AA friends. By concentrating so much time on AA, however, he hurt his other relationships. When his wife, Shirley, asked him to go to a movie or dinner, Del wouldn't because he believed that someone would call looking for help. In time, this was a contributing factor to their divorce. After they divorced Del and Shirley continued to see each other and Shannon told his close friends that he would like to reunite with Shirley.

EUROPE AND GERMANY: ONCE AGAIN RECOGNITION OF DEL'S TALENT OUTSIDE AMERICA

In November, 1979 Shirley joined Del for the West German tour. They drove from Hanover to Berlin. "It was a little intimidating," Shirley recalled, "They held us up at the border for quite a long time." But Del loved to travel in Europe. The German countryside reminded him of Michigan and he was so well known there that he felt like he still had hit records.

As usual the English provided warm hospitality. The club dates that Del played were lucrative ones. He had a strong fan base and the small towns outside London were eager for American rock and roll. The backup band was excellent and the production costs low. So he was assured a substantial concert fee.

This is an important insight into Shannon's business dealings. He always took away a nice chunk of money and made sure that the business end of his concert schedule was handled professionally. What often surprised Shannon about his music was the interest in his early years.

While he was performing in Germany, Del was approached by Meyer Brandenburg who asked him about his Hi Lo Club demo tapes. With a smile, Del informed him that he had sent the tapes to a disc jockey. After listening to them, the DJ was trying to sell the tapes to record labels. That was in the 1960s and Shannon never heard another word about the songs. He also never found out what happened to the tapes. They circulated amongst collectors but no one bootlegged them. This alone is a testimony to the feeling for Shannon's music.

DEL SHANNON ENGLISH-SCOTTISH-WEST GERMAN TOUR, OCTOBER-NOVEMBER 1979

October 12-13, Valentines Club, Manchester

October 15, McTavish's, Boness, W. Lotian, Scotland

October 16-17, Dundee, Scotland

October 18, Kirkleston Bowling Club, Edinburgh, Scotland

October 19 Stuarts and Lloyds Social Club, Bellshill, Scotland

October 20, Marconis Social Club, Dunfermiline, Scotland

October 21, Waverley Castle Hotel, Galashiels, Scotland

October 24, Town Hall, Oakengates, near Telford

October 25, Trentham Gardens, Stoke on Trent

October 26, The Painted Lady, Melton Mowbray, Leicestershire

October 27, St. Helier Arms, Carshalton, Surrey

October 28, The Wookey Hollow, Liverpool

November 1, Bunnies Club, Cleethorpes, Lincolnshire

November 2, Talk of the Midlands, Derby

November 3, Talks of the East, Norwich, Norfolk

November 4, Sparrows Nest Theater, Lowestoff, Suffolk

November 7, Fabrik Club, Hamburg, West Germany

November 8, Waldbune Club, Bremen, West Germany

November 10, Cheetah Club, Berlin, West Germany

November 11, Eisenhutte, Bielefeld, Near Frankfurt, West Germany

---

DEL IN TRANSITION

The disc jockey that shopped the tapes, Ollie McLaughlin, sent them to Irving Micahnik who simply buried them in his drawer. So some of Del Shannon's best music never saw the light of day. From the Hi Lo Club days "Little Oscar" remains a novelty recording. All of these tapes are in Max Crook's possession and need to be released.

DEL IN 1980-1983

In 1980-1981 Del Shannon's career was temporarily on hold. RSO Records had gone bankrupt and his producer, Tom Petty, was searching for a new label. They were in the studio and had the new LP more than 80 percent completed. The problem was that there wasn't a major record label to release Shannon's product. Del wanted a major label because he was sick and tired of the small labels. During the 1980s, Shannon would revitalize his career. Tom Petty turned out to be the major catalyst to a resurgence in Shannon's music.

In June 1980, Del appeared at the Fern Tree Gully Hotel in Australia before a crowd that cheered his new material. He wore a plaid sport coat, a white shirt and a tie. Not only was the show well received but everyone remarked about his energy. It was Del in transition, he was again preparing a new group of hits.

During the next couple of years there was a great deal of new material and a commercial resurgence to Shannon's music. As 1983 concluded, there were a host of new challenges both musically and personally. Del had been in transition since 1979 and he was ready to break out in new career directions.

BIBLIOGRAPHICAL SOURCES

See Graham Gardner's interview with Del in **And The Music Plays On: Del Shannon Magazine**, no. 6, Winter, 1995, pp., 8-11. A series of lengthy interviews with Dan Bourgoise of Bug Music helped to place this period of Shannon's career in perspective.

For Shannon's 1978 British tour see the **New Musical Express**, **Disc** and **Melody Maker** for comments on his appearances in the United Kingdom. Joe Flannery, a Liverpool promoter, helped to place the English rock scene in the 1970s in perspective.

The English side of Shannon's career is covered in a number of newsletters from The Del Shannon Appreciation Society. Shirley Westover also provided some important comments on Del's career in the United Kingdom.

Christopher Meyer-Brandenburg, "Track Talk: What's Buried in the Mole Hole," **And The Music Plays On**, number 14, Summer, 1998, pp. 32-39.

Interviews with Bo Diddley and Delbert McClinton helped to clarify the Surf Ballroom show. Also see, Larry Lehmer, **The Day The Music Died: The Last Tour of Buddy Holly, the Big Bopper and Ritchie Valens** (New York, 1997). Other sources helped to this period in Shannon's career included Steve Chapple and Reebee Garofolo, **Rock and Roll Is Here To Pay** (Chicago, 1977); John Beecher and Malcolm Jones, **The Buddy Holly Story** (MCA Record Box Set); John Goldrosen and John Beecher, **Remembering Buddy Holly: The Definitive Biography of Buddy Holly** (New York,

1985); Alan Clark, **Ritchie Valens: 30th Anniversary Memorial Series** (West Covina, Ca., 1989).

An interview with Bill Griggs helped to clarify the Buddy Holly end of the Clear Lake, Iowa concert. An interview with Maria Elena Holly at the opening of the Rockabilly Hall of Fame in Jackson, Tennessee in the spring of 2000 helped to add material to this chapter.

On the commercial side of the music industry, see R. Serge Denisoff, **Tarnished Gold: The Record Industry Revisited** (New Brunswick, 1986). Other problems with this era are echoed in Chuck Berry's career, see Howard A. DeWitt, **Chuck Berry: Rock 'N' Roll Music** (Ann Arbor, 1985).

On Tom Petty, see, for example, Philip Bashe, "Del Shannon's Comeback a Petty Matter," **Circus** (April 30, 1982), p. 46. Also see, Mitch Cohen, "Del Shannon's Fugitive Kind of Love," **Creem**, volume 14, no. 1 (June, 1982), pp. 24-25, 58-59 and Jon Young, "Del Shannon," **Trouser Press**, volume 9, number 4 (June, 1982), pp. 8, 50.

12: THE ROAD GOES ON FOREVER: AUSTRALIA 1985 ON THROUGH AMERICA TO 1988

"I've taken stock of my life. It used to be drinking and smoking and it was party time all the time. Now I take care of my health. I steer my own ship." Del Shannon in an interview with Leslie Radin of the Battle Creek Inquirer

What did Del Shannon have left? This was a question frequently asked in the 1980s. The answer was that there was plenty of new material in the old rocker. With his new found energy resulting from an end to drinks and drugs, Del wrote some of the best original music of his career. Yet there was an ultimate frustration. While Shannon had a great deal left in his creative soul, it was difficult to find someone to release his music with the proper promotion. The contrived musical sounds of the 1980s were not tuned to Del's music.

The tragedy and irony of Del's career was that he was making some of his best music. The 1980s, however, were a time of techno and pop tunes that had little resemblance to Shannon's music. As a result the major labels believed that he was no longer a hit artist. Although he was signed to a major label, Warner Bros., in the 1980s they did little, if anything to promote his music. It was the ultimate contradiction. He could point with pride to a contract with one of the best U. S. labels but deep down Del knew that he was little more than decoration on their corporate image. This not only created frustration but pigeon holed his music into oblivion.

The irony of this period is that Del had a revived career thanks to the oldies market but he failed to sell his new music. So he experienced both success and failure in the 1980s. It was a dilemma which bothered him and caused Shannon to doubt the industry.

THE FRUSTRATION OF THE MUSIC INDUSTRY

An Australian film, "Street Hero," contained a Shannon song, "Something To Believe In" and when the movie was released the song was bootlegged and available in Sydney record stores. The rumor was that it was a tune destined for the American soundtrack of "Grease 2." Del remarked to a close friend: "the road goes on forever through Australia and back to America." His frustration with the music business was obvious. But the popularity of the tune and Shannon in Australia prompted increased record sales and lucrative touring opportunities.

When Del wrote "Something To Believe In," the song was completed in the Mole Hole. Del's daughter, Jody, often helped her dad out on vocals. As Jody watched her dad in the studio she realized that the old magic had returned. When Del was cutting "Something To Believe In" and it didn't make the "Grease 2" sound track, he went into the studio with Jody and cut a new song he called "When." In an interview with Brian Young's magazine, **And The Music Plays On**, Jody remarked: "We did it together as a demo on a four-track at home. There's a lot of great songs that Dad wrote that didn't get out." Jody believes that "Jaime" and "Till I Found You" are other songs that deserve release. The point is that Shannon was making great music in his last years. The record companies simply could not picture him as anything more than an oldies artist.

The record company attitude ate away at Shannon and he became increasingly frustrated. He was making some of the best music of his career, but no one would listen and few were eager to release it. The only solace that Del received was in the acclaim of the fans. None were more loyal than those in Australia.

DEL SHANNON IN AUSTRALIA, 1985, WARNER BROS. AND ON TO "CRIME STORY" 1986

In 1985, Del Shannon signed for an Australian tour. He would appear throughout Australia from February 24 through March 16, 1985. Not only would Del perform in some of the best spots in Australia, but he was intent upon promoting his recent music. After arriving in Sydney, Del rested for a day. Then he began preparing for his pub and club tour.

Although he had a quarter of a century in the music business, Del practiced with his Australian musicians and carefully plotted his songs. He was intent upon making a series of concerts that would be so strong that the record companies would sit up and take notice.

The Australian tour was a fresh beginning. As Del spent an inordinate amount of time crafting new music for his concerts, he worked in songs like the Rolling Stones' "Satisfaction" and the Los Bravos hit "Black Is Black" to give his shows a harder edge. On stage Del liked to talk about rocking as well as anyone. The Australian tour would prove that point. As he prepared extensively to conquer the down under audiences, Del believed that he had some new hits. It was time well spent as the press reported that Shannon was once again a staple on the Australian rock scene. He was also connected with a major record company, Warner Bros.

The road to the Warner Bros. contact was a calculating one. Del began by flying in his longtime friend and sometimes musical collaborate, Steve Monahan, in from Florida to Nashville. The intent was to showcase his music for the various labels. Dan Bourgoise, now very successful at Bug Music, helped to broker the deal that landed Del with Warner Bros. Shannon and Monahan not only cut what came to be known as Shannon's 1985 Nashville sessions, but they used a local band, the Wolves, to compliment the new sound.

Del With Russell Conran in Coopersville, 1983

Dan Bourgoise remembered that Del played a punk club in Nashville for the various record executives. The show was a smash and a number record companies were interested in Shannon. With his lengthy experience in the music industry, as well as talking at length with Bourgoise, Del used his expertise to select Warner Bros. It was both a wise and unfortunate decision. Warner Bros. was a major label with clout but they didn't like to redevelop artists. A decision was made within Warner that if Shannon's music did not sell instantly, he would be released from his contract. Del, of course, was unaware of this corporate decision.

After a long period without a significant new record release, Warner Bros. released two Del Shannon country singles. These October 1986 releases indicated that his career was once again on the rise. When Warner Bros. released "In My Arms Again" and "You Can't Forgive Me" as a single, this record charted on the **Billboard** Country Top 50. Recording in Nashville, Shannon finally returned to his country roots. This single was followed by "Stranger On The Run" backed with "What You Gonna Do With That Beautiful Body." While this release received substantial airplay, it didn't sell well nor did it chart. The second single was what most of the major labels did with Shannon. They released an old cut and hoped for the best. This was not the road to success. However, there was a fan who loved Del's music, he was a television producer and he brought back "Runaway" as more than just an oldie.

In addition to his Australian success, Shannon's "Runaway" became the theme song for the television show "Crime Story." When Michael Mann's program premiered on September 18, 1986, it featured a newly-recorded version of "Runaway" as the programs theme song. Each show opened with "Runaway" as Michael Torello, played by Dennis Farina and Danny Krychek, portrayed by Bill Smitrovich, began to solve a crime in circa 1963 Miami. The media spent too much time comparing the program to Mann's previous blockbuster TV hit "Miami Vice." Most of the media lauded Shannon's recut version of "Runaway" but had they listened closely, it was virtually the same song. While the critics didn't care for the show, the fans loved it. Largely because "Crime Story" was a fun show. Real-life criminals and con men appeared in cameo roles and such future mega stars as Julia Roberts and Cameron Slater were guests.

The executive producer, Michael Mann, was such a devoted Del Shannon fan that in one episode he featured a three-minute cut of "Keep Searchin' (We'll Follow The Sun)." He also used Bonnie Raitt's "Runaway" on two other occasions. Mann wanted an organ background in "Runaway" and this forced Del to get rid of Max Crook's signature musitron sound. Rumors persist that there is a mix with an organ for Mann but no one has found it to date. Mann remixed "Runaway" for the show and on some of the Dino/Evasound bootleg CDs these television mixes are obvious.

Although "Crime Story" only had a two-season run, it was another example of the innovative nature of Del's music. He could take an old tune like "Runaway" and adapt it to the 1980s market. Not only did Shannon demonstrate that he could work easily within the television industry, but he was able to recast his music in a new and fresh direction. He wasn't the oldies but goodies act that many envisioned. While "Crime

Story" was in production, Del often mentioned that he had other ideas for television music.

Shirley, Del and Rainer Genatowski

When Del shot the "Crime Story" video of "Runaway," the song featured his daughter, Kym, who is an excellent singer and songwriter Although she had never sought the spotlight, Jody Westover remains a talent. She is not only a song writer but her line of greeting cards is an indication of her enormous creative potential.

To celebrate his new record Shannon appeared on Friday, October 3, 1986 at the cavernous Universal Amphitheater. With "Runaway" riding high on the TV show "Crime Story," Shannon was in demand on the concert circuit. As Del sat down for an interview with Todd Everett of the **Los Angeles Herald Examiner**, he remarked that the 130 to 140 concerts a year was wearing thin. As he reminisced, Shannon made it clear that he wasn't an oldies act. "I didn't do these oldies shows for a long time," Del continued. "But I saw Frank Sinatra once and if that's not an oldies show, what're you going to call it." What this interview suggested was a strange duality. Del would do the oldies shows but he still wanted to promote his recent music. This turned out to be a problem.

Warner Bros. didn't seem to know how to promote Del Shannon. One day in sheer frustration, Del stormed into Warner Bros. and let them know that he had a host of new material. Whether or not this helped to end his Warner Bros. deal no one knows but they took little interest in his future music. Always the businessman, Del laid out his future musical plans and pointed out the profit margin. Warner Bros. executives ignored his arguments and Shannon began looking for a new label.

There were new tracks that Warner Bros. didn't release. One was "You Still Live Here" which is a marvelous ballad that English rocker Dave Edmund's covered. Juice Newton was another country artist to discover Shannon's music. She recorded "Cheap Love" and it rose to the country top 10. In 1982 when Del wrote "Cheap Love" he thought of it as a country tune. However, the music industry didn't recognize the song until Juice Newton pulled it out of a remainder bin.

When Del first heard Juice Newton's version of "Cheap Love," he was in the car with his old friend from Indiana, Ray Meyer. Shannon had just arrived in the Middle West for a series of concerts and Ray picked him up at the airport. As they started for the Holiday Inn, the radio began playing Newton's "Cheap Love."

"Turn that up," Shannon said. Since Del was hard of hearing, Meyer turned the volume up to full blast. "I wrote that song," Del shouted. Ray didn't believe him.

"It's a country song, Del," Ray remarked.

"I told you that I wrote it," Del remarked.

"I don't think so," Ray countered.

"Well, I'll show you Ray, let's go to Smokey Montgomery's Record Store. Does he still have it? You know that small store in Fort Wayne."

"We are on our way," Ray said they headed the car to town. Smokey Montgomery's Record Store is located in Fort Wayne, Indiana and sure enough it had a copy of Newton's "Cheap Love." "See," Del told Ray, "I wrote it." "Case closed," Meyer responded.

When Del Shannon recorded "Cheap Love" for the Network label which was distributed by Elektra, he found it shelved for American release when network went bankrupt and Elektra moved its home office from Los Angeles to New York. "Cheap Love" wasn't permanently lost as it was released by Demon Records in England and Line Records in Germany as a bonus track on the **Drop Down And Get Me** album.

It was Juice Newton's success with "Cheap Love" which prompted Del to cut a second version of the song. It may have been intended for the "**Rock On**" album. There was also the possibility of releasing it as a single. This never materialized. The reason may have been the large number of artists releasing Del's material.

In 1986 Shannon's music made a come back when Luis Cardenas, a Latin artist, released "Runaway" on the Allied Artist label. It briefly charted in the 1980s on the Billboard Hot 100 before it vanished from sight. A music video by Cardenas with wildly exaggerated puppets was picked up by MTV and suddenly a new generation listened to Del Shannon. In this music video, Del took on a cameo acting role as a policeman and actor Norman Winter was cast as a bum. Shannon had been friendly with Winter since he drove Brian Hyland and Del to see Elvis Presley in Las Vegas in 1970.

Del With ELO's Jeff Lynne

The "Del Shannon Appreciation Society" Newsletter publicized the 25th anniversary of "Runaway's" release. The numerous cover versions of "Runaway" by Bonnie Raitt, Elvis Presley, Lawrence Welk, the Ventures, Rod Stewart, Narvel Felts and others continued to sell well. Del's concerts were also well attended and he was making an excellent living.

In concert the surf group, the Ventures, featured Don Wilson singing lead vocal on "Runaway." "We loved working with Del," Wilson remarked, "and to this day I can't understand his death." At this point in his career, Del had a revived popularity and was generally in fine spirits.

The 1986 Del Shannon concerts were still strong ones. His favorite place to play was still Battle Creek, Michigan. Since he hit the charts with "Runaway" in 1961 Shannon had found it difficult to book himself into the town where he had begun his career in the notorious Hi Lo Club.

So when Del had a chance to return to his old haunts in Battle Creek he did so. He was part of an April 20, 1986 concert which featured Shannon along with Johnny Tillotson and Chubby Checker. The $10 tickets for seats at the Kellogg Center Arena sold out quickly with the Rock Café, and The Believe In Music store helping to make the event a success.

Such old friends as Sue Gooch, Ginny Gibbs, Susie White, Darr Farr, the Popenhagen family, the DeMott boys, Jim Espy, John Anglin and even the old bouncer from the Hi Lo Club, Rufus Wines, smelling of beer, wandered down to see Del in concert.

Before the show Del sat down with Leslie Rardin, the **Battle Creek Inquirer** lifestyle editor and talked about the old days. "I started to write all of a sudden," Del remarked. "Rock gave me a direction as far as writing goes." With a bittersweet tone, Del suggested that he had both positive and negative memories from the early years. "I wanted to look good and sound good," he recalled. "It was hard, but that was a great training ground for me."

DEL SHANNON: THE 1987 CONCERT SCHEDULE AND PERSONAL EXHAUSTION

As Del Shannon entered his second quarter century in show business, he continued to tour incessantly. Usually, he flew out of Los Angeles and performed on weekends. This allowed him to write new songs Monday through Thursday, and to continue to work on his weight, diet and healthy lifestyle. He attended the AA meetings at the Rafters and often left the house late at night to help other members of AA. Shannon was a giving and caring person who could not say no when fellow alcoholics asked him for help.

A series of concerts with Lesley Gore and the Shirelles during the summer of 1987 made Del a strong draw on the oldies market. After playing in Reno, small venues in Minnesota, the oldies show stopped in Topeka, Kansas. A full house on August 8, 1987 at the Topeka, Kansas Municipal Auditorium was treated to an excellent show. The pace was beginning to show on Shannon. Earlier in the year he had performed in Australia, England and Japan.

By mid August 1987, Del was exhausted from concerts, recording and a revived career. Concerts in Canada, Japan and throughout the United States fueled new record sales. When Del appeared on the Japanese TV show, "Music Fair," he was forced to sit eight hours in the studio prior to his appearance. Johnny Tillotson was with Del and they talked well into the night about the rigor of Japanese touring. Don Wilson of the Ventures had provided Del with a lengthy list of things to do to make touring Japan easier.

Del In England: 1980s

An appearance on Late Night with David Letterman was another boast to his career. The "Crime Story" version of "Runaway" helped Shannon attract a new generation of fans while maintaining the old ones. Although "Crime Story" producer Michael Mann requested some minor lyric changes, the original feel of "Runaway" remained. In addition, Shannon made a video on location with the "Crime Story" cast. Del's daughter, Kym, appeared in the video and MCA announced that it looked for phenomenal sales for the new "Runaway."

In England, Demon Records and in Germany, Line Records released Shannon material. The Demon LP was a 16 cut package featuring hard-to-find Shannon classics. The LP was entitled **Break Up** and included extensive liner notes by Graham Gardner and Dan Bourgoise at Bug Music, which provided some of Shannon's rarest records. The difficulty in finding Shannon titles like "Break Up," "That's The Way Love Is," (with the Young Sisters), "I Won't Be There" as well as Shannon's original recording of "I Go To Pieces" came to an end with this release. Since "I Go To Pieces" was a Top 5 hit in England for Peter and Gordon, Demon spent a great deal of time and money promoting the song and the album in the U. K. Ironically, this success in England diverted attention from the new country music which was changing the direction of Shannon's career.

One of the intriguing aspects of the Demon Record LP was the inclusion of four Doc Pomus-Mort Shuman songs. Also, a Del original "Broken Promises," is included. This is a difficult tune to locate because it was the b-side of "Keep Searchin." Peter and Gordon also recorded " Broken Promises," but it was simply one of many Shannon songs which failed to chart.

Del Shannon

In the fall of 1987 one of Del' strangest career shifts took place when he recorded a commercial for Canada Dry's new soft drink, Wink. The money was not only good for this commercial, but Del was writing successful commercials as well as composing his new music. He had recorded a Pepsi commercial in 1966 and Del remarked to his old friend Charlie Marsh that: "I need a soft drink commercial every 20 years."

Country music remained one of Shannon's passions. He appeared on the television show "Nashville Now" and began to promote his Warner Bros. country singles. Also appearing on the program were Freddy Cannon and the Diamonds. The "Del Shannon Appreciation Society" newsletter for August 14, 1987 announced that a new country album was about to be released and discussed the tracks at length. The newsletter urged members to look for the LP in early 1988.

The Rock and Roll Hall of Fame nominated Del Shannon for the second straight year, but he failed to earn a spot in the coveted rock marketplace. Shannon was disappointed but said little to the press. To his close friends, Del was incensed when Franki Valli was inducted into the Rock and Roll Hall of Fame. Valli asked Shannon to present him during the inauguration, but Del graciously refused. Privately, Shannon was hurt by the snub for a second year in a row. He desperately wanted to be in the Rock and Roll Hall of Fame. Just like so many other slights, Del simply continued to work and ignored the slight. He also made time for his friends and often showed up to play their birthdays.

Ray Meyer and Del Shannon at Ray's 40th Birthday Party

RAY MEYER'S BIRTHDAY PARTY, APRIL, 1988 AND DEL SHANNON'S SURPRISE

Throughout his life, Del Shannon was a considerate person. His family came first, his friends were always granted special favors and he went out of his way to be nice to fans. During the early 1980s when Del played some clubs in Indiana, he met a young banker, Ray Meyer, who also worked for the Midnight Sun Club in Wabash, Indiana, and they became lifelong friends.

When Shannon played the Midnight Sun Club, Meyer was a friend and easy-going companion. Del hated to be alone. Not only did Meyer understand the complex nature of Shannon's personality but he found that he had a lot in common with Del Shannon. They were both basically quiet and introverted. They had a sense of drama and an interest in writing. They were also both frustrated by some of the everyday problems of life. For these reasons, Del and Ray were close when Shannon toured the Middle West.

On April 8, 1988 Ray Meyer turned 40 and his good friend, Del Shannon flew into Wabash to perform at the Moose Lodge. Ray didn't tell his friends that Shannon had agreed to perform for his party. "Just in case something came up and he couldn't make it, I kept that little secret to myself," Ray chuckled.

Del Signing Albums In Milwaukee, Wisconsin, July 1989

Not only did Del perform, but he had a great time. On the way back to the hotel Shannon had Ray stop at a 7-11 so he could buy a yogurt. Del frequently did this after a concert to settle his stomach. Ray wondered if the clerk would recognize Del Shannon. It was Del who had the fun.

"Do you know who this person is," Del asked the clerk. The 40 year old looked bewildered. "Meet my good friend Ray Meyer, he told the clerk. "He threw a great party, he turned 40 tonight." They walked out as the clerk looked quizzically at them. He had no clue that he was talking to Del Shannon.

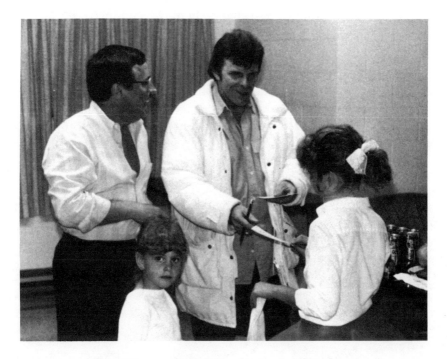

Ray Meyer and Del At a Party, April 8, 1988

DEL SHANNON: CHANGES IN THE LATE 1980s

In the late 1980s, some subtle but obvious changes came over Del Shannon. His mood swings were more pronounced and he experienced tremendous highs and lows. There was strong evidence that Shannon had a manic-depressive disorder. His family and friends were equipped to recognize or handle his mood swings. Much of what Shannon did seemed logical and a part of his personality.

Shannon was also a one-man-money-making machine. So many people depended upon him that it was difficult for Shannon to give up the road. He continued to see both a psychologist and psychiatrist for his emotional difficulties but they didn't seem to help. From time to time the old Del Shannon would emerge, particularly when it came time to buy some new clothes.

By the late 1980s, he was purchasing his clothes at the American Rag company in Newhall, California. This retro store sold old clothing from the past and it was the perfect place for Shannon to pick up new touring costumes. One clerk remembered that Del was happy and on a cloud the day he purchased clothes, and then would come in a few weeks later and talk about people trying to sabotage his career.

Because he was playing 150 to 180 concert dates a year, Shannon continued to make a good income. At Dan Bourgoise's suggestion, Del had increased his minimum guarantee and the result was that he played in high-end clubs or casinos. A good example of this took place at the Club Casino in Hampton Beach, New Hampshire, where Shannon performed resplendent in a red sport coat for $7500. The times were good for Del and he looked forward to returning periodically to Coopersville.

The fans still loved Del Shannon's shows. He was performing at a level which combined the old tunes like "Runaway" with the new songs that he hoped would be hits. The reception for Del's new music was excellent and he was slowly but surely bringing in a new audience. It wasn't just the oldies who came to see Shannon, it was also a growing number of new fans.

Del Shannon: On The Road

By the late 1980s, despite good health and a rigid diet, Shannon was experiencing some unexplained personal problems. When he returned to Coopersville and Battle Creek, his friends noticed a change. Since his divorce and remarriage Del had undergone a great deal of personal turmoil. No one understood the personal demons that beset Shannon. Yet, there still remained moments where he was his old self.

THE COOPERSVILLE HIGH SCHOOL 35 YEAR REUNION, 1988

Del Shannon always felt that Charles Westover didn't get respect. Although he loved his home town, Del often referred to his lack of appreciation. With a Del Shannon Day in 1961 and another celebration in 1983, Coopersville more than paid its respect to their native son. In July 1988, Del returned for a concert at the Coopersville High School football field. The $6 tickets sold out quickly and Del was forced to write some friends that he had no clout in the matter of tickets. The high school reunion was part of the Coopersville Summerfest and Del was more than happy to appear in his old home town.

The 1988 concert was part of a 35 year high school reunion. It featured food booths and a beer tent. Del remarked that the city finally had a beer supply, after he had quit drinking. A pig roast was announced prior to Del's concert and a street dance after the show enlivened the festivities. The event was part of an American Cancer Society fund raiser.

Del Shannon: Playing The Hits, 1987

Del's sister, Blanche Dykehouse, drove down from nearby Spring Lake as did his other sister, Ruth McCuaig of Sparta. They were not only proud of their brother but glad to see him. Since Shannon was on the road a great deal, he didn't have the time to keep in touch. "He was the best brother in the world," Ruth remarked to a Grand Rapids reporter.

John VanDoorn organized the 1988 Coopersville Summerfest and he found Del a jewel to work with during the event. The event was a huge success and everyone remarked that Charles was his old self.

To his close friends who visited with him after the show, Chuck Westover was the same old guy. Sonny Marshall doesn't believe that Del committed suicide. "He was his old self," Marshall recalled, "and to this day I can't believe that he would commit suicide. None of it adds up," Marshall recalled. "He loved life and talked about his future, yet less than two years later he was dead. It beats me."

The 1988 homecoming was special for Del because he was able to visit his old high school principal, Russell Conran, and they laughed about the good old days. For much of his life, Shannon viewed Conran as a surrogate father. He respected his advice and valued his friendship.

DEL SHANNON ON DEL SHANNON

A Michigan disc jockey, Marty Natchez, interviewed Del Shannon in the 1980s about his music and records. In a revealing conversation, Del Shannon talked at length about his music. A record collector, Natchez owned a copy of the **Runaway** LP in stereo and told what it was worth.

Del remarked: "Love to get that from you." Then they began talking about his hits disappearing from the record bins because so many of the companies went out of business. In a joking manner, Shannon remarked, "I broke em all." When the discussion turned to mono records, Del's opinion became firm. "I hate any record that was a mono that is synthetically put into stereo. I think they're a bunch of idiots and they only do it to sell records."

BIBLIOGRAPHICAL SOURCES

Ray Meyer recalled his birthday party and the years he was acquainted with Del.

The "Del Shannon Appreciation Society" Newsletter for October 1986 was important to the country music described in this chapter. The "Del Shannon Appreciation Society" newsletter for August 14, 1987 was helpful. A video of Ray Meter's party and lengthy interviews with Meyer were useful in recreating Shannon's birthday surprise for Meyer.

Interviews with Dan Bourgoise and Dick Schlatter helped to clarify this period of Shannon's career.

Charlie Marsh reconnected with Del in the 1980s and Shannon recounted in great detail his recent career changes.

For Shannon's remarks on Battle Creek, see Leslie Radin, "B.C.'s Rock Runaway is Back," **Battle Creek Inquirer**, April 17,1986.

The **Topeka Capitol Journal**, August 2, 1987 p. 30 contains an excellent story on Shannon. On the 1988 class reunion see Pete DeMaagd, "Spotlight In Coopersville Will Be One Guy Who Made It Big," **Grand Rapids Press**, July 26, 1988.

See "Del Shannon's New Mystery: The Case of the Missing Tapes," **And The Music Plays On: Del Shannon Magazine**, Issue 11, Spring, 1997, pp. 31-39 for Del's comments on his music and the interview with Marty Natchez.

Brian Young, "Kym Wilkerson and Jody Westover: An Interview With Del Shannon's Daughters," **And The Music Plays On: Del Shannon Magazine**, Issue 11, Spring, 1997, pp. 17-22 for key information on the 1980s.

Todd Everett, "Del Shannon Has Never Run Away," **Los Angeles Herald Examiner**, October 3, 1986 is an excellent interview-article on the state of Del's music.

For materials on "Crime Story" see, ' Crime Story' Review," **And The Music Plays On: Del Shannon Magazine**, Issue 9, Fall, 1996, pp. 34-39.

13: DEL ON THE COMEBACK TRAIL: SUMMER 1988 THROUGH THE ROCK ON ALBUM AND SUICIDE

"Now, nineteen months after his death, Del Shannon is making music again," John D. Gonzalez, Grand Rapids Press

DEL SHANNON: THE MYSTERIOUS LAST YEARS

In 1988 Del Shannon was once again on the road. On July 6, he appeared at the Hampton Beach Casino in New Hampshire. The oldies concert included Dion DiMucci and the place was packed. By the following September 1989, Shannon appeared at Kowloon's Night Club in Saugus, Massachusetts. During that year Del continued to make good music. When Dion's close friends asked him about Shannon's death, Dion simply shook his head and couldn't explain how he had gone from the vibrant performer to a man who chose to end his life by his own hand.

In final years, Shannon had a mercurial life. He was happy at one moment and sad the next. No one believed that he would have thought of putting a gun to his head and committing suicide. As 1989 opened, Del was in the midst of a major comeback. He had been working with Tom Petty and Mike Campbell on an album which was released with the title **Rock On**. But nothing was simple for Shannon, not even a comeback LP.

ROCK ON: THE TALES OF A COMEBACK ALBUM

The course of Del Shannon's **Rock On** album was a rocky one. The CD was not released outside the United States until April 1991 when in Europe the Silvertone label agreed to distribute it. In America Tom Petty's private label, Gone Gator, with distribution from MCA, brought Shannon's music back to his fans.

When the **Rock On** LP was recorded in 1989 there was some difficulty getting it into the American marketplace. Despite the success of "Runaway" in movies like "American Grafitti" and "Born On The Fourth of July," the industry didn't think that Shannon produced a viable product. Even with Petty making the rounds of record labels there was little interest in Shannon's music. Then, he committed suicide and the resulting publicity brought back interest in his music.

DEL ON THE COMEBACK TRAIL

The **Rock On** CD featured not only Petty but Electric Light Orchestra's Jeff Lynne. By March 1991, some 14 months after Shannon's untimely death, the CD appeared and the single "Walk Away" was brought out with the Silvertone label providing the European distribution. **Rock On** featured some of Los Angeles' best studio musicians including Benmont Stench on piano, Phil Jones on drums and Campbell played guitar and bass parts. Jeff Lynne and Tom Petty helped out with vocals and selected guitar riffs. They had to finish and mix some of the tunes after Shannon died.

In the press there were tales of a comeback album. The truth was that Shannon had been producing, continuing his song writing, making extensive recordings and performing to large crowds in more than one hundred concert appearances a year since "Runaway" hit the charts in 1961. There were no comebacks because Del had never gone anyplace. He was always on the road and in the middle of the music business.

There were other problems too. The industry pigeon-holed Shannon as an oldies act and this cut into his sales. His concert appearances were strong ones, but there was often a predictable nature to his shows. After almost 30 years on the road it was hard to vary the hits and everyone came to hear them. It was the new material that Shannon tried to showcase and often he was frustrated by the inability of the fans to see beyond the early hits.

Despite his continued creativity and extraordinary songwriting, the **Rock On** album didn't sell very well. The reason was a simple one, it was too carefully intertwined with the influences of Tom Petty, Jeff Lynne and Mike Campbell. While this trio added a great deal to Shannon's music there was concern among the industry that his old fans would desert the new material. Whether or not these fears were significant ones no one knows because the CD didn't sell.

During this time there was a great deal of speculation that Shannon would replace Roy Orbison in the Traveling Wilburys. This rumor was fueled by the fact that the only non-original tune the Traveling Wilburys cut was a version of "Runaway." There was no credence to the rumors and Del would not have been a member of the group. At least this is the view of Dan Bourgoise. He should know because he remained Del's closest friend. Although Bourgoise was busy with his publishing firm, Bug Music, he spent an inordinate amount of time talking with Shannon.

From Bourgoise's viewpoint all Del wanted to do was to continue to make new and original music. So he spent as much time as possible crafting the **Rock On** CD and then he hoped to promote it with a vengeance. Shannon's untimely suicide ended the dream of another hit LP.

On the first cut from **Rock On**, Shannon wrote "Walk Away," which he co-authored with his new musical partners who also played acoustic guitar. It has the feel of a Traveling Wilburys single. It also owes its soul to "Runaway." Shannon was unhappy with his current career and this song demonstrated that fact.

The 10 songs from **Rock On** were among the strongest and most innovative in Shannon's career. He wasn't an oldies singer simply going through the motions. Among the best original tunes is the haunting "Callin' My Name" and the country edged "Let's Dance." One reviewer, John Young, called Shannon's singing as that of "a great rock 'n' roller with a honky tonk soul." The twangy nature of "Lost In Memory" prompted Young to conclude, "**Rock On** makes a fine farewell for an artist who never held back."

One of Shannon's great strengths as a performer and recording artist was his knowledge of the old music. On the **Rock On** CD, he had excellent covers of the Tams' 1963 hit, "What Kind of Fool (Do You Think I Am?)" and Peter and Gordon's 1965 hit, "I Go To Pieces." When Del wrote "I Go To Pieces," he wasn't sure it was right for his style. So he didn't record it. This version is the master interpreting his own work.

Del Shannon's untimely death killed the commercial potential of **Rock On**. The nineteen months between his death and the release of **Rock On** was enough to make the fickle rock music world all but forget Shannon. He had not released an LP since the Tom Petty produced **Drop Down and Get Me**. Shannon's untimely suicide obscured many of the changes which had taken place in his career. There was much more to Del's life than people realized. He was never one to seek media publicity and the result was that many of his charity ventures helping the sick, his work with AA guiding alcoholics and his substantial donations to various charities never were publicized.

During Shannon's career, Canada was one of his fondest places to play, travel and unwind. Like England and Australia, Shannon was a super star that the Canadians appreciated and this led to many successful tours.

CANADA: A PLACE WHERE DEL SHANNON FOUND HAPPINESS

Canada had always been one of Del Shannon's favorite places. The music scene was still fresh in the small, rural provinces. Del loved Calgary, Winnipeg, Ottawa, Victoria, Vancouver and Edmonton. These quaint towns were viewed by the Canadians as the ideal place to live and Shannon couldn't have agreed more with this conclusion. Shannon hadn't played all of these towns, but he had traveled throughout Canada and loved it.

There was little pretension from the local media and the Canadian fans were loyal ones. He had fond memories of his concerts. Early in the afternoon of Saturday, September 16, 1989, Shannon walked into Ottawa's Municipal Auditorium. He looked around and his eyes drifted to the balcony. Suddenly, down the stairs from the upper balcony a young man with a welding kit emerged. He walked toward Del.

"Hello, can I get you to sign this paper?"

"Sure," Del responded.

"I love those old songs Mr. Shannon," the young man remarked.

"You do," Del smiled. "Would you like to hear some new Del Shannon hits?"

"You really mean it, you still write songs."

"Just yesterday, I finished two," Shannon remarked. "See you kid." As he walked away, Del resolved to increase his song writing schedule. What no one knew is that for the past eight months, Shannon had written an entire collection of tunes.

The itch to write new songs had hit Del Shannon on New Year's day 1989. He was sitting in front of his television set watching the football games. He jumped up and went to his study. That was it. Shannon was going to write the material for a new album. He sat down amidst the upcoming recording sessions and in a few weeks wrote all the songs which would appear on his **Rock On** album.

Shannon was tired of seeing "Runaway" released over and over again. In 1989, he remarked that he had seven separate "Runaway" releases and he wanted to make some new music. Clearly, Del was frustrated by the oldies but goodies label which haunted his music.

The background to the **Rock On** album began in 1987 when Shannon asked Tom Petty and Jeff Lynne to help him create a "new and contemporary sound." In response to Shannon's call they brought along the former Beatle, George Harrison, to craft the new album. It would take another two years to bring the LP to fruition and it was not until that New Years day that the writing bug hit Del; he was then ready to go into the studio. Once Shannon got into the studio the **Rock On** CD flowed with ease.

Del Shannon spent the first seven weeks of 1989 in the recording studio with Tom Petty, Mike Campbell and Jeff Lynne working on the single cut of "Walk Away." However, it wasn't a traditional recording studio. The **Rock On** sessions were cut in Mike Campbell's garage with Tom Petty recording the sessions on a video camera.

Everyone anticipated a big hit, and Petty's band loved working with Shannon. The Del Shannon Appreciation Society Newsletter was exuberant about the future. In addition to his studio work, Del was preparing to release a series of singles in Australia. This was part of a deal in preparation for another Australian tour.

DEL SHANNON'S 1989 AUSTRALIAN TOUR: A TRIUMPH

During the early weeks of 1989, Del Shannon prepared for another Australian tour. His records had sold well for almost 30 years down under and he had performed there many times. The Australian tour was scheduled from February 24 through March 16, 1989 and the financial arrangements were among the most lucrative in Del's career.

When he opened with three days of concerts, February 24 -26 at the Seagulls Leagues Club on the Australian Gold Coast, he was met by sold-out audiences. These shows were followed by four engagements in Melbourne, two in New South Wales and Del concluded with two shows at Rote Hill in Sydney. The Australian fans, press and record executives who followed the tour praised it. Once again Del Shannon was at the top of his performing peak.

While in Melbourne, Shannon played at one of his favorite clubs, Swagman's, and the February 28 date was a high point for Australian fans. It also provided an opportunity for some bootleg CDs.

The release of a CD, **Del Shannon Live**, on the AVM label was one of the special treats from this Australian tour. The AVM CD is a bootleg but the quality and concept are excellent. This 14 song set was from a March 11, 1989 show in Sydney and featured the usual Shannon hits, but "Runaway" was done as the theme from "Crime Story" and the Rolling Stones' "Satisfaction" was a strong surprise. AVM of Australia didn't include Shannon performing "Walk Away" but the chance to hear Del perform a medley of "Pretty Woman" segued into "Satisfaction" and then ending with a few bars of "Pretty Woman" makes this now out-of-print disc a collectable.

Another AVM CD bootleg, **Del Shannon: Greatest Hits Live**, was released in December, 1995. This March 1989 concert had also been bootlegged on the Dino and

Evasound labels. All the cuts on this CD are in stereo and the sound quality is excellent. In many respects, this CD is better than Shannon's 1972 **Live in England** release. The irony was that the bootlegger was doing a better job producing his material than Shannon's record label.

DEL SHANNON'S 1989 AUSTRALIAN TOUR

February 24-26, Seagulls Leagues Club, Gold Coast

February 28, Swagman, Melbourne

March 1., T.B.C., Melbourne

March 2, Pitrones, Melbourne

March 3, St. Kilda Town Hall, Melbourne

March 7, Ettalong Beach Memorial, New South Wales

March 8, Sawtell, New South Wales

March 11, Rote Hill (2 Shows) Sydney

A few days after he returned from his Australian tour, Del was resting at home and turned on the television. He accidentally turned on the local PBS station and watched himself in a live show from the Los Angeles Coconut Grove. This TV special included the Dixie Cups, the Tokens, Little Peggy March, Mitch Ryder, Mary Wells and Dodie Stevens among others. Del smiled at his strong performance. He felt on top of things.

Then his good friend, Tom Petty, released his **Full Moon Fever** CD which contained some vocal accompaniment by Del Shannon. The friendship with Petty helped to make the music interesting once again. Del eagerly looked forward to making some new records.

On April 8 and 9, 198, Del appeared at Disneyland. His backup band, the Monte Carlos, was a well-known oldies act and the shows were well received. Not only did the Monte Carlos know his songs but they loved playing with Shannon, and it showed during the concert.

The summer of 1989 seemed to be a relaxing and happy time. He attended weekly meetings at the Rafters and religiously followed the AA creed. Alcohol was no longer a problem for Shannon. Depression, however, was another matter. He frequently talked about Coopersville and Battle Creek and suddenly developed a long lost nostalgia for Michigan. To combat his depression, Del was seeing Dr. Elliott Phillips, a psychiatrist, and also a family counselor, Barry Levine. During this period, Dr. Curt Olson-who lived nearby on Sand Canyon Road-was a close family friend who watched Del's deteriorating mental health. Both doctors became his friend and did everything in their professional capacity to help Del survive. No one seemed to be able to help Shannon. Work was his only solace.

Del Shannon: The Late 1980s

Some of Shannon's old friends were concerned about him. Ginny Gibbs, an acquaintance from the Hi Lo days in Battle Creek, remembered: "Del didn't seem to be himself in the late 1980s. He seemed distracted and concerned about other things."

More than 20 of Shannon's friends remarked on his state of mind in the late 1980s. They saw a different man-one who was a shell of his former self. "I don't know what it was, but he was different," Darr Farr recalled. Others like John Anglin wondered if the "ghost of Coopersville was haunting their old friend."

THE GHOST OF COOPERSVILLE AND PUSHING DEL'S CAREER BUTTONS: 1989

One of Del Shannon's pastimes was to talk about his old hometown Coopersville. In lengthy conversations with old friends, Del mentioned the comfort that he derived from the small Michigan city.

During the first three months of 1989, Del continued working on new songs. He was adamant about having more hits. His collaboration with Tom Petty, Mike Campbell, Jeff Lynne and George Harrison fueled the creative juices. He told close friends that he was pushing his career buttons hard. He mentioned to everyone who would listen that his emphasis was on "roots rock." "I really like drums and real bass," Del told a reporter for the **Seattle Post-Intelligencer**, and he continued by suggesting that the Las Vegas-style rock and roll would never enter into his music.

To his close friends Del seemed frantic. He was at a crisis point. At this point in his career, Del was determined to forge ahead. But there were other problems. He was touring too much and he still remained in contact with his former wife, Shirley, and his three grown children Jody, Kym and Craig. They offered him support as did his mother Leone. There was one special person that Del could write a letter to expressing his thoughts and desires.

The person who remained his chief Coopersville contact, former high-school principal Russell Conran received regular letters from Shannon. These heartfelt missives offer some interesting insights into his career. On March 30, 1989, Shannon wrote Conran:

Mr. Conran:

Just thought I'd drop you a line. When I awoke this morning. I thought of something you said to me many years ago in high school. It had to do with giving up. You said to me once: 'Charles your a quitter, you start something and then stop doing it.' Well many times in life I have thought about what you said and today it came to mind again, for I am going to England in May, they want me to do a project with the number one producer of records in the nation. Well, I was really into it, but this morning. I thought of quitting, of calling my manager and telling him I'm fifty-four years old and maybe it will fail and who needs it anyway. But that's old high school thinking for me, so here I am not calling my manager, I'm writing to you to say thanks once more for caring so many years ago, because you cared, where most people today don't care. So thanks to you and your advice, which I have used many and many times. I have passed it on to others in my family and business, with me it started with you-DON'T BE A QUITTER. So I'm off to England. Thanks, Russ,
　　　　　Your friend,
　　　　　Charles Westover
P.S. Love to your wife and family.

This heartfelt letter to Conran suggests the degree to which Shannon used Coopersville as a psychological ballast. "I think that Chuck needed to go back to his old hometown to recharge the batteries," Chuck Marsh remarked. "When he came to see me in Kalamazoo, he talked about Coopersville all the time."

In late March 1989 when Shannon appeared on the late night interview show with Bob Costas he talked at length about Michigan in general and Coopersville in particular and how they buoyed his spirits.

THE FALL OF 1989 AND A NEW DEL SHANNON

In September 1989, Del Shannon appeared as one of the headliners at the Puyallup Fair outside of Seattle, Washington. He turned in a stunning concert and talked at length about his new album. The crowd was large and the reception was a great one.

When Del came out to perform he remarked: "How's everybody?" and then he went into a concert that featured all of his hits. What made the Puyallup Fair show special was that there was a new and improved Del Shannon. He had energy, his new music was timely and hit oriented, and he appeared to be on top of the world.

An interview with the **Seattle Post Intelligencer** provided some important insights into Del's current music. He talked about his new album and suggested that the emphasis would be upon "roots rock." Del went on to praise Tom Petty, Jeff Lynne and Mike Campbell for helping him put together his new album.

While in the Seattle area, Del was writing furiously backstage before the concert and he had also written on the flight to and from Seattle. Del didn't stay in a hotel but returned home shortly after his show. He had to return to his home in Valencia to begin to finalize the songs which he hoped would bring him back to the mainstream of the rock and roll marketplace. The **Rock On** CD was foremost in his mind.

During the fall of 1989 Del sat around the studio with Tom Petty, Mike Campbell, the leader of the Heartbreakers and Jeff Lynne of Electric Light Orchestra fame. In less than five months Shannon would kill himself in the study of his Santa Clarita, California home. In the months before his death, Shannon appeared back on the road to mainstream stardom.

What was life like for Del Shannon during the five months prior to his death? It was a commercially successful time. Because of the shrewd business skills of his long-time friend, Dan Bourgoise, Shannon received $35,000 for small portions of "Runaway" which were sung by Bruce Springsteen in the hit movie "Born On The Fourth of July." Ron Kovac, the movies hero-who also wrote the screenplay-was partial to "Runaway." "It was a song that was personal to me," Kovac remarked. "I had to include it in the movie."

As Del finished the songs for his new CD, **Rock On**, he was writing the best music of his career. When the hits stopped, Shannon wasn't worried. He had confidence in his song writing and performing abilities and continued to make a good living. He was still a star on the oldies or rock-revival circuit and he loved to play these shows. "He never felt that he'd failed when the hits stopped," Bourgoise remarked.

Tom Petty was the most important person in Del's later musical life. When Petty mentioned Shannon's influence in the song "Runnin' Down A Dream," he suggested the influence of "Runaway" to fledgling young rockers like Petty. "Me and Del were singing 'Little Runaway," Petty sang whimsical.

There was also integrity to Shannon's approach to the music which often made it difficult for him to release his material. When he recorded some country songs for Warner Bros. they remastered the tunes and took off the fiddles and steel guitar. Strings were added in the new mix, but Shannon refused to allow Warner Bros. to release it. "He could afford to turn on his heels and walk out," Bourgoise remarked, "so he did."

While Del Shannon recorded his last album, he was battling personal demons. In an attempt to recreate the past, Shannon re-recorded the 1960s hit he wrote for Peter and Gordon "I Go To Pieces." He loved the song but thought that the English duo gave it a lightweight sound. So Del cut a version that he believed was an example of his poignant lyrics and forceful musical direction.

DEL SHANNON IN SANTA CRUZ CALIFORNIA 1990

In August 1989, an evening with Del Shannon was presented in the beach community of Santa Cruz. With its pier and amusement park atmosphere the concert was a tribute to the oldies sound. The California All Stars opened the show and after an hour set, Del came out for a 45 minute set. When Del got to the end of the concert he left for a brief break. Then he came back and did "Runaway," "Hats Off to Larry" and "Little Town Flirt." He also did "Under the Boardwalk" because he was performing on the Santa Cruz boardwalk.

The Santa Cruz show was one of the best of Del's career. The open-air forum with a bevy of fans of all ages prompted him to put on an excellent performance. With the roller coaster as a back drop, the Santa Cruz Beach Boardwalk reminded Del of the 1960s when he toured to adoring crowds in rustic settings.

That evening Shannon enjoyed himself. He was worried about his new home. He lamented to one California All Star: "All I seem to be doing is moving from one house to another." Then Shannon went to downtown Santa Cruz and had dinner. He walked over to a local music club on Pacific Avenue and listened to a surf band.

While he was in Santa Cruz, Del talked at length about his new album. He was sure it would bring him back into the musical mainstream. How could it miss with friends like Tom Petty, Mike Campbell, George Harrison and Jeff Lynne?

ROCK ON: THE ALBUM THAT WOULD BRING DEL INTO THE MAINSTREAM

Rock On, the album that Shannon was working on during the last months of his life, was not only well produced, it had some new directions for Del. The song writing continued to be personal but demonstrated growth and maturity. Tragically, before the **Rock On** album was released, Del committed suicide. Steve Simels in **Stereo Review** remarked: "Ten seconds into it (Rock On) you realize that Shannon's powers were utterly undimmed, before the awful moment, something induced him to blow his brains out." The critics also agreed that "Let's Dance" was the cut from the **Rock On** CD which deserved airplay. With its catchy Cajun musical flavor and simple words, the song indicated that Shannon was still a premier songwriter.

There were other parts of **Rock On** which indicated that Shannon had an extremely commercial sense. The falsetto hook on "Are You Lovin' Me Too" is as good as his "Runaway" falsetto. Always a student of the old music, Shannon dug into his archives and recorded a cover version of the Tams "What Kind of Fool Do You Think I Am?" The influence of former Wall of Sound producer, Phil Spector, and Lynne's own Electric Light Orchestra is evident in "Walk Away."

Del Shannon and Tom Petty In The Studio

Del Shannon was back on the road. On February 2, 1991, he was scheduled to play in Grand Forks, North Dakota and the following night in nearby Fargo. Shannon was part of an oldies show which included Bobby Vee and the Crickets. Unwittingly, Del held his last press conference during these shows. He didn't look well and everyone remarked that he gave short, non-communicate answers to the press. Nyal Peterson of the Buddy Holly Memorial society taped the show and there was little doubt that Shannon was troubled.

Del, who was unusually cooperative with the press, provided brief answers in his response to questions about Tom Petty. Perhaps he was upset that not more questions were directed toward his own contribution to rock and roll history. Del retold the story of how Petty called him up and asked to collaborate with him. One result was Shannon's hit "Sea of Love" was a new phase of Del's career. But Shannon was obviously uncomfortable answering these questions.

As the press conference continued, Del talked about Max Crook's synthesizer sound and jokingly said: " I apologize for it." In a more serious vein, Shannon lectured the reporters on his pioneering contribution to rock music. The synthesizer was now commonplace. Del was obviously bitter about not being in the Rock and Roll Hall of Fame.

A Promotional Photo for the "Rock On" Album

Letting his guard down a bit, Del continued the press conference by listing "I Go To Pieces" as his favorite song. He talked about going under a bridge and hearing a Motown song. He scrambled the lyrics in his head and they sounded like "I Go To Pieces." "I went home and wrote it," Shannon concluded. Then Shannon told the story of meeting Peter Asher and feeling good over Asher's ecstatic response to the tune.

Shortly after this press conference Del gave his last performance in Fargo, North Dakota.

DEL SHANNON COLLECTIBLE RECORDS: THE BURST OF A NEW INDUSTRY

One of the ironies of Del Shannon's last few years, prior to his untimely suicide, was the rise of collectible records and CDs. Del had no way of knowing that there was a renewed world wide interest in his material. There were also a series of bootlegs which added to Shannon's recording luster.

The collectable phase began when Demon Records issued the album **Runaway Hits** (Edsel 121) on its Edsel label. Leasing the master tapes from Dan Bourgoise at Bug Music, the Demon family selected not only the best of Del's hits but included such sought after b-sides as "Jody," "Kelly" and "The Answer To Everything." The liner notes by Graham Gardner were excellent ones that put Shannon's career in proper perspective. For the time being, a real label had rescued Del from the bootleggers.

In Hamburg, Germany, the Line Record Company issued a mono album and CD of the early material. The masters, licensed from Bug Music, give this LP an excellent sound. This was the first of six reissues from Rainer Genatowski, a longtime Shannon fan, and a record company executive who believed that everyone should hear the best of Del Shannon, no matter what his records sold. One of the most interesting tunes to come from Genatowski was "The Wamboo." This was featured in an album entitled **A Portrait of Del Shannon** (Revival BCD 01789) which was a 1989 Holland release.

The following year **Let The Good Times Roll** (BCD 01789) was issued on Double D records. This CD featured all ten a and b sides from the Big Top label.

Shannon's untimely death didn't end his career. Like Elvis Presley, the demand for Del's music increased with time. His posthumous releases, thanks to Dan Bourgoise, were ones that enhanced his reputation as a serious artist. The irony was that the industry didn't take Shannon seriously until he died. It was other artists who came to recognize and appreciate Del's songwriting genius. Suzy Boguss, a country singer, included "Runaway" in her stage show. Bonnie Raitt had recorded it and the signature Shannon tune was part of her concert act.

Lurking in the background of Del's fans was a balding, bespeckled mild mannered Battle Creek businessman. His name was Dick Schlatter and he had a mission. It was to secure a historical market for Shannon and his song "Runaway." When his friends told him that this had never been accomplished for any Michigan rock and roll artist, Schlatter remarked with a smile: "We'll see."

BIBLIOGRAPHICAL SOURCES

Shirley Westover also provided an excellent perspective on Shannon's life after his divorce, and she had a more mature and balanced perspective. Dan Bourgoise also helped immensely in putting together Del's final months. An interview with Ron Kovic was important in placing "Runaway" in his life. Eric "Dr. Rock" Isralow also helped out in this area by recalling his experiences filming Salvador with Oliver Stone and showing how rockers like Del Shannon were part of the creativity of people like Stone. Conversations with screenwriter Richard Boyle helped to shape this look in the 1980s.

Matt Lucas spent an inordinate amount of time analyzing the Canadian music scene and his comments added a great deal to this chapter.

Garr Farr, Ginny Gibbs, John Anglin, Dick Schlatter, Dick Parker, Charlie Marsh and Sue Gooch provided brief interviews on their impressions of Del in the late 1980s. In Coopersville Sonny Marshall, Dick Nash, Bud Taylor and Jim Budzynski helped to piece together aspects of Shannon's life. They were particularly helpful in suggesting that when he returned to Coopersville as late as the year prior to his suicide, he was a normal person. They do not believe that he committed suicide.

On Shannon collectibles see Mike Wilson, "The Del Shannon CD Jigsaw Puzzle," **And The Music Plays On**, Issue 5, Fall, 1995, pp. 37-39.

For reviews of the **Rock On** CD see, for example, Steve Simels, "Del Shannon: Rock On," **Stereo Review**, September, 1991; Ken Barnes, "Del Shannon: Stranger in Town Departs," **R & R**, February 23, 1990.

For the Australian tour see the **Del Shannon Appreciation Society Newsletter** for February 1989.

Mark Glubke, "Special Events Planned to Mark Music History," **Battle Creek Enquirer**, September 23, 1990 is important in understanding the continued Michigan interest in Shannon's career.

See the **Seattle Post Intelligencer**, September 8, 1989, p. 5 for a description of Del Shannon's Puyallup Fair date.

For Bob Dylan's influence see, for example, Michael Gray, **Song And Dance Man III: The Art of Bob Dyla**n (London, 2000); Clinton Heylin, **Bob Dylan: Stolen Moments** (Essex, 1988); Clinton Heylin, **Bob Dylan Behind The Shades: A Biography** (London, 1991); Clinton Heylin, **A Life In Stolen Moments: Bob Dylan Day By Day, 1941-1995** (New York, 1996) and Greil Marcus, **Invisible Republic: Bob Dylan's Basement Tapes** (New York, 1997).

Also see, Howard A. DeWitt, **Chuck Berry: Rock 'n' Roll Music** (Ann Arbor, 1985); Howard A. DeWitt, **Van Morrison: The Mystic's Music** (Fremont, 1983); Howard A. DeWitt, **Sun Elvis: Presley In The 1950s** (Ann Arbor, 1992); Howard A. DeWitt, **The Beatles; Untold Tales** (Fremont, 1985) and Howard A. DeWitt, **Paul McCartney: From Liverpool To Let It Be** (Fremont, 1993) for influences upon Shannon's music as well as how the times shaped his career.

The MCA release sheet for **Rock On** provided some important information. For Jon Young's review of **Rock On** see **And The Music Plays On: Del Shannon Magazine**, Issue 4, Summer, 1995, p. 36.

On The Travelin' Wilburys, see, Howard Sounes, **Down The Highway: The Life of Bob Dylan** (New York, 2001), pp. 384-385, 390-391.

14: THE DEL SHANNON MEMORIAL AND DICK SCHLATTER

"Del Shannon did a lot for Battle Creek. His song 'Runaway' put us on the map. I realized that he would never get full recognition for his songwriting efforts without a state marker. It is a tribute to Del the man and the artist," Dick Schlatter, Memorial organizer

Richard Schlatter moved to Battle Creek from Chicago in the late 1960s. He became a respected local businessman as the art director for Hilltop Advertising. After three years of success, the demand for Schlatter's product was so great that he formed the Schlatter Group. This graphic design company quickly became one of Battle Creek's most profitable and respected businesses. When the marker to Del Shannon was dedicated a number of people wondered about Schlatter. "It was an odyssey to honor Del," Dick Nash remarked. Who is Dick Schlatter?

THE ODYSSEY OF DICK SCHLATTER

The locals often called him a businessman with skill. He was much more than a local entrepreneur. Not only was the Battle Creek entrepreneur a shrewd advertising impresario but he was also a rock and roll fanatic. Once he left work, Schlatter went home and played his Del Shannon records. He also talked to anyone who would listen about the Battle Creek music scene. As Schlatter haunted the clubs that Shannon frequented and played in during the late 1950s, he developed a Walter Mitty fantasy. He would establish a state historical marker. His friends urged him to drop the notion. Michigan had never recognized any local music artist with a marker. Dick was urged not to waste his time. Therefore, Schlatter persisted and steeped himself in the local music lore.

During lunch and sometimes in the evening, Schlatter heard tales of the Hi Lo Club and its raucous music atmosphere. Schlatter was an unlikely person to pursue a memorial to Del Shannon. He wore glasses and was a conservative, church going family man. But Dick was also an underground rock and roll fan. He loved roots music. None more so than Del's music.

As a young family man with two children, Schlatter found himself increasingly drawn to the rock music of his youth. His favorite song was Shannon's "Runaway." For years Dick had listened to Shannon's other hits "Hats Off To Larry," "Little Town Flirt," "Keep Searchin' (We'll Follow The Sun)" and "Two Kinds of Teardrops" among others. Schlatter's wife, Linda, actually owned the record player that he used, but, as Schlatter remarked, "I didn't marry her just for the record player." She could also buy beer a couple of years before Dick. Schlatter is typical of Del Shannon fans. He is educated, prosperous and addicted to old time rock music. He also believed that it was incredible that no one had honored Shannon's legacy.

THE LURE OF THE OLD HI LO CLUB AND SCHLATTER'S RESOLUTION TO HONOR DEL SHANNON

One night Schlatter was having a drink in the old Hi Lo Club, now known as the Gilbert Lounge, and he wondered why no one had immortalized Del Shannon's influence on local rock and roll music. He talked to everyone in the club. When someone mentioned Charlie Johnson's Band, Schlatter asked: "Who?" The response was that Charlie Johnson became Del Shannon. Dick didn't realize this and it piqued his interest. Suddenly Schlatter realized that Shannon was a complete local music product. He found out everything he could about Del and became a rock and roll historian. Schlatter figured that he would file the information away and enjoy using it. Then Shannon committed suicide. This is what brought Schlatter out of the woodwork. The mild mannered head of the Schlatter Group began a one-man crusade to acquire a historical marker for Del Shannon.

After putting on his Del Shannon superman outfit, Schlatter attacked the problem of a memorial. One problem was that there was no longer a vibrant music scene in and around Battle Creek. So Schlatter began a crusade to have a marker erected for Del Shannon. The quest seemed formidable as the Michigan Historical Commission wrote Schlatter suggesting that there had never been a historical marker for a rock star.

THE SCHLATTER MEMORIAL CAMPAIGN BEGINNINGS AND EARLY PROBLEMS

When Schlatter began his campaign to place a memorial in downtown Battle Creek to commemorate Del Shannon's music, it looked like a long and impossible task. He organized a group known as "The Friends of Del Shannon." Then Schlatter found a spot at the corner of Hamblin and Capital, near the old Hi Lo Club, and he urged the city to donate this land for a Del Shannon/Runaway Memorial. Most people ignored Schlatter, but they didn't realize his persistence.

The initial reaction was a mixed one. Many of the so-called-civic-minded local politicians saw the Del Shannon Memorial Plaque as a political issue. They cried out against drugs, rock and roll and the general craziness middle aged people associate with rock and roll. Had they done their homework, they would have realized that little of this criticism applied to Shannon. The opposition to the marker demonstrated the volatile feelings that rock and roll music continued to evoke.

It was mid-February 1990, just days after Shannon's death, when Schlatter introduced the memorial resolution to Del Shannon. At first, he tried out the idea on his friends. "They all agreed," Schlatter remarked, "that Del Shannon did as much to put Battle Creek on the map as anyone." Then Schlatter began researching and found out that memorials to dead or living rock and roll stars were virtually nonexistent. This was a challenge that Dick Schlatter could not pass up.

The first thing Schlatter did was to go to a Battle Creek City Commission meeting to ask for a Del Shannon Memorial. He presented them with a letter requesting that the City Commission memorialize Shannon's life. They came back to Schlatter and put him in charge of the memorial. After the City Commission asked Schlatter to take charge, a reporter from the **National Enquirer** called to inquire about the Shannon memorial. The wire services picked up the story and it appeared in the **Lansing State Journal**. The head of the Michigan State Historical Commission called and asked Schlatter to apply for a state historical marker. The historian agreed to meet with Schlatter and they talked about the procedure to secure the Del Shannon Memorial.

Schlatter went home and began to set up the criteria, which he believed would help him secure the Shannon Memorial. Then Schlatter went back to the City Commission and asked for a piece of city land to erect the memorial. The City Commission pointed out that Schlatter had to pay for the actual building of the memorial. Dick immediately began to raise money for the project.

BILL BOARDS: A BATTLE CREEK COUNCILMAN OPPOSES THE SHANNON MEMORIAL

When the City Commission met to approve the Del Shannon Memorial only five of the nine city commissioners showed up. To pass the memorial five votes were needed, but that evening the issue became political. The city commissioner for the Second Ward, Bill Boards, an African American who was a small businessman, saw an opportunity to make a moral issue out of the Shannon Memorial. With the indignation of a Baptist preacher, Boards decried the evils of rock and roll.

The newspaper interest in the Del Shannon Memorial emboldened Boards to point out the dangers that such a plaque allegedly presented to the young people of Battle Creek. When pressed to state what he disliked about Shannon, Boards confessed that he knew little about Del Shannon's personal life or his career. Like many politicians, Boards was well aware of the impact that the dispute might have on potential voters. Fortunately, Battle Creek citizens saw through the arguments against a memorial, and the opposition provided Schlatter with a reason to fight.

In late March 1990, Boards led a movement to defeat the proposal to honor Shannon's memory. In an emotional speech, Boards was critical of Shannon's suicide and made references to drugs, sex, and a rock and roll lifestyle. Many who had known Del Shannon were upset over these criticisms. These inadvertently turned many in the town in favor of the memorial. When Boards termed Shannon's suicide "an unforgiveable sin", there were outbursts of disagreement from the audience at the City Commission meeting. Soon the newspapers were flooded with letters praising Shannon and his music.

The day before the Battle Creek City Commissioners met to reconsider the plaque, Shirley Westover, Del's first wife, was in nearby Coopersville for a memorial celebration. Walking had in hand with her brother, Dick Nash, Shirley had strong memories of the old days. Coopersville hadn't changed much since she met young Charles Westover in the early 1950s. "I walked around the streets where Del and I dated and had fun and couldn't believe that strangers were besmirching my husband's memory."

Now, just a few years after her husband died, Shirley had to face this attack upon his character. But Shirley has one quality, she is a woman of character and integrity. So she held up well against this attack and carried off her duties to honor Del with style and grace. The **Battle Creek Inquirer** covered Shirley's visit to Coopersville and the publicity strengthened Dick Schlatter's bid for a Del Shannon Memorial Plaque.

To some people in Coopersville and Battle Creek who knew Del and Shirley, they found them the perfect couple. They were also aware of Del's wandering eye, his tendency to compulsively chase hit records and his up and down mental state. But what truly mattered is that most people believed they had a solid marriage. So these rumors and innuendo years later stung Shirley.

After a great deal of debate-both pro and con-over Schlatter's Del Shannon Memorial proposal, the Battle Creek City Commission met on Tuesday, April 10, 1990 for a final vote. The city manger, Rance Leaders, was inundated with mail in support of the plaque. Locals recalled that "Chuck," as Del Shannon was then known, was a down-to-earth and hard-working businessman-entertainer. This time the City Commission voted eight to one in support of the memorial. Only Boards cast the dissenting vote.

Despite the overwhelming support of the community and the Battle Creek City Commission, Boards continued to criticize Dick Schlatter's efforts. He called the land, which the city donated for the memorial, "a giveaway of taxpayers' money". At the same time he continued to criticize Del Shannon.

Shirley Westover quieted the criticism with a simple comment. "The memorial is going to give us something to come back and see year after year." The mild-mannered and scholarly-looking Schlatter agreed. Throughout the ordeal, Schlatter restrained himself. Boards often attacked Schlatter personally, but this did very little to anger the Battle Creek businessman. He had a mission and was determined to accomplish it.

The integrity that Schlatter displayed was important. There were events in Boards' personal life that locals urged Dick to use to win his argument for a memorial. "No way," Schlatter replied. "I will never engage in character assassination." Like Shirley, Schlatter is a man of integrity.

On June 26, 1990, a letter from John B. Swainson, a commissioner with the Michigan Historical Commission, informed Richard Schlatter that the Del Shannon/Runaway Information Site was to be located at 45 Capital Ave., S.W. and has been listed in the Michigan State Register of Historic Sites. Schlatter went home, got his wife, and went out for an expensive dinner. Schlatter had accomplished the impossible. Del Shannon was the first rock and roll star in the United States to be awarded an official state plaque.

DICK SCHLATTER'S PERSONAL QUEST TO BUILD THE MEMORIAL TRIUMPHS

After he received the letter, Schlatter took matters into his own hands. He organized a hole digging ceremony on the spot where the Del Shannon/Runaway Memorial would be erected. A picture in the **Battle Creek Shopper News** on August 3, 1990 showed a smiling Schlatter along with a fan, Brad Latty, and Jim and Mike Popenhagen. The story proudly announced that on September 29, 1990, the dedication would take place. The publicity was an important part of Schlatter's ploy to raise the rest of the memorial money.

Then donations began pouring in to help Schlatter and the Michigan Historical Commission to fund the plaque. A "Saturday Lost in the 50s Party" at Kalamazoo's Wings Stadium brought in more than $2000. This was added to the $1500 donated from private citizens. As a graphic designer, Schlatter donated his time and paid for the production costs to create a 45 RPM record of "Runaway" on the Big Top label which was used as the marker. A shy, retiring kind of person, Schlatter simply shrugged and said: "I am happy to do it for Del."

When local newspapers placed the cost of the Shannon memorial at $11,000 with the city providing the land, the rest of the amount was raised only by Schlatter's diligent efforts. This speculation was not factual and it demonstrated once again that the press didn't have accurate information. The news story was designed to defeat and depress Schlatter. He never gave up and continued to raise money even when it looked like the memorial would fail. Naturally, Schlatter was exhausted, but he had accomplished the impossible task of setting up the first marker issued by a state historical commission for a rock and roll star.

Shirley Westover forwarded a large check in which she requested anonymity. Not eager to enter the public limelight, Shirley made Schlatter promise not to publicize the amount. Shirley's contribution, as well as fund raisers and other donations, made the marker a reality.

There was a local celebration when Laura Ashlee, state historical marker coordinator for the Michigan State Bureau of History, officially informed the Battle Creek City Commission that the state board voted unanimously to approve the marker and it would take four to six weeks for the $1215 marker to be manufactured and delivered. At that point, Richard Schlatter announced that he would schedule the ceremony and attempt to place the Del Shannon Memorial in the proper place.

In mid-September 1990, the dedication ceremony was planned. Gary Mallernee, the president and general manager of WNWN radio, was ecstatic about the Del Shannon Memorial and he began rounding up guests to make the celebration special. A young guitarist, Michael Popenhagen was on hand to watch Mallernee present the remainder of the memorial money to Schlatter on a little hill next to where the plaque would be erected. His grandfather was the guitar player in the Charlie Johnson Band, Del's first group at the Hi Lo Club.

Young Mike's voice was eerily like Del's and he sang "Runaway" with all the same inflection. Popenhagen's band, Last Request, was scheduled to play at the memorial and for young kids they sounded like a band from Shannon's day.

Dick Parker was one of the unseen benefactors to Shannon's Memorial. He was Del's original drummer and he quietly provided the bulk of the remaining money needed for the memorial. Parker wrote out a check for $1000 and looked at Mallernee and remarked: "It's your ass, if you tell anyone about this contribution." Parker had lifted weights for years, rode a motorcycle and works in the computer industry. He is also a highly private person who is also an accomplished writer. A brilliant man who continues to go his own way in the world, Parker along with Shirley Westover quietly kicked in the money necessary to complete the Del Shannon/Runaway Memorial Plaque.

Over the years, Parker has had some great experiences. While on vacation in Florida, Dick was having a drink in a bar when the person next to him told Parker that he had played the drums on Shannon's "Runaway." Parker smiled and remarked: "Great man, it's good to meet you." This is typical Dick Parker. Quiet, calm, laid back and there is not a mean bone in his body. He was one of Shannon's best friends and continues to honor his memory.

ANOTHER CONTROVERSY SURFACES TO CHALLENGE THE SHANNON MEMORIAL

After all the problems with the Del Shannon/Runaway Memorial, just as it looked like everything was in place, there was one last controversy. The Calhoun County Commissioners where Battle Creek is situated were asked to declare Saturday, September 29, 1990 as Del Shannon Day. As the local county commissioners debated the issue, Tino Smith, a Democrat from Battle Creek, asked for a roll-call vote and stated that he was opposed to the day because Shannon committed suicide. Then in the roll-call vote, five commissioners, sensing political problems, voted against the proposed Del Shannon Day. Gary L. Beard who represented District 5 as a Calhoun County Commissioner came out strongly against the Del Shannon Memorial. Beard suggested that Shannon's place in history was "not an appropriate one". Beard spoke profusely about Del Shannon but had difficulty placing the issue appropriately within the context of the general history of the Kellogg Corporation or Battle Creek. Richard Schlatter once again answered these attacks in a emotional letter, some time later, to the **Battle Creek Inquirer** since the incident had obviously upset Del's wife, Shirley, and his daughters, Jody and Kym, who were on hand at the event. In some respects, Beard's criticism ensured the success of the Del Shannon/Runaway Memorial. The opposition to Beard was staggering and helped carry the day for Schlatter's committee.

Commissioners with a sense of dignity and propriety. One of them, County Commission Chairperson, Robert Huntington, a Republican from Battle Creek, suggested that the commissioners reconsider their vote as Shannon did bring fame and fortune to Battle Creek. There were others who reconsidered because of Beard's ineloquent and unfair attack upon Shannon.

Around town the defense of Del Shannon's life and reputation was complete. Most everyone loved Chuck Westover and when he became a star they recalled his positive comments about Battle Creek and his frequent visits to the city.

Beverly Riskey, a Democrat from Battle Creek, believed that drugs and alcohol were never a part of Shannon's mystique. Riskey pointed out that for some time Shannon had been clean and sober. So why bring up the past? She also remarked to the County Commissioners that literally hundreds of local citizens expressed their support for a Del Shannon Memorial. It seemed logical to include a day to commemorate the plaque.

The County Commissioners weren't stupid, they needed votes to remain in office. Then the audience began murmuring their support for Shannon's marker, the political winds shifted to his favor. When the County Commissioners asked the audience for its opinion, there was no doubt that the citizenry supported a Del Shannon Day. Just as quickly as they opposed the event, the County Commissioners, sensing a loss of votes, agreed to support it. It was a strange meeting and suggested the tumultuous controversy often surrounding Del and his music. The final vote was five to four and the debate left rancorous feelings. Even after his death, Del Shannon remained a source of controversy. There was no one that could ruin the perfect weekend which inaugurated the Del Shannon/Runaway Memorial.

The controversy, however, didn't die down. Del Shannon's fans were so furious with the politicians that hundreds of letters, telegrams and personal complaints were delivered to the Calhoun County Commissioners. The tide was so strong in Del's favor that Commissioner Beard wrote a letter to the **Battle Creek Inquirer** and asked the newspaper to include the headline "Yes I Am A Del Shannon Fan!"

THE CELEBRATION OF THE DEL SHANNON MARKER

The night before the formal celebration for the Shannon marker, Bobby Helms of "My Special Angel," "Fraulein" and "Jingle Bell Rock" fame brought his band into the W.K. Kellogg center for a benefit concert. Mike Popenhagen was one of the opening acts and performed his tribute tune "My Special Friend, Charlie." In addition to the music, Del's daughters, Jody and Kym performed two songs "Sweet Dreams" and "I Go To Pieces" for the sold-out crowd.

The September 29, 1990 Del Shannon/Runaway Memorial celebration was a momentous event. Richard Schlatter knew Shannon's past and picked the best of his friends to address the throng. Del's principal at Coopersville high school, Russell Conran, was a marvelous speaker who had the crowd in constant laughter with his tales of Shannon's guitar playing and general lack of interest in high school. Dan Bourgeois, Shannon's former manager and lifelong friend, added a great deal to the festivities. Even John B. Swainson, representing the normally staid Michigan Historical Commission, got caught up in the spirit and wowed the crowd with a number of interesting anecdotes. On the sideline, Dick Schlatter orchestrated the festivities like the coronation of a King, after all Charlie Johnson was Battle Creek's first rock and roll king.

The Del Shannon Memorial was particularly pleasing to Shirley Westover. "I only wish that my husband were alive to see it," Shirley continued. "It would have made a lot of difference to him. He loved both Coopersville and Battle Creek. They were always his home."

BIBLIOGRAPHICAL SOURCES

Interviews with Richard Schlatter helped to focus the memorial issue. Ginny Gibbs, Darwin Farr, Don Rogers, Charlie Marsh, the Popenhagen family and others helped to clarify the memorial controversy. The former Mayor of Battle Creek, Al Brodofsky, helped to parcel out the politics of the time and Larry Gilbert, son of Ma and Pa Gilbert, kindly recreated some of the tensions surrounding the Del Shannon issue. Also important to this chapter were anonymous interviews with a number of politicians who opposed the Shannon memorial. Dick Parker talked at length about the memorial and others mentioned his financial contribution. When asked if he gave money, Parker simply smiled.

The **Battle Creek Inquirer**, February 24, 1990, p. 5a, and April 11, 1990, p. 3a discusses the Del Shannon Memorial controversy in detail. Also see the **Battle Creek Shopper News**, May 31, 1990, p. 16 and August 30, 1990, p. 6.

On the plague see a letter from John B. Swainson to Richard Schlatter, June 26, 1990 for the memorial commission award.

EPILOGUE

In his life and musical journey, Del Shannon often lacked confidence. His first wife, Shirley, recalls that he never felt like that he deserved fame and fortune. During his lifetime, Del lived like an average person, while carefully investing his money, and he was never at ease in the public eye. What is intriguing about Shannon is his level of creativity. He wrote some of the songs, which identify the teen angst of the early and mid 1960s, and he remained a strong concert attraction until his untimely suicide. Shannon's creativity was never questioned but his personal instability and a poor decision made his life at times an unbearable one. Few people took time to recognize Del's enormous creativity and this hurt him.

The beat poet, Kenneth Patchen, summed up the career of most creative people by suggesting that no matter what an artist achieved, there were still new heights to scale. Patchen's words were prophetic. Throughout his life no matter what Shannon accomplished, he still retained thoughts of failure and insecurity. These feelings were the product of his childhood and early adult years. However, over time he partially overcame some of these feelings and emerged as a confident, serious adult.

If he was killed by anyone, it was the music business and the milieu surrounding fame. When his wife, Shirley, asked him to go to a movie or dinner, Del refused. Not because he didn't love her, not because he didn't want to go out, he was simply tired of fame and fortune.

No matter how hard he tried after "Runaway," Del never had another number one **Billboard** hit. He came close but this wasn't enough for him. The elusive search for a gigantic hit record was one of the themes that encompassed his life.

What bothered Shannon was the public perception of his music. The myths that followed him and haunted his very existence were ones surrounding the notion that he was a one-hit artist. He wasn't an oldies act and he wasn't a one hit artist. Yet, the rock critics often persisted in picturing him this way. He endured endless interviews with the same questions and inane comments, but Del always did it with a smile. With an unusually high degree of intelligence, Shannon learned to play the record company game, but he was unhappy with the tales that grew up around his music. The career myths threatened to destroy his self-confidence and undermine his future music.

EPILOGUE

DEL SHANNON'S CAREER: THE MYTHS

The serious Shannon fans realized that he charted tunes in every decade. Generally, "Runaway," "Hats Off To Larry," "Stranger In Town" and "Little Town Flirt" were the tunes that most people recalled. This fact obscures his hit-making ability. From 1961 to 1983, Del placed nine tunes on the **Billboard Top 40** chart. So he was a consistent hit maker.

From the time that "Runaway" hit the charts and went to number one in both America and the U. K., Shannon's hits continued to flow. After "Runaway," he charted in the Top 40 from 1961 to 1965 with "Hats Off to Larry," a number five hit, "So Long Baby," a number 28 tune, "Hey! Little Girl," settling in at 38, "Cry Myself To Sleep," which was 29 in England, "The Swiss Maid," a number two U. K. chart buster, "Little Town Flirt," which was number 12 in the U. S. and four in the U. K., "Two Kinds of Teardrops," a number five English hit, "Two Silhouettes," a number 23 English hit, "Sue's Gotta Be Mine," number 21 in England, "Mary Jane," a non-U. S. chart song that rose to number 35 in England, "Handy Man" charted at 22 and 36 in the U. S. and U. K. respectively; "Keep Searchin' (We'll Follow The Sun) hit number ninie and "Stranger in Town" was number 30 in the U. S. and 40 in England. Del's career slowed down after 1965, but he had established his hit-making potential.

Adam Komorowski, a leading British music critic, summed up Del's career: "Shannon was a popular visitor to the U.K. in the 60s, and along with Roy Orbison, established himself as one of the leading American artists in an era where being British was almost a prerequisite for success in the pop world." Komorowski recognized Del's crossover musical appeal. He was at home in the pop, rock, country, jazz or even blues marketplace. To some performers this would have been the kiss of truth, but Shannon thrived in this milieu.

Shannon was a complex individual, a great songwriter, an excellent performer and a man of many contradictions. He was also an artist who was judged by his times. When Del became a star, there was a tendency to downgrade or ignore the intellectual side of rock and roll music. Few people paid attention to the lyrics. If they had realized the plaintive wail in "Stranger In Town," they would have looked at Del the same way that the critics glorified Bob Dylan. But rock music writers often pigeon holed artists, like Del, into an inescapable time warp. Del Shannon fell into the early 1960s time warp thanks to these critics. The established view is that Shannon was part of the teen crooner explosion that brought Frankie Avalon, Fabian, Bobby Rydell and Bobby Darin among others to the top of the charts. What is often ignored is that the early 1960s was a time of continued musical ferment. In 1960, Gene Vincent's "Pistol Packin' Mama" and Eddie Cochran's "Cut Across Shorty" were released to heavy sales in England but to little interest in America. The following year, Jerry Lee Lewis' cover of Ray Charles' "What'd I Say" became a British hit and such artists as Brenda Lee, Gary U. S. Bonds, the Everly Brothers and Freddie Cannon among others kept the roots style of rock and roll alive. It was in this mix that Del Shannon became a major star. What has been missing from serious analysis of Shannon's career is his ability as a storyteller.

Like Bob Dylan, Shannon electrified audiences with his pop tales. "Little Town Flirt" had its genesis in the Hi Lo Club and the other numerous musical dives that Shannon played early in his career. It was in this training ground that the local bar flys, the would-be musicians, the story tellers, the local toughs and the middle-class guy out for a night, told stories that found their way into songs.

It is in the themes to Del's songs that one finds his greatest contribution. "Keep Searchin' (We'll Follow The Sun)" was an appeal to find his way in the mindless jobs that young men were forced into during the late 1950s and early 1960s. Many tunes were personal. "Jody" was written for a girl who hung out at the Hi Lo Club and "Hats Off To Larry" was a tribute to producer, Harry Balk. When Del teamed up with Tom Petty and Mike Campbell in the 1980s, this technique continued as "Liar" and "Sucker For Your Love" offered a Dylaneseque look at Del's life. "Little Town Flirt," written with Maron McKenzie, distilled the tales of young girls in the bars all over Battle Creek. It was these experiences which created Shannon's musical mystique. There were also many myths about his career.

The myth that Del was one of the slick, pop crooners of the early 1960s was not entirely inaccurate. He had the looks, the style and at times the direction of the mindless bobby boys. These Philadelphia, American Bandstand created teen idols had little songwriting talent, average voices and drop dead good looks. Yet, Del competed with them and carried his loyal fan base for the next 30 years. This picture ignores his varied and vivid career. It also fails to recognize his ability to weave magical lyrics. The reality is something quite different. Del Shannon had the pulse of the mid-west in his songs, the teen angst of the times and the natural talents of a person who could tell a tale. More often than not, it was a story of local lore and personal anguish.

DEL SHANNON AS A STORY TELLER

Like Bob Dylan and John Lee Hooker, Del had a way of using his personal experiences and the trials and tribulations of the times to mold and weave his tales. Unfortunately, the pop pundits and academic critics have paid little attention to Shannon's story-telling abilities. They have insisted upon focusing upon his career. Often the critics have paid more attention to Del's declining period of hits than to his 30 year contribution.

By 1965, Shannon's top ten hit career was on the decline, although he continued to chart periodically until his death. What set Shannon apart from his contemporaries was his ability to tell a story. As he grew up in the small, remote town of Coopersville, Michigan, he was Charles Westover. There were no bars in town. There were spots though where local storytellers relived the good old days. At restaurants like Tiny and Tink's, a bar without alcohol where the locals gathered, there were constant tales. The storyteller was often a farmer who talked of the local who milked his cows and then shot himself. As the person relating the tale suggested, he didn't want the wife to have a dead husband and ruined milk cows. So he kept the cows alive to guarantee her livelihood. To the sophisticated city dweller, this was a ridiculous tale. To Del it was a statement of folk history. One that he could use in a song. What enthralled young Chuck was that the storyteller seemed more interested in the cow than in the widow. It was tales like these that inspired Chuck Westover to write his own stories. But his were set to music.

When "Runaway" raced to number one on the **Billboard** chart, Shannon wrote about a confused person running from life. With "So Long Baby," "Hey! Little Girl" and "Little Town Flirt," all Top 40 hits from 1961 to 1963, Shannon developed the themes of teen angst that propelled his career to the top of the charts.

The best examples of Del's song-poet influence came when he wrote "Keep Searchin' (We'll Follow The Sun)" and "Stranger On The Run." These tunes produced a moody, apocalyptic sound, which placed Del's music into a genre more like Bob Dylan's than Bobby Vee's did. It frustrated Del that his story telling wasn't taken seriously by the critics or the public. His tales were ones of the bleak existence of people in his Coopersville youth or of similar types in his Battle Creek early adult years. The foibles and frailties of those around Shannon found their experiences rewritten in songs with a poetic quality and a lyrical sophistication.

Rock and roll lyrics are generally not considered poetry. Del's song are reflective of the times. What Shannon did was to talk about the girl everyone knew in "Little Town Flirt," or the person who changed your life in "Hat's Off To Larry." The philosophical musings of the times were handled in "Keep Searchin' (We'll Follow The Sun)," and in obscure tunes like "The Wamboo," Del let you know that young people were still having fun. Though few, if any, off the rock critics paid attention to Shannon's story telling. Had they, a litany of problems, influences and good with bad times would have been the subject of record reviews. Unfortunately, rock criticism was in its infancy and Shannon was treated as just another early 1960s idol. One exception was Dave Marsh who recognized the moody, eerie and prophetic nature of Shannon's songs.

DEL SHANNON: A SINGER- SONGWRITER'S LEGACY

Del Shannon's legacy rests on his song writing. The eerie falsetto, the roaring music and the sensitive lyrics established Shannon's singer-songwriting legacy. Not only was Del not appreciated in the manner of his contemporaries but also his ability to sketch a tune and produce it is lost to history.

Another problem with the Shannon story was the myth-making machinery attached to the rock and roll industry. When "Runaway" hit the charts, five years were shaved from his age. He was not 21 and a single, swinging bachelor, but a family man from Battle Creek, Michigan. Of course this image would not sell with **16 Magazine**. The result was that Charles Westover became Del Shannon and never looked back to his old life.

As Charles Weedon Westover, he had experienced a degree of fame and happiness at Battle Creek's Hi Lo Club. Once he went on the road, Del's life was never the same. Coming of age musically in the early 1960s, Del faced the onslaught of the teen idols, Frankie Avalon, Fabian and Bobby Rydell and then the Beatles and the English Invasion. He survived both and remained a star.

"The Schizoid Heritage" is a term often used to describe Shannon's music. He was caught between two generations. Del grew up listening to the music of Chuck Berry,

Little Richard, Dion and the Belmonts, the Big Bopper, Elvis Presley and Jerry Lee Lewis among others. He became a star as 1950s rock and roll faded and a highly programmed, predictable type of rock music surfaced. Fortunately, Del was anything but predictable and he began a career which demonstrated his musical versatility.

THE IMPACT OF DEL'S FIRST ALBUM

When Del's first album, **Runaway With Del Shannon**, was released, he had written eight of the 12 tracks. The tragedy of Shannon's career is that he released the perfect song, "Runaway" on his initial album. Listening to the **Runaway** LP suggests Del's enormous talent. The initial cut, "Misery," is an up-tempo tune with Max Crook's signature musitron sound adding to the mix. But it is Del's falsetto sound and lyrical beauty, which makes "Misery" a winner. A slow tune, "Day Dreams," is an example of a versatility, which made the Shannon sound unique.

A cover of Doc Pomus and Mort Shuman's "His Latest Flame" took place prior to Elvis Presley placing the tune on the charts. "The Prom" was a Shannon song that received enough mid-west radio play for the Robbs to cover it. The talking bridge in "The Prom" is a perfect example of how the teen angst mode of song writing influenced Shannon. It is the fifth song on the LP, "The Search," which has classic Shannon imagery. "I Wake Up Crying" is a typical teen anthem of despair, which puts Del squarely into the camp of the agony songwriters of the day.

In the next song, "Wide Wide World," Shannon creates a chalypso beat, which was a popular dance, and he talks about a lost love. The influence of Mickey and Sylvia subtly seeps into the song but it is vintage Del Shannon. "I'll Always Love You" is a song, which shows off Del's crooner style. The slow ballad tells another story of lost love. This theme is one, which recurs throughout his early music.

The up-tempo "Lies" is a lyrical masterpiece which has a controlled vocal style backed by Harry Balk's energetic production. With "He Doesn't Care," a song which sounds like a cross between Paul Anka and the Skyliners and the dreamy "Jody," Shannon finished off an LP which was a first release masterpiece.

Adam Komorowski, a noted British rock historian, wrote in his notes to **Del Shannon: The EP Collection**, released in England in 1998 by See For Miles, that 'Del's soaring lyrics' produced a pop classic "Runaway." While this is correct, the remainder of the songs on the first Shannon LP remain classic ones. When "Runaway" topped the British chats during the first week of July 1961, Shannon was a bona fide international pop star. There was a question whether or not the magic would continue. It did. Del Shannon's second album demonstrated that he was no one-hit wonder.

THE MASTERPIECES CONTINUE: THE HATS OFF TO DEL SHANNON LP

The second LP, **Hats Off To Del Shannon**, began strangely with a cover of Roger Miller's county tune, "The Swiss Maid" which was cut in Nashville. While in Nashville, Shannon was able to team up with the famed country musician, Owen Bradley and the

Jordanaires. Initially, Del was not happy about the song but it became a huge English hit. This quickly quieted his fears that the song was too country. A Shannon original "Cry Myself To Sleep" and a Pomus-Shuman song "Ginny In the Mirror" which was featured in the movie "It's Trad Dad" were tunes that found a ready English market. "You Never Talked About Me" was the b-side of "Little Swiss Maid" and as a result was a popular U. K. song. "Don't Gild the Lily, Lily" was a non-Shannon written tune but once again the English audiences loved it. The b-side "I Won't Be There" was another teen angst tune with a controlled falsetto and minimal soaring violins.

Looking back on the second LP, Del remarked: "I was forced into recording 'Ginny In The Mirror' for a movie deal. I had to cut it and it had to be a single. I hated that record." "Hats Off To Larry" was of course the hit from the LP. But such obscure songs as "The Answer To Everything" suggests the depths to which Shannon could interpret a song. "Hey! Little Girl" was a radio friendly tune, which was both an American and British, hit. "I'm A Gonna Move" complete with a female back up, bears testimony to Shannon's country music roots blended with the teen anthems of the early 1960s.

The country sound of "I Don't Care Anymore" suggests the versatility in Del's musical bag. The **Hats Off To Del Shannon**, ends with "So Long Baby" which establishes Del not only as a highly commercial songwriter, but a singer who has a penchant for spirited lyrics. The use of a kazoo harkens back to Del's days in Coopersville and is another example of this musical dexterity.

When the British-based Beat Goes On Records label reissued the **Runaway With Del Shannon** LP backed with the **Hats Off To Del Shannon** LP, bonus stereo cuts of "Runaway," "Hats Off To Larry" and "Hey! Little Girl" added to Shannon's musical legend.

There was much more great Shannon music, but the first two LPs were so carefully crafted by producer, Harry Balk, that Del's songs took on a highly commercial direction and while he continued to make good music, the first two albums stand out as examples of his creative genius.

STEVE MONAHAN: LOOKING BACK ON DEL SHANNON'S LIFE

Steve Monahan was a young kid who had just graduated from MacKenzie High School in Detroit. One night he and his father drove down to the Southwind Bowling Alley and Night Club in Southfield, Michigan. They were celebrating Steve's high school graduation. It was 1962 and Monahan was not only a fan of Del Shannon's music but he was also a singer and songwriter. That night Steve met Del and Shirley. "It was like a dream come true," Monahan continued, "I couldn't believe it."

"We went to the bowling alley to see Doug Brown and the Omens. Then I found myself sitting next to and bonding with Del Shannon. He was one of the most caring people I have ever met. Shirley was a jewel and they treated me like family."

For the next 38 years Del Shannon was Steve Monahan's best friend. They stayed in constant contact. Del also supported all of Monahan's endeavors. When Steve attended the Henry Ford Community College for three years, Del was there in his corner. There was also a musical side to Monahan. He was signed to Vee Jay Records in Chicago and later recorded an album for Kapp. When Del and Shirley moved to California, Monahan relocated to the Golden State. It was 1965 and they were all young and having fun. Monahan even provided backup vocals on Del's cover of Bobby Freeman's "Do You Wanna Dance."

THE REAL DEL SHANNON

Shirley Westover remarked that her husband never believed that he deserved his fame and fortune. This comment provides an interesting insight into Del's psyche. The real Del Shannon was always Chuck Westover the kid from Coopersville. The reception to his records, positive or negative, never deterred Del from continuing to write and produce new music. What made Shannon significant was his ability to produce new music. At the end of his life the collaboration with Tom Petty and Mike Campbell brought a new sophistication and lyrical magic to his work.

The negative side to Shannon's life was that he made poor decisions during his last decade. He created a mountain of debt with the new houses, he was on the road too much and he was increasingly unhappy. Yet, despite these shortcomings, he found a renewed vigor in the 1980s music world.

In 1981, the Tom Petty album collaboration, **Drop Down And Get Me**, produced a minor hit with a remake of Phil Phillips' "Sea of Love." This album contained a number of excellent songs. "Cheap Love," for example, crossed over into the country market. In the mid-1980s when Del went to Nashville to cut some new records, he was recognized for his country musical skills. But Warner Bros. released two singles to insignificant sales. It never dawned on Warner Bros. to spend promotional money. Part of the problem was Shannon's musical direction. When he covered Nazareth's "Broken Down Angel," Del believed that he had a country hit. Internal Warner Bros. memos were skeptical of Shannon's musical direction.

The ability to experiment was demonstrated in 1984 when Del arrived in Sydney, Australia and cut some sides with Jeff "Skunk" Baxter and members of the Divinyls. The result was a song entitled "Something To Believe in" which was intended for the movie "Street Hero." A decade earlier, Shannon had cut some sides with Air Supply pianist, Frank Esler-Smith. Their song, "Help Me," was a b side that was pressed in small numbers. What was strange was that few people recognized these efforts. So it was back to the oldies circuit.

The real mystery of the last years centered on the rumor that Shannon would replace Roy Orbison in the Traveling Wilburys. Dan Bourgoise claims there was nothing to the rumor. Yet, "Runaway" was the only song by another artist that the Wilburys recorded.

DEL SHANNON: AN OVERVIEW OF A HIT MAKING LIFE

Del Shannon wasn't perfect as a husband, father, singer, songwriter or businessman. Yet, he accomplished so much and made some many people happy.

Perhaps this is what contributed to his ultimate demise. He was too nice. He tried to please too many people. He never found happiness. He was not content with his string of hits. No one knows for sure and Del took his secrets to the grave.

What Del left behind was a magnificent musical legacy. He was a carpet salesman playing nights at Battle Creek's Hi Lo Club when "Runaway" raced to number one on the **Billboard** pop chart. On July 1, 1961, "Runaway" reached number one and remained there for almost a month. It sold more than half a million copies and also topped the English charts. By August, "Hats Off To Larry," which bore an eerie resemblance to "Runaway" began climbing the charts, and with Max Crook's musitron influenced solo, it hit number five on **Billboard**. This provided the first sign of Shannon's mysterious personality. According to close friends, he was depressed that "Hats Off To Larry" didn't reach number one.

By November 1961, the album **Runaway** was released on the Big Top label. Because Irving Micahnik was an amateur, only 10,000 copies of the album were produced. There were 9,000 pressed in mono and 1,000 in stereo. The result was that Shannon lost a substantial royalty. The producer, Harry Balk, had nothing to do with this decision. Micahnik ran the business end of Embee Production and he doubted that Del could sell more than 10,000 albums.

What made the **Runaway** album unique was the song selection and production. Using four of the songs that he had written and practiced in Battle Creek's Hi Lo Club, "Day Dreams," "The Prom," "Lies" and "He Doesn't Care Anymore," Shannon crafted the perfect 1961 LP. "The Prom" and "He Doesn't Care Anymore" caught the essence of the teen angst mood of the early 1960s.

There were some legendary songwriters who helped with Del's first album. Doc Pomus and Mort Shuman were Brill Building songwriters in New York who had two songs for Shannon. "Misery" was written after the pair listened to "Runaway" and "His Latest Flame." This allowed Del to cover the song before Elvis Presley made it a massive hit.

The hidden ingredient in the **Runaway** LP was the musicians. With Bill Ramal arranging the songs, Al Caiola and legendary jazz guitarist, Bucky Pizzerrelli, helped Max Crook on piano and musitron, Milt Hinton on bass and Joe Marshall on drums. From time to time Ramal joined in on saxophone. The result was a perfect twelve song LP with a sound, which established Del Shannon as a three-decade hit act.

When his second hit, "Hats Off To Larry," hit the charts, there was little doubt as to Shannon's commercial staying power. He was also an English star. By his third single "So Long Baby" and his fourth release "Hey! Little Girl," Del was touring in a world-wind manner. When his second album, **Hats Off To Del Shannon**, was released, it became what some have described as a lost album. It didn't sell well in America, but in England it was a smash. Once again the nefarious hand of Irving Micahnik is seen in the background. This LP was something of a greatest hits and it included the first six singles with both a and b sides. Only small numbers of the **Hats Off Del Shannon** album were printed and Del became bitter and frustrated with Embee Productions. Strangely enough, the British did appreciate the second or lost Del Shannon LP.

By 1963, Embee Productions and Del were on the verge of a divorce. Although 1962 was a banner year with hits in Japan, Australia, Europe and the U. K., producer

EPILOGUE

Harry Balk was worried about the decline in Shannon's 45 sales. Balk realized that Max Crook's musitron sound was passé and Del needed to find a new hit direction. It was at this point that Balk introduced Del to Maron McKenzie, an African American songwriter working in a Detroit candy factory, and they proceeded to cowrite "Little Town Flirt," "Two Kinds of Teardrops," "Kelly," "Two Silhouettes" and "My Wild One." These songs made up the essence of Shannon's next album **Little Town Flirt**.

There were some musical surprises in the **Little Town Flirt** LP. The backing vocals by the Young Sisters added a soulful touch to Shannon's music. There were also some excellent cover tunes. The Beatles' "From Me To You" charted in America for Del at number 77 and it came a year prior to the British Invasion. With covers of Dion's "Runaway Sue" and Bruce Channels' "Hey Baby," Embee Productions was attempting to cash in on the current hit market. This strategy deflected interest away from Del's original songs. It also prevented such strong tunes as "The Wamboo" from being included on the album.

It was in England that Shannon reached true superstar status. In 1962-1963, he was selected as the premier male vocalist by a leading London music magazine. His album, **Little Town Flirt**, was the ninth best selling LP in the United States and the increased international touring market guaranteed Shannon's future success. There is a tendency among rock and roll historians to ignore American acts in the wake of the 1964 British Invasion. Del Shannon fared just fine as the English invaded the colonies.

The 1964 album, **Handy Man**, was another winner. Once again Harry Balk's production magic helped Del to withstand the onslaught of British acts. In the midst of this LP, unfortunately, Shannon and Talent Artists Inc. became embroiled in a fractious legal dispute. When Del broke away from Balk and Micahnik, he was blackballed from signing with other labels. "He had a contract with us," Balk remarked in an interview, "and we made sure he honored it." To counter what he considered a low and unfair royalty, Del formed his own label, Berlee. The label named after his parents, Bert and Leone, issued two singles "Sue's Gotta Be Mine" backed with "Now She's Gone" and "That's The Way Love Is" b/w "Time of the Day." Shannon learned quickly that it was difficult to sell records. "Sue's Gotta Be Mine" did chart at 71 in the U. S. and 21 in the U. K. But Del quickly found that the business end of the industry was a precarious one. By March 1964, Del was back with producer, Harry Balk, and his business partner, Irving Micahnik.

In England, two Shannon singles were released on the same day. "That's The Way Love is" came out on the London label and "Mary Jane" on Stateside Records. At this point, producer Balk was keeping Shannon's career running in high gear. Harry had an ear and eyes for the marketplace. So he took Del's magnificent falsetto and paired it with Jimmy Jones' "Handy Man." The result was a new-sounding hit. It was Balk who reasoned that Shannon wasn't writing with his usual flair and so he brought in Maron McKenzie to help and continued to search out cover tunes. Harry also brought the Royaltones to New York City and they had the sound that made Del a hit once again. Eventually, Shannon and Dennis Coffey of the Royaltones wrote the pre-punk tune "Move It On Over."

Shirley Westover remembered this period. She recalled that Del almost cried when he heard Roy Orbison's "Crying" and he couldn't wait to put it on record. He also selected the Impalas' "Sorry (I Ran All The Way Home)" and the Isley Brothers', "Twist and Shout" to complete his cover tunes. With the Royaltones backing, Del was on the edge of a new stage of musical creativity.

By 1965, Del's music was moving in new directions. "Keep Searchin' (We'll Follow The Sun)" came in at number nine on the **Billboard Top 40** ending Shannon's three year Top Ten drought. With a story and musical line similar to "Runaway," the "Keep Searchin' (We'll Follow The Sun)" single also hit number four in the U. K. Del was once again back on top. Steve Monahan and Dan Bourgoise recalled the song. It was one that came together while the three sat in the basement of Shannon's Southfield, Michigan home. "Monahan, Del and I were sitting in his basement studio." Bourgoise continued, "We were drinking a little and I asked Del what was the funny thing at the beginning of 'Runaway.' Del told me it was A minor. He played the lick and the song developed." This story suggests the spontaneous creativity that characterized Shannon's early career.

Just two months later "Stranger In Town" was a Top 40 hit in both the U. S. and U. K. and Shannon toured incessantly. By September, 1965 an album, **One Thousand Six Hundred Sixty Five Seconds With Del Shannon** was released with covers of Jay and the Americans "She Cried," Roy Orbison's "Running Scared," the Searchers "Needles and Pins," the Four Seasons "Rag Doll" and Bobby Freeman's "Do You Wanna Dance." With this album, Shannon's hits ran their course. He would remain a strong concert act for the next twenty-five years and he continued to sporadically chart. The only days of mega hits were over but, in some respects, this was a blessing. Del continued to tour and make a fine living.

In 1982, a comeback when Tom Petty produced the **Drop Down and Get Me** album and reminded his fans that Shannon was still around and making good music. Unfortunately, few people beyond his immediate fans listened to Del's new music. This is unfortunate because they missed some great sounds. When the Canadian-based Unidisc Music Inc. label rereleased the album in 2000, they included bonus cuts of "Cheap Love," "Help Me" and "Distant Ghost." This reissue suggests the depth of Shannon's musical artistry.

In February 1982, "Sea of Love" reached number 33 on the American chart and Del was back with a hit. By this time his concert pace had lessened and he seemed to be enjoying his place in the musical pantheon of stars. But the end was near. Increasing depression, a divorce and some poor personal decisions drove Del to suicide. When he died on February 8, 1990, the self-inflicted gunshot wound that ended his life mystified his family and friends. What no one could take away was his musical accomplishments and the legacy that he left behind. Del Shannon remains one of the classic rockers of the 1960s who continued to make fine music. He was always a "Stranger In Town" but perhaps this was his legacy. He was an outsider from the small town of Coopersville, Michigan who took the music world by storm and lasted in the business for 30 years. Not a bad legacy for a rock and roller.

As Brian Young suggests in his liner notes to the CD, **Del Shannon: All The Hits**, "Shannon was one of the few singers of the early 1960s manufactured pop star era who really had the talent." When Mark Knopfler of Dire Straits suggested that Del Shannon was the reason that he picked up his first guitar, there is no finer compliment. The legacy that Shannon left to the music world is enduring. To his family and friends he will always be remembered as "Chuck," the person who did as much as he could for everyone.

DEL SHANNON IN THE ROCK AND ROLL HALL OF FAME

On March 15, 1999 at New York's Waldorf-Astoria Hotel, Del Shannon was inducted into the Rock and Roll Hall of Fame. It was a fitting tribute to Del's influence and lengthy career. Along with other 1960s icons Paul McCartney, Dusty Springfield and Curtis Mayfield, Shannon shared center stage. Del's first wife, Shirley, his daughters, Jody and Kym, his son, Craig and his daughter, Amanda Sarver, and her husband, Jeff and Craig's wife, Nancy were joined by Dan Bourgoise, his wife, Kelley Ryan, Kym's husband, Ray Wilkerson, and Brian Young to celebrate the event.

The vote to place Shannon into the Hall of Fame was extraordinary. The reason is that the Cleveland-based Hall of Fame is dominated by Atlantic Record, Motown and other major label artists. Most of Del's hits were with minor labels and his foray with the larger record companies did not bear gigantic hits. So Del's inclusion in the Rock and Roll Hall of Fame was one based on merit.

The Rock and Roll Hall of Fame Induction is the final award, which posthumously cements Del Shannon's reputation in the pantheon or roots rockers who continued to influence succeeding generations of rock and roll performers. It was not only an important honor but also a capstone to an illustrious career.

BIBLIOGRAPHICAL ESSAY

GENERAL REFERENCE MATERIALS: HISTORIES

Nick Tosches, **Unsung Heroes of Rock: The Birth of Rock in the Wild Years Before Elvis** (New York, 1991) is a collection of essays suggesting some influences on Shannon. Also see, Harry Sumrall, **Pioneers of Rock and Roll: 100 Artists Who Changed The Face of Rock** (Boston, 1994); Lester Bangs, **Psychotic Reactions and Carburetor Dung** (New York, 1988) is a brilliant collection of essays on rock and roll.

On the rising influence of rock music see, for example, Simon Frith, **Sound Effects: Youth, Leisure and the Politics of Rock 'n' Roll** (New York, 1981); Peter Guralmick, **Feel Like Going Home: Portraits in Blues & Rock 'n' Roll** (New York, 1971, 1981 edition) and Robert Palmer, **Rock & Roll: Unruly History** (New York, 1995).

For text book histories, see, for example, Charles T. Brown, **The Art of Rock and Roll** (Englewood Cliffs, N. J., 1987, 2nd edition); Joe Steussy and Scott Lipscomb, **Rock and Roll: Its History and Stylistic Development** (Upper Saddle River, N. J,. 1999, 3rd edition); Don Hibbard and Patricia Kaleiahola, **The Role of Rock** (Englewood Cliffs, 1983); Ed Ward, Geoffrey Stokes and Ken Tucker, **Rock of Ages: The Rolling Stone History of Rock and Roll** (New York, 1986); John Tobler and Peter Frame, **Rock 'N' Roll: The First 25 Years** (New York, 1980); Arnold Shnaw, **The Rock Revolution** (London, 1969) and David P. Szatmary, **Rockin' In Time: A Social History of Rock and Roll** (Upper Saddle River, N. J., 1991, 3rd edition). Also useful are Irwin Stambler, **Encyclopedia of Pop, Rock and Soul** (New York, 1989, revised edition); Arnold Shaw, **Dictionary of American Pop/Rock** (New York, 1982); Lillian Roxon, **Rock Encyclopedia** (New York, 1969); Norman Nite, **Rock On: The Illustrated Encyclopedia of Rock 'N' Roll: The Sold Gold Years** (New York, 1978, volume l) and **Rock On: The Illustrated Encyclopedia of Rock 'N' Roll** (New York, 1984, volume 2). Also see Brock Helander **The Rock Who's Who** (New York, 1982).

For an academic history of rock and roll see, Theodore Gracyk, **Rhythm and Noise: An Aesthetics of Rock** (Durham, N. C., 1996) and Charlie Gillett, **The Sound Of The City: The Rise of Rock and Roll** (New York, 1983, revised edition).

Michael Bane, **White Boys Singing The Blues** (New York, 1982) and D. Laing, K. Denselow and R. Shelton, **The Electric Muse: Folk Into Rock** (London, 1975) are important to understanding the 1960s.

Also useful were Carl Belz, **The Story of Rock** (New York, 1972); Peter E. Berry, **And the Hits Just Keep On Comin'** (Syracuse, 1977); Bruce Chipman, ed., **Hardening Rock: An Organic Anthology of the Adolescence of Rock 'n' Roll** (Boston, 1972); B. Lee Cooper, **Images of American Society In Popular Music** (Chicago, 1982); Jonathan Eisen, ed., **The Age of Rock** (New York, 1969); John Gabree, **The World of Rock** (Greenwich, 1968); Lloyd Grossman, **A Social History of Rock Music** (New York, 1976); Brock Helander, **The Rock Who's Who** (New York, 1982); Michael Shore with Dick Clark, **The History of American Bandstand** (New York, 1984) Michael Uslan and Bruce Solommon, **Dick Clark's The First 25 Years of Rock & Roll** (New York, 1981); Ian Whitcomb, **After**

The Ball: Pop Music From Rag To Rock (NewYork, 1972) and Paul Williams, **Outlaw Blues** (New York, 1969).

Larry Lehmner, **The Day The Music Died: The Last Tour of Buddy Holly, the Big Bopper and Ritchie Valens** (New York, 1997) was an important source as was John Beecher and Malcolm Jones, **The Buddy Holly Story** (MCA Record Box Set-Booklet); John Goldrosen and John Beecher, **Remembering Buddy Holly: The Definitive Biography of Buddy Holly** (New York, 1985) and Alan Clark, **Ritchie Valens: 30th Anniversary Memorial Series** (West Covina, Ca., 1989).

GENERAL REFERENCE MATERIALS: AND ARTIST PROFILES

For the influence of rock drummers see Bob Cianci, **Rock Drummers In The Sixties** (Milwaukee, 1989). See Nik Cohn's **Rock From The Beginning** (New York, 1984) for some profiles and a history of early rock music.

See John A. Jackson, **Big Beat Heat: Alan Freed and the Early Years of Rock and Roll** (New York, 1991) for an excellent study of how the rock concert business started.

GENERAL REFERENCE MATERIALS: CHARTS AND CHRONOLOGIES

Fred Bronson, **The Billboard Book of Number One Hits** (New York, 1992, 3rd edition); Fred Bronson, **Billboard's Hottest 100 Hits: Revised and Enlarged Edition** (New York, 1995); Paul Gambaccini, Tim Rice and Johnathan Rice, **British Hit Albums** (New York, 1992); Paul Gambaccini, Tim Rice and Johnathan Rice, **British Hit Singles** (New York, 1991, 8th edition); Frank Hoffman and George Albert, **The Cash Box Album Charts, 1955-1974** (Boulder, 1994); Dave McAleer, **The All Music Book of Hit Albums: The Top 10 U. S. and U. K. Album Charts From 1960 to the Present** (San Francisco, 1995);Dafydd Reed, Barry Mazell and Roger Osborne, **The Complete NME Singles Charts** (London, 1995); Craig Rosen, **The Billboard Book of Number One Albums: The Inside Story Behind Pop Music's Blockbuster Records** (New York, 1996); Joel Whitburn, **The Billboard Book of Top 40 Albums** (New York, 1995, 3rd edition) and Joel Whitburn, **The Billboard Book of Top 40 Hits** (New York, 1996, 6th edition); Joel Whitburn, **Billboard's top 2000** (Menomonee Falls, Wisc., 1985) and Joel Whitburn, **Top Pop Albums, 1955-1985** (Menomonee Falls, Wisc., 1985).

Important chronologies include Paul DeNoyer, editor, **Rock 'N' Roll: The Year By Year Illustrated** (Miami, 1995); Editors of Rolling Stone, **Rolling Stone Rock Almanac: The Chronicles of Rock and Roll** (New York, 1983); Frank Laufenberg and Hugh Gregory, **Rock and Pop Day By Day** (New York, 1992); Norm Nite, **Rock On Almanac: The First Four Decades of Rock 'N' Roll** (New York, 1992, 2nd edition); John Tobler, **This Day In Rock: Day By Day Record of Rock's Biggest News Stories** (New York, 1993) and Michael Shore with Dick Clark, **The History of American Bandstand: From the 1950s to the 1980s** (New York, 1985).

BIBLIOGRAPHICAL ESSAY

Anthony DeCurtis and James Henke, (with H. George-Warren, editor), **The Rolling Stone Album Guide** (New York, 1992) and **The Rolling Stone Illustrated History of Rock And Roll: The Definitive History of the Most Important Artists and Their Music** (New York, `1992) are two excellent source volumes.

B. Lee Cooper and Frank Hoffman, **The Literature of Rock II** (Metuchen, 1986) is a pioneering bibliographical effort that aided this book immensely.

ACADEMIC ARTICLES ON ROCK AND ROLL

B. Lee Cooper "Teaching American History Through Popular Music," **AHA Newsletter**, no. 14 (October, 1976), pp. 3-5' Richard Aquila, "Images of the American West in Rock Music," **Western Historical Quarterly**, no. 11 (October, 1980), pp. 415-432; Richard Aquila, "Rock Music: A Source Guide For Collection Development," **Indiana Media Journal**, no. 5 (Spring, 1983), pp. 6-15 and David Manning White, "Popular Culture: The Multi Faceted Mirror," in **Popular Culture: Mirror of American Life** (Delmar, 1977).

Also see, Steve Chapple and Reebee Garofalo, **Rock 'n' Roll Is Here to Pay: The History and Politics of the Music Industry** (Chicago, 1977) and Herbert Gans, **Popular Culture and High Culture** (New York, 1974). Peter Guralnick, **Feel Like Going home: Portraits in Blues and Rock 'n' Roll** (New York, 1971) is a solid, scholarly look at people and issues peripheral, but important, to Del Shannon.

DEL SHANNON'S SUICIDE: THE PRESS COVERAGE

For newspaper and magazine coverage of Shannon's death from the sensational press, see, for example, "Sad Star Who Couldn't Runaway From His Hit," **Today**, February 10, 1990, p. 7; **London Daily Mirror**, February 10, 1990, p. 5;; **London Daily Star**, February 10, 1990. p. 4; **London Daily Sun**, p. 1, 4; **London Guardian**, February 10, 1990; **London Daily Express**, February 17, 1990; **London Daily Mail**, February 10, 1990; "Split Personality Drove Rock Idol Del Shannon to Shoot Himself," **London Star**, February 27, 1990, p. 29; "Del Shannon's Murder Probe-Widow Says: I'I Cannot Believe He Killed Himself," **National Enquirer**, February, 1990. The above stories bore little resemblance to fact but they are important in suggesting one of the reasons for Shannon's death. That reason was his difficulty coping with a savage and often untruthful media.

For more balanced accounts from the Michigan press see, for example, **Fruitport News**, February 10, 1990:

For editorial reflections on Shannon's death see, for example, John D. Gonzalez, "Del Shannon's Best Known Work," **Grand Rapids Press** Michael Goldberg, "Del Shannon: 1934-1990," **Rolling Stone**, March 22, 1990, pp. 20, 124.

Michael Tennesen, "Did Charles Westover Kill Del Shannon?" **Los Angeles Magazine**, September, 1990, pp. 132-140. David Hinckley, "Time Ran Out For Runaway Man," **New York Daily News**, February 19, 1990.

BIBLIOGRAPHICAL ESSAY

THE DEL SHANNON MEMORIAL

On the Del Shannon Memorial see, "Shannon Tribute Tuned Out," **Battle Creek Enquirer**, March 28, 1990; "Benefit concert Planned for 'Runaway' Marker," **Battle Creek Shopper News**, September 6, 1990, p. 26.

MAX CROOK

The material on Max Crook is voluminous. For early coverage of his career with Del Shannon, the White Bucks and as Maximilian, see, for example, Allen T. Conn, "Maximilian: Man With A New Sound," **Kalamazoo Gazette**, May 21, 1961, p. 38;

For later developments in Crooks life and career see, Bob Baker, "He's Serious About His Music," **Thousand Oaks, California News Chronicle**, January 18, 1974, pp. A-3,A-6; Useful in understanding Crook's genius is David Crombie, **The Synthesizer and Electronic Keyboared Handbook** (New York, 1984).

Stan Martin, "The Rise and Fall of the White Bucks," **Musitrons, Moogs, and Maximilian: Max Cook Music Magazine**, volume 1, no. 1, 1999, pp. 12-15 and Brian Young, "Maximilian's Story," **Musitrons, Moogs, and Maximilian: Max Crook Magazine**, volume 1, no. 1,1999, pp. 19-35 are important to the Max Crook story. Also, see, Howard A. DeWitt, Dennis M. DeWitt and Brian Young, "Max Crook: The Maximilian Story," **Rock & Blues News**, April-May, 2001, pp. 27-32.

THE BEATLES AND DEL SHANNON

For key materials on the Beatles and Del Shannon see, for example, Nicholas Schaffner, **The British Invasion: From the First Wave To The New Wave** (New York, 1983); John Blake, **All You Needed Was Love: The Beatles After The Beatles** (New York, 1981); Hunter Davies, **The Beatles** (New York, 1968) 8is an authorized biography which shows how Shannon influenced the Fab Four. Philip Norman, **Shout: The Beatles In Their Generation** (New York, 1982) remains the standard history of the group. Howard A. DeWitt, **The Beatles: Untold Tales** (Fremont, 1985) contains vignettes of how Shannon influenced the Mersey Sound and the Beatles.

An interesting source is Arthur Aron, **Not Just The Beatles...The Story of How Legendary Impresario Sid Bernstein Brought The Beatles To America, and His Association With The Show Business Greats Of Our Time** (Teaneck, 2000).

ROOTS ROCKERS WHO INFLUENCED DEL SHANNON

For the roots rockers who influenced Del Shannon see, for example, Howard A. DeWitt, **Chuck Berry: Rock N Roll Music** (Ann Arbor, 1985); Charles White, **The Life and Times of Little Richard** (New York, 1984); Howard A. DeWitt, **Sun Elvis: Presley In the 1950s** (Ann Arbor, 1992); Peter Guralnick, **Last Train To Memphis: The Rise of Elvis Presley** ((London, 1994); Myra Lewis (with Murray Silver), **Great Balls of Fire** (New

BIBLIOGRAPHICAL ESSAY

York, 1982). Also see, Margaret Jones, **Patsy: The Life and Times of Patsy Cline** (New York, 1994) and Ellis Nassour, **Honky Tonk Angel: The Intimate Story of Patsy Cline** (New York, 1993, first edition, 1991) for helpful information on country influences.

For teen idols and the American Bandstand influence, see, for example, Noel Coppage, "The Bandstand That Wouldn't Grow Up," **Stereo Review**, number 41 (September, 1983), pp. 88-89; Dave Samuelson, "And Now For The Kiddies: Ed Sullivan and Rock and roll, 1954-1971," **Goldmine**, number 64 (October, 1981), p. 179; Lynn Van Matre, "Those Early-60s Heartthrobs: Where Are They Now?" **Chicago Tribune Arts and Books** (May 31, 1981), p. 15 and Howard A. DeWitt, "Chuck Berry and the First Golden Age of Rock and Roll Music, 1956-1957," **Record Profile Magazine**, number 2 (September, 1983), pp. 43-48.

On Johnny Tillotson, who was a close friend of Del's, see, Graham Gardner, "Johnny Tillotson: The Johnny Tillotson Story," **Goldmine**, number 89 (October, 1983), pp. 59-60, 62, 64.

THE INDUSTRY AND DEL SHANNON

A key to understanding the impact of the music industry upon Shannon is Frederic Dannen, **Hit Men** (New York, 1990). This volume examines the inside business dealings that left so many artists destitute. For inside the industry by an honest and talented producer see Joe Smith, **Off The Record: An Oral History of Popular Music** (New York, 1989).

Dennis DeWitt, "Harry Balk Interview," **And The Music Plays On**, Summer, 1995, is an important source. For other material on Balk, see, for example, Bill Millar, "Blowin' Up A Storm," **Melody Maker**, number 54 (March 24, 1979), p. 42, Bill Millar, "Johnny And The Hurricanes," **Goldmine**, number 57, (February, 1981), pp. 10-11; Lou Holscher, "Little Willie John-- Fact or Fiction," **Goldmine**, number 72 (May, 1982), p. 189 and Steve Propes, "Little Willie John: King of Detroit Soul Music," **Goldmine**, number 171 (February 13, 1987), p. 22.

On Shannon's royalties see, Bob Fisher, "Writs and Royalties," **And The Music Plays On**, number 1 (Fall, 199), p. 16 and Marc Elliot, **Rockonomics: The Money Behind The Music** (New York, 1989).

For Harry Balk and Motown see, for example, Nelson George, **Where Did Our Love Go? The Rise of the Motown Sound** (New York, 1985) and Gerri Hirshey, **Nowhere To Run**(New York, 1984). Also see, Berry Gordy, **To Be Loved: The Music, The Magic, The Memories of Motown** (New York, 1994).

Other useful studies of the industry included R. Serge Denisoff, **Tarnished Gold** (Brunswick, N. J., 1986) and Simon Garfield, **Money For Nothing** (London, 1986).

On censorship see, Eric Nuzum, **Parental Advisory: Music Censorship In America** (New York, 2001). The Nuzum book deals with contemporary censorship but has an excellent section on the Beatles.

Clive Davis, **Inside The Record Business** (New York, 1976) was a valuable insider look at the industry.

SPECIALIZED ARTICLES ON DEL SHANNON

For specialized articles on Shannon, see, for example, Dennis DeWitt, "Del Shannon: Stranger In Town," **Blue Suede News**, number 14, Spring, 1990, pp. 7, 11. Prof. Fred Hopkins "Hats Off To Del Shannon," **Blue Suede News**, number 14, Spring, 1990, pp. 4-5; Marc Bristol, "Chuck Westover Comes Home," **Blue Suede News**, number 14, Spring, 1990. pp. 8-9.

Sue Worden and Brian Young, "Wes Kilbourne Interview," **And The Music Plays On**, no. 14, summer, 1998, pp. 26-31 recalls the Battle Creek Hi Lo Club days. Christoph Meyer-Brandenburg's article "Track Talk: What's Buried In The Mole Hole," **And The Music Plays On**, no. 14, Summer, 1998. Todd Everett, "Del Shannon Has Never Run Away, **Los Angeles Herald Examiner**, October 3, 1986, p. 32.

Howard A. DeWitt and Dennis M. DeWitt, "The Recording of Runaway," **Rock & Blues News**, April-May, 2000, pp. 5-12 provides the background to Del's seminal tune.

For unreleased Shannon tracks see, Christopher Meyer-Brandenburg, "Track Talk: What's Buried In The Mole Hole," **And The Music Plays On**. Number 14 (Summer, 1998), pp. 32-39. On Del's comeback with Tom Petty see, Philip Bashe, "Del Shannon's Comeback a Petty Matter," **Creem**, volume 14, no. 1 (June, 1982), pp. 24-25, 58-59 and Jon Young "Del Shannon," **Trouser Press**, volume 9, number 4 (June,1982), pp. 8, 50.

On Del Shannon collectibles see, Mike Wilson, "The Del Shannon CD Jigsaw Puzzle," **And The Music Plays On**, Issue 5, Fall, 1995, pp. 37-39. Also see, "Del Shannon's New Mystery: The Case of the Missing Tapes," **And The Music Plays On**, Issue 11 (Spring, 1990), pp. 17-22 for tapes missing in the 1980s.

The **Rock On** CD drew a lot of attention, see, for example, Steve Simels, "Del Shannon: Rock On," **Stereo Review**, September, 1991 and Ken Barnes, "Del Shannon: Stranger In Town Departs," **R & R**, February 23, 1990.

LOCAL MICHIGAN PRESS ARTICLES ON DEL SHANNON

Leslie Radin, "B. C.'s Rock Runaway Is Back," **Battle Creek Inquirer**, April 17, 1986 features quotes from Del on Michigan. For the Coopersville class reunion of 1988 see, "Pete DeMaagd, "Spotlight In Coopersville Will Be One Guy Who Made It Big," **Grand Rapids Press**, July 26, 1988. The **Topeka Capitol Journal**, August 2, 1987 contains an excellent Shannon story.

On the Del Shannon Memorial see, for example, Mark Glubke, "Special Events Planned to Mark Music History," **Battle Creek Inquirer**, September 23, 1990. Also see the **Battle Creek Inquirer**, February 24, 11990, p. 5a and April 11, 1990, p. 3a for the controversy over the Del Shannon Memorial.

GENERAL MICHIGAN HISTORY

For Coopersville history, see, Jim and Lillian Budzynski, **Chronicles of Coopersville** (Coopersville, 1996); **The First Hundred Years** (Coopersville Area

Centennial, 1971); **History of Muskegon and Ottawa Counties, Michigan Illustrated, 1882** (Chicago, 1882); **Standard Atlas of Ottawa County Michigan** (Chicago, 1897); Gayl VanDoorn, **The History of Coopersville** (Handwritten document, n. d.) and Adrian Van Koevering, **Original Pioneer Settlers in Ottawa and Northern Allegan Counties** (Zeevland, Michigan, n. d.).

The roots of the Westover, Cooper and Mosher families can be traced in M. M. Bagg, **The Pioneers of Utica** (New York, 1977); Fred C. Hockenbary, **Descendants of the John Cooper Family** (Mantawan, New Jersey, 1976) and **Oneida County And Its People** (ONeida County, New York, 1876). Also, the **Coopersville News** and the **Coopersville Observer** were used to add in depth information.

See Richard Schlatter, **The Del Shannon Memorial and State Historical Marker Dedication** (Battle Creek, 1990) for the historical marker. Also, see, James Clinton, James McClurken and George Cornell, **People of the Three Fires** (Grand Rapids, 1986) and C. Fred Rydholm, **Superior Heartland: A Backwoods History** (Marquette, 1989) for the influence of the Ottawa Indians.

ACKNOWLEDGMENTS

Biography is a shared experience. By putting together materials from the subject's life, notably letters, journals, manuscripts, newspaper interviews, the recollections of friends, the intimate memories of spouses and children and the business side of life, the biographer assembles the material. In the case of Del Shannon his two wives, close friends, business associates and those in the press were unwavering in their support.

In the lengthy and elaborate process of writing a biography there is a tendency to found more material than is significant. For that reason we have left many of the tales untold about Shannon's private life. Like most figures in the rock and roll community, his actions are often difficult to separate from fact and myth. Since he committed suicide shortly before we began work on the book, the press was filled with half-truths and much guesswork. Since the days of Dr. Samuel Johnson biography has tended to sway between two poles-hagiography and character assassination. This book is an attempt to bridge that gap. The closer that a book remains to the details of a public life the better chance it has of making the subject come alive. As a result we have tried to tell the story through Shannon's music and his public life as a rock and roll star.

My earlier biographies of Chuck Berry, Van Morrison, Paul McCartney and Elvis Presley were happy ordeals. The loneliness of the writer often makes he or she a bit cranky. I confess this happened to me. As I sat writing the final version of this book my brother Dennis didn't call or contribute. In the end that worked out fine as I took the earlier manuscript and refined it.

In the case of Del Shannon, I do not know the man. He died before I began the project. His first wife, Shirley Westover, his children Jody, Kym and Craig were unusually helpful. His mother, Leone, was a jewel who talked at length about her son. Among those close to Del no one was more helpful than Dan Bourgoise. He is an important player in the music industry with a great deal of business. Yet, when I called, he was gracious and took time from his busy schedule to help put the book together. Harry Balk, Del's producer, was equally gracious with his time and opinions. He had never talked to a rock and roll journalist at length. Max Crook helped us ferret out the "Runaway" story. Dick Parker, the drummer at the Hi Lo Club, was an unusually great source and he is a walking encyclopedia of Shannon facts and ideas.

Dennis and I began this book in 1991. Dennis collected the music, the videos, the pictures and the clippings. We then proceeded to interview more than a hundred people close to Del Shannon. Howard wrote the book with some criticism from Dennis and a page by page detailed critique by Brian Young, Shirley Westover and Dan Bourgoise. It was Brian Young who facilitated this book by providing access to people, information and the music. In particular, it was Brian who led us to Bourgoise and Balk. Young is truly a co-author, even though he was barely old enough to shave when we met him, Brian had knowledge of Del's career second to none. He runs the Del Shannon

Appreciation Society and its magazine **And The Music Plays On**. Without Brian we couldn't have completed this book. His name deserves to be on the title page.

In Battle Creek Dick Schlatter facilitated our research and helped with interviews of the locals. Dick also took Howard to some of his favorite spots. People providing important information on the local music included Sue Gooch, Susie Forrest, the Popenhagen family, Karl Palmer, Peter Vice, Charlie Marsh, Ginny Gibbs, Darr Farr, Rufus Wines, the DeMott family and the patrons of numerous clubs helped a great deal.

Some of Del's early friends notably Steve Monahan, Fontaine Brown, Chuck Marsh and Peter vice helped out immensely. Ray Meyer was a later friend who knew Del well and shared his stories with us.

In Coopersville Jim and Lill Budzynski were helpful. Others who gave us insights into Coopersville included Sonny Marshall, Russell Conran, Dick Nash, Ken Pottiger, Bud Taylor and Earl Meerman.

In Indiana Ray Meyer gave insights into Del as did the Detroit based Maron McKenzie.

In California Mayf Nutter helped to recreate the days at the old Hi Lo Club. Glen Glenn recalled some key meetings with Shannon.

Musical figures who gave their opinions on the music scene of the day on some opinions of Del Shannon included Don Wilson, Bob Bogle and Nokie Edwards of the Ventures, Freddy Cannon, Brian Hyland, Johnny Tillotson, Delbert McClinton, Jimmy McCracklin, the late Charles Brown, the late Lowell Fulson, Johnny Otis, Bobby Vee, Guitar Mac, Johnny Powers, Vernon Taylor, Hank Ballard, W. S. "Fluke" Holland, Mary Wells, Tommy Roe, Tommy Sands and Ike Turner.

In England Sam Leach, Joe Flannery, Clive Epstein, Brian Kelly, Bob Wooler, Ray Coleman, Alistair Taylor, Billy J. Kramer, Jerry Marsden, Eddie Hoover, Kingsize Taylor, Charlie Lennon, Allan Williams, Tony Bramwell and David Williams helped with the book. Les Collinson, the rocking vicar, added some useful anecdotes.

In Germany Horst Fascher, Astrid Kircheer, Tom Shaka and Tony Sheridan were important sources in describing Shannon's European popularity.

In the pulishing world Lee Cotten of **Rock N Blues News** provided a forum for our material on Del Shannon. Lee is a first rate editor and a fine scholar. This magazine which covers the working performers of rock and roll helped us formulate our ideas. Lee is a good friend and helped on all parts of the book. Marc Bristol, the boss at **Blue Suede News** was another source for our writings. This rockabilly-roots rock magazine provided a great deal of information and published many of our efforts. Our thanks to Marc and Gaby. **Discoveries** was another important source and John Koenig's skillful editorial handling makes it a marvelous souce. Dennis Loren, the editor of the now defunct **Record Profile Magazine** was an early supporter of the book. Also, the former editor of **Discoveries** helped to facilitate projects important to this book. A previous editor of **Discoveries**, Wayne Jancik, also publishing some of my material and became a good friend along the way. Opal Louise Nations provided important ideas and criticism on the early roots of rock and roll. Opal, who is a fountain of rock and roll knowledge, provided many significant research clues. Don Kirsch provided key research materials. Jeff Miller

ACKNOWLEDGMENTS

was another important research source form Wiley's Golden Oldies in Tacoma, Washington. Prof. Fred Hopkins was a constant fountain of knowledge and help. Duane DeWitt provided an overview of Pacific Northwest rock and roll as did Ron Peterson, Little Bill Engelhardt, Warren Johansen, Bert Hamstad, Grady McCart and George Palmerton.

The Battle Creek Public Library provided early materials. The Del Shannon Museum in Coopersville was another source of material. The Michigan Department of History and Archives had a great deal of useful material on Shannon's roots.

For providing coffee, work space and constructive criticism Don and Gael Stewart helped to make the book a joy to write.

Bryan Thomas at Del Fi Records was an important source for the early history of rock and roll.

Professor B. Lee Cooper not only provided encouragement his books and research were a constant help. Perhaps the finest academic scholar in American on matters of popular culture, Professor Cooper's erudite writings were an important source. At the Bowling Green University Popular Culture Archives, Bill Schurck, was helpful in many ways.

Among the writers and music scholars who were generous with their time were Bill Griggs, Jim Hannaford, Jim Dawson, Steve Propes, Steve Marrinucci, Duane DeWitt and Bob Hover.

Glinda Wertenberger reconstructed the mansucript and acted as a co-editor and writer. Thanks to Glinda for her help. My good friend of forty-three years, David Page provided wise counsel and helpful suggestions.

Dr. Paulette Profumo, the Dean of Instruction, at Ohlone College provided the work atmosphere, which made this book possible. Everyone should work for a boss with such grace and skill. Eleene Kraft and Judy Smith offered a great of personal advise on the writing techniques. W. Reed Severson recalled his Del Shannon concerts and Daryl Myers suggested some of the key rock and roll influences upon Shannon.

If we have forgotten anyone, please accept our apologies. Thank all for your help and remember all errors are the responsibility of the authors. For suggestions for the next edition send them to P. O. Box 3083, Fremont, California 94539. Or e mail to Howard217@aol.com

Howard A. DeWitt
Dennis M. DeWitt
April 30, 2001
4:45 A. M.

ABOUT THE AUTHORS

Howard A. DeWitt is Professor of History, Ohlone College, Fremont, California. Her received his B. A. from Western Washington University, a M. A. from the University of Oregon and a Ph. D. from the University of Arizona. Professor DeWitt has also taught at Cochise College, Chabot College and the University of California, Davis. His two course in the History of Rock and Roll, established in 1975, became the prototype for similar courses at the college level. He is the author of 15 books and more than 300 articles and reviews. His rock and roll articles have appeared in **DISCoveries, Rock 'N' Blues News, Blue Suede News, Juke Box Digest, Record Profile Magazine, Audio Trader** and **Good Day Sunshine**. His book, **Sun Elvis: Presley in the 1950s**, was a nominee in 1993 for the RIAA rock music book of the year. For additions and corrections to the book write Howard at P. O. Box 3083, Fremont, California 94539 or e-mail to Howard217@aol.com

Currently, Howard is preparing the first of four volumes of a monumental Van Morrison biography. He also has another Beatle book, much like his earlier well received tome, **The Beatles: Untold Tales**. This book, **The Beatles: Please Don't Pass Us By**, is another collection of pathreaking essays.

Dennis M. DeWitt is a Seattle, Washington based journalist. He writes a regular column and articles for **Blue Suede News**. His work has appeared in **Rock 'N' Blues News** and **Juke Box Digest** as well as a host of European and English magazines. Dennis is also a promoter and has brought such acts as Robert Gordon, Janis Martin, Joe Clay, Ray Condo and Kim Lenz among others to the Pacific Northwest. He is presently working on a manuscript which brings his columns together from **Blue Suede News**.

A hard working and industrious writer, Dennis specializes in roots rock and the rockabillly music scene. He is continually on the outlook for new material for his column. Anyone with material for his "Juke Box Tidbits" column which is a regular feature in **Blue Suede News** can send their suggestions to Dennis at 14801 Interlake Ave. N., Seattle, Washington 98133. When not researching and writing, Dennis enjoys gardening and playing his records and CDs in his own mole hole. He also has one of the best collection of reocrds andhis Pacific Northwest Greatest Hits is second to none. At present Dennis is also working on a book on rockabilly music. He will combine his publications in liason with new research and present a fresh look at this genre.

CONSULTATIVE RESEARCH ASSOCIATES

Brian Young is the editor of the Del Shannon fanzine **And The Music Plays On**. He was the primary research person for the book. In addition, Brian provided criticism of the manuscript and discographical information. He has written extensive liner notes for CD reissues of Del Shannon's materials and he has published his articles on Del in DISCoveries. Brian is currently involved with extensive research on Del's relationship with the Beatles and the Merseyside sound. In addition to this project, he is working on a book length study of Del Shannon which will examine the influence that Del had upon Bob Seger and Tom Petty as well as other early rock and roll artists. Brian can be contacted at the Del Shannon Appreciation Society, P. O. Box 44201, Tacoma, Washington 98444. Brian's e-mail is **brianyoung@delshannon.com**

Inaddition to editing and writing for the magazine **And The Music Plays On**, Brian is a well known liner note author. His notes to the eight CD reissue of Del Shannon material by the Canadian based Unidisc Music Inc. conglomerate is a piece of scholarship that every Shannon fan treasures.

Glinda Wertenberger is a Fremont, California educator and free lance critic. She was instrumental in reshaping the mansucript and provided a great deal of research help. Glinda was also responsible for final revisions of the manuscript. She is presently working on a textbook for a college level geography course. Her academic specialty is Native American education and she is working in that field.

A specialist in Native American educaiton, Ms. Wertenberger is destined for a career on a major Indian reservation. She has studied ethnic history and remains a influential educator in that area.

OTHER BOOKS BY HOWARD A. DEWITT

Jose Rizal: Philippine Nationalist As Political Scientist (1997)

The Fragmented Dream: Mulitcultural California (1996)

The California Dream (1996)

Sun Elvis: Presley In The 1950s (1993)

Paul McCartney: From Liverpool To Let It Be (1992)

Beatle Poems (1987)

The Beatles: Untold Tales (1985)

Chuck Berry: Rock N Roll Music (1985)

Van Morrison: The Mystic's Music (1983)

Jailhouse Rock: The Bootleg Records of Elvis Presley (with Lee Cotten) (1983)

Readings in California Civilization (1981)

Violence In The Fields: Filipino Farm Labor Unionization During The Great Depression (1980)

California Civilization (1979)

Anti Filipino Movements in California: A History, Bibliography and Study Guide (1976)

Images of Ethnic and Radical Violence in California Politics, 1917-1930: A Survey (1975)

WORK SHEET 1
CHAPTERS 1-5

NAME_____

1. Briefly explain the role that Max Crook played in Del Shannon's music.

2. What is the importance of Doug DeMott to the Battle Creek years?

3. Identify the significance of Charlie Marsh?

4. What role did Ollie McLaughlin play in Del Shannon's music?

5. What background did Harry Balk have that helped him in the music business?

6. Briefly explain the production techniques of Harry Balk.

7. What was the reason for the English strategy from Balk and Micahnik.

8. Who was Irving Micahnik and why was he important?

9. What was the musitron?

10. What impact did Max Crook have upon Del Shannon''s music?

11. Explain how "Runaway" became a hit. What was the making of "Runaway?"

12. Analyze Del Shannon's career after "Runaway" to 1965.

WORK SHEET 2
Chapters 6-10

Name:_____

1. What influence did Dan Bourgoise have upon Del Shannon's career?

2. How did the name Bug Music originate?

3. Who was Bones Howe?

4. What was the role of Snuff Garrett at Liberty Records?

5. Describe the period from 1971 to 1977. What is meant by "Lost In The Musical Ozone?"

6. Analyze Del Shannon's relationship with the Beatles and the Merseyside sound.

7. What Beatle song did Del Shannon record?

8. What is the missing second album and what does it suggest about Shannon's career?

WORK SHEET 3
Chapters 11-15

Name:_____

1. Explain the transition in Del Shannon's life from 1978 to 1983.

2. What was Tom Pettty's relationship to Del Shannon?

3. Who was Mike Campbell and why was he important?

4. What was the importance of the Rock On Album?

5. Discuss the key points in chapter 12. What is meant by "the road goes on forever?"

6. Discuss the issues surrounding the Del Shannon Memorial. Why was there resistance?

7. Identify the importance of Dick Schlatter.

8. Who was Dick Parker?

9. From reading this book assess the role of Del Shannon in rock and roll music.

INDEX

INDEX